Making Sense of Data and Statistics in Psychology

Making Sense of Data and Statistics in Psychology

2nd Edition

Gerry Mulhern

School of Psychology
Queen's University Belfast
UK

Brian Greer

Graduate School of Education
Portland State University
Oregon, USA

palgrave
macmillan

First edition 2001
Second edition 2011

Published by
PALGRAVE MACMILLAN

Palgrave Macmillan in the UK is an imprint of Macmillan Publishers Limited, registered in England, company number 785998, of Houndmills, Basingstoke, Hampshire RG21 6XS.

Palgrave Macmillan in the US is a division of St Martin's Press LLC, 175 Fifth Avenue, New York, NY 10010.

Palgrave Macmillan is the global academic imprint of the above companies and has companies and representatives throughout the world.

Palgrave® and Macmillan® are registered trademarks in the United States, the United Kingdom, Europe and other countries.

ISBN: 978–0–230–20574–1

This book is printed on paper suitable for recycling and made from fully managed and sustained forest sources. Logging, pulping and manufacturing processes are expected to conform to the environmental regulations of the country of origin.

A catalogue record for this book is available from the British Library.

A catalog record for this book is available from the Library of Congress.

10 9 8 7 6 5 4 3 2 1
20 19 18 17 16 15 14 13 12 11

Printed and bound in Great Britain by
MPG Group, Bodmin and Kings Lynn

Short Contents

Contents

Preface

The first edition of this book was prompted by our perceived need for a textbook that would present the essentials of statistics and research methods in the style in which we wished to teach our own students. This remains our overwhelming aim in this new edition.

The challenges confronting those who teach and learn quantitative methods in psychology remain stubbornly similar to those we described in 2002. Psychology has continued to burgeon as a discipline and there is unprecedented demand to study the subject at university. Internationally, large class sizes remain a feature of the student experience and the discipline continues to attract students with diverse mathematical backgrounds. Some will have studied mathematics and statistics to a relatively advanced level, while many more will have a more modest background. Some will relish the prospect of learning about the quantitative aspects of psychology, while others will harbour reservations.

In our preface to the first edition, we pointed out that one of the challenges of larger class sizes was the increased anonymity of students and the greater sense of 'distance' between teacher and pupil. As we wrote then, 'students may seldom have an opportunity to discuss ideas or problems with their lecturers ... and lecturers may not easily be able to identify students who are experiencing difficulties'. In the nine years since our first edition, we have not had the sense that the distance between teacher and pupil has decreased appreciably, and as such, we have sought to tailor this new edition to this reality as far as possible.

A further challenge we identified back in 2002 was related to the use of statistical packages such as SPSS, which can often generate a 'distance' between students and their data, giving rise to incorrect or inappropriate analyses. Our response to this in the first edition was to eschew statistical packages in our content. *This time we have taken a different tack, resulting in an important new feature of this edition in which we present SPSS implementations of the examples used in the text. Crucially, these are presented as standalone inserts which can be skipped over by students or instructors if they prefer, so the conceptual flow of the text can be retained without reference to computational details.* We accept that the inclusion of SPSS in this edition will reflect more closely how statistics is typically taught, while also giving students the conceptual tools to use statistical software packages with appropriate insight and judgement.

We have received many good wishes and positive comments from readers of the first edition and reviewers of early drafts of this second edition, along with some extremely useful feedback. Some have pointed out minor errors in the original text for which we are both apologetic and grateful. Others have made more wide-ranging suggestions for change and we have taken many of these on board, although some may have to await a third edition!

A consistent theme to emerge from reader comments was the extent to which the book was being used in a range of teaching and learning contexts. Some instructors were using it at introductory level only, others were using it at both introductory and post-introductory levels, and still others were using it with postgraduate students. This we found extremely heartening since one of the original aims was to produce a text that resonated with learners at different levels. By the same token, we came to realize that we needed to introduce additional material to cater for different levels of engagement. This has led to several further new features in this edition. In addition to the *'Before reading on ...'* feature from the first edition, we have introduced *'Making links'* boxes, which we recommend all readers should use: these are designed to help students identify connections between statistical ideas that may not be readily apparent, and to adopt a more integrative perspective when trying to make sense of their own data. We have also introduced a further new boxed feature, entitled *'For those who wish to dig a little deeper'*: these boxes are optional and intended mainly for post-introductory readers, although introductory readers should also find them useful. Both of these new features are intended to enhance students' understanding through broadening and deepening ideas. *We have also increased the number of 'Socratic' dialogues which proved such a popular feature of the first edition.*

Finally, we have introduced additional material to expand on the coverage of the first edition. Notably, *we have included a new Chapter 10 dealing with effect size and confidence intervals and have included treatment of these topics with examples in subsequent chapters.* We also offer a *companion website to help extend, consolidate and illustrate ideas in the textbook.* This has the added advantage of allowing content to be added more flexibly, so we are happy to include web features suggested by readers where we can.

Note to Teachers

As in the first edition, we hope that you encourage your students to engage with the old and new features described above. We have strived to ensure that the 'Socratic' dialogues have been presented in a natural, informal style and we have taken great care to identify and ventilate the conceptual challenges that the reader is likely to face – many are based on actual conversations with our own students. We have also endeavoured to ensure that the *'Making links'* and *'For those who wish to dig a little deeper'* features are as accessible as possible to students at all levels.

The *'Before reading on ...'* exercises are also based directly on our experience of teaching undergraduates. Typically, these are the short tasks with which we have punctuated our own lectures and tutorials over the years. We would urge you to make use of them in your own teaching and to ensure that students engage with the tasks where they appear in the text, rather than coming back to them later or skipping over them altogether.

As in the first edition, we have grouped statistical tests within chapters on the basis of what they *do* rather than on the basis of their parametric status. With few exceptions, authors of statistics texts in psychology have tended to deal with parametric and non-parametric methods separately. Here, you will see that, following three introductory chapters, most of the rest of the book divides into two strands, based on the two main functions of statistical tests – *comparing* data sets and *relating* data sets.

A further important feature of the book is that, in each strand, chapters are organized in such a way that concepts introduced at an earlier stage are later revisited and elaborated upon. Using this approach, examples are first presented descriptively and graphically, while later chapters present a more advanced statistical treatment of these examples.

Thus, in the *comparing* strand, Chapter 4 introduces key concepts relating to the description and graphical display of comparisons between two data sets. These ideas are an extension of those presented in Chapter 3, which deals with the description of single variables. In turn, Chapter 7 shows how these concepts and examples can be extended to formal statistical tests of comparisons between two data sets. In Part II of the book, the ideas are extended further to include comparisons of more than two data sets, first descriptively (Chapters 11 and 13), then in terms of statistical tests (Chapters 12 and 14).

In the *relating* strand, Chapter 5 also builds on ideas from Chapter 3 by discussing methods for displaying and describing relationships between two variables. Chapter 8 extends the concepts to formal statistical tests of correlation between two variables, and these are further elaborated in Chapter 15 to include correlation and regression analysis in a multivariate context.

Chapters 6, 9, 10 and 16 straddle both strands. In Chapter 6, the relationship between probability and statistical testing is introduced, which is a necessary preparation for moving from the descriptive statistics in Chapters 4 and 5 to statistical testing in Chapters 7, 8 and beyond.

Chapter 9 is a somewhat pivotal chapter, in which ideas are revisited, drawn together and elaborated. Here key concepts in experimental design, such as control, causation and validity of experiments, are discussed. The inextricable link between specific research designs and choice of statistical test is also discussed, as is the logic of statistical inference. Chapter 10 encourages readers to think about statistical results more broadly by considering effect size and confidence intervals as alternative perspectives in judging the importance of data. Chapter 16 concludes matters by drawing together the key themes of the book, including variability, statistical inference and a discussion of some of the controversies surrounding the null hypothesis testing approach to significance testing.

GERRY MULHERN
BRIAN GREER

Acknowledgements

Warmest thanks to Joanna McGarry for her charming and efficient approach to this second edition and for having demonstrated just the right blend of support and subtle pressure. Thanks also to Neha Sharma for her excellent editorial assistance at an earlier stage of the process, and to Vidhya Jayaprakash, head of the project management team at Newgen Imaging Systems, Chennai for looking after the day-to-day production details so efficiently. To Maire and Swapna, much love and thanks for your unswerving support and forbearance. Finally, our thanks to the three anonymous reviewers of this revised edition for their stunningly detailed, constructive and apt comments. We were delighted to be able to incorporate changes based on their feedback and the final product is all the better for it. Any errors or omissions that remain are of course our own.

GERRY MULHERN
BRIAN GREER

About the authors

GERRY MULHERN is Senior Lecturer in Psychology at Queen's University Belfast, UK and was President of the British Psychological Society from 2010 to 2011. He has previously taught at the Universities of Edinburgh and Ulster and has published widely in the areas of applied cognition and mathematics education.

BRIAN GREER is Adjunct Professor in the Graduate School of Education at Portland State University, USA. He has taught statistics to psychology students for many years and has published widely on mathematics education.

Both authors have conducted research into how people learn mathematical concepts and they bring this knowledge to bear in the explanations contained within *Making Sense of Data and Statistics in Psychology*.

Statistics in psychology

In this chapter

... we describe our approach to the book and our aims and expectations for its readers. The status of psychology as a science is examined, and the importance of statistical methods within psychology discussed. The nature of variability in psychological research data is also examined, and four main sources of variation are identified.

What does this book offer?

This textbook is intended to achieve something that many of its predecessors have promised, but too often have failed to deliver; that is, to present a clear, concise, nontechnical explanation of statistical and methodological concepts in psychology at an introductory level (Part I), and, similarly, to explore key concepts at the post-introductory level (Part II).

Our approach is to enable you to acquire a 'feel' for data, as well as a pragmatic competence in statistical techniques. We aim to provide a conceptual framework that allows you to get the most from your data. Since nowadays students seldom – if ever – need to compute statistics by hand, we stress an understanding of principles and concepts, rather than procedural or technical understanding. Throughout the book, we place considerable emphasis on principles of *exploratory data analysis* (EDA) and on encouraging you to acquire fluency in the use of visual representations which we consider to be the most powerful tools for making sense of data.

Since we are psychologists, our focus is more on data analysis than on statistical theory, and therefore, on occasion, we have chosen to simplify concepts that a 'hard' statistician might wish to elaborate or qualify. We make no apology for this.

Our philosophy and approach

In writing this book, we have attempted to strike an appropriate balance between the curricular imperatives of psychological statistics and the need to acknowledge the realities of life as a psychology student coming to terms with statistics, probably for the first time.

We recognise that the majority of students using this text will be members of large classes, learning statistics in the relatively impersonal setting of lectures and large laboratory classes. Many students, rightly or wrongly, find large classes intimidating and unconducive to asking questions. A consequent risk of students' failure to clarify important concepts as the need arises may be slow progress, reduced momentum and, in some cases, disenfranchisement. This is a reality.

We are also conscious that, in general, groups of psychology students tend to be heterogeneous in terms of ability, motivation and academic background. While, for some, psychology may be their main academic interest, others will be taking it as a minor or subsidiary subject. Moreover, at school, some students will have studied science and mathematics to an advanced level, while many more will have taken humanities and social sciences. A substantial proportion of the latter will, to a greater or lesser extent, find the idea of learning statistics daunting, if not aversive. This too is a reality.

Our aim in writing this book is to present statistical concepts in a way that will engage all students, irrespective of ability, academic background or attitude to learning statistics. In doing so, we have adhered to the following principles:

- We have kept the written text relatively short and to the point, liberally peppering it with figures and illustrations.
- In order to help orientate the reader, new concepts and terms are printed in **bold** type.
- As far as possible, we have avoided technical jargon, mathematical symbols and formulae – many other textbooks state this aim but merely pay lip service to it.
- We have gone even further by limiting the arcane terminology of psychological statistics, such as 'central tendency', which is an unnecessary legacy of the past.

- In order to avoid getting in the way of the statistical concepts under consideration, we use vivid, simple examples.
- Similarly, we use real data sets for authenticity, as well as smaller bespoke, though plausible, sets designed to make a specific point. On occasion, we juxtapose two alternative or contrasting data sets in order to emphasise a particular concept.
- Through the use of dialogues, we discuss, in everyday language, the sorts of questions that typically occur to students.
- Active learning is encouraged through regular use of *'Before reading on ...'* activities sandwiched within the text.
- In this second edition, we have introduced a *'Making links'* feature to help draw together ideas from different parts of the text or to emphasise the overlap between statistics that are generally considered as separate approaches.
- We have also introduced some short sections entitled *'For those who wish to dig a little deeper'*. As the title suggests, this material deals with important ideas in a little more depth, and it can be skipped over, although we would suggest that you study it.
- From our experience gained over many years, we try to anticipate and pre-empt the conceptual difficulties that students may encounter.
- We assume that all students will have ready access to one of the popular computer-based statistical packages and although we have used SPSS (Version 18) to illustrate examples, *'Making sense of SPSS'* sections have been presented as stand-alone optional extras which can be ignored by students or instructors if they wish. These are clearly marked so that readers can use them or choose to ignore them as they see fit. For those who require more detailed descriptions of SPSS than those offered here, we recommend the excellent *SPSS for Psychologists* (4th edition) by Nicola Brace, Richard Kemp and Rosemary Snelgar, published in 2009 by Palgrave Macmillan. Where appropriate, we offer page references to this book.

Figure 1.1 presents a schematic guide to chapters. You will see that, following this introductory chapter, the rest of the book divides largely into two strands, based on the two main functions of statistical tests – *comparing* data sets and *relating* data sets (more of this later). An important feature of the book is that, in each of these two strands, chapters are organised so that ideas introduced at an earlier stage are later revisited and elaborated. We hope you will find this approach to learning effective, as you are encouraged to progress gradually with an opportunity to revise and build upon earlier material.

How to use this book

This text is neither a 'cookbook' nor an instruction manual. Those intending to whip out a calculator and set about finding out *how to do* a particular statistical test will be disappointed much of the time. Such is the ubiquity of information technology that the days of having to carry out your own calculations have well and truly gone. In any case, we take the view that working through calculations by hand is over-rated as a means of gaining an understanding of a test. Recognising this, we focus instead on the rationale underlying statistical tests and on statistical interpretation of results. That said, we recognise that there are different styles of learning and that some students may find working through a calculation helpful. Consequently, we have included calculations among our online support materials to which those who wish can refer.

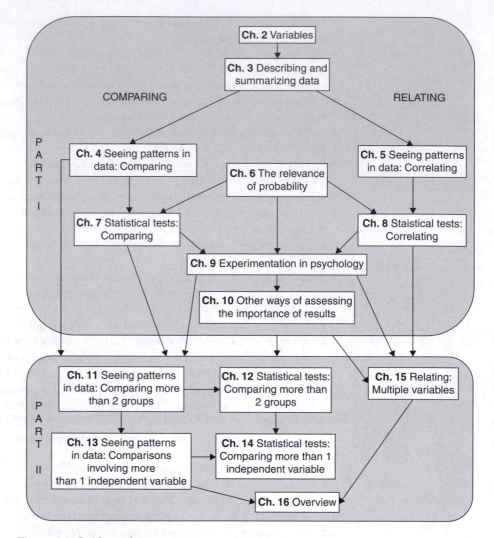

Figure 1.1 Guide to chapters

The book has been written as an integrated whole, with the sequencing of material carefully planned. Students with little statistical knowledge and limited experience of data handling are strongly advised to start at the beginning and work through to the end. Experienced readers may prefer a more flexible approach, although we would advise that they too should adhere more or less to the intended sequence.

As has already been indicated, we have punctuated the text at regular intervals with *Before reading on ...* activities and questions. Please resist the temptation to skip over these. They are an essential part of our pedagogic approach, intended to encourage you to process information actively. Similarly, we consider the *Student/ Lecturer* dialogues to be an extremely important pedagogic vehicle. The fact that they appear informal and possibly at times not obviously relevant is their strength. They have been written carefully for a specific purpose and each contains powerful ideas.

OK, so why statistics?

Student: I became a psychology student because I'm curious about why people behave as they do. I'm not even sure I will want to become a psychologist when I graduate – at the moment, I'm interested in a career in advertising.

Lecturer: That's not unusual; many psychology graduates use their degree as a basis for pursuing a career outside psychology.

Student: I have to say I'm a bit surprised and daunted by the amount of statistics and research methods we're expected to learn. I'm really only interested in the subject matter of psychology, and so are a lot of the other students I've spoken to. We have no interest in statistics, or anything mathematical. So, why are we expected to study statistics?

Lecturer: First, let me reassure you that statistics is not some arbitrary hurdle you have to jump over at the whim of your tutor or lecturer. Although you may not realise it just yet, statistics and research methods are among the most valuable subjects you will learn.

Student: Why is that? They don't interest me and, besides, I'm not sure that it's right for psychologists to reduce people to numbers.

Lecturer: Spend a moment or two thinking about some of the psychological facts you have learned on your course so far.

Student: Actually, I've found there aren't too many facts as such. There are lots of theories and ideas, and some major disagreements and controversies.

Lecturer: Why do you think that is?

Student: Well, because researchers have different ideas about the processes underlying behaviour.

Lecturer: And how do they go about forming and developing these ideas?

Student: Usually, they carry out, or read about, research to test their ideas.

Lecturer: You've basically answered your own question. In a nutshell, the reason why you need to learn about statistics and research methods lies in the fact that psychology is first and foremost an **empirical** discipline. By that I mean that psychological knowledge is acquired through systematic gathering of data, in a variety of forms, and the subsequent analysis and interpretation of these data. Think about some of the major debates in psychology.

Student: What, like nature versus nurture, or different theories of schizophrenia?

Lecturer: What do you notice about the substance of these debates?

Student: Now you mention it, the discussion nearly always focuses on the way the research was carried out, or what the results mean.

Lecturer: True. Indeed, much of the debate in psychology consists of critiquing methods and procedures used by researchers to support their own ideas or to counter someone else's. Wouldn't it be more satisfying if you knew something about experimentation and statistics, so that you could do some critiquing of your own?

Student: I suppose so, but two researchers holding incompatible views can't both be right, can they?

Lecturer: It's not so much a question of right and wrong in any absolute sense. As you will see, it has more to do with interpretation. In studying psychology, your task is to evaluate the evidence and come to your own conclusions. Sometimes you will agree with psychologists' interpretations of their findings; at other times you will be less convinced.

Student: But, in order to do that, don't I need to be able to make an informed judgement about the quality of the research and the strength of the data?

Lecturer: Precisely! In order to interpret empirical findings and evaluate the researcher's methods, it's essential that you know statistics and research methods. Incidentally, this expertise will prove useful far beyond the realm of psychology. You need the same powers of critical evaluation and probabilistic reasoning in everyday life, and in virtually every area of employment, including advertising.

Student: Since you put it that way ...

Do you recognise yourself in any of the above? The chances are that you do. Having taught statistics for more than sixty years between the two of us, if we had a pound (or a dollar) for every time one of our students asked why they had to study statistics, we would be very wealthy!

Variability in psychology

Of course, the fact that psychology is an empirical discipline is a necessary but not sufficient reason for needing to use statistics. Imagine if we lived in a world in which everybody was the same, so that people were identical in every respect, with the same genetic code, physical characteristics, mental capacities, opinions, tastes, ambitions, socioeconomic status, lifestyle, personality, health, lifespan, educational qualifications, environmental influences and so on. Imagine too that all other animals were similarly uniform. Furthermore, suppose we were able to measure or quantify every one of these features with complete precision. In such a world, psychologists would have little need for statistics. Research would merely involve measuring some characteristic or other. What is more, since there would be no variation, measurements of a single person would generalise with complete precision to the entire population. The only statistics that would be required would be the most rudimentary description of these measurements. Even the most basic summary statistics would be redundant.

Hence, it is not the empirical nature of psychology *per se* that gives rise to the need for statistics and research methods; rather, it is the fact that psychology is an empirical discipline in a world of variability, uncertainty and inaccuracy. Given the nature of living things, such variability is inherent in all human, biological and social sciences. Indeed, more generally, the popular view of science as yielding definitive answers has long been untenable, even in the so-called pure or natural sciences, where results are seldom conclusive and frequently contradictory. One only has to think of currently hotly debated topics in physics, such as worm holes, dark matter, string theory, supersymmetry and the like.

Taming variability

In studying behaviour, psychologists must somehow cope with the variation and uncertainty that is such an essential characteristic of the world in which we live. That is where both **research methods** and **statistics** come in. As you will see later, the two go hand in hand. The term 'research methods' refers to a set of procedures and techniques for data collection in situations of variability, while 'statistics' is a set of techniques for exploring, summarising and making sense of the data collected. A host of statistical techniques have been designed to cope with variation and uncertainty in data, and each is linked inextricably to the particular research method used to generate the data in the first place. In later chapters, you will see how various statistical techniques are linked to specific research designs.

In statistics, the essential tool for coping with the variation and uncertainty that are such essential characteristics of our world is **probability** theory. Chapter 6 describes in some detail how knowledge of probability helps us to draw conclusions about data.

Everyday statistics

While a term like 'probability' is technical and mathematical, you should bear in mind that we all use ideas of probability regularly in our daily lives. Upon hearing a weather forecast of a 70% chance of rain, you are much more likely to reach for your umbrella than for a forecast of a 5% chance of rain. You would also have an intuitive sense of the likelihood of it snowing on Midsummer's Day. You may be familiar with dilemmas faced by investors as to whether to buy shares or to put their money into lower-risk options. In deciding to travel on an aeroplane, or not to eat beef, or to give up smoking, or not to practise safe sex, or to buy a lottery ticket, you are intuitively making probabilistic judgements.

Individuals who apparently flout the risks may be considered by others, and perhaps even by themselves, as behaving irrationally. More often, however, it is simply that people have different thresholds for what they consider to be 'acceptable risk', or they may weigh the risk against competing factors.

A possible exception may be the decision to buy a Lotto ticket. In the UK, the chance of winning the jackpot is approximately 14,000,000 to 1. Put into context, this means that, if you buy a ticket two hours before the draw, you are more likely to be dead by the time the draw is made than you are to have won the jackpot. Despite these widely publicised odds, millions of people opt for a weekly flutter (including one of the authors of this book, though emphatically not the other – a clear illustration of human variability!).

The important point is that we all appear to make these probabilistic judgements quite naturally. Clearly, the better informed we are about the processes underlying uncertainty, the more likely we are to make sound decisions. In the context of psychological research, statistics provides a formal framework to enable you to make similarly sound judgements about data.

Causes of variability

Among the many sources of variation that afflict psychological research, we can identify four broad clusters.

Measurement variation

Errors in measurement, perhaps the most obvious causes of variability in data, are present in all empirical disciplines. Indeed, variations in astronomical measurements were one of the first contexts within which statistical theory developed. One source of variation is the sensitivity, or calibration, of measuring instruments. Put simply, a measurement is only as good as the instrument that produces it. Even for physical characteristics, such as weight or height, instruments have limited sensitivity, and measurements are recorded to the nearest unit of calibration, for example, grams or millimetres.

Variation may also occur due to inaccuracies in measuring instruments. These may be systematic (leading to consistent overestimation or underestimation), or they may be random (leading to unsystematic variation from one measurement to the next). The former is likely to prove less problematic than the latter in research, in that systematic measurement errors do not affect the overall pattern of measurements. Indeed, if the magnitude of the error is known, it can be corrected readily by addition to, or subtraction from, the measurement as appropriate.

Situational variation

It may be stating the obvious to suggest that the behaviour of individuals can be affected by environmental conditions, such as time of day, room temperature, appearance of the researcher or test instructions. Again, these may have a consistent effect on all participants, particularly if the researcher makes an effort to keep situational factors constant. More problematically, conditions may vary randomly from one participant to another, sometimes unavoidably. It may, for example, be a practical necessity to schedule participants throughout the day.

Individual variation

It is self-evident that, on any measure, whether physical or psychological, people display substantial **individual differences**, a term used widely in the psychological literature. Such differences are undoubtedly the most important source of variability in psychological research. Much of the variation is the result of physical and psychological 'traits', which can be considered fixed within, but which differ between, individuals. Many research designs and statistical methods originated from the necessity to cope with individual differences of this sort.

There is, of course, another important cause of individual variation, namely the tendency for individuals to vary in their own behaviour or performance from one occasion to another. For example, if you were to measure a person's reaction time on ten successive occasions, you would find differences in performance across the ten sessions. Similarly, you might assess a person's mood on a particular day, only to find it had changed markedly the next. This within-individual 'state' variability can arise from natural cycles and rhythms, or from a host of situational factors within a person's everyday life. Of course, since participants are often tested on a one-off basis, performance reflects an individual's state at one, somewhat arbitrary, point in time.

You may find a golfing analogy useful for contrasting between- and within-individual differences. In a tournament, such as the US Masters, competitors play a round of golf on each of four successive days. Between-individual variation is reflected in all golfers' scores after each round, and more especially their overall position on the leader board at the end of the tournament. Within-individual variation, on the other hand, is indicated by the change in each golfer's individual scores across the four days, *irrespective* of those of other competitors.

Sample variation

As you will see in later chapters, most psychological research involves using data from **samples**, drawn from a **population** in order to form general conclusions about the population as a whole. Just as in the case of individual variation, the data from one sample can differ markedly from the data from another sample because of differences between the individuals making up the samples. Moreover, some samples may give a fair reflection of their parent population, while others may provide a distorted picture. In psychological research, great care must be taken to try to ensure that samples are **representative** of their populations, so that variability across a number of samples is minimised. Again, as you will see later, various research designs and statistical techniques have been designed to help researchers cope with **sample variation**.

Psychology as a science

In the past, some psychologists have tended to get bogged down with the well-trodden question of psychology's scientific credentials. In our view, it is not particularly helpful to think along these lines since, by necessity, the argument centres on the definition of the term 'science'. Of course psychology is a science, and the criteria for regulation of undergraduate psychology programmes by professional bodies across the world reflect this. More important than its scientific status, however, is the empirical nature of the discipline, guided by the scientific principles of objectivity, replicability and rigour. While the collection and analysis of quantitative data play a central role, we should bear in mind that psychology is an eclectic, interdisciplinary subject that relies on a wide range of methodological approaches, including experiments, surveys, case studies, questionnaire studies, test construction, discourse analysis, semi-structured interviews, ethnography, meta-analysis and computer modelling.

These different empirical approaches all involve the systematic gathering and objective analysis of evidence. As such, each has its role in the science of behaviour and mental life. In this book, we do not attempt to cover the full gamut of empirical approaches to psychological research. Our primary focus is on quantitative methods and analysis, which are by far the most common. In particular, we are concerned with the empirical approach represented in Figure 1.2.

In its basic form, the researcher (i) identifies a topic and specifies the goals of the research; (ii) formulates one or more precise research questions (called **hypotheses**); (iii) devises a study to address these questions (called **research design**); (iv) gathers

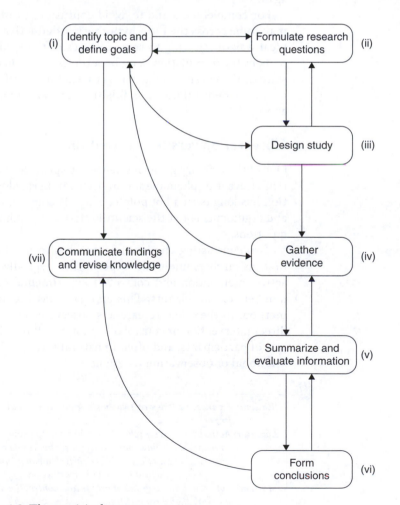

Figure 1.2 The empirical process

numerical information about these questions (called **data collection**); (v) summarises and evaluates this information (called **statistical analysis**); and (vi) draws appropriate conclusions (called **interpretation**). Finally, (vii) the results of the study are communicated (called **dissemination**) and integrated with existing knowledge. As the various arrows on the diagram suggest, the process is not necessarily sequential, but may involve iteration and feedback between the various sub-stages. In this book, we focus on the basic cycle in (i)–(vii).

Interrelationship of theory and experimentation

The iterative processes of feedback and modification, as well as the revision of existing knowledge on the basis of new findings, typify empirical research in psychology and other similar disciplines. Indeed, without this 'experimentation/theory cycle', psychological research would fail to progress. Instead, we would be left with a collection of fragmented facts. In order that research on any topic can move forward, hypotheses must be rooted in current knowledge of the topic, the data collected must allow the predictions contained in the hypotheses to be tested, and the outcomes must be assimilated into the current body of knowledge, so that the process can begin again.

For completeness and to avoid confusion, we should note that, elsewhere, you may come across the term **hypothetico-deductive method**, which is a more technical way of referring to several stages of the empirical process described above, namely, the formulation of an hypothesis based on existing theory, data collection, statistical analysis, conclusion as to whether to refute existing theory or not based on the evidence (known as **falsification**) and modification of existing theory as appropriate.

Observation versus intervention

One of the primary goals of science is to provide explanations of what *causes* a particular event or phenomenon to occur. In psychology, the issue of **causal explanation** has long been a hot potato. There is considerable overlap between this debate and arguments about the scientific status of psychology, although they are distinct questions.

Two contrasting empirical approaches in psychology may be identified. In the first, researchers undertake experiments, typically laboratory-based and involving active intervention and control of experimental conditions, with relatively small numbers of participants. This approach has become known as the **experimental method**. In the other, researchers observe or measure people's behaviour without direct intervention or control of conditions, typically involving relatively large samples of participants, and often in natural settings. These studies are known as **correlational** or **observational** designs.

Student: I can see there are two basic approaches, but I don't see why the distinction is important.

Lecturer: Actually, as a researcher, it is important to know which method you are using, and that your choice can have important consequences. Let me give you an example. Say you are interested in the effect of sleep deprivation on people's speed of response. How might you use the experimental method to investigate the effect?

Student: You would take a group of people and control the amount of sleep they could have, then measure their response times.

Lecturer: Explain how you would do that in a little more detail.

Student: Well, say you had twelve people and you allowed four of them to sleep for two hours before wakening them, another four could be wakened after four hours, and the remaining four after six hours. You would also measure each group's response times when they woke up and look to see if there were differences between the groups.

Lecturer: OK, say you found quite large differences – what would you conclude?

Student: That the amount of sleep affected people's speed of response.

Lecturer: Can you think of any other explanation?

Student: All things being equal, no. That's to say, assuming the three groups were broadly similar in terms of general characteristics, and providing I was sensible and careful about how I treated the people, I think it's a pretty safe conclusion.

Lecturer: Now, how would you go about investigating the same question using observational methods?

Student: Well, you would just have to find people who had slept for different periods of time and measure their reaction times. I'm not quite sure how you would ensure a spread of sleep deprivation – maybe you could wait outside a local factory and ask people who had just come off the night shift.

Lecturer: So, you're saying that you would end up with a group of people, all of whom had slept for different lengths of time? How, then, would you examine the relationship between sleep deprivation and response time?

Student: Basically, by looking to see if, in general, those with less sleep had different response times from those with lots of sleep and those with middling amounts.

Lecturer: Say you found large differences. What could you conclude this time?

Student: Pretty much the same as last time – that the amount of sleep affects reaction time.

Before reading on...

Think about the dialogue so far. Do you agree with the student's conclusions?

... now read on

Lecturer: Let's look again at your last conclusion. Might there be other explanations for the differences?

Student: Hmm, not sure.

Lecturer: Well, remember you said that, for the experimental approach, as long as you could assume that the three groups were equivalent in everything except amount of sleep, you could assume that sleep deprivation affected reaction time.

Student: Yes – ah, so you're asking me the same question again. Right, well, since I did not intervene by manipulating the amount of sleep, I just had to take whoever came along.

Lecturer: Can you safely assume that those people with less sleep were otherwise equivalent to those with moderate sleep, and in turn to those with more sleep?

Student: No – for a start, the ones with little sleep might have come from the night shift, or a club, or whatever.

Lecturer: Indeed, or some may have been rampant insomniacs out looking for a drugstore.

Student: Or werewolves, even!

Lecturer: Hmm! The important thing to remember is that, in the observational study, there may have been some underlying factor, or factors, that influenced both the amount of sleep participants had and their response times. For example, suppose the sleep-deprived individuals tended to be older than their well-slept counterparts.

Student: So, while it might seem that sleep deprivation had influenced reaction time, in reality there is no direct link between the two.

Lecturer: Right – put another way, it might not be a **causal** relationship.

Student: And that's because the study was observational? So the fact that I could infer a causal link in the experiment was because the amount of sleep was carefully manipulated, and this allowed me to assume that any differences in the speed of response of my groups were caused by this intervention?

> *Lecturer:* Correct – assuming you took the necessary precautions to ensure that your three groups were equivalent in all other relevant respects.
>
> *Student:* What precautions are those?
>
> *Lecturer:* We'll see in Chapter 9.
>
> *Student:* Incidentally, does that mean that the observational approach is not scientific, but the experimental one is?
>
> *Lecturer:* That's an interesting question, and there's no simple answer. Certainly, it's true that one approach is called experimental, and the other non-experimental, and some psychologists equate this with the former being scientific and the latter unscientific. Personally, I think this is wrong. I can think of some observational studies that make very good science and some experimental studies that make very bad science. The important thing in all empirical work, whatever the approach, is to strive for rigour and objectivity in the methods used.

Chapter review

Following a discussion of our philosophy and ambitions for the book, we introduced a number of key issues relating to research methods and statistics within psychology. We argued that it is essential to have a sound grasp of statistical concepts in order to understand the empirical aspects of the discipline, as well as a pragmatic sense of how to deal with the ubiquitous influences of variability and uncertainty in psychological data. We also suggested that arguments about the scientific nature of psychology are less important than those about the various empirical methods used by researchers to advance psychological knowledge.

Part I

Making sense of basic designs

Variables

In this chapter

...the methods used to generate the raw material for statistical analysis, namely numerical data, are described and discussed. We consider the range of ways in which researchers go about measuring what they are interested in, and the types of numbers that are produced by these measurement procedures. The key concept of a **variable** as a theoretical entity that can be measured and expressed as a number on a single scale is introduced, and the concept is illustrated by typical examples from psychological research. The basic idea of psychological research as the exploration of relationships between variables through data is outlined, with examples.

Ways of measuring people (and other animals)

For statistical analysis you need numerical data, and for numerical data you must have ways of measuring what you are interested in. A great deal of effort on the part of scientists in general, and psychologists in particular, goes into devising ways of measuring. Physicists apply theoretical and technical expertise in measuring the temperatures of distant stars and the properties of subatomic particles; psychologists must be equally ingenious in measuring subtle aspects of the behaviour, abilities, personality, feelings and mental life of humans (and other animals).

Here are some examples – intended to provide a representative rather than an exhaustive survey of all possibilities from the measurement repertoire of empirical psychology.

Direct physical measurements

Historical examples include phrenology (the study of the supposed links between areas of the brain and human propensities through the measurement of parts of the skull) and anthropometry (the study of body measurements). While such approaches have now been largely discredited, they are of great historical interest and made very important contributions to the development of psychological theory and statistical methods.

In some areas of applied research, such as ergonomics, body measurements such as height, weight, grip strength, heart rate are of interest and can be measured using appropriate apparatus. More indirect physiological measures include galvanic skin response (which may give an indication of level of stress, for example) and scans of brain activity (which researchers link to a variety of mental states and processes).

Observations

The behaviour of animals, children or adults can be observed in environments varying from **naturalistic** to highly **controlled**, and with or without direct **intervention** by the experimenter. Such observations may be **qualitative** and described in verbal terms (as in a great deal of Piaget's work on cognitive development) or **quantitative**. For example, the frequency of occurrence of a predefined behaviour may be noted, as in counting the number of times a boy or girl playing in a school interacts with 'male' and 'female' toys. Another example would be measuring the amount of time mice placed in the same cage spend fighting with each other.

Performance measures

People can be asked to perform a variety of tasks, and aspects of their performance such as speed, accuracy or productivity can be measured. For example, typing skill could be measured by the amount of text typed in a given time, in conjunction with the number of errors made. A rat could be 'asked' to run a maze with a food reward at the end, and its performance measured by the number of wrong turns and the time taken. Exams might be thought of as a particular, and complex, form of performance measure.

Self-reports

As long as they have the necessary skills, people can be asked to report things about themselves either verbally or in writing (or using some other form of physical recording). A simple example would be a perception experiment in which the participant has to judge whether two stimuli are the same or different on some dimension and report that judgement to the experimenter. A more complex example would be if the participant is asked, say, 'On a scale of 1 to 10, how anxious are you?'

A more developed form of this approach is the questionnaire aimed at measuring something in particular. You may be familiar with this sort of exercise in the popular press. For example, under the headline 'How sensitive are you to others?' you might be asked to answer questions such as the following:

> You are eating out with a number of friends, and one of them asks, 'Do you mind if I smoke?' You do mind.
> Do you say:
> (a) Yes, it's bad for my health.
> (b) No, that's okay.
> (c) You should have more concern for others.

At the end, there is a key that awards points for each answer chosen. You add them up, and are told how, if you obtained a certain score, you are too good to be true; how, for a different score, you are quite sensitive; and so on. Questionnaires used in psychological research (apart from some technical refinements) are not all that different; see the example below on measuring attitude to computers.

Subjective ratings

Clearly, some characteristics of people are more difficult to measure than others. In many cases, you can at least ask a panel of people to make subjective judgements, and combine their judgements into a single figure (as is done in scoring performance in ice skating or gymnastics competitions). For example, videotapes of pupils in a classroom could be shown and the panel asked to rate how well each pupil behaved, say on a scale of 1 to 10. Averaging the ratings would give overall measures that could be used in statistical analysis.

Nature of data generated

Consider a particular number, say 4. If you think about it, we use 4 in many different ways. For a start, we can distinguish between counting items and measuring quantity (compare *there are 4 bottles of milk* with *there are 4 pints of milk in the jug*, for example). When a child says 'I am 4 years old', she does not mean exactly 4 (unless it happens to be her birthday), but rather somewhere between 4 and 5 years old. Four can also be used to indicate position in a sequence, as in Henry the Fourth. It can be used for identification purposes (for example, a No. 4 bus). It can be a number on a footballer's shirt. And so on.

Note that the way in which the number is used defines the properties of the number and, in turn, determines which arithmetical operations can validly be applied. It makes sense to say that 4 bottles of milk is 1 fewer than 5 bottles of milk, and twice as many as 2 bottles. It makes sense to say that 4°C is 1°C less than 5°C, but actually it does *not* make sense to say that 4°C is twice as warm as 2°C (think about why not; this will be discussed below). The player in a football team wearing the number 4 shirt is not twice as *anything* as the player wearing the number 2 shirt. You should be able to think of many examples – often they are turned into jokes of a kind, as in 'If Henry the Eighth had six wives, how many did Henry the Fourth have?'

The most natural use of numbers is for counting discriminable entities (not necessarily physical objects). That's why the positive whole numbers, 1, 2, 3, 4 … are called *natural numbers*. Very often the collection of data in psychological experiments involves counting the number of times something happens – for example, the number of errors a pupil makes on a test, the number of times a rat stands on its hind feet during a given period of time, the number of different uses a person can think of for a brick (a measure of creativity).

Other numbers represent quantities that can vary continuously and *fill in* the gaps between the natural numbers. An obvious example of something that varies continuously is weight. Intuitively, you can think of weight increasing slowly as you grow, and corresponding to a continuum of numbers associated with some unit of measurement, such as grams. A number line provides a powerful way of forming an image to think about it. For statistical purposes, the numbers between whole numbers can be represented as decimals, to any given level of accuracy. However, data such as weights and heights are often measured to the nearest gram or centimetre.

Levels of measurement

The numerical data generated by measuring take many different forms. As will become clear throughout this book, this diversity has crucial implications for the design of experiments and the types of statistical analysis that are appropriate. The various types of number, with differing properties, that are generated by measurement procedures are often referred to by statisticians in terms of four so-called **levels of measurement**, corresponding to measurement scales with increasingly strong properties, as follows.

Nominal scale

This level corresponds to measurement in a minimal sense, in which numbers are used merely as names to distinguish categories and have none of the properties we would normally associate with numbers (such as rank or relative size). In this case, numbers are used merely as labels for categories into which people may be divided. An example would be nationality. If an experimental investigation of humour was targeting English, French, German and Italian people, then, for convenience, the numerical labels 1, 2, 3 and 4 might be attached to people of each of these four nationalities respectively. Any distinguishable symbols could be used just as well, but numerical coding is convenient (and is required for some statistical computer packages). Which numerical label goes with which nationality is entirely arbitrary, and of course there is no sense in which the particular labelling above implies that Italians are higher than Germans on anything, or that Italians are twice as anything as the French.

The simplest case of a nominal measure is when there are only two categories – **dichotomous** data, to use the technical term ('dichotomous' meaning 'cut in two'). An obvious example is sex. The data to be analysed would consist merely of the number of cases that were found in each category.

Ordinal scale

At this level, the extra ingredient is that the numbers in this scale have a definite order and appropriate inferences can be drawn because of that order. By way of example, an investigator looking at the mathematical ability of children in a class might ask the teacher to use subjective judgement to rank the children in this respect. Incidentally, alphabetical ordering, letters A, B, C ... could be used just as well as numbers (as long as the class didn't have more than 26 members). For an ordinal scale such as this, it is appropriate to conclude that the child ranked 4 (starting from the best) has been judged better than the one ranked 5, but not as good as the one ranked 3. However, it is not appropriate to conclude that the differences between the children ranked 3 and 4 and those ranked 7 and 8, for example, are the same – it could be that the third best child is *just* better than the fourth, but the seventh is a *lot* better than the eighth. That is, we cannot assume that the intervals between points across the scale are equal. Similarly, it would be nonsensical to conclude that the child ranked 4 is half as able (whatever that would mean) as the child ranked 2. That is, it does not make sense to compare points on the scale in terms of their ratios.

In the example just discussed, there is a single ranking of all the cases, and each rank corresponds to one case. In other situations, the same ranks may be applied to each case separately. For example, suppose the teacher was asked instead to assess each child on mathematical ability as follows: 1, outstanding; 2, above average; 3, average; 4, below average; 5, weak. Here again, a rank of 4 is between 3 and 5, but the differences between 3 and 4, and 4 and 5 cannot be assumed to be equivalent, and in no sense does a rank of 4 represent twice as *anything* as a rank of 2.

Assigning numbers to ranks facilitates the calculation of various statistics and the coding of data for computer analysis.

Interval scale

Measurement on an interval scale implies all the properties of an ordinal scale, but in addition it has the property that differences, or intervals, are considered equal. An example is temperature, as measured in degrees Centigrade, say. The difference between 8°C and 12°C is equivalent to that between 33°C and 37°C. It would take the same amount of heat energy to raise the temperature of a fixed amount of water by 4°C in both cases. However, it does not make sense to say that 8°C is twice as warm as 4°C, since Centigrade is not measured on a scale with an absolute zero; rather, zero on this scale is the temperature at which water freezes. Hence, while we can assume equal intervals between points anywhere on the scale, it does not make sense to compare points on the scale in terms of their ratios.

Ratio scale

Finally, on a ratio scale, it does make sense to compare two numbers on the scale in terms of their ratio, because zero on such a scale really means 'nothing' of what is being measured. Weight is a clear example – zero is the weight of nothing, the reading on a balance when there is nothing on it. As a consequence, the ratio of two measures is meaningful – a baby mouse of 40 grams is twice as heavy as one of 20 grams (two of the lighter mice would balance one of the heavier on a balance, for example).

Derived values

Many numbers that become the grist for statistical mills are not simple direct measurements as such, but rather the results of more or less complex procedures. Consider an experiment in which reaction time is being measured (that is, the time it takes someone to react to a stimulus – for example, by pressing a button when a light comes on). It would be possible simply to measure the time that this takes (for example, by using apparatus interfaced with a computer that can determine when the light went on and when the button was pressed, and working out the time interval between these events). The disadvantage is that you would be relying on a single measurement of a capability that is subject to considerable fluctuation, as can be demonstrated by asking someone to carry out this task repeatedly. Accordingly, it is much better to make the measurement several times and take one of several possible averages of the results. This average can be considered a more accurate measure of the individual's speed of reaction in general than any single measurement. By way of analogy, in ice skating, the marks of several judges are combined, albeit in a somewhat complex way, into a single overall mark. You will be able to think of many other situations in sport and other contexts where this sort of procedure is followed.

Another example, to be dealt with in more detail below, is the derivation of an IQ score as a complex overall summary of performance on a variety of tasks.

The idea of a variable

In thinking about data, the notion of a **variable** is absolutely central. The term refers to any aspect of interest that varies (hence the name) among people, animals or other units of analysis (for example, countries). Thus, we can conceive of *aggressive-ness* as something that a person, an animal or a country possesses to a greater or a lesser degree.

In determining what counts as a variable, culture plays a major role. In particular, we tend to attribute the status of variable to any quality that has a name. Indeed, new names may be invented for this purpose, either in the wider culture, such as the relatively recent term 'male chauvinism', or within a more specialized scientific field, as in the less recent introduction of the introversion/extraversion dimension in psychology.

There is a very strong psychological tendency, once something is accepted implicitly as a variable, to assume that it has strong structural properties. Consider an abstract quality such as 'tolerance'. In the ways in which people talk about tolerance we may detect many implicit and debatable assumptions, in particular the following:

(a) People differ in their level of tolerance.
(b) Each person can be considered to have, in some sense, a basic overall level of tolerance. Of course, it is recognized that this level is not constant over time and is relative to target groups; for example, a person could be differentially tolerant in relation to race and religion (though these attitudes tend to be related).
(c) As a consequence, we are often prepared to make comments such as 'A is more tolerant than B'. More generally, the level of tolerance can be conceived of as lying somewhere on a single dimension.
(d) The level of tolerance of each individual can be measured with some degree of precision and expressed numerically.

Here are some illustrative examples of variables and their associated measurement procedures.

Handedness

This is a simple example but not as simple as you might think at first sight. It would be possible to simply ask each person 'Are you right-handed or left-handed?' But, in fact, handedness is not such a clear-cut matter. A person may be right-handed for some actions (opening a door, say), and left-handed for others (writing, say); or they may be ambidextrous. In practice, handedness is measured by means of a sample of behaviours. The *Edinburgh Handedness Inventory*, for example, asks the respondent to indicate whether they have an absolute preference, or a preference for one hand or the other, or are indifferent, for activities such as writing and drawing, using tools and utensils, and striking a match. Foot and eye preference are also taken into account. The responses are used to determine a single score reflecting the degree of left- or right-handedness. (Note that this procedure assumes that a measure of handedness on a single dimension makes sense.)

Reaction time

Speed of reaction is of importance in many situations, including driving, and a considerable amount of research has been devoted to studying the factors that influence it. In the simplest experimental set-up, the participant waits for a stimulus to appear (a light coming on, say) and then makes a response as quickly as possible (by pressing a button, for example). Many more complex variants of this basic set-up may be used. For example, there may be several alternative stimuli and several alternative responses, and the participant is required to make a specific response corresponding to each specific stimulus. As already mentioned, repetitions of such a task typically show considerable variation in the measured reaction times for the same participant, so it is normal to average over a number of repetitions to obtain a more stable measure.

Attitude to computers

It is very common to measure attitudes through questionnaires. By way of a specific example, one measure of attitude to computers works as follows. The respondent is asked to report his/her feelings by reacting to twenty statements such as:

a. Computers help people have easier lives.
b. Computers help to create unemployment.
    The response is made by circling one of the numbers from 1 to 5, where:
    1 = strongly agree
    2 = agree
    3 = undecided
    4 = disagree
    5 = strongly disagree.

For statements like **b** above, the higher the number circled, the more positive the feeling reported. In this case, the numbers circled are added when calculating the total score. Conversely, for statements like **a**, the higher the number circled, the more negative the feeling reported. In this case, the scale is reversed: 5 becomes 1, 4 becomes 2, and so on, for the purposes of calculating the total score. Since there are twenty statements to be responded to, a total somewhere between 20 (the extreme negative response) and 100 (the extreme positive response) is obtained.

Intelligence

Tests of intelligence originated in France; but much of their subsequent development has taken place in the USA and the UK. The basic principle behind most such tests remains the assessment of performance on a variety of tasks, each assumed to require intelligence. More or less complex procedures are used to score the component tasks and then to combine those scores into a single measure of IQ (you can easily find out details on specific IQ tests).

Beyond issues of what types of ability are indicative of intelligence, and what constitutes an adequate selection of the vast range of candidate tasks, there are deep controversies about the nature of intelligence testing, notably in relation to its cultural bias. Further, the assumption that it is appropriate to measure intelligence on a single dimension is itself controversial.

Variables under experimental control

The above examples – handedness, reaction time, attitude to computers and intelligence – are all cases in which the value of the variable is a measure of an individual's *performance* (or score) on the construct in question. Such measures of performance are known as **dependent variables** (note the spelling of the adjective 'dependent', not the noun 'dependant' – a common error by students).

By contrast, there is another family of variables in psychological research that do not function as measures of performance. Instead, these variables are under the control of the researcher, so-called **independent variables**. Here participants can be assigned by the researcher to different values of the variable; that is, the variable in question is systematically manipulated, or controlled, by the researcher and participants are assigned to one of the values of the variable. For example, if an investigation were being carried out as to whether children performed better on a memory task if they were offered a reward for a good performance, then for each child tested, the researcher would decide which value of the **dichotomous** variable *reward/no reward* to assign to that child.

In many instances, the distinction between these two types of variable is entirely clear. There are cases, however, where it becomes blurred and you need to be alert to this (indeed, initially, this can be a source of confusion for some students). The blurring occurs when the researcher uses a measure of performance to categorize participants into one of a number of groups defining an independent variable. In such cases, for any given person, the value of the independent variable is inherent to that person, and not under the control of the experimenter.

Take handedness, for example. Suppose participants were scored using the *Edinburgh Handedness Inventory*. These scores can of course be used in their own right as a dependent variable to provide a numerical measure of individuals' handedness and analysed accordingly. But suppose that instead the researcher used the scores to assign each person to one of three categories – left-handed, right-handed or ambidextrous. In this case, the dependent variable has been used to create an independent variable with three values. Clearly, although the researcher can allocate participants to one of these values, this must be done of the basis of an individual's score, and the experimenter cannot simply decide which handedness group that participant should be assigned to. For fairly obvious reasons, these kinds of independent variable are called **subject variables** (although, given the trend away from using the term 'subject', they may increasingly become known as **participant variables**).

To illustrate the importance of **experimental control**, suppose a researcher wants to investigate the hypothesis that drinking coffee improves reaction time. Consider the differences between the following two approaches.

Approach 1

Experimental participants turn up in the morning. The experimenter asks them whether they drank coffee for breakfast. Their reaction times are measured subsequently and the values compared between the group that had drunk coffee and the group that had not.

Approach 2

Experimental participants are asked not to drink coffee for 24 hours before the experiment. When they turn up for the experiment, they are divided *randomly* into two groups. Here 'randomly' means that any individual participant is equally likely to be assigned to either group, which could be done by tossing a coin, for example. The participants in one group are given two cups of coffee prior to having their reaction times measured and those in the other group are not given any coffee to drink.

> **Before reading on …**
>
> Think carefully about these two approaches. What implications do the differences between the approaches have for the interpretation of the data?
>
> … **now read on.**

There are many aspects to consider about these two approaches, but the key point we want to make here is the contrast between the researcher merely *measuring* the value of a variable (here the dichotomous variable *coffee/no coffee*) and being able to *control* the variable. In the former case, the independent variable is a subject variable, since participants bring their coffee-drinking status with them. In the latter, the researcher controls who should be assigned the value *coffee* and who the value *no coffee*. This distinction has a crucial importance when it comes to interpreting the results, even though the data will look exactly the same in the two cases.

Suppose the data suggest that coffee-drinkers do, in fact, have quicker reaction times. If these data have come from an experiment based on *Approach 1*, we cannot with total confidence attribute the difference to drinking coffee.

> **Student:** *Why not? It seems clear to me that the coffee-drinkers have faster reaction times, so coffee makes you faster.*
>
> **Lecturer:** *Well, that's one possible scenario. But, let's just suppose, however implausibly, that intelligence is related to coffee drinking, specifically that more intelligent people are more likely to drink coffee for breakfast. So, in* Approach 1, *when the participants turned up, and were divided into groups, the coffee-drinking group would contain, in general, more intelligent people than the non-coffee-drinking group.*
>
> **Student:** *So what?*
>
> **Lecturer:** *Now suppose that intelligence is also related to reaction time, specifically that more intelligent people have faster reaction times, in general.*
>
> **Student:** *Ah, so the coffee-drinking group is loaded with more intelligent people, according to your scenario, and they also tend to have faster reaction times. And that's an alternative explanation for the difference in reaction times noted in the data.*
>
> **Lecturer:** *Exactly! That's the point. We say that the samples of coffee-drinkers and non-coffee-drinkers are biased – in particular, if the hypothetical scenario holds, they are biased with respect to intelligence, which in turn is related to reaction time.*
>
> **Student:** *OK, I'll buy that. So* Approach 1 *isn't a very good way to do an experiment, since you can't interpret the data with confidence?*
>
> **Lecturer:** *That's right. Do you think* Approach 2 *is better?*
>
> **Student:** *Well, I can see that randomly assigning participants to the two groups should mean that there would be no systematic differences between the two groups – in particular, they should be of about the same intelligence overall.*
>
> **Lecturer:** *And the same goes for any other possible complicating factor. One of the important skills of being a good experimenter is designing your experiment so that the story told by the data is not open to multiple interpretations.*

The distinction highlighted in the above example, between simply measuring independent variables as opposed to having them under experimental control, is a theme that recurs at many points in this book. Also, issues to do with dependent and independent variables are covered in greater detail in Chapter 9.

Investigating relationships between variables

Psychological research concerns itself with general questions, of which the following are not untypical:

• Do students with previous experience of using computers have a more favourable attitude towards them than those with no such previous experience?
• Does coffee improve reaction time?
• Do typists work faster in the morning than in the afternoon?
• Is reaction time related to intelligence?

Each of these questions can be seen as a question about the relationship between two variables. In the first example, the two variables are:

• attitude to computers and
• previous computer experience (a yes/no dichotomous variable).

The relationship between the two variables is investigated by comparing the scores for attitude to computers between the two groups of participants – those with previous computer experience and those without. Note that previous computer experience is a subject variable, not under the control of the experimenter.

In the second example (assuming *Approach 2* as described above is used) the two variables are:

• reaction time and
• consumption/non-consumption of coffee.

Again, the relationship between the two variables is investigated by comparing the reaction times between the two groups of participants. Here consumption/non-consumption of coffee is under the control of the experimenter (an independent variable).

In the third example, let us assume that the approach adopted is to test a group of typists both in the morning and in the afternoon. The two variables are:

• typing speed and
• time of day (morning/afternoon).

Note a major contrast with the first two examples. Here there is only one group of participants, each of whom is tested twice, and the comparison is *within* this group of participants, comparing their morning typing speeds and their afternoon typing speeds. The difference between comparisons made *between* groups of participants and comparisons made *within* a single group of participants is another key distinction that will recur throughout this book.

In the final example, the two variables are:

• reaction time and
• intelligence.

Again, there is a contrast between this example and the preceding ones. Here, both variables are multi-valued, whereas in all the previous cases one of the variables was dichotomous. In this case, the question of interest is whether or not there is a relationship between reaction time and intelligence – is it the case that, in general, people with faster reaction times have higher intelligence and, conversely, that people with slower reaction times have lower intelligence?

In each of these four examples, we are considering a possible relationship between two variables. Such a relationship cannot be observed directly. Instead, we must find some way to measure or assign each of the variables so that data relating to the hypothesized relationship can be collected and subjected to statistical analysis. Our interpretation of this analysis then has implications for our view as to whether the relationship between the variables is important or not.

Part I of this book shows how relationships between two variables of various types, including those illustrated in the four examples above, can be investigated through the design of appropriate experiments, the collection of data and the statistical analysis of those data. In Part II, statistical methods for analysing more complex relationships between more than two variables are introduced.

Chapter review

In this chapter, we introduced, through examples, the key idea of variables as theoretical building blocks, and we considered the types of variable experimental psychologists study, the procedures devised to measure these variables and the nature of the numbers produced. We introduced initial ideas about dependent and independent variables and, in the latter case, distinguished between those variables under the direct control of the experimenter and those that the participant brings with them and which therefore cannot be manipulated, known as subject variables. We briefly discussed the different types of relationship between variables and noted how the investigation of such relationships is central to psychological research.

Describing and summarizing data

In this chapter

... ways of organizing a set of measurements for a group of participants on a single variable are set out. The first part deals with summary statistics; that is, numbers derived from the data that reflect important aspects of those data, namely, averages and the amount of variation within the data set. Then various graphical ways of displaying data are introduced.

Summary statistics

Summary statistics describe data in terms of three main aspects – average, variability and shape. Below is a data set representing the scores of a class of 27 students on the *Attitude to Computers Scale* described in Chapter 2 (see p. 21). The 27 numbers are initially written in no particular order.

60 62 62 47 63 69 68 46 70
60 56 54 48 50 49 58 49 66
54 53 56 52 57 63 71 61 43

An undigested list of numbers like this calls out for some organization to bring out its salient features and patterns. We begin with numerical summaries, called *summary statistics*, before considering a variety of graphical methods for displaying the data set revealingly.

Averages

The most familiar summary statistic is the *average*, as in figures such as the average number of children per married couple, average amount of rainfall in Manchester in June, average contents of a box of paperclips and so on. In these cases, the average referred to is technically called the **mean**, which is calculated by adding all the cases and dividing by the number of those cases. Note that, though 'average' is often taken to mean 'mean', it is a more general term, and there are several other types of average.

The total of the 27 *Attitude to Computers* scores listed above is 1547, which, when divided by 27, gives 57.3 (to one decimal place). (In passing, note that if you do this calculation on a calculator, you will get an answer like 57.296296 and, similarly, output from a statistical package may give the answer to many decimal places. In general, for values greater than 1, it is sufficient to round answers to one or, at most two, decimal places. For answers less than 1, three or, at most four significant figures – that is, digits other than leading zeros, will provide sufficient precision, for example, 0.573, 0.0573 ...)

One way of thinking about the mean is as a point of balance (see Figure 3.1). If each number is thought of as a ball of standard weight placed on a (weightless) bar according to its value, then the mean is the point at which the configuration would be perfectly balanced.

Another property of the mean is that the distances of the balls on either side of the mean balance out – that is, the sum of the positive differences (above) and the sum of the negative differences (below) are equal. Put another way, *the sum of differences between the individual scores and the mean always equals zero*. This is a key

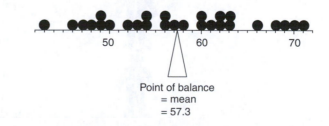

Point of balance
= mean
= 57.3

Figure 3.1 **Mean as a point of balance**

property of the mean and, in fact, is why the balance model just illustrated works (think about it!).

Here's another example that may help to give you an intuitive feel for what 'the mean' means. Consider a group of five people varying in height (given in centimetres), as indicated in Figure 3.2, which also shows the mean height. Two people are above the mean height for the group and three are below. These differences above and below the mean balance out to give a sum of zero (check this numerically for yourself). If the people are thought of as acrobats standing vertically on top of each other, the total height is the same as it would be for another group of acrobats achieving the same feat but consisting of quintuplets all equal in height to the mean of the first group.

As already noted, however, the mean is just one form of average. For our purposes, of the other types, there is one in particular that is important. It is called the

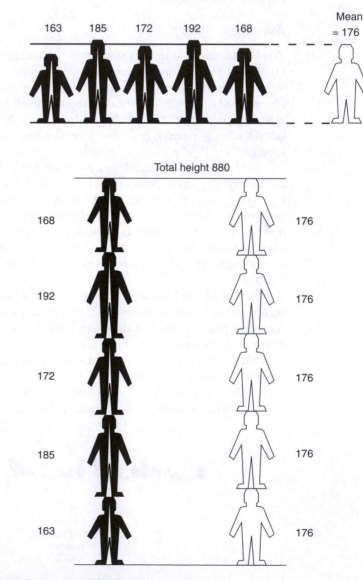

Figure 3.2 Two ways of thinking about the mean

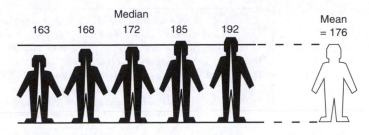

Figure 3.3 Median height of five people

median and is calculated by ranking the measurements and taking the one that comes right in the middle. For example, if we rank the five people just discussed in terms of height, the median is the height of the one in the middle (see Figure 3.3). Note that it is different from the mean, though not by much in this case.

Before reading on...

Find the median for the 27 *Attitude to Computers* scores listed on p. 27.

... now read on.

We hope you got a median of 57. Here's how. Let's take our *Attitude to Computers* scores and sort them by size from smallest to largest:

43 46 47 48 49 49 50 52 53 54 54 56 56 57 58 60 60 61 62 62 63 63 66 68 69 70 71

The median is simply the middle number in this ordered set. Since there are 27 values, the median is the 14th value, 57. It might occur to you to ask 'What if there were an even number of data, so there isn't *one* in the middle?' How do *you* think the procedure to calculate the median might be modified to take account of that? (The answer will be revealed later.)

There is an important reason for having the median available as an alternative to the mean, as illustrated by the following example.

Worker:	*My boss says the average salary in the company is £56,000 per year, but my union says the average salary is only £24,000. Who's lying?*
Statistician:	*It's possible neither is lying.*
Worker:	*I've heard the one about 'lies, damned lies and statistics', but that's ridiculous.*
Statistician:	*Let me explain. Your boss may be talking about one sort of average and your union about another.*
Worker:	*Go on.*
Statistician:	*Let's suppose your boss pays himself £320,000 and the other eight workers £32,000, £27,000, £26,000, £24,000, £22,000, £20,000, £18,000, and £15,000 respectively. Add those sums altogether, and it comes to £504,000. Divide by 9 – the average is £56,000, as your boss says.*
Worker:	*But that's not fair! He's the only one earning more than £56,000 – a lot more – and the rest of us are nowhere near £56,000.*
Statistician:	*That's why your union chooses not to use the same average as your boss, which is called the* mean *(not because it* is *mean, though you might well consider it so).*
Worker:	*So how does the union make it £24,000?*
Statistician:	*They have used a different average called the* median. *This is the one that comes in the middle when the numbers are put in order. You can see that it is £24,000. Most*

> people would agree that this is a more sensible average to use in these circumstances – unlike the mean, it represents a more typical sort of salary in that firm, and it is not distorted by the anomalously high salary of the boss.
>
> Worker: And they say figures can't lie!
> Statistician: I prefer to put it this way – figures can't lie, but liars can figure. Remember that most statistics are presented by people with a vested interest in persuading you in one way or another. Even if you are not going to be a researcher, it's important that you know how to think critically about the statistics that you'll meet in your everyday life.

A single number within a set that is very different from most or all of the general run of numbers in that set – such as the boss's salary in our example – is called an **outlier** (of which more later). When a data set contains one or more outliers, it will often be more reasonable to use the median as an average rather than the mean.

One other average is commonly mentioned in statistics books (and thereafter ignored). For the sake of completeness, we shall do the same. It is called the **mode**, which is simply the value that occurs most often. It is not very useful, especially if you don't know how your scores are distributed, though for variables measured on a nominal scale, it can be considered as a rudimentary average.

The three averages that we have introduced can be linked with scales of measurement as follows:

	Few/no outliers	*Some/many outliers*
nominal scale ⟷	mode	mode
ordinal scale ⟷	median	median
interval scale ⟷	mean	median
ratio scale ⟷	mean	median

Measuring variation

As summary statistics, averages are very useful. An average provides a single number that gives a general idea of the size of the numbers across the set as a whole. In particular, this makes it possible to make comparisons between sets of data, and averages are very often used in this way in many contexts – education, business, sport, national characteristics and so on. However, an average has a major limitation, illustrated by the following example. If you are told the average temperature of a place over the year, this is not necessarily a good guide for deciding whether or not it is a good holiday destination – it could be that it is sometimes very hot and sometimes very cold, or it could be that it is moderately warm throughout the year, with little variation. There are a number of corny jokes on the same theme, such as the definition of a statistician as someone who thinks that if you stand with one foot in a bucket of boiling water and the other in a block of ice, then on average you are comfortable!

These examples remind us that, as well as an average, it is also usually essential to take into account how much the data vary. It is necessary, therefore, to have methods of quantifying the amount of **variation**, or **spread**, as it is sometimes called. A very simple way to do this is to calculate the **range**, which is just the difference between the highest and lowest values in the data set. However, you should be able to see that this is not a particularly sensible way of measuring spread since it is based on only two values.

Instead, let's consider two other ways of measuring variation that reflect more of the information available in the data set. The first is called the **standard deviation**. The term itself is a bit of a mouthful, but it's pretty straightforward to understand. Think about our 27 *Attitude to Computers* scores again. We already know that the mean of these data is 57.3, to one decimal place. Now, what about the variability of the data? Actually, we have already touched on this indirectly earlier in this chapter. Recall that in Figure 3.1 we represented the *Attitude to Computers* scores as balls representing the 27 scores distributed according to their values and balanced on the mean. Recall too that we referred to the distance of each ball from the balance point. Clearly, the more spread out the data, the greater the distances of the balls from the balance point. Similarly, the less variable the data, the smaller the distances.

Student: So, actually, these distances can be used to quantify the overall variability of the data?

Lecturer: Indeed – how might you use these distances to calculate a single measure which would reflect the overall variability?

Student: Well, you could take each score and subtract the mean from it to give the distance between that score and the mean. Then, you could work out the average of all these differences by adding them up and dividing by 27.

Lecturer: That's good, but remember that some of these distances will be positive, because they are above the mean, and others will be negative because they lie below.

Student: Ah yes, and the sum of the distances will always be zero, so that's no good. How about if you ignore the minuses and just calculate an average distance regardless of whether the distances are positive or negative?

Lecturer: Yes, you could do that. In fact, you have just re-invented a measure known as the **average deviation**. Well done!

Student: So what's this thing called standard deviation? Why not just use the average deviation?

Lecturer: Well, to put it in non-technical terms, statisticians don't really like it when you just ignore something that is there, like a minus sign. It's fine if you are just using the average deviation as an indication of variability in its own right, but, if you wished to include it as a measure of variability in some other statistical calculation, that's when statisticians get a little uncomfortable.

Student: Yes, but, if you keep the minuses, you'll always have a value of zero as your measure of variability.

Lecturer: The solution that statisticians prefer is to get rid of the minuses, not just by ignoring them, but by using a more mathematically 'respectable' method.

Student: Oh – what's that then?

Lecturer: Think about it – what mathematical operation can you do that gets rid of negative numbers?

Student: The only one I can think of is by squaring them.

Lecturer: Got it in one!

Student: So we calculate the distance of each score from the mean, square it and then work out the average of all the squared distances?

Lecturer: Exactly, each squared distance is known as a **squared deviation**, and you have just re-invented a measure known as **variance** – the average of the squared deviations. Well done again!

Student: I've heard of variance – but what about standard deviation?

Lecturer: Well, because we squared all the distances and worked out the average, that gives us a pretty big number. So we can take the square root of the variance to undo, to some extent, the original squaring. This is the **standard deviation**, and it has some interesting properties which make it a little more useful than the 'un-square-rooted' variance.

An example on standard deviation follows.

Figure 3.4 shows how to work out the standard deviation of the 27 *Attitude to Computers* scores.

X	$X - \bar{X}$	$(X - \bar{X})^2$
60	2.7	7.29
62	4.7	22.09
62	4.7	22.09
47	−10.3	106.09
63	5.7	32.49
69	11.7	136.89
68	10.7	114.49
46	−11.3	127.69
70	12.7	161.29
60	2.7	7.29
56	−1.3	1.69
54	−3.3	10.89
48	−9.3	86.49
50	−7.3	53.29
49	−8.3	68.89
58	0.7	0.49
49	−8.3	68.89
66	8.7	75.69
54	−3.3	10.89
53	−4.3	18.49
56	−1.3	1.69
52	−5.3	28.09
57	−0.3	0.09
63	5.7	32.49
71	13.7	187.69
61	3.7	13.69
43	−14.3	204.49
1547		**1601.63**

$$\bar{X} = \frac{\Sigma X}{N} = \frac{1547}{26} = 57.3$$

$$sd = \sqrt{\frac{\Sigma (X - \bar{X})^2}{N - 1}} = \sqrt{\frac{1601.63}{26}} = \sqrt{61.60} = 7.85$$

Figure 3.4 Calculating the standard deviation

The steps in the calculation are as follows:

1. The first column contains the set of 27 numbers. For convenience, let's use '*X*' to stand for any number in that set. As noted earlier, the sum of the numbers is 1547. You will often see this sum abbreviated to the somewhat scary mathematical looking 'ΣX'. Don't panic! The Σ is a universal abbreviation which simply means *add up all the X's* (Σ is the Greek capital letter *sigma* corresponding to our letter S).

2. Again, as noted earlier, the mean of the scores is 57.3. Let's abbreviate this to $\bar{X}$, which again is standard notation for the mean of the X scores. So, we can say in this case that:

$$\bar{X} = \frac{\sum X}{N}$$

where N is the number of scores.

3. Next, subtract the mean from each score in turn (this sometimes yields a negative number and sometimes a positive number). Each $X - \bar{X}$ is called a **deviation from the mean**. Remember, the sum of these deviations is, of necessity, zero (actually, if you calculate it by hand, you should obtain a sum of -0.1 – this is due to rounding error associated with using the mean correct to 1 decimal place).

4. Next, square each deviation.

5. Then add up the squared deviations, which give a total of 1601.63 in this case.

6. Standard deviation (sd) is calculated by dividing $N - 1$ (26) and taking the square root of the result. Again, this calculation may be abbreviated as follows:

$$sd = \sqrt{\frac{\sum (X - \bar{X})^2}{(N - 1)}}$$

The calculation gives the value **7.85** (calculated to two decimal places) to the standard deviation as shown in this example.

It should be clear that the standard deviation works as an overall measure of spread because it is based on how much the data points spread out around the average value represented by the mean. By squaring each deviation, dividing by $N - 1$, and then taking the square root, a sort of average of the deviations is obtained. You might well be wondering at this point why we have divided by $N - 1$ rather than simply N. Good question! The habit of using, not quite N, but something very close like $N - 1$, $N - 2$ and so on, crops up consistently when we are calculating a statistic (like standard deviation) from a sample of data rather than from the entire population. We shall come back to this point regularly in later chapters.

One alternative way of measuring spread that we need to introduce is, like the median, based on ranking procedures. The basic approach is to sort the scores according to size (as you would to calculate the median) and chop them up into four quarters. For any set of data sorted in order of size, the **lower quartile** comes a quarter of the way along, and the **upper quartile** comes three-quarters of the way along – these definitions need to be made more precise, as you will see shortly. The **interquartile range** – quite a mouthful, but not as complicated as it sounds – is the difference between these upper and lower quartiles. The statistically more informative **semi-interquartile range** – even more of a mouthful – is half the interquartile range, that is, half the difference between the upper and lower quartiles. Thus, it is somewhat like the range, but not based on extreme values, so it is much better, since it will not be distorted by a few unusually large or small extreme values.

A quarter of the way along is, of course, too vague to specify how the calculation is actually done. Again, let's take our 27 *Attitude to Computers* scores and sort them by size from smallest to largest:

43 46 47 48 49 49 50 52 53 54 54 56 56 57 58 60 60 61 62 62 63 63 66 68 69 70 71

Now work out the 'location' of the lower quartile, which is given by the formula ¼(N+ 1), where N is the number of scores. That comes to 7 in this case, and so the

7th number along – which is 50 – is the lower quartile (see Figure 3.5). Similarly, the location of the upper quartile is given by ¾ $(N + 1) = 21$, and so the upper quartile is 63. The interquartile range is $63 - 50 = 13$, and the semi-interquartile range is therefore ½$(63 - 50) = 6.5$.

You may be wondering what happens if ¼$(N + 1)$ and ¾$(N + 1)$ do not conveniently turn out to be whole numbers. Suppose we add an extra score, 40, to our data, so it is now:

40 43 46 47 48 49 49 50 52 53 54 54 56 56 57 58 60 60 61 62 62 63 63 66 68 69 70 71

The formula for the location of the lower quartile now gives 7.25 – what does this mean as a location? Reasonably enough, a location of 7.25 is taken to mean a quarter (.25) of the way along from the seventh number towards the eighth number (see Figure 3.6). Because the seventh number is now 49 and the eighth number 50, this comes to 49.25 since the difference between 49 and 50 is 1, and a quarter of this is .25. Similarly, you should be able to see that the location of the upper quartile is now at position 21.75, giving a value of 62.75 for the upper quartile, and so the inter-quartile range is $62.75 - 49.25 = 13.5$ and the semi-interquartile range is ½$(62.75 - 49.25) = 6.75$ for the expanded data set.

Remember we asked you earlier how you would calculate the median for a set of data with an even number of data points? What you do in such a case is to define the median as midway between the *two* middle scores. This is precisely equivalent to defining the location for the median by the formula ½$(N + 1)$, whether N is odd or even (you

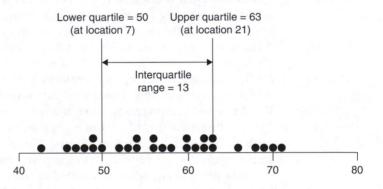

Figure 3.5 *Attitude to Computers*: **Quartiles and interquartile range**

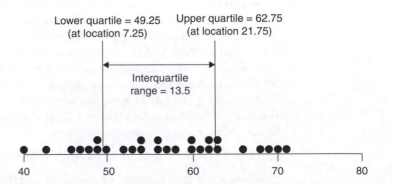

Figure 3.6 *Attitude to Computers*: **Quartiles and interquartile range (expanded data set)**

should check that out to your satisfaction). For the expanded *Attitude to Computers* data, since there are 28 scores, the middle value will lie between the 14th and 15th values (56 and 57) giving a median of 56.5 (check this for yourself using the formula).

The quartiles we have just considered, and the median before that, are special cases of a more general statistic known as **percentiles**. Roughly speaking, the kth percentile is such that in the data set, k per cent of the data are less than it, and the rest ($100 - k$ per cent) are greater. To be precise, the formula for the location of the kth percentile is $k/100(N+1)$, and the number corresponding to this is worked out in the same way as in the examples for the quartiles. If you think about it, lower quartile, median and upper quartiles are other names for the 25th, 50th and 75th percentiles, respectively. Percentiles are useful for gauging where a particular score lies in relation to the set of scores as a whole. For example, if you were told that your mark of 67 in a statistics test was at the 94th percentile for the class, you would know that, roughly speaking, 6% of the class scored higher and 94% lower than you in the test.

Figure 3.7 summarizes the four main summary statistics covered in this chapter. The rank-based summary statistics share the property that they are not very much affected by outliers in the data set. For this reason, they are called **resistant** statistics. (An alternative term for the same idea that you may come across is **robust**.) By contrast, the mean and standard deviation affected more strongly by outliers and so are called **non-resistant** or **less resistant**. You will see that this theme of non-resistant statistics and alternative, rank-based resistant statistics recurs frequently in subsequent chapters.

	Non-Resistant	Resistant, Rank-Based
Average	Mean	Median
Measure of spread	Standard deviation	Semi-interquartile range

Figure 3.7 **Resistance of summary statistics**

Making sense of SPSS

Coding data and obtaining summary statistics

Note: We recommend you also consult Brace et al. (2009), pp. 26–63 and 72–76 who present further information on this topic.

1. Creating a data file

First, we begin with some basic guidance on creating a data file in SPSS. As you progress through the book, you will be provided with further information on how to code data appropriate to the type of statistical analysis you need at each stage.

The golden rule for coding any data in SPSS is that *each individual participant (case) occupies a single row of their own in the data file*. This is known as a **casewise** data structure. So, the first question you must ask yourself before coding any data is "How many different participants (cases) are there in the study?" The answer to this question will tell you instantly how many rows your data file will contain.

Let's take the *Attitude to Computers* scores. We know that 27 different participants make up these data. So we know straight off that there will be 27 rows in the
data file. Also, since each participant produced only a single score, there will only be
a single column of scores in the data file.

OK, let's create this data file in SPSS. Although we are using SPSS 18, virtually all
of the information here applies equally to all other versions, including Versions 16
and 17, used by Brace et al. (2009). Any important differences will be highlighted.

Launch SPSS by clicking or double-clicking on the SPSS program icon.

The following screen will appear. Select **Type in data** and click **OK**.

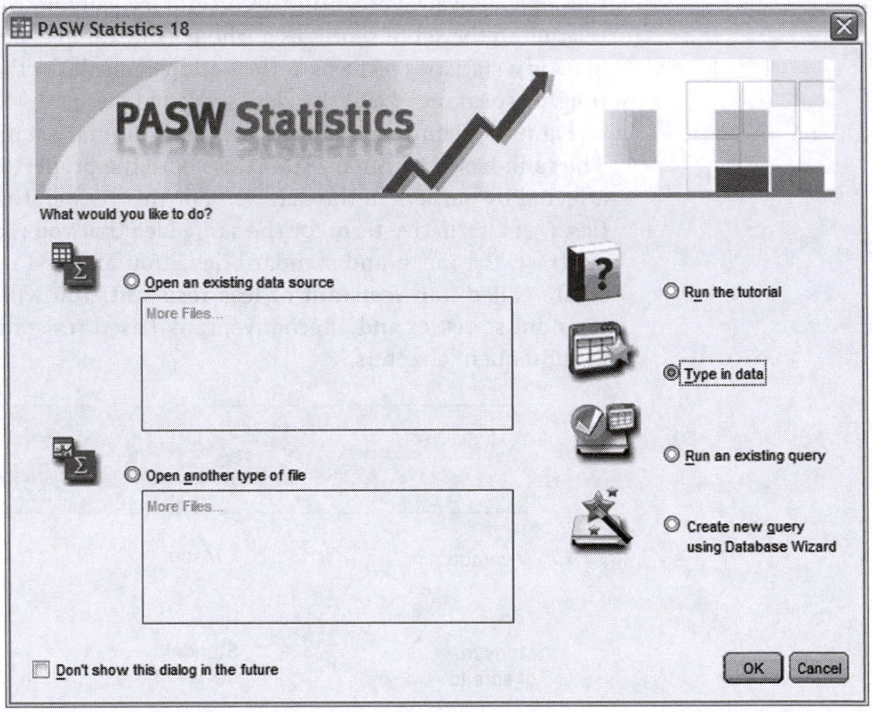

The next screen to appear will be the following. This is basically a blank data
table. First, click on **Variable View** to tell SPSS about the data you wish to input.

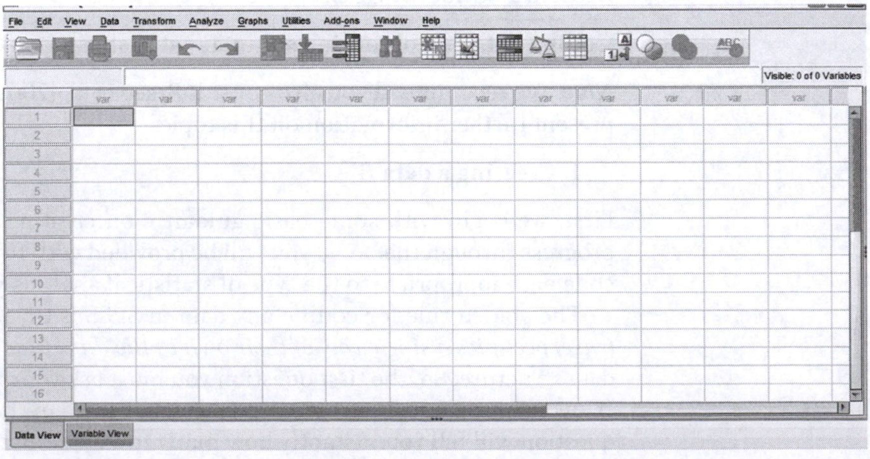

In the **Variable View** window, fill in some (you do not need to fill in everything) as below. Note that we have arbitrarily given the variable a short **Name** *attcomp* and fuller **Label** *Attitude to Computers*.

Now click on '**Data View**' to reveal the blank data table again. You will see a single column entitled *attcomp*. The data are entered into this column, row by row until you have all 27 rows filled in, as follows (Note, the figure only shows the first 16 rows, but you can scroll down to reveal all 27 rows):

At this stage, it's always a good idea to save your data as soon as you have finished coding it, though not absolutely essential if it's a one-off calculation. We recommend that you always save your data. To do this, click on **File** in the top menu bar and drag down to **Save As ...**

In the dialogue window, enter a **File name:** of your choice and ensure that the appropriate location in the **Look in:** bar has been selected before clicking **Save**.

2. Calculating summary statistics

First, let's calculate the mean and standard deviation for our sample.

To begin, click on '**Analyze** in the top menu bar.

Next drag down to select **Descriptive Statistics** and **Descriptives...** from the drop down menus.

The following dialogue box will appear. Simply move *Attitude to Computers* from the box on the left to the one on the right by highlighting it and clicking on the arrow. Click **OK**.

An **SPSS Statistics Viewer** window will appear containing a summary table of mean, standard deviation and, for good measure, the minimum and maximum scores. This is the SPSS default option – by clicking on the **Options** box in the above dialogue window, you can exclude some statistics or include others as you wish.

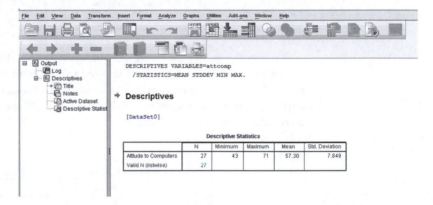

One of the somewhat frustrating features of SPSS is its unwieldy nature on occasions. There is often more than one way to obtain the statistics you want, and some of the statistics you require cannot be found in the routine you might intuitively expect. This is the case even for descriptive statistics. For example, it is not possible to obtain the median or upper and lower quartiles using the **Descriptives...** routine. Instead you have to choose **Frequencies...** from the **Analyze > Descriptive Statistics** menus (see below). Move *Attitude to Computers* into the right-hand box as before.

Now click on the **Statistics...** button and select the desired statistics from the dialogue window (incidentally, you will notice that you can also choose mean and standard deviation from this routine). Note that we have also added two percentile points (10th and 90th) corresponding to the whiskers in Figure 3.11 below. We could also have chosen mode, sum, minimum, maximum and variance. Click on **Continue** followed by OK.

Frequencies: Statistics

Percentile Values
- ✔ Quartiles
- ☐ Cut points for: 10 equal groups
- ✔ Percentile(s):
  - Add
  - Change
  - Remove
  - 10.0
  - 90.0

Central Tendency
- ✔ Mean
- ✔ Median
- ☐ Mode
- ☐ Sum

☐ Values are group midpoints

Dispersion
- ✔ Std. deviation ☐ Minimum
- ☐ Variance ☐ Maximum
- ✔ Range ☐ S.E. mean

Distribution
- ☐ Skewness
- ☐ Kurtosis

Continue　Cancel　Help

Among the rather excessive output, even at this descriptive stage, you will find the chosen summary statistics displayed in a table in the **SPSS Statistics Viewer** as below. Note that you can easily work out the interquartile range by subtracting the 25th percentile value from the 75th (63 – 50 = 13) and the semi-interquartile range by dividing this result by 2 (6.5).

Statistics

Attitude to Computers		
N	Valid	27
	Missing	0
Mean		57.30
Median		57.00
Std. Deviation		7.849
Range		28
Percentiles	10	46.80
	25	50.00
	50	57.00
	75	63.00
	90	69.20

Before reading on ...

The mean (57.3), median (you should have obtained 57 earlier), standard deviation and the semi-interquartile range (6.5) for the 27 *Attitude to Computers* scores listed on p. 27 have already been calculated. Now add three new numbers to the data set – 22, 23 and 20 – and recalculate the four summary statistics (use computer software or pencil-and-paper methods as you prefer). Look carefully at what happens.

... now read on

You should have found that the addition of the three outliers had a big effect on the mean and standard deviation, but little effect on the median and semi-interquartile range, illustrating the point about non-resistant and resistant statistics.

Graphical representations of distributions

Summary statistics are useful, but even an average and a measure of spread together give limited information about the characteristics of data in the set as a whole. Graphical representations are extremely valuable for examining the data set in more detail and making its main features salient, and statistical software offers a range of these representations. Figures 3.8 to 3.11 illustrate several alternative ways of displaying the data set of 27 *Attitude to Computers* scores.

Dot plot

This simply plots a point along an axis for each of the numbers in the data set. The mean, median, standard deviation and interquartile range have been added here. Note that it makes sense to think of the mean and median as **points**, but the standard deviation and semi-interquartile range as **intervals**. One rough, but sometimes useful, rule of thumb is that *the standard deviation will tend to be about one-and-a-half times as big as the semi-interquartile range*. Another frequently cited rule of thumb is that about two-thirds of the scores will usually lie within 1 standard deviation above and 1 standard deviation below the mean (and about 95% within two – 1.96 to be precise – standard deviations above and below).

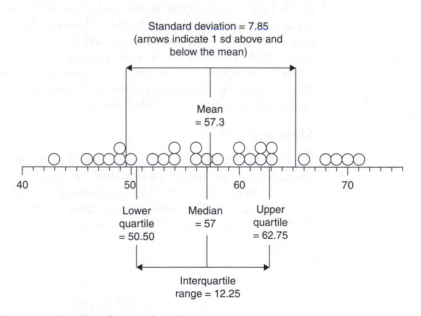

Figure 3.8 Dot plot of *Attitude to Computers* scores

Bar chart (or histogram)

The axis is divided into a number of intervals and the number (frequency) of data falling in each interval is represented by a column of the corresponding height. The columns collectively show the 'shape' of the distribution. You will also see this graph

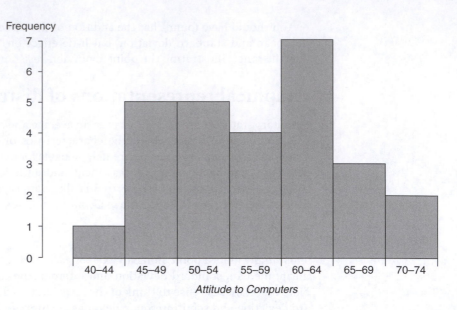

Figure 3.9 Histogram of *Attitude to Computers* scores

referred to as a **histogram**, which strictly is incorrect, since, in a histogram, frequency is represented by the *area* of the bars, rather than their height. This only becomes problematic in the rare instances where class intervals (given by the width of the bars) are not equal. In the vast majority of cases where class intervals are equal (as in our example), the height and area of the bars are directly proportional and, therefore, the shape of the graph will be the same regardless of whether height or area has been used to represent frequency. For this reason, we tend to prefer using the term 'bar chart' to refer to frequency graphs of discrete categories of data, such as males and females, or various faculties, and 'histogram' for continuous data, divided into (usually) equal class intervals.

Stem and leaf

This is a quick back-of-an-envelope method of summarizing data. Each number in the data set is split into two parts, *stem* and *leaf*. In the case of 2-digit numbers, as here, it's obvious how to do that – if there are more than 2 digits you would round to the first 2 or 3. The stems are presented vertically – here, an extra feature has been introduced to spread the data out more, in that each of the stems has been

```
7 *  0 1
6 •  6 8 9
6 *  0 0 1 2 2 3 3
5 •  6 6 7 8
5 *  0 2 3 4 4
4 •  6 7 8 9 9
4 *  3
```

Figure 3.10 Stem-and-leaf plot of *Attitude to Computers* scores

subdivided. The number 4* is used for the range 40–44, and 4• for 45–49, and so on. The leaves are then placed, in order, opposite to their stems. The shape of the distribution is again shown – in fact, the stem and leaf is rather like a histogram turned through a right-angle, with the added advantage that it is possible to extract the exact values of the numbers using the stem and leaves. Another advantage is that the data are ordered, making it easy to determine, say, the median.

Box-and-whisker

This is a more detailed graphical summary of the data and, in our view, one of the most useful of all. Put simply, the 'box plot' (as it is often known, for example in SPSS) is a graphical method for chopping up the data, in much the way that we saw for the special percentile points of median, lower and upper quartile. The **box** part of the display extends from the lower quartile to the upper quartile, with the median marked as a line within it. From each end of the box a **whisker** is drawn, the top one extending up to the 90th percentile and the bottom one down to the 10th

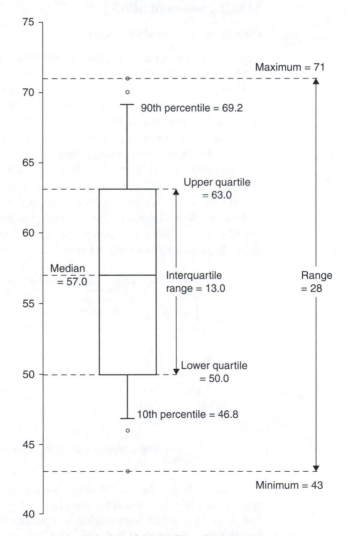

Figure 3.11 Box-and-whisker plot of *Attitude to Computers* scores

percentile. Any points lying beyond these limits are plotted individually. Note that the actual percentile points for the whiskers are somewhat arbitrary and different in some computer packages, for example, in SPSS (actually, the whiskers in SPSS are rather arcane for the scope of this book).

Figure 3.11 shows an annotated example of a box plot for our *Attitude to Computers* data. Actually, if you rotate your head 90 degrees clockwise while looking at it, you should see strong links between this plot and those in Figures 3.6 and 3.8. Try it.

> **Before reading on …**
>
> If you add the three extra data – 22, 23 and 20 – to any of these representations they will show up clearly as outliers. To check that you understand how to construct a box-and-whisker plot, sketch out a box plot for the enlarged set of 30 data (and compare it with the one for the 27 data in Figure 3.11).
>
> **… now read on.**

Making sense of SPSS

Obtaining graphical summaries

Note: We recommend you also consult Brace et al. (2009), pp. 77–79 who present further information on this topic.

Here, we use the same *Attitude to Computers* scores as we used in the *SPSS summary statistics* example earlier in this chapter. Just to remind you that twenty-seven different participants make up these data.

Launch SPSS in the usual way and open the data file you had saved with the 27 *Attitude to Computers* scores. (More conveniently, simply double click on the data file icon, and this will both launch SPSS and load the data file.)

As before, you will see a single column entitled *attcomp*.

Let's produce the relevant graphical displays that SPSS offers.

First, click on **Graphs** in the top menu bar and drag down to **Legacy Dialogs**. The list of available plots is shown in the drop down menu below. From this list, only three displays are informative **Error Bar …** , **Histogram …** and **Boxplot …**

Let's choose **Error Bar …** first. Drag down and select it. The dialogue box below will appear. In this case we want a **Simple** chart (since there are no variables to cluster) and we need to select **Summaries of separate variables** we are summarizing a single variable here. Now click **Define**.

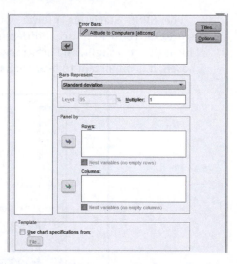

A further dialogue box will appear. Simply highlight the *Attitude to Computers* variable in the left hand box and move it to the box labelled **Error Bars:**. Then click on the drag down box labelled **Bars Represent** and showing **Confidence interval for the mean**. Select **Standard deviation** and, in the same window, change the **Multiplier:** from **2** to **1**. Click **OK**.

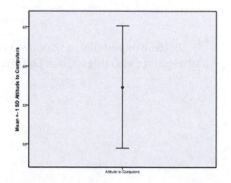

An **SPSS Statistics Viewer** window will appear showing the following graph. The small circle in the centre shows the mean score for the sample, and the **Error Bar** shows one standard deviation (previously calculated as 7.85) above and below the mean (57.3). Thus, approximately two-thirds of the scores lie within this bar, that is, between 49.45 and 65.15.

Now let's draw a **Histogram…**. In the dialogue window, move *Attitude to Computers* to the **Variable:** box as shown and click **OK**.

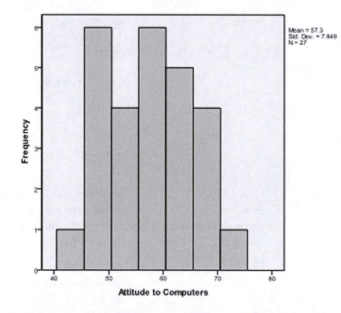

The **SPSS Statistics Viewer** will show the histogram below. Look back at Figure 3.9. You will notice a difference between the shapes of the two histograms. This is due to a slight, and arbitrary, difference in the class intervals that have been chosen. It is important to bear such factors in mind when interpreting histograms.

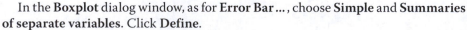

In the **Boxplot** dialog window, as for **Error Bar…**, choose **Simple** and **Summaries of separate variables**. Click **Define**.

In the resulting dialogue window, move *Attitude to Computers* to the box labelled **Boxes Represent:** and click **OK**.

The box plot will appear in the **SPSS Statistics Viewer** window. In our opinion, this is the most informative graphical display of all. Look back at Figure 3.11, and use the information in that figure to interpret the new Boxplot.

Shapes of distributions

As mentioned, histograms in particular are useful in displaying the shape of a distribution. A number of general shapes may be distinguished, as indicated in Figure 3.12. In each case, a typical histogram is shown, together with a schematic indication of the general shape.

The normal distribution

Many variables found in psychological research produce distributions conforming, at least approximately, to this shape (sometimes called the **Bell Curve**). Graphical

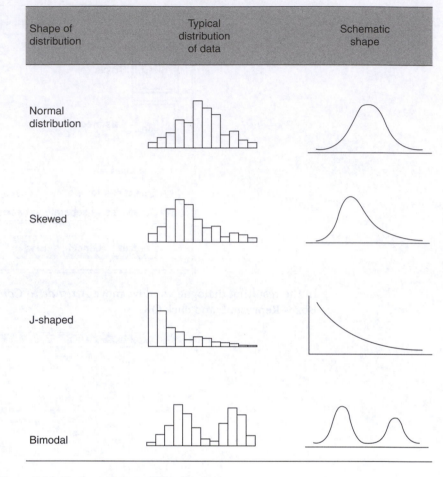

Shape of distribution	Typical distribution of data	Schematic shape
Normal distribution		
Skewed		
J-shaped		
Bimodal		

Figure 3.12 Various shapes of distribution

displays of data showing physical characteristics, such as height, often conform very closely to this shape. Intelligence is assumed to be distributed in the same way, and measures of intelligence are scaled accordingly. As we shall see later, many statistical approaches require your data to conform pretty closely to a normal distribution, with the most important feature being its symmetry either side of the mean.

Skewed

This shape is like a normal distribution that has been stretched out more at one end than the other. In this case, unlike the normal distribution, the data are not symmetrical about the mean. Reaction times tend to produce this sort of shape – there is clearly a lower limit (zero, ultimately) but no upper limit, and in any set of reaction times there may be some that are high relative to the rest.

J-shaped

In this case, values taper off very quickly. An example of a variable that would tend to yield such a distribution is the number of accidents in a year for workers in a factory, in which case most of the workers might well have 0, some would have 1, and the frequencies would tail off quickly thereafter. (The shape is supposed to resemble a reflected letter J.)

Bimodal

Here, the distribution has two 'peaks' when represented as a histogram, indicating relative concentrations of frequencies at two separate places on the scale ('mode' in this context refers to high points in the histogram). This sort of shape is relatively rare. An example would be handedness, where people tend to be either predominantly left-handed or predominantly right-handed (there are more of the latter).

An important general point to understand is how the various shapes of distribution reflect the nature of the variable whose data are being displayed. Many characteristics of people naturally lead to a normal distribution (at least approximately) but, as examples above show, there are other variables which equally naturally lead to very different shapes of distribution.

Chapter review

In this chapter, summary statistics – numbers derived from the data reflecting salient aspects of the data – were introduced. We began with two sorts of average, mean and median, with discussion of when the median is a more sensible option. Similarly, two measures of spread, standard deviation and semi-interquartile range, were defined. It was stressed that the median and semi-interquartile range are more resistant (robust) than the mean and standard deviation, in that outliers have a much weaker effect on them.

In the second part of the chapter, a variety of graphical methods for displaying sets of data for a single variable were illustrated. We concluded by briefly pointing out the logical relationship between the nature of a variable and the shape of the distribution of scores that it typically produces.

Seeing patterns in data: Comparing

In this chapter

… ways of organizing and displaying data to reveal important patterns are shown. All the examples in this chapter are about making comparisons between two sets of measurements, using data taken from samples of people. In this way, it is possible to investigate empirically questions such as the following:

- Do Arts and Science students differ in their preferences for various courses in psychology?
- Do squash players react more quickly than chess players?
- Does drinking coffee improve speed of reaction?

A key point of the chapter is that data from samples can only offer evidence in relation to such questions, not definitive answers.

Comparing proportions: hint, hint

One of the Gestalt psychologists who studied problem-solving more than fifty years ago was N.R.F. Maier. Figure 4.1 is based on one of the problems he investigated. Can you see a solution?

One line of investigation is to see whether a hint would help participants find the solution. Accordingly, for half the participants tested, the experimenter contrives to brush against one of the hanging strings to set it swinging. For the other half, this hint is not given. (The solution – or, at least, *one* solution – to the problem is to tie the hammer to one of the strings, set it swinging, hold the other string and wait for the hammer to swing close enough to be grabbed.) Accordingly, data in the four cells of a 2 × 2 table can be collected and might look like those in Figure 4.2 for a total sample of 80 participants.

Note that the table shows a relationship between two variables of a simple type not considered previously, in which both variables are dichotomous. The variable *without hint / with hint* is under the control of the experimenter through, for example, random assignment of participants to the levels.

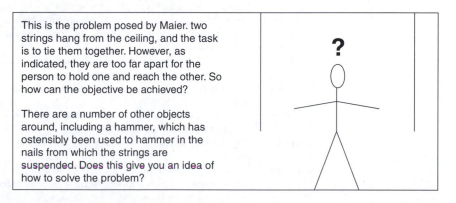

This is the problem posed by Maier. two strings hang from the ceiling, and the task is to tie them together. However, as indicated, they are too far apart for the person to hold one and reach the other. So how can the objective be achieved?

There are a number of other objects around, including a hammer, which has ostensibly been used to hammer in the nails from which the strings are suspended. Does this give you an idea of how to solve the problem?

Figure 4.1 The Maier problem

	No. of successes	No. of failures
Without Hint	15	25
With Hint	31	9

Figure 4.2 2 × 2 frequency table – Maier data

Before reading on...

Do *you* think that these data would prove that a hint helps to solve the problem? Think carefully about how you would justify your answer to someone who was sceptical about this conclusion.

... now read on

More participants in the group given the hint solved the problem (31 out of 40) than in the group not given the hint (15 out of 40). That is clear. Expressed in percentage terms, the difference is 78% as against 38%. (Note: the exact percentages are 77.5% and 37.5%, but we shall generally round percentages to the nearest percentage.)

> **Student:** So, that would appear to prove that giving the hint helps people to solve the problem.
> **Lecturer:** It depends what you mean by 'prove'. Nine people who were given the hint still didn't solve the problem, and fifteen people who weren't given the hint did.
> **Student:** OK, what I mean is that people given the hint are more likely to solve the problem.
> **Lecturer:** Do you think everyone is equally good at solving problems in general, or this one in particular?
> **Student:** No, clearly some people are generally better than others.
> **Lecturer:** So, some people would solve Maier's problem easily, while at the other extreme, some would never get it?
> **Student:** Yes.
> **Lecturer:** What if, by chance, the people Maier put in the hint group were mostly smart, while those in the no-hint group were mostly poor at solving problems? Wouldn't that be an alternative explanation for the results?
> **Student:** I see what you mean. But that's unlikely to happen. By the law of averages, since he assigned people randomly to groups, the two groups are bound to be of the same overall level of smartness.
> **Lecturer:** It's true that there is a good chance that the groups will be roughly equal in smartness, but there remains the possibility that they are not.
> **Student:** So, why bother doing an experiment if you can't reach conclusions when you've got the data?
> **Lecturer:** It's not as bad as that. The data strongly support the hypothesis that giving the hint helps. But we cannot say that they prove it. See the difference?
> **Student:** Okay, but aren't you being vague? Just how strong is the evidence in support of the theory?
> **Lecturer:** That is a very complex and controversial issue. Statistical theory has a number of suggested procedures to lend more precision to such statements, and this is mostly what statistics books are about.

A question of taste

In a psychology course, all students in two faculties were asked to nominate their favourite among four modules given in one session – Psycholinguistics, Social Psychology, Statistics and Human–Computer Interaction (HCI). The collated data are as shown in Figure 4.3.

	Psycholinguistics	Social	Stats	HCI	Total
Arts	27	35	3	8	73
Science	13	9	3	18	43

Figure 4.3 Frequency table (*Faculty × Favourite Module*)

Here, the two variables being related are *Favourite Module* (on a nominal scale, with four values) and *Faculty* (dichotomous). Incidentally, *Faculty* is an example of what we defined in Chapter 2 as a subject variable.

Before reading on...

Study the data, and note down the main points of interest.

... **now read on**

Compare the notes made by two students, shown in Figure 4.4. We hope it is clear to you that the second student's interpretation is much more sensible. Remember the old riddle: why do white sheep produce more wool than black sheep? Because there are more of them! Where the total numbers differ, proportional rather than absolute numbers are more helpful for making comparisons. Following the second student's lead, the data can be converted systematically to percentages, as shown in Figure 4.5.

Instead of a table of percentages, various graphical devices are available for making patterns in the data visible to the eye, including pie charts, strip charts and composite (or clustered) bar charts (see Figures 4.6 to 4.8).

Of the various tabular and graphical representations shown, which do you think is easiest to use? Indeed, maybe *you* could invent a better way of showing the data.

Psycholinguistics – twice as popular for Arts students (27 v 13)
Social Psych much more popular among Arts students
Stats – equally unpopular
HCI about twice as popular for Arts students

No real difference for Psycholinguistics
(about 1/3 in each case choose it)
Social Psych more popular with Arts
(about 50% v 20%)
Few in either faculty like Stats best
Much higher proportion of Science students voted for HCI

Figure 4.4 Two interpretations of *Favourite Module* data

	Psycholinguistics	Social	Stats	HCI	Total
Arts	37%	48%	4%	11%	100%
Science	30%	21%	7%	42%	100%

Figure 4.5 Percentage table (*Faculty* × *Favourite Module*)

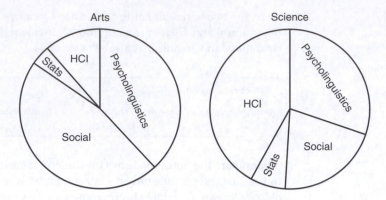

Figure 4.6 Pie charts (*Faculty × Favourite Module*)

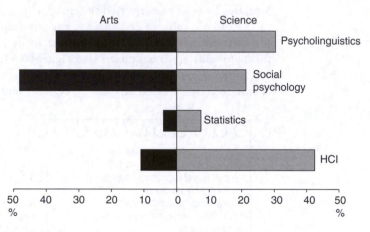

Figure 4.7 Strip chart (*Faculty × Favourite Module*)

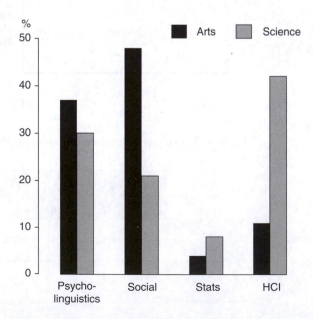

Figure 4.8 Composite bar chart (*Faculty × Favourite Module*)

Student: I thought the table was easiest to use and interpret, but my friend preferred the composite histogram.

Lecturer: Well, there is no 'right answer' here. People differ in their preferences.

Student: Anyway, however you look at them, the results are clear here. All the students were tested, so there is no sample involved.

Lecturer: That's true. If you are only interested in these students in their own right, then the results seem pretty clear-cut – but not entirely.

Student: Why not? It seems pretty cut-and-dried to me.

Lecturer: Well, consider this, for example. If the students were tested again three months later, mightn't at least some of them have changed their opinions?

Student: That is possible, but it seems unlikely that more than a few would.

Lecturer: Fair enough. Notice, by the way, how often you are using words such as likely and unlikely in our discussions. Now, here is another major point. Suppose the focus is not on this class of students specifically, but on Arts and Science students in general – for simplicity, let's confine it to the single university in question.

Student: Ah, so if the survey was done the next year, the results might be different.

Lecturer: You've got it! It's the same message again. The data are suggestive – maybe very suggestive – but not conclusive.

Comparison between independent samples

Quick on the draw

Squash is a fast game. The ball travels at very high speeds, giving players fractions of a second to make decisions and carry out complex motor movements. By contrast, in an untimed match, chess players may take as long as an hour thinking about a single move. It is plausible to conjecture that squash players may have faster reaction times than chess players, on the grounds of the following observations:

only people with fast reaction times will play squash

OR

playing squash improves reaction time

OR

a combination of the two

OR

another explanation entirely.

To investigate the question, reaction times for groups of participants from a squash club and a chess club were measured in seconds. The data are as shown in Figure 4.9.

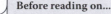

Before reading on...

Do these data support the hypothesis that squash players have faster reaction times than chess players? How could you display the data to make a visual comparison easy?

... now read on

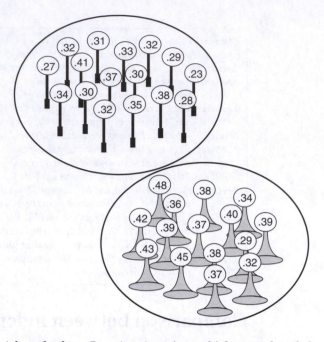

Figure 4.9 *Quick on the draw*: Reaction times (seconds) for squash and chess players

A variety of graphical representations, involving extensions of methods introduced in Chapter 3, can be used to provide visual comparisons between those on the court and those on the board (see Figures 4.10 to 4.12). Consider each graphical representation in turn. What specific features of each one suggest that, overall, squash players do have quicker reaction times?

A complementary approach is to calculate and compare averages.

	Mean	Median
Squash players	0.32	0.32
Chess players	0.39	0.38

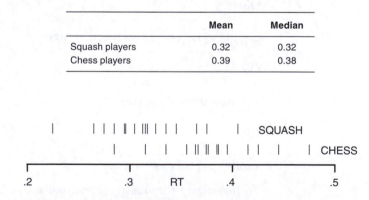

Figure 4.10 Multiple line plots for *Quick on the draw* data

Before reading on...

Look back to the graphical representations of the data. Note the place where the mean and median for each group are located on these graphs.

... **now read on**

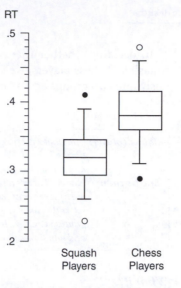

RT

Squash Players   Chess Players

Figure 4.11 Box-and-whisker plots for *Quick on the draw* data

Squash		Chess
	.4 *	5 8
1	.4 ●	0 2 3
8 7 5	.3 *	6 7 7 8 8 9 9
4 3 2 2 2 1 0 0	.3 ●	2 4
9 8 7	.2 *	9
3	.2 ●	

Figure 4.12 Back-to-back stem-and-leaf plots for *Quick on the draw* data

Figure 4.13 shows yet another way to look at the data. Are the faster people predominantly squash players and the slower ones chess players? A simple way to get a handle on this is to rank them. To do this, we treat all of the reaction times as a single data set, irrespective of whether each score was produced by a squash or a chess player (although we continue to keep note of each score as either squash (S) or chess (C)). Now, we simply rank this combined set. Note that the three fastest times are .23 (squash player); .27 (squash player); .28 (squash player); and then come a squash player and a chess player tying on .29. Continuing the analysis leads to the sequence:

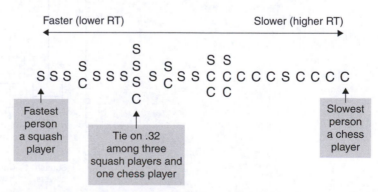

Figure 4.13 Combined ranking of squash and chess players' scores

In deciding whether there is a meaningful difference in the reaction times of squash and chess players, we simply look to see if the single ranking falls out obviously into two groups again, or whether they are totally jumbled up.

> *Squash player:* That looks pretty conclusive to me. Although not all the squash players are faster than all the chess players, the trend is clear. The faster ones are mostly our guys, and the slower ones are the pawn-pushers.
>
> *Statistician:* I agree. There's a remote technical possibility that very unrepresentative samples were picked, but the data look very strong. Having put all of the times into a single set and ranked them, the data do appear to have separated into the two original groups very clearly, with the exception of a couple of unusually fast chess players and one slow squash player.

What if?

What if two more squash players had been tested and their reaction times measured at 0.55 seconds and 0.58 seconds? These way-out data could arise in a number of ways. If it is decided to take them seriously, then each of the graphical representations can be amended accordingly as in Figures 4.14 to 4.16. Note how the two extra data stand out like sore thumbs. Consider also the effect on the mean. Revised to take account of the two new data, the mean for the squash players becomes 0.36, which is only marginally faster than the mean of 0.39 for the chess players. Would it make sense, in that case, to conclude that there is really no evidence for a difference between the groups? By contrast, adding new data generally has a small effect on the median, and, in fact, in this case it doesn't change it at all! (Check this out for yourself to see why.)

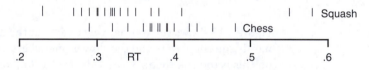

Figure 4.14 Multiple line plots of squash and chess scores (with outliers)

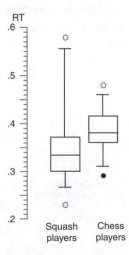

Figure 4.15 Box-and-whisker plots of squash and chess scores (with outliers)

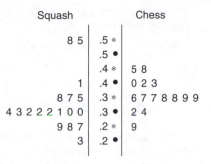

Figure 4.16 Back-to-back stem-and-leaf plots of squash and chess scores (with outliers)

Squash player: *These two extra guys have really let us down. Couldn't we just ignore them? Obviously the apparatus was faulty, or they didn't understand the instructions, or they weren't paying attention. Surely we shouldn't take them seriously!*

Statistician: *The technical name for such data is outliers. When a few really way-out data like this occur, it's right to be careful. First, it should be considered whether something did go wrong that would justify ignoring these data as outliers. That is one possible course of action. Another is to use a different statistic that is more resistant, namely not so markedly affected by outliers. In this case, it can be argued that the median is preferable to the mean if we wish to compare the average speed of the two groups.*

Comparison within paired data

Coffee time

Whether coffee quickens reaction time or not can be tested empirically. One approach would be to set up separate groups of participants, and test reaction times for both groups. One group would receive coffee, and the other group would not. In such a situation, the group that is treated in some way is generally called the **experimental group**, and the group not treated is called the **control group**.

An alternative approach is to use just one group of people, but to test each person in the group on two occasions, once with and once without-coffee. The contrast between the two approaches is shown schematically in Figure 4.17.

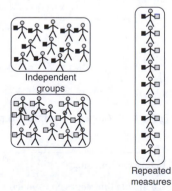

Independent groups

Repeated measures

Figure 4.17 Two designs – independent groups and repeated measures. Each little 'box' represents one score.

The second design is more incisive, in general. This is because it compares the same individuals under the two conditions, rather than unrelated people. On the other hand, care should be taken to make sure when this design is used that the testing of an individual on the first occasion does not affect their performance on the second occasion – unlikely, in this case.

Figure 4.18 presents some data for such a study. They could be displayed using one of the representations introduced earlier, such as a back-to-back stem-and-leaf plot. However, there is a major drawback of such a representation in that it loses important information in the data, namely, which *with-coffee* measurement is linked with which *without-coffee* measurement. In short, we should try to retain the paired information in any graphical representation – this will allow us to observe the *change* in each individual's performance between the two conditions, something not possible for unrelated groups. Figure 4.19 gives an alternative representation which retains that information; we call this a **related line chart**.

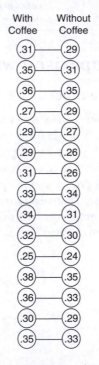

Figure 4.18 *Coffee time* **data – repeated measures (reaction time in seconds)**

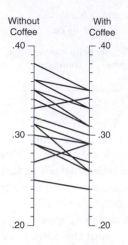

Figure 4.19 Graphical display of repeated measures data (*Coffee time*)

If the line slopes up, it means that the RT with-coffee is higher; that is, the person whose two measurements are represented by that line was slower with-coffee than without. Conversely, if the line slopes down, it means the *with-coffee* RT was faster.

Figure 4.20 shows another possible way to show the data. Each individual tested has two measures – RT *without-coffee* and RT *with-coffee*. Each such pair of data can be represented by a point on a two-dimensional graph, with RT *without-coffee* on the horizontal axis and RT *with-coffee* on the vertical axis. The collection of such points gives an overall picture of the data. Note that a diagonal line has been added, which passes through all the points in the plane where RT *without-coffee* and RT *with-coffee* would be the same (referred to as the **line of equality**).

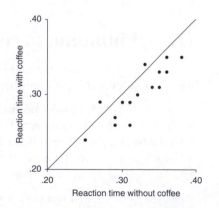

Figure 4.20 Alternative graphical display of *Coffee time* data

Actually, this is an extremely useful and versatile form of graphical representation which will crop up in a variety of contexts in this book. When interpreting the graph, you should be aware of the question which *you* want answered. Here, we are interested in the *difference* between individuals' performance in two conditions. In the next chapter, we shall see how this type of graph can be used to answer a different question.

Before reading on...

What do points *above* the diagonal line have in common? What do points *below* the diagonal line have in common?

... now read on

The diagonal line passes through all the points of equality for the two measurements. A point above the diagonal line corresponds to an individual with a slower RT *with-coffee* than *without-coffee*, and a point below the diagonal line corresponds to an individual with a faster RT *with-coffee*. Moreover, the further any point is from the diagonal line, the bigger the difference between the two RTs, in one direction or another.

A different approach is to carry out a pair-by-pair comparison. As a simple first step, count the number of cases where the person performed faster *with-coffee* and the number where the person performed slower *with-coffee*. In fact, you can do this directly from either of the graphical representations – there are 13 of the former type, and 2 of the latter.

All of the representations tell a consistent story. For the sample of participants tested, in most cases, reaction time is faster after coffee.

Student: But there were two people who performed less well with-coffee. Maybe the world is made up of two sets of people – those whose reaction times are speeded up by coffee, and those whose reaction times are slowed down.

Lecturer: That is possible. In that case, the data provide some support for the hypothesis that the former type is more frequent. There are other possibilities though. It could be, for example, that the two people who were slower with-coffee just happened to have unusually slow reactions for some of those particular trials. Remember that there will always be variation in reaction times measured repeatedly for the same individual.

On not jumping to conclusions

In all of the above cases, it should be clear that the data being presented offer evidence for judging the questions being posed and suggest the following:

- Hints help people to solve problems.
- There are marked preferences for certain subjects over others among psychology students, and the patterns differ for Arts and Science students.
- Squash players have faster reactions times than chess players; and
- Coffee speeds up reaction time.

At the same time, it has been pointed out repeatedly that absolute, cut-and-dried answers are not forthcoming. The main reason for this is the fact that the data are only a sample of all the possible data. For example, in the problem-solving experiment involving hanging strings, only 80 people were tested. Let's suppose these 80 people were first-year university students. Then there is a much larger group of all first-year university students, even if we restrict it to the country in which the study was carried out. Moreover, the potential pool of participants would be widened even more if first-year students over many years were included. The technical term for such a complete potential pool, however defined, is **population**. Studies of this sort, therefore, are based on testing a **sample** from a very much larger population, with the hope of being able to make general statements about the population on the basis of the sample.

Thus, on the basis of the data described, it would be reasonable to state a conclusion such as 'there is some evidence that hints can help people to solve problems'. However, caution is needed. Not only have we data restricted to a sample of the target population, but it also only relates to one particular hint and one particular problem. Similar studies would be needed with other problems and other hints to build up a general picture. Only if a consistent trend emerged would we be justified in making a general statement about the efficacy of hints in problem-solving.

Similar cautionary remarks apply to the other examples. In Chapter 7, we shall start to show some approaches that give a handle on the general problem of **statistical inference**, namely the making of inferences about populations on the basis of data for samples.

Making links: Comparisons as relationships between variables

The examples discussed above fit into the general framework described in Chapter 2, of relationships between variables. They have in common also that at least one of the variables in each case is dichotomous; that is, it has only two values. For this reason, the relationship between the variables in each of these cases can be explored by comparisons between two sets of data. In the next chapter, by contrast, we consider relationships between variables, both of which take multiple values.

Although this may appear to labour the point, it is important to be clear about the terms 'relationship' and 'comparison'. This can be a source of confusion for students and justifiably so since, later, we will see a blurring of the two. In a sense, 'relationship' is the more general terms since it includes both comparisons and relationships. We shall revisit this issue at various points later in the book.

Chapter review

This chapter has presented the following examples of ways of looking at data:

- Comparing percentages of responses from different groups.
  Example: *Do the percentages of students preferring various courses differ between two faculties?*
- Comparing two groups' measurements on some variable.
  Example: *Do squash players tend to have faster reaction times than chess players?*
- Comparing performances of one group of people under different conditions.
  Example: *Do people react more quickly after drinking coffee than without coffee?*

Throughout the chapter, the absolutely central point has been stressed that data for a sample do not offer an absolute answer to any experimental question about a general population. Data for a sample must always be considered against the background of what might have been.

Seeing patterns in data: Correlating

In this chapter

... more ways of organizing and displaying data to reveal important patterns are shown. Whereas Chapter 4 was about relationships between variables in terms of *comparisons* between two sets of data, this chapter deals with relationships between two variables, bearing on such questions as the following:

- Is it generally true that the taller people are, the heavier they are?
- Is it true that people's intelligence relates to the size of their head?
- Do tests that are intended to measure the same variable present a consistent picture?
- Does the academic performance reduce as the number of parties attended by students increases?

As in the previous chapter, it is emphasized how data from a sample can only offer degrees of evidence in addressing these questions, and not definitive answers.

The concept of correlation

Proverbial wisdom has it that 'the bigger they come, the harder they fall' and 'more haste, less speed'. Whether or not these are generally true, there are very many situations that can be characterized in the form *the more of A, the more of B* or, conversely *the more of A, the less of B*. For example, it is accepted that the richer people are, the more conservative they are politically. Of course, this is just an overall trend, since we can think of rich people with left-wing views, and poor people with right-wing views. Similarly, in general – but by no means universally – the more education you have, the more you will earn.

Within psychology, there is a large number and variety of situations in which the relationship between two variables is of interest. Here is a selection of illustrative examples.

A matter of opinion

Social psychologists are interested in postulated personality traits such as authoritarianism and conservatism. One form of evidence in support of such claims is when stated opinions can be shown to be related. For example, supporting harsher sentences for criminals and corporal punishment in schools might both be considered indicative of authoritarianism. Figure 5.1 presents a set of possible data relating to this question in the form of a 2 × 2 table. It can be seen that more of those tested either support both views or oppose both views than support one and oppose the other. These data therefore represent some evidence for the hypothesis that the views are related, and the underlying hypothesis is that there is a trait accounting for this relationship.

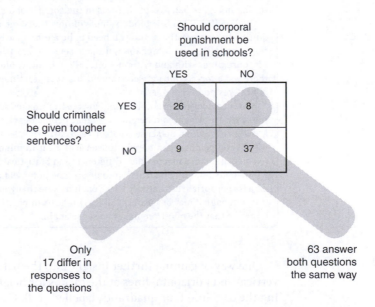

Figure 5.1 2 × 2 frequency table: Sentencing and corporal punishment data

> *Person in street:* So what? People who want to punish criminals want to punish schoolchildren. I could have told you that.
>
> *Social psychologist:* Bear in mind that this is just a small example to illustrate how we build up a picture of a theoretical construct such as authoritarianism. These data are just one piece of the jigsaw that allow us to theorize about the nature of authoritarianism and the ways in which it is manifested – some of which are not obvious – as well as providing ways of measuring the strength of the trait as it differs from individual to individual.

Height and weight

Whereas the previous example was about the relationship between variables taking only two values, this one is about the relationship between two variables measured on a continuous scale. The data are for 60 male psychology students. To investigate the relationship between the two variables, an excellent graphical resource is to hand (see Figure 5.2). For each student in the sample, there are two data – height and weight. Each such pair of measurements can be represented by a single point on a two-dimensional graph, where height is measured on the horizontal axis and weight on the vertical axis. A complete display of all such points for the sample is called a **scattergram** or **scatterplot**. In the scattergram you can see a trend whereby weight tends to be greater (but by no means always) if height is greater. A relationship of this sort is called a **positive correlation**.

Making links

Recall that, in the last chapter, we presented a graphical representation (Figure 4.20) very similar to that in Figure 5.2, except that was in the context of a *comparison* of reaction times with and without coffee. This is a good example of how the same representation can be used to answer quite different questions, and you need to be alert to the question you wish to ask. In the *Coffee time* example in the last chapter, it made sense to ask whether there was a difference between response times with and without coffee. Equally, it would also have made sense to ask whether there was a *correlation* between individuals' reaction times with and without coffee, but we were not interested in that question then.

Now consider the example here. Obviously, it makes sense to ask whether there is a correlation between weight and height. Are taller people heavier and shorter people lighter? However, it makes absolutely no sense whatsoever to ask whether there is a difference between people's weight and height – completely nonsensical. Bear in mind, however, that it is perfectly possible to calculate such a meaningless difference, and Statistical Package for the Social Sciences (SPSS) will happily obey any instruction to do so. The judgment as to whether or not a question about data is appropriate lies entirely with you. It may be that you are simply not interested in the question, although it may be entirely valid, as in the example from the previous chapter. Alternatively, it may be that the question makes no sense at all.

One way of gaining further insight into the pattern in the scattergram is to draw vertical and horizontal lines at the means for height and weight, respectively, dividing the data into four quadrants, labelled A, B, C and D as in Figure 5.3. The points in quadrant A correspond to the individuals in the sample who are of above-mean height and above-mean weight. The points in quadrant B correspond to those of below-mean height but above-mean weight ... and so on. The cases that fall in quadrants A and C are in line with the general trend that relatively tall people tend to be

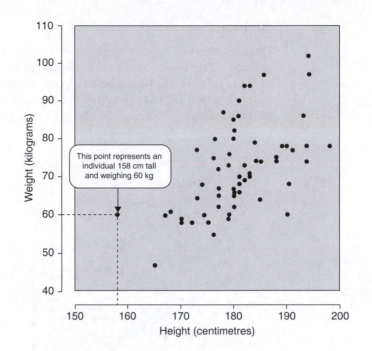

Figure 5.2 Scatterplot of height/weight

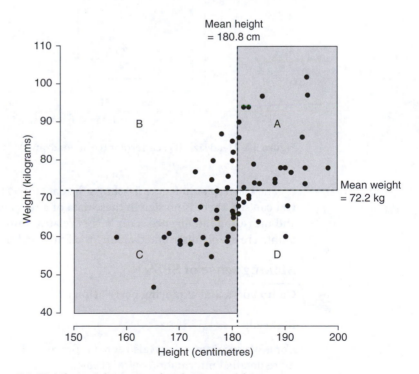

Figure 5.3 Height/weight scatterplot slowing quadrants

relatively heavy, and relatively short people tend to be relatively light; the less numerous cases in quadrants B and D correspond to the exceptions to the general trend who are smaller but heavier, or taller but lighter, respectively.

Bigheads

Does intelligence depend on the size of your head? Many people have thought so, including Paul Broca, a medical professor who founded the Anthropological Society of Paris in 1859. He firmly believed that intelligence depended on the size of the brain – hence, for example, men are more intelligent than women because their brains are larger.

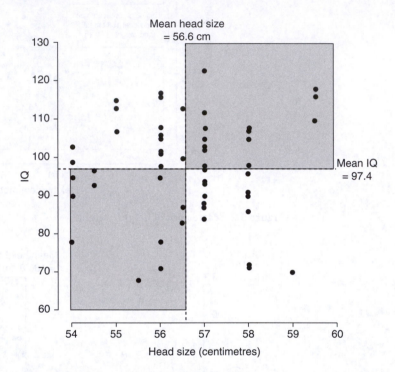

Figure 5.4 Head size/IQ scatterplot (with quadrants)

The scatterplot in Figure 5.4 shows the data for 54 female psychology students. As you can see, there is no sign in these data of a relationship between the size of head and measured intelligence. This lack of relationship is reflected in the fact that the points are evenly distributed among the four quadrants.

Making sense of SPSS

Coding data and exploring correlation

Bigheads

Note: We recommend you also consult Brace et al. (2009), pp. 154–161, who present more detailed information on this topic.

1. Creating the data file

We remind you of the golden rule for coding data in SPSS, namely that *each individual participant occupies a single row of their own in the data file*. In the *Bigheads* example we have 54 participants, so we know that there will be 54 rows in the data file. Also, since each participant produced two scores, there will be two columns of scores in the data file.

Launch SPSS and bring up the data window as you were shown in Chapter 3 (p. 36). Click **Variable View**. Complete the details as below.

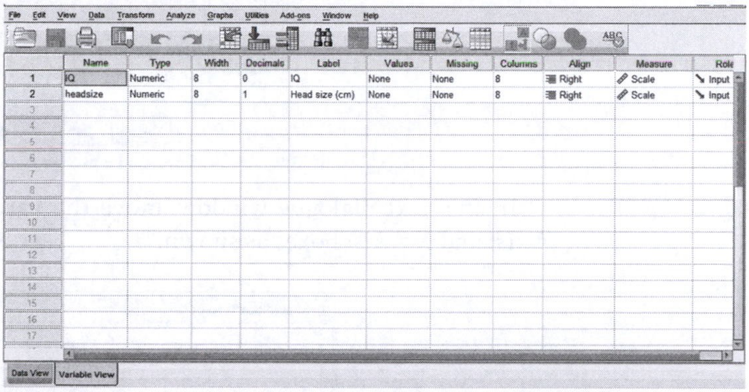

Now click on **Data View** to reveal the blank data table again. You will see two columns labeled *IQ* and *headsize*. The data are entered as indicated below (rows 1-16 displayed). Remember to save the data giving the file an appropriate name.

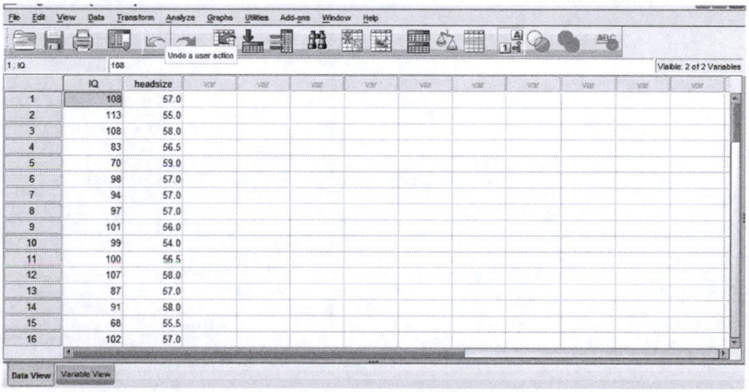

2. Exploring the correlation

In this chapter, since the emphasis is on descriptive aspects of the relationship between variables, we merely draw a scatterplot.

Select **Graphs** > **Legacy Dialogs** > **Scatter/Dot...** as shown below.

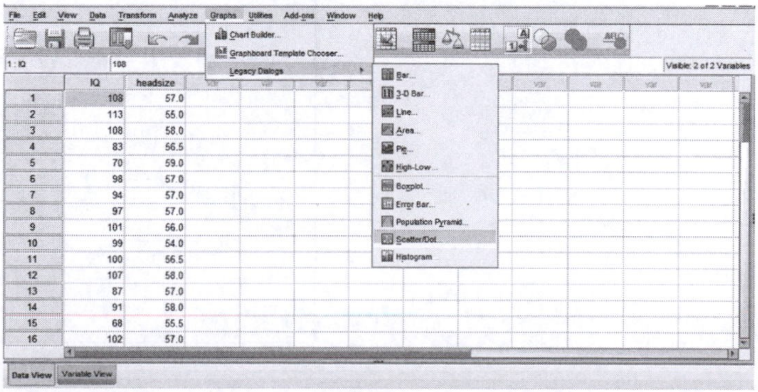

The following dialogue box will appear. Select **Simple Scatter** and click **Define**.

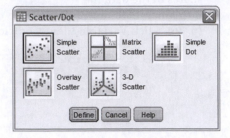

In the next dialogue window, move the variables *IQ* and *Head size* into the **Y Axis:** and **X Axis:** boxes as shown.

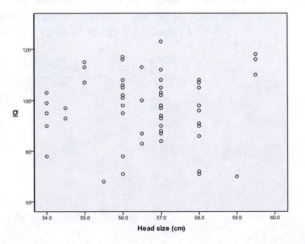

In the **SPSS Statistics Viewer** window the graph below will appear. Note the similarity of the scatterplot to that in Figure 5.4. It is possible to improve the look of the graph by double-clicking on it and using the graph editor (have a go).

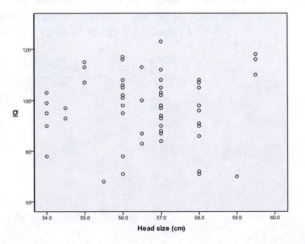

Consistency

As was discussed in Chapter 2, psychologists devote considerable time and ingenuity to devising variables to measure complex behaviours, assuming that these variables can be measured on a single numerical scale. One of the examples of such a construction was a test for measuring attitude towards computers. One way of evaluating whether such tests are appropriate is to see how much consistency there is between two such tests, each of which purports to measure a given variable. If the variable is a viable construct, and each of the tests does indeed measure it, then the results should be consistent – individuals scoring high on one test should also score high on the other, and individuals, scoring low on one test should also score low on the other.

The scatterplot in Figure 5.5 shows data for a sample of 58 male students for two tests designed to measure their attitude towards computers. As can be seen, there is an overall relationship between the two sets of scores, though the pattern is by no means perfect.

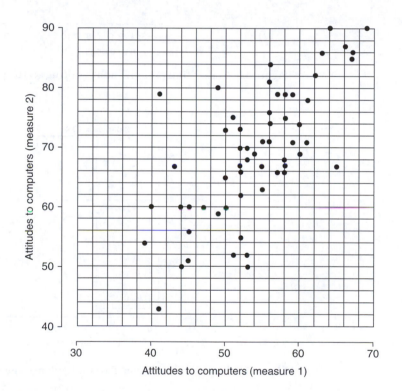

Figure 5.5 Scatterplot of two measures of attitude towards computers

Critical thinking

Another example of using correlation to examine consistency is when the judgements of two people are considered to see how consistent they are. Figure 5.6 presents data on the rankings of three people of a selection of ten classic movies. Using scatterplots to examine the consistency, it becomes clear that A and B have rather similar views on the relative merits of the movies, whereas those of A and C are very different. Looking at the data in the table, would you say that the judgements of B and C are similar or not?

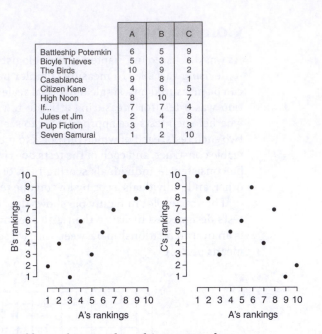

Figure 5.6 Classic film rankings and resulting scatterplots

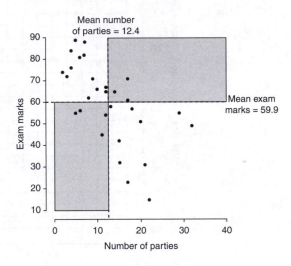

Figure 5.7 Negative correlation: Party attendance and exam performance

Party time

Figure 5.7 presents some data for 30 students about the number of parties attended by them during an academic year, and the average marks obtained at the end of that year. (These data are, of course, *entirely* fictitious.) From the scattergram, we see that there is an overall relationship whereby the greater the number of parties, in general, the lower the marks. When there is a relationship between two variables of this sort, with high scores on one variable tending to go with low ones on the other, it is called a **negative correlation**. Note how, in this case, the majority of the points lie in quadrants B and D.

Making sense of SPSS

Coding data and exploring correlation

Party time

Note: We recommend you also consult Brace et al. (2009), pp. 154–161, who present more detailed information on this topic.

1. Creating the data file

In this example, we have 30 participants; therefore, we know that there will be 30 rows in the data file. Again, since each participant produced two scores, there will be two columns of scores.

Launch SPSS and bring up **Variable View** as in the previous example (p. 69). Complete the details as before, this time for the *Party time* data. Then click on **Data View** to reveal the blank data table. You will see two columns labeled *parties* and *marks*. The data are entered as indicated below (rows 1–16 displayed). Remember to save the data by giving the file an appropriate name.

Exploring the correlation

Select **Graphs > Legacy Dialogs > Scatter/Dot…** as shown below.

The following dialogue box will appear. Select **Simple Scatter** and click **Define**.

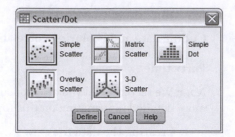

In the next dialogue window, move the variables *Exam marks* and *Parties attended* into the **Y Axis:** and **X Axis:** boxes as shown.

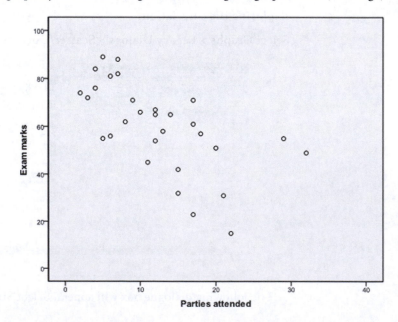

In the **SPSS Statistics Viewer** window the graph below will appear. Again, note the similarity of the scatterplot to that in Figure 5.7. It is possible to improve the look of the graph by double-clicking on it and using the graph editor (have a go).

Correlation and causation

Suppose – for the sake of argument – that the last set of data presented for party-going and academic performance was authentic. What conclusions would be suggested by such data?

> **Student A:** *It looks like going to parties causes you to do badly in your course. I can buy that. If you want to do well, cut down on socializing is the message.*
>
> **Student B:** *That's one possible explanation, but I can think of others. It's a matter of personality. Some people are serious and work hard, others like to enjoy themselves. This is the underlying cause for both the amount of partying and the level of performance.*
>
> **Student C:** *Here's another theory. We all have a fair idea of how we're doing. Maybe the ones who know they aren't going to do well go to parties to cheer themselves up. So the level of performance influences the social behaviour, not the other way round.*

This example illustrates a very general point about correlation. The mere existence of an empirical relationship between two variables, X and Y, for a sample of data may be suggestive of a causal link, with X causing Y. However, the correlation by itself cannot establish such a link and, among other potential explanations, the possibility must be considered that Y causes X, or the existence of another variable Z, underlying both X and Y and accounting for the relationship between them.

By its nature, a correlation between variables taking multiple values involves subject variables, not variables under the control of the experimenter. The fact that causation cannot be inferred directly from a correlation can be seen as a consequence of this lack of experimental control.

On not jumping to conclusions

In all of the above cases, it should be clear that the data presented offer some evidence for judging the questions posed. At the same time – as for the analyses of comparison discussed in Chapter 4 – absolute, cut-and-dried answers are not forthcoming.

Again, the main reason is the fact that the data are only a sample of the potential data. Consider the set of data for two unidentified variables presented as a scatterplot without scales in Figure 5.8. It suggests a positive correlation between the variables. Yet, this sample *might* have come from a population where there is no relationship between the variables, as shown in Figure 5.9. In turn, different samples from that population might have suggested quite different relationships, even possibly a negative correlation.

As in this example, and more generally, the key question in much of the statistical analysis in psychological research boils down to this:

> *How can the evidence from a sample be evaluated with a view to addressing questions about the population from which the sample came?*

Calculations about chance play a central role in trying to get a handle on this problem and that is why the next chapter is about probability.

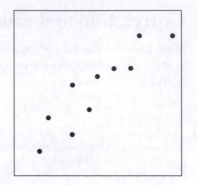

Figure 5.8 'Sample' scatterplot

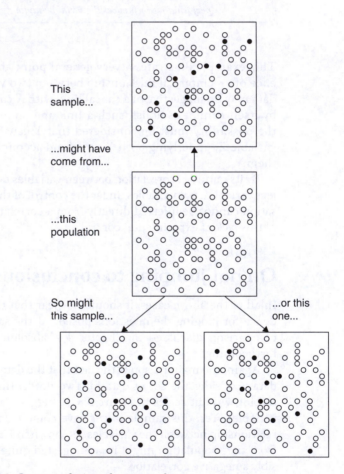

Figure 5.9 One population, three samples

Chapter review

This chapter has presented the following examples of ways of looking at relationships between variables.

- Relating yes/no responses to questions of opinion.
  Example: *Do people who think that criminals should get harsher sentences approve of corporal punishment in school?*
- Relating one variable to another that might plausibly be causally related.
  Example: *Is IQ dependent on size of head?*
- Relating different ways of measuring the same variable.
  Example: *Do two measures of attitude yield consistent results?*
- Relating subjective judgements made by individuals.
  Example: *Do people rank movies consistently?*
- Relating variables that exhibit a trade-off.
  Example: *Does party-going affect academic performance?* As in the previous chapter, it was pointed out repeatedly that absolute answers to such questions are not forthcoming from data collected only for samples of the population of interest.

The relevance of probability

In this chapter

... relevant ideas about probability are introduced. Why a chapter on probability? The short answer is that research in psychology invariably involves using sample data to make inferences about populations, so uncertainty is inherent to this research, and judgments are therefore intrinsically probabilistic. Some knowledge of probability is central to allowing you to make such judgments. Accordingly, the necessary groundwork is laid, and then straightforward examples are worked through to demonstrate how samples can vary from one to another, and how knowledge of this can allow us to use sample data to make inferences about populations.

Measuring probability

Most people have some notion of probability, even if it's only in connection with forecasting weather, gambling or predicting outcomes of sporting contests. Everyday language includes many terms indicating varying levels of likelihood of something happening which is more or less probable, that is, lying somewhere between 'impossible' and 'certain' – for example, 'unlikely', 'improbable', 'possible', 'likely' and 'almost certain'. Such terms are used routinely in trying to predict events, such as marks in examinations, elections, success in relationships and so on.

What people mean by verbal probabilistic statements is generally vague and subjective. Indeed, research shows that how different individuals interpret a term such as 'probable' varies across a wide spectrum. Similarly, in a court of law, the interpretation of 'beyond a reasonable doubt' varies enormously. The vagueness can, in some circumstances, be replaced by mathematical precision (but this precision should not foster the illusion that probabilistic analysis is cut-and-dried – this is far from being the case).

Although people must have been aware of probability, in some sense, since essentially the start of civilization through observations from everyday life, and although games of chance have been around in most cultures for millennia, a more formal treatment of probability is a late development within the history of mathematics. What is recognized widely as the first major contribution came as the result of French gamblers in the seventeenth century appealing to their mathematical friends for practical advice. Such chance procedures as tossing a coin, throwing dice or picking a card at random, offer familiar contexts for illustrating how probability can be measured, and this is where we start.

Before reading on...

Try these to see how much you know. What is the probability of the following?

1 Getting heads if you toss a fair coin?
2 Getting 1 head and 1 tail if you toss a fair coin twice?
3 Getting a 6 if you roll a fair die?
4 Getting a score of less than 3 if you roll a fair die?
5 Picking a club at random from a pack of 52 cards (no jokers)?
6 Picking a card that is *not* an ace if you pick a card at random from a pack of 52 cards (no jokers)?
7 The first spinner in Figure 6.1 ending up pointing to 1?
8 The second spinner in Figure 6.1 ending up pointing to 1?

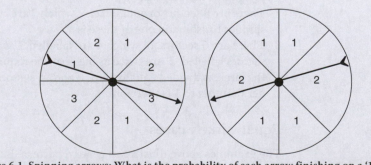

Figure 6.1 Spinning arrows: What is the probability of each arrow finishing on a '1'?

... now read on.

The answers to the questions follow. If you weren't able to answer most of them with confidence, you may want to brush up on basic probability.

1 The probability of getting heads if you toss a fair coin is $^{1}/_{2}$. In fact, that is what is meant by it being 'fair' – there are equal chances of a head and a tail.
2 For the tossing of a coin twice, Figure 6.2 shows two different points of view. Are you convinced by either? Think about it before moving on.

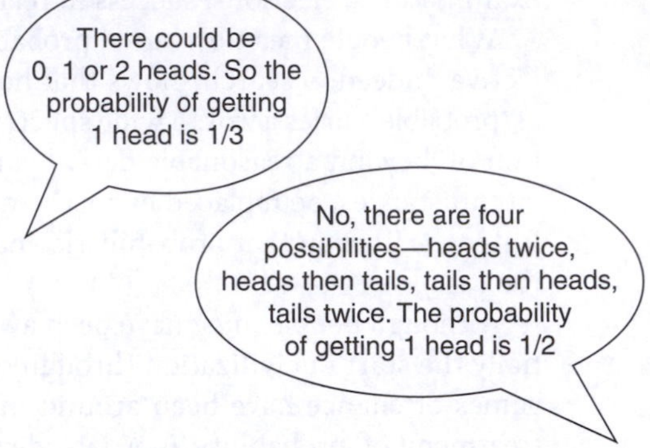

Figure 6.2 Tossing a coin twice – what are the possible outcomes?

The second explanation is the correct one. There are four equally likely outcomes, not three. (The misconception that there are three, as illustrated in the first argument in the figure, is common. If you are not convinced, you could carry out an experiment. Toss a coin twice a large number of times (at least 300), and observe on how many occasions you get one head and one tail (in either order). For a large number of coin tosses, we confidently predict it will be close to ½, rather than ⅓, of the number of times you did it).

3 Again, a 'fair' die means that all six numbers are equally likely, so the probability of getting a 6 (or any other particular number) is ⅙.
4 A score of less than 3 means either 1 or 2. There are two chances out of 6 equal chances, so the probability is $^{2}/_{6}$, or ⅓.
5 To pick 'randomly' means, by definition, that each card has an equal chance of being picked. Since there are 52 cards, of which 13 are clubs, the probability of picking a club is $^{13}/_{52}$, or ¼.
6 There are only 4 aces in a deck and 48 cards are not aces, so the probability of not picking an ace is $^{48}/_{52}$, or $^{12}/_{13}$.
7 There are 8 sectors of equal size, of which 3 are labelled '1', so the probability of the spinner finishing in one of these is ⅜.
8 There are 6 sectors, of which 4 are labelled '1', *but they are not of equal size* – the sectors labelled '2' are twice as big – so the required probability is *not* 4/6. In fact, the circle is divided equally into '1' and '2' sectors, and the probability of the spinner pointing to 1 is therefore ½.

Equally likely cases

The examples above illustrate a general pattern. Except for the final example, where the outcomes as originally defined by the sectors on the spinner are *unequal*, there are a number of possible outcomes (heads or tails, numbers on dice, cards in a pack, sectors of a circle where the spinner may come to rest), each of which is equally likely. Why do we believe they are equally likely? Because there is no reason to believe any one is more likely than any other. For example, a die is as perfectly precise a cube as the limitations of manufacture allow and therefore is symmetrical. Similarly, thorough shuffling of a pack of cards means that we have no basis for saying that any one card is more likely to be picked than another.

In these circumstances, if n is the number of possible outcomes ($n = 2$ for a coin, 6 for a standard dice, 52 for picking a card, 8 for the first spinner) then

the probability of a particular outcome is $\frac{1}{n}$

We may be interested in the probability, not of a single outcome, but of a set of outcomes – for example, what is the probability of getting an even score with a die? Such a set of outcomes is called an *event*. The event 'even score on a die' covers three outcomes – 2, 4 and 6. Similarly, for picking a card, the event 'a spade', covers 13 outcomes. If m is the number of outcomes in an event (out of n equally probable outcomes) then

the probability of the event is $\frac{m}{n}$

(This includes the special case when the event consists of just a single outcome, in which case the probability is, of course, $\frac{1}{n}$.)

Sometimes, we are interested in the probability of an event *not* happening. In that case, if the event corresponds to m outcomes, there are $n - m$ outcomes corresponding to the event not happening, so

the probability of the event not happening is $\frac{(n-m)}{n}$

It should be starting to become clear that all probabilities must lie between 0 and 1. The closer the probability is to 1, the higher is the chance of the event happening. If the probability is nearer 0, the less is the chance of the event happening. In the extreme, the probability of an 'impossible' event (such as getting a score of 7 on a die) is 0 (since $\frac{0}{n} = 0$), and the probability of a 'certain' event (for example, getting a score of less than 7 on a die) is 1 (since $\frac{n}{n} = 1$).

Long-run frequency

It is only in special cases that it is reasonable to assume equal likelihoods for the different possible outcomes. Even a coin or die may be biased (that is, have unequal probabilities for different outcomes). A simple example is the following. If a tack is thrown in the air and allowed to fall on the ground, it can land on its back with point straight in the air, or at an angle, with point facing down. Intuitively, we feel that there is a probability for each of those outcomes, but we have no reason to assume that each has the probability ½. While we cannot determine the probabilities by argument, we can estimate them by experimentation. The tack is thrown many times, and the proportion of times it falls in each of the two positions provides an estimate of the respective probabilities.

In this situation, we can think about tossing the tack an infinite number of times. This represents the population of all possible tosses of the tack. Conceptually, there is a fixed probability, p, for this population, that the tack will land point up (and conversely, a probability $1 - p$ that it will land point down). Any experiment with a number of tosses of the tack provides a sample from this population. From that sample, p can be estimated. Figure 6.3 shows how one such sampling might conceivably go (but, of course, it will happen differently every time it is done). For each set of 10 trials, the number of times the tack lands point up is recorded. Twenty batches of 10 trials are performed and the percentage 'up' of the total number of trials to date is recorded and plotted on the graph. In the short run (say the first eight batches of trials), the relative frequency may fluctuate considerably, but in the long run, it can be expected to settle down within a relatively small interval close to the (idealized) true probability.

For this conceptualization of probability to be applicable, it is necessary that the following are true:

- Essentially the same procedure can be repeated over and over (the technical term for each repetition is a **trial**); and
- it is reasonable to postulate that the probability of the event of interest on each trial is independent and constant.

'Independent' means that what happens on any one occasion is not dependent in any way on what happened before.

If these conditions are met, and if the event of interest occurs k times in n replications, its probability, p, can be estimated as k/n. *In general, the larger the number of replications, the better the estimate will be.* It should be clear that a probability estimate derived in this way must lie between 0 and 1.

If the probability of an event is known, or estimated, to be p, then in N independent trials, the event can be expected to happen *about $p \times N$ times.* For example, if a student is postulated to guess every answer in a 40-item multiple choice test with four alternative answers on each item, then the probability of a correct choice for each

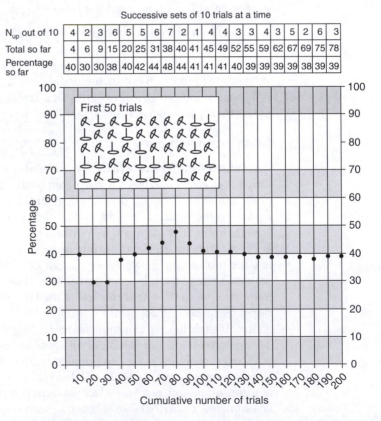

Figure 6.3 Throwing a tack in the air: Which way up will it land over 200 trials?

item is ¼, and the student would be expected to get *about* 10 (¼ × 40) answers right 'just by chance'.

Subjective probability

There are other situations where we feel that we can subjectively make a probabilistic statement; yet, there is no basis for doing so, either on grounds of equal probability, or by reference to replications. For example, we may believe that it is almost certain that our team will beat the opposition in a sports event, or that a certain actor will win an Oscar. Such a judgement is called a **subjective probability**, and the person making it could be asked to convert it into a numerical value between 0 and 1. Subjective probabilities play no essential part in this book, however, and are mentioned here only for completeness.

Examples

As you will see later, in interpreting results of statistical tests, a probability of $\frac{1}{20}$ or less is conventionally taken as meaning 'unlikely' ($\frac{1}{20}$ can alternatively be expressed as a decimal, 0.05, or as a percentage, 5%). Conversely, a probability of $\frac{19}{20}$ (.95 or 95%) or greater represents a conventional standard for 'likely'. Figure 6.4 presents some examples to give you a feel for what such probabilities mean. In the first example, the probability of picking a black ace (ace of spades or ace of clubs) from a properly shuffled pack of 52 cards is $\frac{2}{52}$, or approximately .038, which is less than .05

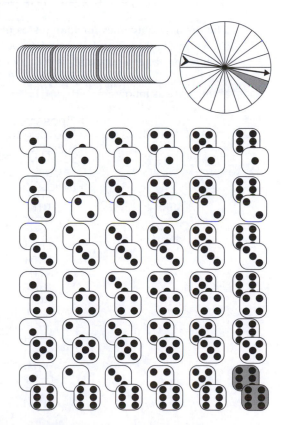

Figure 6.4 'Likely' and 'unlikely' events

(½₀). In the second example, with twenty equal sectors on the spinner, the chance of the pointer finishing on the shaded sector is $\frac{1}{20}$. The third example shows the 36 possible outcomes if two dice are thrown. The probability of a total of 12 is $\frac{1}{36}$, = approximately .028, since in only one case is the total 12 (6 and 6). Conversely, the probability of not picking a black ace is approximately .962, the probability of not landing on the shaded sector is $\frac{19}{20}$ or .95, and the probability of getting a total less than 12 is approximately .972.

Counting heads

As has already been discussed, if a coin is tossed twice, there are four possible outcomes, namely HH, HT, TH and TT. If we are interested in the number of heads (regardless of order) then the probabilities are the following:

Prob (0 heads) = ¼
Prob (1 head) = ½
Prob (2 heads) = ¼

Now, consider what happens if a coin is tossed four times.

> **Before reading on...**
>
> Can you work out for yourself the probabilities for getting different numbers of heads for four tosses of a fair coin?
>
> **... now read on**

The possible outcomes for four tosses of the coin can be set out systematically as shown in Figure 6.5 and grouped according to the number of heads in each case. Each of the sixteen outcomes is equally likely, with a probability of $\frac{1}{16}$, so taking the number of outcomes corresponding to 0, 1, 2, 3 and 4 heads into account, the probabilities are as follows:

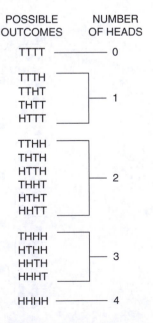

Figure 6.5 Possible outcomes of tossing a coin 4 times

Number of Heads	Probability	Decimal Equivalent
0	$\frac{1}{16}$	0.063
1	$\frac{4}{16}$	0.250
2	$\frac{6}{16}$	0.375
3	$\frac{4}{16}$	0.250
4	$\frac{1}{16}$	0.063

As shown in Figure 6.6, the same information can be presented graphically as a **probability distribution**. Without going into details, the same procedure gives the probability distributions in Figures 6.7 and 6.8 for 8 and 16 tosses of the coins respectively.

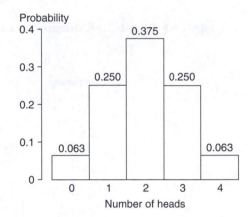

Figure 6.6 Probability distribution of the 4-coin toss

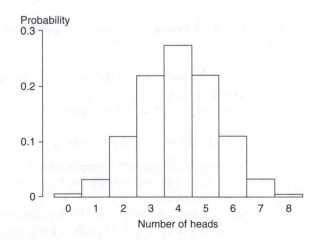

Figure 6.7 Probability distribution of an 8-coin toss

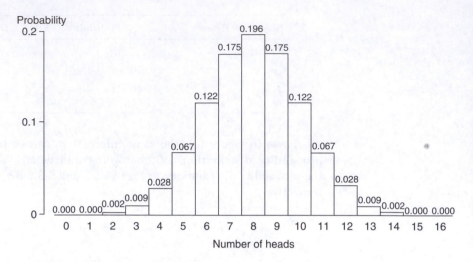

Figure 6.8 **Probability distribution of a 16-coin toss**

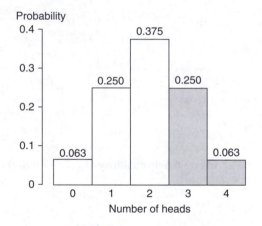

Figure 6.9 **Probability of at least 3 heads in a 4-coin toss**

A further property of the probability distributions is that if each column is taken to have unit width, the area of the column equals the probability it represents. Further, we can represent the following probability

Prob (at least ¾ of tosses come up heads)

by shading the corresponding parts of the probability distributions – the shaded areas equal the required probabilities, as in Figures 6.9 to 6.11. We can then see that the probability of at least ¾ of the coin tosses coming up heads is .313 for 4 tosses, .144 for 8 tosses, and .039 for 16 tosses. This illustrates yet again the effect of increasing sample size. With only four coin tosses, getting at least ¾ heads is quite common, with 8 it is still not particularly unusual, but with 16th it is less than 5%. In general, the larger the number of tosses, the more likely the proportion of heads is to be close to ½.

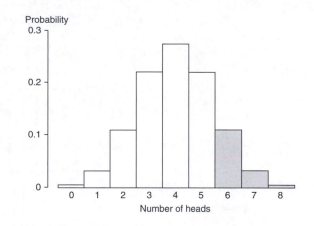

Figure 6.10 **Probability of at least 6 heads in an 8-coin toss**

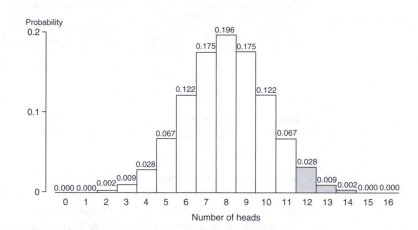

Figure 6.11 **Probability of at least 12 heads in a 16-coin toss**

The role of the normal distribution

In the examples just considered, the probability distributions have a striking resemblance in shape to the theoretical smooth curve that defines the so-called **normal distribution** (or *Bell Curve*). Indeed, as illustrated in Figure 6.12, the probability distribution for tossing a coin *n* number of times starts to resemble closer and closer the *normal* distribution as *n* gets bigger.

As mentioned in Chapter 2, many variables of interest in psychology, when measured for representative samples, produce empirical distributions that reasonably conform to the shape of the *normal* distribution. (It is also important to remember that many other variables produce shapes of distribution which differ markedly from the *normal* distribution in various respects.)

The occurrence of roughly *normal* distributions for empirical distributions of variables such as height can be linked to the shapes of distributions presented in the previous section. The number of heads obtained when one tosses a fair coin 16 times may be thought of as arising as the overall result of 16 small causes operating independently, namely the 16 tosses, each of which contributes either 0 or 1 to the total number of heads. The shape of the resultant distribution reflects the fact that there is only one way of obtaining 0 or 16 heads, whereas there are very many ways

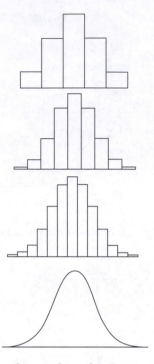

Figure 6.12 Tossing coins: As the number of coins tossed increases, the probability distribution increasingly resembles a normal distribution

of obtaining 8. More generally, the number of ways increases towards the middle of the distribution and falls away to the extremes. A physical characteristic, such as height, could be considered, analogously, as the result of a large number of small causes operating more or less independently – hence, the good approximation to the *normal* distribution when height measurements are presented for a sample from a homogeneous population. While this argument is plausible, it should be noted that it is somewhat controversial.

The *normal* distribution is of central importance for another, theoretical, reason. Many of the statistical tests used in psychological research are based on the assumption that the distribution of the variable in question in the population approximates well the normal distribution. The technical term for such tests is **parametric** tests. An implication is that, if the distribution of data departs markedly from the *normal* shape, alternative **non-parametric** (or so-called **rank-based**) tests should be considered. This aspect will be discussed at more length in the course of the next two chapters.

Predicting an election: a sampling example

When an election is taking place, attempts to predict the result on the basis of polls of samples of the electorate are common. Such polls are often badly reported, in the sense that little attention is drawn to sampling variation, although sometimes undefined *margins of error* will be quoted. If one party's estimated share of the vote differs by a few per cent from one week to the next, it is usually analysed on the assumption that there has been a shift in support within the population, whereas the difference may well be attributable to sampling variation; that is, to the fact that the results from different samples of the same population will vary, sometimes considerably.

Before reading on...

Try working through the following exercise that simulates the situation where the voting preferences of a population are being estimated on the basis of a sample. The preferences for three parties – A, B or C – for an entire population of 2000 electors are represented by the array of letters in Figure 6.13. Obviously, the numbers of As, Bs and Cs in the grid could be ascertained simply by counting. For the purposes of the exercise, however, the whole array of letters will not be counted, only samples. Here's what you should do.

1 Choose a letter, at random, somewhere on the page. Consider the 25 letters forming a 5 × 5 square for which the chosen letter lies at the centre.
2 Count and record the number of As, Bs and Cs in this sample of 25 letters. On the basis of this sample, what percentage of the letters on the entire page would you estimate are As, Bs or Cs? Record your estimate.
3 Now choose another 5 × 5 square (not overlapping the first), and repeat the process. Record the results again. What would your estimates now be for the percentages of letters on the entire page?
4 Repeat the process another eight times, recording the results each time.

Look carefully at all the data you have collected. What do you make of it? Jot down some thoughts.

... now read on

Here are the most salient points we would expect you to notice.

- The percentages of support for parties A, B and C vary quite a bit over the 10 samples.
- The predicted order of support for the three parties varies from sample to sample, although one party may come out on top more often than the other two.
- By combining all your samples you get, in effect, a sample of 250. You may have more confidence in the predictions made on the basis of this larger sample.

Now repeat the whole exercise using samples of 49 each time (use a 7 × 7 square of numbers).

Before reading on...

Look carefully at the data from both parts of the exercise. What differences does a larger sample size make? On the basis of all the information to hand now, how would you estimate the support for the three parties in the population?

... now read on

Here are the most salient points we would expect you to notice:

- The variation from sample to sample is almost certain to be less for the samples of 49 than for the samples of 25.
- With the larger samples, there is a good chance that the indications are that B is the most popular party, followed by A, then C.

If you combined all the samples, you have a total sample of 740 (250 from the first part and 490 from the second). This should give you a fairly good estimate of the actual percentages in the population (which you can find at the end of the chapter).

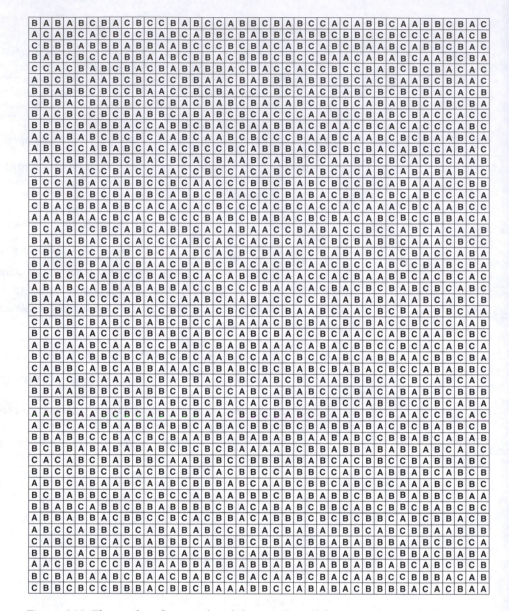

Figure 6.13 Electoral preferences (candidates A, B or C) for a population of 2000 voters

This example makes a number of absolutely vital points in relation to using samples to make inferences about populations (which is what lies at the heart of statistical methods most commonly used in psychology):

- A sample should always be interpreted in relation to *what might have happened* with lots of different samples of the same size.
- Different samples may point to conflicting results (this is really a specific aspect of the previous point).
- The larger the sample, the more stable estimates become, and the more confidence can be placed in them.

Making links

Sampling distribution and standard error

At this point, we introduce some ideas that link to much of what you will encounter later in the book. Towards the end of the last chapter, and in some of the sections above, we have raised the issue that a single sample of data drawn from a population may or may not reflect that population well. In the above example, we saw that, when several samples of a given size were taken from a population of 2000 voters, the percentages of support for different parties could vary considerably, although less so for larger sample sizes.

Let's now consider this key idea in more detail. We know that, in general, if we were to draw several samples of the same size from any population, the summary statistics for each are likely to differ from the others and, in relatively rare cases, may differ markedly. An important question is whether it is possible to say something definitive, or even to quantify, the 'behaviour' of lots and lots of samples of a given size drawn from a population. In order to explore this point, let's look again at the *Attitude to Computers* data from the class of 27 students first shown in Chapter 3 (p. 27).

    60 62 62 47 63 69 68 46 70
    60 56 54 48 50 49 58 49 66
    54 53 56 52 57 63 71 61 43

Recall that we calculated various measures of average (mean, median) and spread (range, standard deviation, percentiles) for this sample. We also provided a method for obtaining these summary statistics using SPSS. Two of the summary statistics obtained were a mean of 57.3 and a standard deviation of 7.85. Actually, it should be noted that, when we collect a sample of data such as this, the sample mean is regarded as our best (indeed, our only) single estimate of the population mean, referred to as a **point estimate**. This approach is used widely in psychology. Clearly, however, it is extremely unlikely that the true mean for the population will be exactly equal to this point estimate. An important question is how accurate is our estimate? More generally, how **representative** of the population is this sample?

One way of getting a handle on this question is to consider how lots of similar samples from the same population might be expected to behave. For example, if we were to take repeated samples of size 27 and calculate the mean, how would all of the means be expected to vary? Fortunately, due to the hard work of clever statisticians, we can construct a distribution of these sample means, known as a **sampling distribution**. You may be relieved to learn that you do not need to know the technical details, nor indeed, to construct the distribution. All you do need to know is that you can easily work out the spread of sample means (the **standard error**, or *SE*, for short) within the sampling distribution using the standard deviation (SD) of the original sample of scores. We simply do this by dividing our sample SD by the square root of the sample size.

Let's do this for the 27 *Attitude to Computers* scores whose *SD* was calculated as 7.85:

$$SE = \frac{SD}{\sqrt{N}} = \frac{7.85}{\sqrt{27}} = \frac{7.85}{5.196} = \mathbf{1.51}$$

Thus, for a theoretical sample of means for lots of different samples of size 27, the standard deviation of the sample means (standard error of means) is 1.51. This standard error is like any standard deviation measure and, given what we have learned about the properties of standard deviation, we know that 95% of the sample means lie within the range of ±1.96 standard errors around the sample mean, as follows:

    Range = 57.3 ±1.96 × 1.51 = 57.3 ±2.96 = **54.34 to 60.26**

Using some technical assumptions that you need not know about, we can also conclude that there is a 95% probability that the population mean will lie in this range. This approach of providing an **interval estimate** of the population mean rather than a single point estimate is a key idea that we shall return to in Chapter 10.

For those who wish to dig a little deeper

Conditional probability

The probability of an event may or may not be changed if we are told that another event has occurred. Examples will make this clearer. If I pick a card at random from a pack (no jokers), the probability that it is an ace is $\frac{4}{52}$, or $\frac{1}{13}$. If I don't look at it, but show it to you and you tell me it's a spade, then, since there are thirteen spades, of which one is the ace, the probability that the card is an ace is still $\frac{1}{13}$. Thus:

Prob (ace given spade) = Prob (ace) = $\frac{1}{13}$

in which the first expression means *the probability of picking an ace, given that the card picked is a spade*.

On the other hand, if in the same situation you tell me that the card picked is a court card (jack, queen, king or ace), the probability now that it is an ace is $\frac{4}{16}$, or $\frac{1}{4}$, since the possible outcomes have been narrowed down to sixteen, of which four are aces. So:

Prob (ace given court card) ≠ Prob (ace)

If we reverse the order of the events within the conditional probability, in general we get a different value. For example, the probability of picking a spade given that the card is an ace is 1/4, since the possible outcomes have been reduced to four (the four aces), of which one is a spade. This is different from the probability of picking an ace given that the card is a spade, which we have already seen is $\frac{1}{13}$.

Similarly, the probability of picking a court card, given that the card is an ace, is 1 (since if it is an ace, it is by definition a court card). Thus:

Prob (court card given ace) ≠ Prob (ace court card)

There are many cases where people get confused about the opposite forms of the conditional probabilities. It may be, for example, that the probability that someone who takes hard drugs previously took soft drugs is high. *It is fallacious to argue from this statement that the probability is high that someone who takes soft drugs will later take hard drugs*. As another example, it is highly probable that a soccer team will win a match, given that they score five goals in the first 15 minutes, but it is *highly improbable* that the team will score five goals in the first 15 minutes, given that they win the match.

Before reading on ...

Consider the following information about testing for the HIV virus in a certain population:

• The probability of a positive test result from a person who has the virus = 0.999.
• The probability of a negative result from a person who doesn't have the virus = 0.99.
• The proportion of people in the population who have the virus = 0.006.

Now suppose a person is diagnosed by the test as HIV positive. What is the probability that the person actually is HIV positive? Make an estimate and record it.

... now read on.

You may be surprised at the answer. Given the information as stated above, the probability that a person, testing positive, truly is positive is only 0.375, as shown by the following informal proof (it can be proved more formally, but that is beyond the scope of this discussion). Suppose that 1000 people are tested. Then among those 1000 there are about 6 who are HIV positive (given that the proportion in the population is .006). Let us assume that 6 are HIV positive, and the remaining 994 are not. Of the 6 who are HIV positive, the chances are that all 6 will be diagnosed as positive by the test. Of the 994 who are not positive, about 1% will be wrongly diagnosed as positive (see the second piece of information above) – say 10 people – and the other 984 will be correctly diagnosed as negative. Thus, in all, 16 people are diagnosed as positive, of which 6 actually *are* positive, and 10 are not. So, if a person is diagnosed as positive, the probability that they in fact *are* positive is only $^6/_{16}$ = 0.375 (we repeat, this is not a mathematically impeccable proof, but the same result is obtained by using such a proof). The argument is probably easier to follow through by looking at the diagram in Figure 6.14.

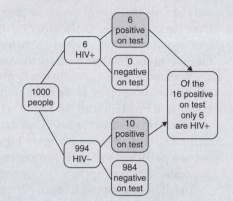

Figure 6.14 What is the probability that someone diagnosed HIV+ *actually is* HIV+?

The chances are that your estimate was much higher. If so, you may have been confusing two conditional probabilities. The probability of a positive diagnosis, given the person has the virus, is 0.999 (as initially stated) – using notational shorthand:

Prob (positive diagnosis given person has virus) = 0.999

However, the conditional probability you were asked to estimate was the opposite one – the probability that the person *has* the virus, given a positive diagnosis, and as shown, this is very different:

Prob (person has virus given positive diagnosis) = 0.375

Confusing one conditional probability with its opposite is very common even among relative experts (and can have serious consequences if used to guide social policy or make decisions, such as in court cases). The reason for analysing this particular example of fallacious probabilistic reasoning is that it is important to be aware of it for a full understanding of the standard method of statistical inference used in psychology, as illustrated in the example that follows.

Inference from sample to population: an example

Having laid some groundwork, we are now in a position to work through a straightforward example that illustrates in detail the logic of standard statistical tests used in psychological research.

In *Gulliver's Travels* by Jonathan Swift, the author satirizes political and religious dissension by describing the controversy between the Big-Endians, who asserted that a boiled egg should be broken at the big, more rounded end, and the Little-Endians, who equally stoutly maintained that it should be broken at the little, more pointed end. Suppose we wanted to investigate the balance of Big-Endians and Little-Endians in the population at large. (Admittedly not the most earth-shattering question open to psychological research, but chosen for the sake of a clear example to lay bare the logic of the procedure.) We would check a sample of the population and find out for each person which type they were – 'B' or 'L', for short. On the basis of the results for the sample, we would consider whether a justifiable conclusion could be made about the population as a whole.

Let us assume that data are collected for a sample of 16 (rather a small sample, given that the information should not be too hard to come by, but easier to deal with in terms of working through the details). There are 17 possible results of such data collection: namely, the number of Bs in the sample could turn out to be any number from 0 to 16 (that makes 17 possibilities, including 0). If all 16 in the sample turned out to be Bs, that would clearly be pretty strong evidence that there are more Bs than Ls in the population. At the other extreme, if none of the sample turned out to be Bs, that would be strong evidence that there are more Ls than Bs. If the sample turned out to contain 8 Bs and 8 Ls, there would clearly be no indication of an imbalance in the population either way. So far, so obvious. The intermediate cases represent varying degrees of support for Bs or Ls being more prevalent in the population. All of this is summed up graphically in Figure 6.15.

Where do we draw the line? How extreme does the imbalance between the number of Big-Endians and the number of Little-Endians have to be before we consider that the sample offers serious evidence that one group or the other predominates in the population?

To follow one approach to answering this question, we introduce a technical device called the **null hypothesis** at this stage. Before proceeding further, however, it is necessary to distinguish two meanings of the word *hypothesis*. Sometimes, it is used to indicate something that the speaker believes to be true (but has not yet been proved) as in 'It is my hypothesis that the world is round', or 'It is my hypothesis that English people have a poor sense of humour'. In other circumstances, however, it is a device of formal argument not necessarily believed by the speaker to be true, but taken to be true, literally for the sake of argument.

In the context of statistical research, the null hypothesis, in general, asserts that no specific effect is in operation (this will become progressively clearer as you encounter

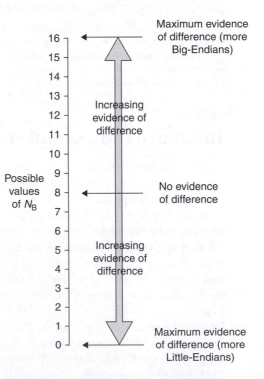

Figure 6.15 Possible numbers of Big-Endians in a sample of 16

more and more examples). For shortness, we use H_0 as notation for the null hypothesis. In the context of the present example, H_0 is that there is no difference either way, that Bs and Ls are equally represented in the population. Here 'hypothesis' is being used in the second sense – for the purposes of following through the argument, it is irrelevant whether or not the experimenter believes it to be true.

The argument now proceeds by asking:

If H_0 is true, what implications follow from that?

Now, we can start to apply some of the probability theory developed earlier. H_0 states that, for each individual in the sample, the probability that they are a B is the same as the probability that they are an L:

Prob (B) = Prob (L) = ½

We are now in a position to state what the probability is of the sample containing any specific number of Bs if H_0 is true. The situation resembles exactly that already analysed of the tossing of a coin 16 times – each toss of the coin, with a 50/50 chance of heads or tails, corresponds to one person being tested, with a 50/50 chance of being a B or an L (that is, given that we assume H_0 to be true). So the probability distribution for the number of Bs that potentially might be found (let's abbreviate it to N_B) in a succession of random samples of 16 under the null hypothesis, looks like that in Figure 6.16.

The probability distribution shown in Figure 6.16 is called the **sampling distribution** for N_B. From the sampling distribution, we can tell that, if H_0 is true, the probability of N_B taking either of the extreme values is (to three decimal places) .000 (the exact value is 1/32768 or .000031 to 2 significant figures). Indeed, the probability of N_B taking a value as extreme as, or more extreme than, 3 or 13, is only .022 (.009 + .009 + .002 + .002) corresponding to the shaded areas in Figure 6.17 and the sum of the corresponding probabilities).

We can thus argue that if H_0 is true, the probability of a result as extreme (in one direction or the other) is very low. We have now reached the pivotal point of the argument. If the experiment is carried out, and the actual result for the sample of 16 is that N_B takes any of the values 0, 1, 2, 3, 13, 14, 15, 16, we consider that doubt has been thrown on the original assumption of the truth of the null hypothesis. The grounds for so doing are that the probability of the null hypothesis generating any of

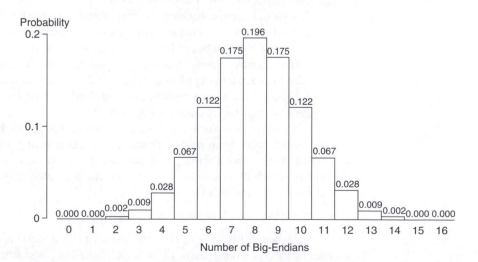

Figure 6.16 Probability distribution for the number of Big-Endians in a sample of 16

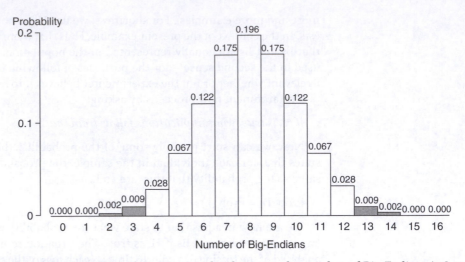

Figure 6.17 Probability that, in a sample of sixteen, the number of Big-Endians is 3 or less, or 13 or more

these extreme values is very low (.022), so low in fact that we would reject the null hypothesis as an explanation for our result. Recall from earlier that, by convention, our 'likelihood' cut-off value is .05 (expressed alternatively as $\frac{1}{20}$ or 5%). If the value of the statistic lies in sections of the tails of the sampling distribution for which the total probability .05 or less, it is sufficiently unlikely that the null hypothesis (H_0) would have produced our result that we reject it. That is, we reject the suggestion that there is no preference for B or L in the population. Here, .022 is less than our cut-off likelihood of .05, so the result is said to be *statistically significant at the .05 level*.

If we had included a little more of the tails of the distribution, namely the values 4 and 12, the total probability would have risen to .078 (.028 + .028 + .009 + .009 + .002 +.002), as you can work out from the figure. Thus, in this example, a result for N_B of 4 or less, or of 12 or more would be deemed to be *statistically non-significant*. That is, it is too likely that the null hypothesis could have produced this result to allow us to reject H_0 as the explanation for our result. We therefore cannot conclude that there is a tendency in the population towards B or L.

This is one approach, therefore, that provides a criterion for answering the question posed earlier, namely: how extreme does the imbalance between the number of Big-Endians and the number of Little-Endians have to be before we consider that the sample offers serious evidence that one group or other predominates in the population?

The logic underlying all of the statistical tests considered in this book is the same as for this example. The steps of the logic, both in terms of the specific example, and in general, may be set out as in Figure 6.19.

The notion of statistical significance, introduced through the example, is very easy to misinterpret. Even many statistical texts get it wrong. In particular, people (often quite expert) have a strong tendency to confuse two conditional probabilities. What the approach described here does is to work out statements about the data, given that the null hypothesis is true. Thus:

Prob (N_B is ≥ 13 or ≤ 3 given H_0 true) = .022

In other words, if H_0 is true, the value of the statistic is unlikely to be as extreme as, or more extreme than, 13 or 3. *BUT, the test for statistical significance does not say anything about the probability that the null hypothesis is true, given these data.*

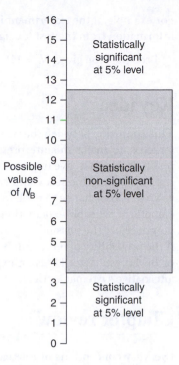

Figure 6.18 Big-Endians and Little-Endians – significant imbalance or not?

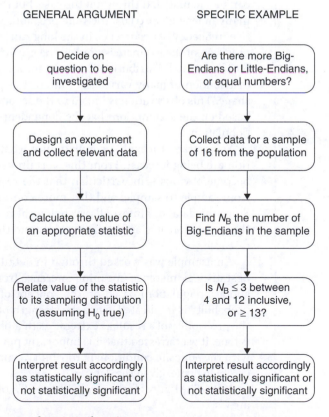

Figure 6.19 Logic of statistical testing

For example, if the experiment is carried out and it is found that $N_B = 14$, we have no information from the test for significance about:

Prob (H_0 true given $N_B = 14$)

Key idea

This confusion between the two conditional probabilities is rife and leads, as has been stressed, to major misinterpretations of what is meant by a statistically significant result. It does not give us a handle on the probability that the null hypothesis is true. Instead, a more modest claim can be made. We begin by giving the null hypothesis, as it were, the chance to explain the data. If the data are such that the null hypothesis can offer a plausible explanation, then we give it the benefit of the doubt, or at least we do not reject the possibility that the null hypothesis accounts for the data. However, if the probability of our result being plausibly explained by null hypothesis is low (.05 or lower), we reject H_0 as an explanation for the data and conclude that there is an alternative systematic effect.

Chapter review

Everyday conceptions of relative likelihood can be converted into precise measures of probability if certain conditions are met. If there are grounds for assuming that outcomes can be assigned equal probabilities, then probabilities of specific events can be calculated. If this is not the case, but the same situation can be replicated over many independent trials, then the probability of an event can be estimated by relative frequency of occurrence in the long run. A crucial point in this regard is that the precision of the estimate is greater, the greater the number of trials.

The normal distribution is important for two main reasons. The first is that the distribution of many variables of interest in psychology at least approximates to its shape. This observation is linked to the second reason, that many statistical tests are based on the assumption that the dependent variable is normally distributed in the population.

You worked through a simulation of what happens when the results of an election are being forecast. From this, certain key characteristics of sampling will have become obvious – in particular, that the results obtained vary, often considerably, from sample to sample, and that more confidence can be placed on larger samples. Since the data for almost all psychological research is collected only for a sample of the population, it is essential to understand these ideas for the interpretation of such research.

An example was worked through in detail to show the basic logic of the method of statistical inference (meaning inference from results from a sample to conclusions about a population) based on the concept of the null hypothesis. This shows how probability is implicated, since the strength of the evidence is gauged by considering the probability of a result as extreme as that obtained occurring if the null hypothesis is true. It was stressed that it is important not to confuse this conditional probability with the opposite conditional probability, namely, the probability of the null hypothesis being true, given the data.

Note: The figures for Figure 6.13 are: 29% of the letters are As; 40% are Bs; and 31% are Cs.

7

Statistical tests: Comparing

In this chapter

... we show how the process of testing for statistical significance, introduced through a simple example in the previous chapter (refer back to the figure on p. 97 for an overview) is applied to the kinds of question of *comparison* treated graphically in Chapter 4. Specifically, appropriate statistical tests are described for the following:

- comparing proportions of participants falling into independent categories;
- comparing scores between two independent groups; and
- comparisons based on paired data.

Comparing proportions

The first type of comparison to be considered is for experimental designs in which participants fall into one of several discrete categories (that is, where the variables are *nominal*). The resulting data are in the form of frequencies or proportions. Figure 7.1 presents some data from a sample of students, male and female, concerning whether or not they had used computers before coming to university. Note the totals at the ends of the rows and bottoms of the columns – the overall total of 159 students included 103 females and 56 males, and split into 77 who had used a computer before and 82 who had not.

	Yes	No	Total
Females	43	60	103
Males	34	22	56
Total	77	82	159

Figure 7.1 Experience of computers (Yes/No) by gender – frequencies

In order to explore the patterns within the data more fully, it makes sense to recast these data as percentages, as shown in Figure 7.2. Note that there are two tables of percentages, depending on which way we look at the data (make sure you understand what is going on here). The first table of percentages is more interesting. It shows that while just under half (48%) of the sample had used computers before, proportionately more males (61%) than females (42%) had done so. This imbalance can be shown diagrammatically as in Figure 7.3.

Is this degree of imbalance indicative of a gender difference in the population from which the sample was drawn, or is it attributable simply to sampling variation? The next step should be clear by now – we need a statistic that the extent of the imbalance and which can in turn be judged in terms of how likely it is that we could have obtained this result if we assume at the outset that there is no such gender imbalance in the population (i.e. that H_0 is true). Thus, the H_0 states that there is no gender imbalance in the use of computers before coming to university, and we begin by assuming this to be true for the population.

	Yes	No			Yes	No	Total
Females	41.8%	58.2%		Females	55.8%	73.2%	64.8%
Males	60.7%	39.3%		Males	44.2%	26.8%	35.2%
Total	48.4%	51.6%					

Figure 7.2 Row and column percentages

In order to assess any imbalance, therefore, we first need to establish what a balanced situation would look like (that is, what values we might expect in each cell of the table if the null hypothesis were true). Then, we measure how far our observed data are away from that balance. Let's look again at the frequency table. The important point to keep in mind is that, overall, there are different numbers of males and females in the sample, and that, overall, different numbers of individuals had and

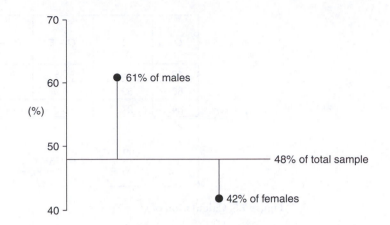

Figure 7.3 Experience of computers – graph of 'Yes' responses showing gender imbalance in relation to overall sample

had not used computers before coming to university. Therefore, the balanced situation must reflect these inequalities.

Given that, in the sample as a whole, 48.4% of participants did have experience of computers, we would expect 48.4% of males and 48.4% of females to have answered 'yes' if there were no effect of gender on such experience. Since there was a total of 103 females, we would expect 49.9 females to have answered 'yes'. Similarly, of the 56 males, we would expect 27.1 to have answered 'yes'. (Note here that .9 or.1 of a person has no practical relevance, but as theoretical value, it is entirely acceptable.) This gives a table of **expected** values that we can set alongside the table of **observed** values, as shown in Figure 7.4. (The term *expected* here can be interpreted as meaning *what would have expected if the overall percentage had applied uniformly across the board.* Another way to think about expected values is as *those values we would expect assuming the null hypothesis to be true.*)

To measure the discrepancy between these two tabulated sets of figures, the steps in Figure 7.5 are followed to calculate the statistic, which is call **chi-squared** (pronounced 'khy', as in 'kite', 'squared') denoted by χ^2. Before going on to consider the calculation of the statistic, a cautionary note should be sounded regarding data in the form of percentages. While the *column* and *row* percentages shown in Figure 7.2 are useful for assessing the degree of imbalance between males and females, and for calculating expected values, they must *not* be used in the calculation of the χ^2 statistic. Instead, only *raw frequencies*, like those shown in Figure 7. 1 may be used.

It should be clear to you now that χ^2, because of the way it is defined, cannot be negative. Second, you should be able to see that χ^2 would be zero if, and only if, the

Observed frequencies   'Expected' frequencies

	Yes	No	Total
Females	43	60	103
Males	34	22	56
Total	77	82	159

	Yes	No	Total
Females	49.9	53.1	103
Males	27.1	28.9	56
Total	77	82	159

Figure 7.4 Observed and 'expected' frequencies

O	E	$O-E$	$(O-E)^2$	$\dfrac{(O-E)^2}{E}$
43	49.9	−6.9	47.61	0.954
60	53.1	6.9	47.61	0.897
34	27.1	6.9	47.61	1.757
22	28.9	−6.9	47.61	1.647

$$\chi^2 = \sum \frac{(O-E)^2}{E} = 5.255$$

Figure 7.5 Calculation of χ^2

observed and expected values were exactly equal – an unusual and implausible situation indicating perfect balance in the sample, and hence no evidence whatsoever of any imbalance in the population. It should then be clear that the larger the value of χ^2, everything else being equal, the stronger the evidence from the sample of an imbalance in the population. Figure 7.6 sums it up graphically.

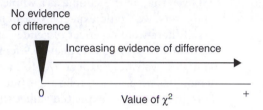

No evidence
of difference

Increasing evidence of difference

0   Value of χ^2 +

Figure 7.6 Value of χ^2 and strength of evidence

Clearly, the smaller the overall discrepancy between the observed and expected frequencies, the more the observed frequencies (our actual data) resemble those predicted by the null hypothesis. The greater the discrepancy, the less our data resemble H$_0$. Furthermore, the smaller the overall discrepancy, the smaller the value of our statistic (χ^2). The greater the discrepancy, the larger the value of χ^2.

The question that remains to be answered is: how large does our χ^2 value have to be before we take it seriously? As in Chapter 6 (see p. 93), this is where the device of the null hypothesis proves useful. We begin by assuming there is no imbalance in the population. We then consider the likelihood that our sample data (and resulting χ^2 value) could have occurred, given this assumption. Using the cut-off, or significance, level of 0.05 discussed in Chapter 6 (see p. 96), we identify the threshold, or criterion, value of χ^2 at this level of significance. This is the threshold which our obtained value must equal or exceed to be deemed **statistically significant**. Such threshold values are known as **critical values**, since they are critical in determining whether or not the obtained value of χ^2 is statistically significant. Here, we do not attempt to explain any of the technical aspects of how the critical value of χ^2 is derived. In fact, the value will change with the number of rows and columns in the data table. Suffice it to say that, in the case of a 2 x 2 table, as in our example, the critical value of χ^2 is 3.84 at the conventional cut-off probability of .05 (as discussed on p. 96). Since, in the example, the value of χ^2 was found to exceed this critical value, the result is deemed to be *statistically significant*.

A point to which we need to alert you is that, rather than simply confirming whether or not your χ^2 exceeds the critical threshold at .05 level of significance, as you will see below, statistical software packages like SPSS tend to do it the 'other way around', so to speak. That is, they give the level of significance as an *exact* probability value associated with the obtained value of χ^2. Naturally, this is a more precise way of conveying information about statistical significance, but is not feasible when calculating the statistic by hand. If the exact probability value given is .05 (or less), you can conclude that the result is significant.

A further technical point we need to mention is that for the 2×2 case, something called a **correction for continuity** is often applied. This represents a slight change to the formula (which we are not going to detail) for certain mathematical reasons (which we are not going to go into either). We are making the usual assumption about access to software that will incorporate the correction for continuity for you.

Making links

The following issue was first raised in Chapter 4 (p. 63), where we indicated that we would revisit it from time to time. It may be apparent to you that we have studiously avoided using the term 'relationship' above. Instead, we described the *comparison* between males and females and discussed whether any *imbalance* between the groups was indicative of a gender *difference*. Of course, we could legitimately have expressed these ideas by asking if there was a *relationship* between gender and computer experience. At this stage, however, we have chosen to keep some clear water between tests of comparison and tests of relationship which we come on to in the next chapter. As the book progresses, you will notice that we begin to blur the two in order to make sense of the data more fully.

Making sense of SPSS

Coding data and computing χ^2

Note: We recommend you also consult Brace et al. (2009), pp. 180–189 who present further information on this topic.

1. Creating a data file

Remember the golden rule that *each individual participant (case) occupies a single row of their own in the data file*. We know that there are 159 different participants, so there will be 159 rows in the data table. This seems a bit daunting, but it's quite easy to code.

Launch SPSS and bring up the data window as you were shown in Chapter 3. Click **Variable View**. Here we have to code two variables, one for gender and the other for computer experience, so there will be two columns in the data table. Complete these details in the **Variable View** window, as follows:

	Name	Type	Width	Decimals	Label	Values	Missing	Columns	Align	Measure	
1	gender	Numeric	8	0		{1, male}...	None	8	Right	Scale	In
2	compexper	Numeric	8	0	Computer experience	{1, yes}...	None	8	Right	Scale	In

Note that, although the variables are numeric (which they should be in the vast majority of cases), the values are merely codes for different nominal categories. By clicking in the appropriate box under **Values**, we can code what each value stands for. Here, we have coded 1 = female, 2 = male for the gender variable (see below), and 1 = yes, 2 = no for computer experience. Click **OK** when you have finished coding each variable.

Now click on **Data View** to reveal the blank data table again. You will see two columns entitled *gender* and *compexper*. The data are entered into these columns, first for *gender* and then for *compexper*. This can be speeded up by using copy-and-paste. Again, the figure only shows 16 rows (we have chosen to show rows 38 to 53), but you can scroll down onscreen to reveal all 159 rows). Remember to save the data giving the file an appropriate name.

2. Calculating χ^2

Now for one of the quirks of SPSS. You must *not* use the **Chi-square...** function which appears under **Analyze > Nonparametric Tests > Legacy Dialogs**. This refers to a different type of χ^2 which we do not cover in this text.

Instead, we have to dig out the χ^2 we need from **Analyze > Descriptive Statistics > Crosstabs...**

The following dialogue box will appear. Although it is entirely arbitrary, for consistency with the example, move *gender* into the **Row(s):** box and *compexper* into the **Column(s):** box.

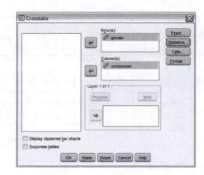

Click on the **Statistics...** button, then select **Chi-square**, ignoring all other options, and click **Continue**.

Next, click on the **Cells...** button and select **Expected** (**Observed** is already selected by default). This will produce a frequencies table with both observed and expected frequencies displayed (actually, you could also have selected row and column percentage, but this creates quite a crowded table for our present purposes – see Brace *et al.* (2009) p. 183 for an example).

Click **Continue** followed by **OK**.

The **SPSS Statistics Viewer** displays the following output, along with some other bits and pieces:

Gender * compexper Crosstabulation

			Compexper		
			Yes	No	Total
Gender	Female	Count	43	60	103
		Expected count	49.9	53.1	103.0
	Male	Count	34	22	56
		Expected count	27.1	28.9	56.0
Total		Count	77	82	159
		Expected count	77.0	82.0	159.0

Chi-Square Tests

	Value	df	Asymp. Sig. (2-sided)	Exact Sig. (2-sided)	Exact Sig. (1-sided)
Pearson chi-square	5.255[a]	1	.022		
Continuity correction[b]	4.493	1	.034		
Likelihood ratio	5.253	1	.022		
Fisher's exact test				.031	.017
Linear-by-linear association	5.192	1	.023		
N of valid cases	159				

[a]0 cells (.0%) have expected count less than 5. The minimum expected count is 27.12.
[b]Computed only for a 2x2 table

Compare the top table with Figure 7.4 (p. 101) to confirm that the observed and expected frequencies are the same.

The bottom table contains details of the χ^2 calculation. Characteristically, the table contains much more than you need, and the labelling is somewhat cryptic. We have shaded the relevant information for you. In fact, it is only the top row of the table labelled *Pearson Chi-Square* that you need (Pearson is the surname of the statistician who developed the statistic). The *Value* column shows the obtained χ^2 statistic (5.23 to two decimal places); *df* refers to the degrees of freedom (1) discussed in this chapter; and the hideously named *Asymp. Sig. (2-sided)* is merely the exact probability value referred to earlier in this chapter, namely the probability that we could have obtained this result assuming the null hypothesis is true – since this value is less than .05, we can reject the null hypothesis as an explanation for the result and therefore conclude that there is a significant association between gender and computer experience.

Before we finish, we should describe the pattern of this association by referring to the observed and expected frequencies. Thus, fewer females had computer experience before university than would be expected if the null hypothesis were true, while more males than expected had computer experience.

Reporting χ^2

You might not be surprised to learn that there is no single exact convention for reporting any statistical result, although any methods must report the important details of the analysis. For consistency, here and elsewhere, we use the convention adopted by Brace et al. (2009).

Thus, when reporting a result such as this in a practical write-up, a thesis or, indeed, in a published paper, the following convention should be observed:

The association between gender and previous experience of computing was significant: $\chi^2(1, N = 159) = 5.255$, $p < .05$ (or $p = .002$). You should then indicate the nature of the association by referring to the discrepancies between your observed frequencies and those expected by chance.

A question of taste

The χ^2 statistic generalizes easily to larger data tables. Figure 7.7 again presents the data introduced in Chapter 4 (see p. 52) for preferences for psychology courses, comparing students in two faculties. Overall, 62.9% of the students were in Arts and 37.1% in Science. If this balance applied uniformly to all the courses considered, the 'expected' figures would have been those shown in Figure 7.8.

As in the simpler case above, the χ^2 statistic measures the discrepancy between the eight observed and expected values as follows:

$$\chi^2 = \frac{(27-25.5)^2}{25.2} + \frac{(35-27.7)^2}{27.7} + \ldots + \frac{(18-9.6)^2}{9.6} = \mathbf{17.52}$$

As noted previously, the *critical value* for the statistic depends on the size of the table, since, all other things being equal, the more cells there are in a table, the larger the value of the statistic. This is simply because more numbers are involved in the calculation. So, when assessing the significance of our statistic, we need to modulate its value to take account of different sizes of table.

At this point, we need to say more about the term **degrees of freedom** (often abbreviated to *df*). This is a rather technical idea which is seldom well explained in textbooks. We don't propose to add to the confusion in this book. At this stage, suffice it to say that *df* is the value used to adjust your statistic for the number of values used in the calculation. If you think about it, that is a sensible thing to do, since, if you had a lot of cells in your frequency table, all other things being equal, your statistic would be greater than if you had relatively few cells, simply because there would be more $(O - E)$ values to square and add up. In the case of χ^2, *df* uses the number of

	Psycholinguistics	Social	Stats	HCI
Arts	27	35	3	8
Science	13	9	3	18

Figure 7.7 Observed frequencies (*Faculty × Favourite Module*)

	Psycholinguistics	Social	Stats	HCI
Arts	25.2	27.7	3.8	16.4
Science	14.8	16.3	2.2	9.6

Figure 7.8 Expected frequencies (*Faculty × Favourite Module*)

rows and columns in the data table to give an indication of its size. In precise terms, *df* is calculated as follows:

$$df = (r - 1)(c - 1)$$

where *r* is the number of rows (horizontal lines of data) in the table and c the number of columns (vertical lines of data). Thus, for a 2 × 2 table, *df* = 1 and for a 2 × 4 table, *df* = 3. There are technical reasons why we use the number of rows (and columns) minus 1, but it is not necessary for you to know these. As we shall see, most statistics that we encounter have a specific method for calculating associated degrees of freedom.

The following 'mini-table' indicates how the critical value for χ^2 depends on the degrees of freedom:

df	Critical value for χ^2 (at 5% level of significance)
1	3.84
2	5.99
3	7.82
4	9.49
8	15.51
16	26.30

Since, for *df* = 3, the critical value for χ^2 is 7.82, the value 17.52 of χ^2 for the example is statistically significant.

Reporting χ^2

Using Brace et al.'s (2009) convention, we would say that there was a significant association between faculty and preferred module: $\chi^2(3, N = 116) = 17.52, p < .05$. Again, you should describe the nature of the association.

Before reading on...

Code the data for this example, and carry out a χ^2 analysis. Notwithstanding the rather student-unfriendly nature of the output, note the value of the statistic and the associated probability (*p*) value. Describe the nature of the association between faculty and favourite module.

... now read on

Alert

It's very easy to abuse the χ^2 test, and computer software will do it for you gladly. The test is only valid when the appropriate conditions apply. These are that the data within the table should be frequencies, and each observation should be divided among the cells of the table such that each case contributes precisely 1 to precisely one cell (**mutually exclusive**), and these observations are made *independently*. Thus, for the example of course preference just dealt with, each of the 116 students was in one faculty and chose one course as their favourite, so each student contributed 1 to just one cell of the table. Also, it is reasonable to assume that the preferences held by the students were **independent**.

If, instead, each student had been asked, for each of the courses, whether they liked each course (scored as 1) or not (scored as 0), and the totals had been tabulated, a very similar looking table would have resulted, and the data could have been fed into a computer for analysis. However, the χ^2 test would not be appropriate for data collected in the way described, because the observations are neither mutually exclusive, nor independent. For example, a student might indicate that she liked Psycholinguistics, Statistics and Human–Computer Interaction. This student would then be contributing 1 to three of the cells of the table, and these contributions are not independent, as they come from the same person. One check to make is that the total of all the cells in the table equals the total number of cases (usually participants) in the study.

Importantly, you should also be cautious if any of your cells contain expected frequencies lower than 5, or, at the very most, no more than one-fifth of your cells should do so. This can affect the stability of the χ^2 calculation. When you encounter such a problem, you must be extremely cautious in interpreting your result, especially if it is marginally significant or non-significant. Common solutions include combining some categories to increase expected frequencies (but only if it makes *logical* sense to do so), or use of an alternative statistic that is more resistant to this violation (known as the Fisher Exact Probability Test, not described here). Unfortunately, this second solution is only possible for 2×2 or 2×3 frequency tables. Packages like SPSS will automatically provide this statistic if the expected frequency requirement is violated.

As mentioned previously, another careless error (occasionally seen in published work) is to apply the statistic to row or column percentages rather than to the original frequencies. This is plain wrong! What's more, if you think about it logically, you should be able to see why.

Assumptions underlying χ^2

Data are in the form of **frequencies**
Observed frequencies are **independent**
Observed frequencies are **mutually exclusive**
There are no (or *very* few) **expected frequencies lower than 5**.

Comparison between independent groups

The next type of comparison to be considered is for cases where numerical (that is, at least ordinal) data are collected on some **dependent variable** of interest for two *separate* groups. This type of experimental design is referred to as an **independent groups** (or **between groups) design**. When such data are collected, the comparison between the two groups can be brought out by comparing averages (means and medians) and measures of spread (standard deviations and semi-interquartile ranges) and by a variety of graphical methods, including multiple line plots, back-to-back stem-and-leaf plots, frequency diagrams, box-and-whisker plots, and a ranking of the combined data (see Chapter 4, pp. 56–59). Now we want to go beyond comparisons, based on summary statistics and graphs, to consider whether any differences evident from the summary statistics are meaningful, that is, *statistically significant*.

At first sight, the obvious candidate for a statistic, reflecting the difference between the two groups, is simply the *difference between the means*. The following example is designed to show why that won't work.

Consider the two data sets shown in Figure 7.9. For the sake of concreteness, assume that the data are from an experiment on attitudes towards computers among females. One group of ten females watched a video intended to promote a positive attitude towards computers among females, while a separate group of ten females were not shown the video. (Note: for simplicity, we have used equal group sizes – often, in real experiments of this type, you are likely to end up with unequal numbers.) *Attitude to Computers* was then measured using the questionnaire described in Chapter 2 (see p. 21). Recall that participants can score between 20 (extreme negative score) and 100 (extreme positive score) on this measure.

For the purpose of illustration, let's consider two *possible* outcomes in which the mean score for the *video* treatment is 72, and the mean for the *no video* control treatment is 64, so the difference between means in each case is 8. However, while the average scores might be identical, there is a noticeable contrast between the two data sets which is of crucial significance in this context.

Before reading on...

Take a good look at the two data sets. Sketch some graphical representation of them. Something should stare you in the face.

... now read on

Data set A		Data set B	
Video	No video	Video	No video
73	63	66	52
72	61	62	66
68	57	74	61
66	69	71	77
77	66	85	70
65	71	79	55
70	58	78	59
78	68	82	79
76	60	65	72
75	67	58	49
Mean = 72	Mean = 64	Mean = 72	Mean = 64

Figure 7.9 *Attitude to Computers*: **Contrasting data sets**

What we hope you noticed is that the scores in data set A show a much smaller spread than those in data set B. In terms of measures of spread, the difference is clear from the summary statistics in Figure 7.10. The contrast is also obvious from the multiple line plots in Figure 7.11.

> **Before reading on...**
>
> Ask yourself this question: Which data set – A or B – if it were presented to you as the result of the experiment, would make you more likely to conclude that watching the video causes a more positive attitude towards computers among females in general? In considering this question, focus on the data – you can assume that the experiment was well designed and carried out.
>
> **... now read on**

It should be clear intuitively that the answer is 'A'. In data set A, for example, there is relatively little overlap between the *video* and *no video* scores, whereas in data set B there is considerable overlap. (If you think about it, you should be able to see that *overlap* is directly related to the much wider *spread* of scores in data set B.) This can be made even clearer by showing the combined scores for each data set ranked as in Figure 7.12. Recall that this descriptive method was introduced in Chapter 4 (p. 57) – the two groups are treated as a single data set and ranked from lowest to highest; then we look to see whether the ranked data 'fall out' into the two groups again, or whether they remain jumbled up.

Data set A			Data set B	
Video	**No video**		**Video**	**No video**
13	14	Range	27	30
4	4	Semi-interquartilte range	7	8.5
4.62	4.88	Standard deviation	9.07	10.45

Figure 7.10 Summary statistics

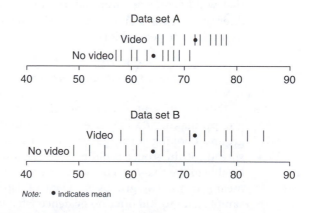

Figure 7.11 *Attitude to Computers* – **line plots**

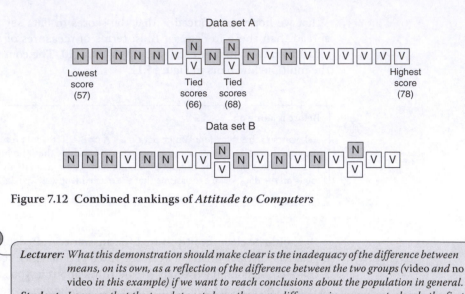

Figure 7.12 Combined rankings of *Attitude to Computers*

> *Lecturer:* *What this demonstration should make clear is the inadequacy of the difference between means, on its own, as a reflection of the difference between the two groups (video and no video in this example) if we want to reach conclusions about the population in general.*
> *Student:* *I can see that the two data sets have the same difference in means; yet, clearly the first data set offers stronger evidence than the second.*
> *Lecturer:* *This example is intended also to suggest to you that the extra aspect that needs to be taken into account is the amount of spread in the data within the groups. The standard way of doing that is to use a statistical test called the **t-test**.*

The independent *t*-test

The foregoing argument is by way of introducing the statistic that is normally used in these circumstances, which is called *t*. You will often see this referred to in textbooks as the **Student's *t*-test**. 'Is there another test called the Lecturer's *t*-test?' we hear you ask! Actually, the *t*-test was devised by William Sealy Gossett who worked for the famous Guinness Brewery. He originally developed the *t*-test to compare batches of 'the black stuff' for quality control purposes. As the company did not permit its employees to publish their work, Gossett published his new *t*-test under the pseudonym 'Student'. More precisely, since there are several *t*-tests tailored to the precise design of the experiment in question, the statistical test for comparing two separate groups is called the **independent *t*-test**, or alternatively, the **between groups *t*-test**, or the **unpaired *t*-test** (the last for reasons that will become apparent later). For any two groups in general, which we shall refer to as Group 1 and Group 2 (with means m_1 and m_2 respectively), the formula for *t* takes the general form:

$$t = \frac{m_1 - m_2}{measure\ of\ spread\ within\ groups}$$

Indeed, $m_1 - m_2$ can be thought of as a measure of 'spread' *between* the two groups, making *t* a measure of spread **between** groups relative to spread **within** groups. Looking at this general formula, and bearing in mind that the measure of spread within groups is defined in such a way that it is always positive, you should be able to see that *t* can be positive, zero, or negative. Clearly $t = 0$ if and only if the means for the two groups are identical (so that $m_1 - m_2 = 0$), and in this case the sample data would offer no evidence whatsoever of a difference in the population. When the means are not equal (which in practice will always be the case) the value of t is positive or negative depending on which group has the larger mean. Note also that if the contrast is between, say, *video* and *no video* groups, it is entirely arbitrary whether *video* or *no video* is designated as the first group. Of course, you have to remember which mean was subtracted from which when it comes to interpreting the results.

For those who wish to dig a little deeper

A simplified independent t formula

In keeping with the philosophy behind this book, we deliberately do not give the precise formula for the bottom line. If you need to calculate t for a given set of data, we assume you have access to computer software that will do it for you (later, we illustrate a calculation using SPSS). It is not necessary for you to know the technical aspects underlying the derivation of the t statistic.

In a nutshell, the independent t statistic is a measure of the difference between the sample means, divided by the variability of this difference for lots of similar samples drawn from the same population, that is, the *standard error of the difference* between sample means:

$$t = \frac{\text{difference between sample means}}{\text{standard error of difference between means}}$$

For calculation purposes, a *simplified approximation* to the precise formula for t is the following:

$$t = \frac{m_1 - m_2}{s_1 + s_2} \times \sqrt{n_1 + n_2}$$

where s_1 and s_2 are the standard deviations for Group 1 and Group 2, respectively, and n_1 and n_2 are the numbers in Groups 1 and 2 respectively. This simplified formula will provide a very good approximation if n_1 and n_2 are equal or roughly equal, and not too small; and if s_1 and s_2 are roughly equal – it's less good otherwise. The advantage of this simplified approximation to the exact formula is that it shows clearly how t is dependent on the relationship between three aspects of the data, namely:

1. Difference *between* groups, as measured by $m_1 - m_2$;
2. Variation *within* groups, here approximated by $s_1 + s_2$, although what is less clear from this computationally simpler formula is that the key measure of variability is the standard error of the difference between means;
3. Total number of cases, that is, $n_1 + n_2$ (all else being equal, the value of t will double if the number of cases is increased by a factor of 4, for example).

The larger the value of t (whether positive or negative) the stronger the evidence would be for a difference in the populations in one direction or another. Figure 7.13 sums this up graphically. The by-now-familiar question that remains to be answered is: *How far away from 0 does t have to be before we take it seriously?* This is where

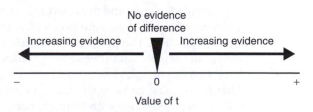

Figure 7.13 Value of t and strength of evidence

the device of the null hypothesis (introduced in Chapter 6) comes in. It will be remembered that, in general, the null hypothesis states that no specific effect is in operation. In the case of the *t*-test for independent groups, this translates into the statement that *the populations represented by each sample have identical normal distributions*, and that any difference observed in the means is simply a result of the sampling that produced the data.

Student: *I find this idea of samples drawn from populations with identical normal distributions a bit technical and confusing. I can grasp what a phrase like this might mean when you have a subject variable, like gender. There are clearly two populations – males and females – in such cases.*

Lecturer: *In your own words, what would be the null hypothesis if gender were an independent variable?*

Student: *In simple language, the null hypothesis would predict that the average scores on the dependent variable are the same for males and females.*

Lecturer: *Now, try to use the technical definition to say the same thing.*

Student: *I would say something like 'the populations represented by the male and female samples have identical normal distributions'. As I said, I'm pretty comfortable with the idea of the entire populations of males and females having the same average scores on a particular measure. But I have real trouble getting my head around what this means in the case of an independent variable that is manipulated.*

Lecturer: *OK. Let's look again at the previous example [see p. 110]. Forget about the technical expression for a moment. In your own words, what is the null hypothesis?*

Student: *I would tend to express it along the lines of 'there is no overall difference in attitude to computers between the* video *and no* video *conditions'.*

Lecturer: *OK, that's quite specific. Now, try to express the null hypothesis in more general terms.*

Student: *That's my problem. I find it quite odd to say something like 'the samples represent populations with identical normal distributions' when there is only one defined population – all females – and both samples are drawn from that population.*

Lecturer: *This is a good example of the rather arcane language that has grown up around statistics. Here, you have hit on a distinction between the everyday and the technical uses of the term* population. *In a technical sense, and for the sake of argument, it is perfectly reasonable to think in terms of two populations in this example – the population of females shown the video and the population of females not shown the video.*

Student: *So, here the population is used in an abstract sense. In my head, this tells me that the* video *sample is drawn from a theoretical population of all females shown the video. The* no video *sample represents another theoretical population of all females not shown the video.*

Lecturer: *It's fine to think of it like that.*

How do t *values vary under the null hypothesis?*

As we have already seen, any two samples drawn from populations with identical *normal* distributions (that is, when the null hypothesis is true) are highly unlikely to have identical means and distributions. They will differ to a greater or lesser extent and, consequently, if we were to calculate the *t* value, we would find it to be greater or less than zero. The problem for researchers is that the only data they can evaluate are the sample data themselves. In order to use the *t* value to assess the likelihood that the samples represent identical populations, we must have some context. That is, we must know what we might expect if two samples were chosen at random from populations with identical normal distributions, or indeed from a single population.

Making links

Just to note at this point that the independent *t*-test is actually a special two-group case of a more general statistical method for comparing differences between more than two unrelated groups. When we encounter this statistic in a later chapter, we shall point out the links between the two statistics.

Getting a handle on t

Let's assume that the null hypothesis is true (remember, this is our starting point for *all* statistical tests). In effect, this means that there are not two populations representing *video* and *no video*, but a single population.

Now, let's draw two samples of 10 from this normal distribution of the population. How large might the value of *t* be purely as a result of this random sampling from the same population? We can use a simulation to get a feel for the answer to this question. For simplicity, let's suppose that the population consists only of 100 discrete values, arranged so as to give a good approximation to the normal distribution. Two random samples of 10 are taken from this set of 100 values (the same value may be taken more than once) and the value of *t* for these data worked out. Figure 7.14 shows one possible outcome of this process, resulting in a value of −0.70 for *t* in this particular case.

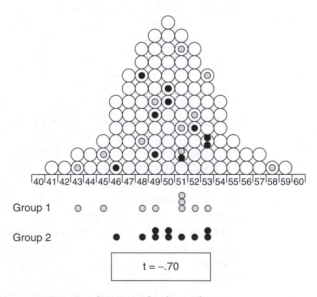

Figure 7.14 Comparing two random samples (*n* = 10)

If the process is repeated with a different random sampling, the data, and of course the resultant value of *t*, will be different. By repeating the process, a very large number of times, a distribution of values of *t* can be built up. Ideally, we would like you to have access to computer software so that you could run the simulation for yourself. If that's not possible, you'll have to make do with results from our running of the simulation. A histogram for 100 samplings looks like the one shown in Figure 7.15. From this diagram, the following important points should be noticed –

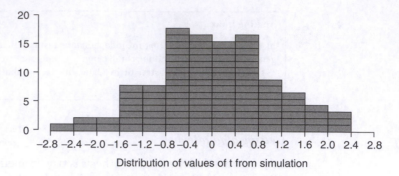

Distribution of values of t from simulation

Figure 7.15 A hundred comparisons of two random samples (*n* = 10)

if *t* is derived from samples from a single population (or, to put it more technically, two populations with identical normal distributions), then

- *t* can be either positive or negative;
- the values of *t* for repeated samplings are distributed approximately symmetrically around 0; and
- values of *t* beyond ±2 are rare.

As stated, the purpose of introducing this simulation is to give you a feel for the distribution of values of *t* if the null hypothesis is true – the technical term for this is the *sampling distribution* for *t*. (Recall, we introduced this term in Chapter 6 when we considered the sampling distribution for means of repeated samples. Here, the logic is identical, but, this time, we have calculated *t* scores from repeated sets of two samples rather than means of single samples).

In fact, as we saw in the example for the sampling distribution for the mean in Chapter 6, it is not necessary to rely on a simulation because the exact sampling distribution for *t* can be derived mathematically, the details of which lie far beyond the scope of this book. The sampling distribution for *t* is similar in shape to, but not exactly the same as, that of the normal distribution. It is symmetrical around the value 0. The distribution produced by a simulation is a good approximation to this precise, theoretically derived sampling distribution. In fact, to be more precise, there is a *family* of *t* distributions, depending on the number in the samples involved. For a total number of 20 cases (10 *video* and 10 *no video*) as in this example, the sampling distribution for *t* is shown in Figure 7.16.

Thinking back to the procedure introduced in Chapter 6, we need to specify extreme intervals (called **tails of the distribution**) which correspond to a probability of .05, or 5%. This means, in graphical terms, cutting 2.5% (or .025, expressing it as a decimal) of the area under the curve from each end of the distribution. This amounts to taking the parts of the distribution that lie beyond ±2.10 as indicated in the diagram. What this means is that, for a total 20 participants, assuming that the null hypothesis is true, the probability of a *t* value more extreme than ±2.10 is 5%, that is, by the cut-off conventionally used, it can be considered unlikely. Accordingly, if such an experiment is done, and the value of *t* resulting from the data is either greater than 2.10 or less than -2.10, the result is said to be statistically *significant* at the.05 level; if not, the result is said to be statistically *non-significant*. Again, the values ±2.10 are called **critical values**, since they are critical in determining whether or not the value of *t* is statistically significant. Figure 7.17 sums this up graphically.

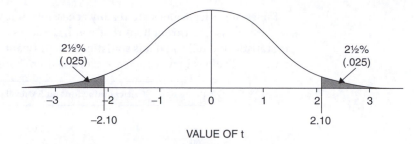

Figure 7.16 Sampling distribution of *t* (*N* = 20)

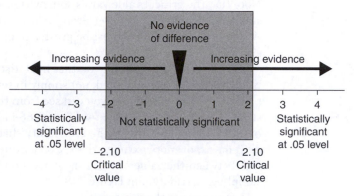

Figure 7.17 Value of *t* and strength of evidence – critical values and statistical significance

Thus, in practical terms, all that needs to be done is to find the value of the *t* statistic and check it against the critical value, which depends on the total number of cases, $n_1 + n_2$. Note that, although we have used examples with n_1 and n_2 equal, there is no requirement for them to be equal.

As was the case for χ^2, the *t*-test has associated *degrees of freedom* (*df*). In the case of the *t*-test for independent groups, df gives a rough indication of the number of scores that go to make up the calculation of *t*. Here:

$$df = n_1 + n_2 - 2$$

For those who wish to dig a little deeper

Logic of degrees of freedom

The basic logic of degrees of freedom is the same as for χ^2 although here we are concerned with the total number of scores, rather than rows and columns. Think back to the calculation of standard deviation (see pp. 32–33). Recall that the sum of the *squared deviations from the mean* is divided by $N - 1$, not N, as might be expected. The reason for this is related to the fact that the sum of the deviations from the mean is, by virtue of the way in which they are calculated, always 0. That means that only $N - 1$ of the deviations are free to vary, since the last one must be equal to 0 minus the sum of the others (in order to make the total for all N equal to 0). In technical language, $N - 1$ is the *degrees of freedom for standard deviation*.

 Now consider the case of data for two independent groups. In calculating the variation within each group, deviations from the mean are used – in fact the formulae above involve the standard deviations for each of the two groups. These deviations must, again, of necessity, sum to 0 for each group. Hence the number of deviations free to vary within the first group is $n_1 - 1$, and similarly $n_2 - 1$ within the second group. Adding these together, the total degrees of freedom when calculating the total variation within groups is $n_1 + n_2 - 2$.

Tables of critical values are readily accessible, but we don't consider them necessary, as we assume throughout that you have access to software that will calculate the statistic and tell you if it is statistically significant. However, to give you a feel for how critical values vary with degrees of freedom, here is a 'mini-table':

df	Critical value for t (at 5% level of significance)
20	2.09
40	2.02
60	2.00
120	1.98

Note that the critical value varies somewhat for relatively low values of *df* but soon stabilizes (and in fact, it never drops below 1.96, no matter how large *df* becomes). A rule of thumb is that *t* must be greater than 2 (or less than −2) to be statistically significant.

Again we need to remind you that in statistical packages, such as SPSS, the significance level is often quoted, not simply in terms of < .05 or > .05, but as an exact probability. For example, as you can see from the SPSS example, should you wish to study it, with $n_1 + n_2 = 20$, a *t* value of 2.66 has an associated probability (*p*) value of 0.016 (remember, this is the probability that we could have obtained a result as extreme as, or more extreme than, 2.66 assuming the null hypothesis is true). The link between the value of *t* and the corresponding *p* can be seen in relation to the sampling distribution in Figure 7.18.

Let's return to the two data sets with which we began (see p. 110). For the first and second data sets, respectively, the approximate formula for *t* gives:

$$t = \frac{8}{4.62 + 4.88} \times \sqrt{20} = \textbf{3.77} \qquad t = \frac{8}{9.07 + 10.45} \times \sqrt{20} = \textbf{1.83}$$

You can see how the greater spread within groups in the second data set, reflected in the larger standard deviations, makes the *t* value much smaller for the second data set. The exact values (to 2 decimal places), as worked out by computer software, are 3.77 and 1.83 (so the approximation works well here) with associated *p* values of .0014 and .0840 respectively. Thus the difference between the groups in data set A, as measured by the *t* statistic, is statistically significant by a wide margin, whereas the difference between the groups in data set B is not statistically significant by a fairly narrow margin, but non-significant nonetheless.

Let's express this in more long-winded terms to drive home the point. We begin by assuming that the null hypothesis is true. For data set A, the probability that we

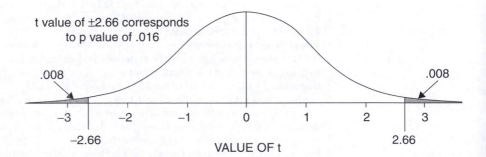

Figure 7.18 Sampling distribution of *t* (*N* = 20), when *t* = 2.66, *p* = .016

would have obtained our result ($t = 3.77$), assuming the null hypothesis were true, is .0014 (14 chances in 10,000, or .14% probability), which is very small and sufficiently small (< .05) to allow us to *reject* the null hypothesis as an explanation for our result. For data set B, the probability that we would have obtained our result ($t = 1.83$), assuming the null hypothesis were true, is .084 (84 chances in 1000, or 8.4% probability), which is too large (> .05) to allow us to reject the null hypothesis as an explanation for our result. That is, we *fail to reject* the null hypothesis and therefore conclude that H_0 is a plausible explanation for out result.

Assumptions underlying the independent t-test

Data are **interval or ratio-scaled.**

Scores in each sample are approximately **normally distributed.**

Scores in each sample are roughly equally spread – known as **Homogeneity of Variance** (actually, if groups have roughly equal numbers of participants, violations of this assumption do not cause too much difficulty for t).

Reporting independent t

(For data set A): An independent t-test showed that the difference between *video* and *no video* conditions was significant: $t = 3.77$, $df = 18$, $p = .0014$ (or $p < .05$). You should also describe the nature (magnitude and direction) of this difference.

(For data set B): An independent t-test showed that the difference between *video* and *no video* conditions was not significant: $t = 1.83$, $df = 18$, $p = .084$ (or $p > .05$, or NS).

Alert

Although we referred to ordinal scale data or better at the beginning of this section, in general, the t-test is intended only for interval and ratio-scaled data. You will have seen from the above description of the t-test that it is a pretty sophisticated statistic that deals with sample data assumed to be drawn from normally distributed populations with specified parameters. In short, t is a **parametric** statistical test and, as such, we should assume that the numbers being analysed have reasonably good scale properties. We should also be concerned that the two samples we are comparing have broadly comparable spread, since the t calculation would be affected by samples with highly heterogeneous spread. (As you can see from the optional example below, SPSS provides a numerical indication as to the relative spread of the two groups and can adjust the t calculation if there appears to be a problem.)

Making sense of SPSS

Coding data and calculating independent t

Note: We recommend you also consult Brace et al. (2009), pp. 128–135, who provide further information.

1. Creating a data file

Again, remember the golden rule that *each individual participant (case) occupies a single row of their own in the data file*. This time there are 20 different participants (10 in each independent group), so there will be 20 rows in the data table. So each participant will have a single *Attitude to Computers* score (column) on a row of her/his own. However, that is not enough information in the data table to allow a comparison of the two groups – we also have to have a column to code the condition (*video / no video*) to which each participant was assigned. *So, the final data table will have 20 rows and two columns.*

Launch SPSS and bring up the data window as you were shown in Chapter 3 (p. 44). Click **Variable View**. Here we have two variables, one for *condition* and the other for *compattA* (that is *Attitude to Computers* scores for data set A), so this gives the two columns in the data table. Complete the details in the **Variable View** window, as below.

You will notice that we have also included a third variable, *compattB* (*Attitude to Computers* scores for data set B). You should do the same. This is a bit naughty, since these are different participants, and so we have broken our golden rule. Do not let this confuse you – simply ignore the fact that it's there for the moment. We have taken a shortcut to save us creating a second data file.

Note that, here, we have coded 1 = *video*, 2 = *no video* for the condition variable (see below). Click on **OK** when you have finished coding each variable.

Now click on **Data View** to reveal the blank data table again. You will see three columns entitled *condition*, *compattA* and *compattB*. So, in effect, we have two separate data files in one, each with two columns. The first data set has *condition* and *compattA*, and the second has *condition* and *compattB*. When we analyse data set A, we will simply pretend that *compattB* does not exist and vice versa.

The data are entered as indicated below. Remember to save the data giving the file an appropriate name.

2. Calculating independent *t*

The specific routine for independent *t* is located in **Analyze > Compare Means > Independent Samples *t* Test ...** (don't ask us why *t* is written as capital T – we don't know either!).

The following dialogue box will appear. As far as you are concerned there are only two variables in the left-hand window (*condition* and *Att to Computers A*). Move condition into the **Grouping Variable:** window and *Att to Computers A* into the **Test Variable(s):** window. (It would have been more student-friendly if these had been labelled 'Independent Variable' and 'Dependent Variable' respectively, or even 'Score' in the latter case.)

You will notice that the **OK** button is not yet active. That is because you have to tell SPSS which conditions you wish to compare. You may consider this unnecessary (and you would be correct!), since there are only two conditions. However, you will see later examples of independent variables with more than two conditions (known as **levels**) for which you need to specify the two levels that you wish to compare.

Click on the **Define Groups…** button to reveal the following little dialogue window. Simply enter the values **1** and **2** into the **Group 1:** and **Group 2:** boxes (the assignment is entirely arbitrary).

Click **Continue** and then click **OK**.

The **SPSS Statistics Viewer** will display the result of the independent t analysis as below. (Actually, it has been necessary to compress the second table in order to fit it on the page – you will see a more elongated table which you will have to scroll across).

Do not be intimidated by the detail presented here – you only require some of it (over-detailed tables with lots of irrelevant information for your purposes is a familiar, unwelcome feature of SPSS).

Let's step through the output. The first table simply presents some descriptive statistics for your two groups (we have shaded the information that is relevant to you). This is useful because, if the analysis suggests that there is a statistically significant difference between the groups, the summary statistics will allow you to see the nature of this difference.

Group Statistics

	Video Condition	N	Mean	Std. Deviation	Std. Error Mean
Att to Computers A	video	10	72.00	4.619	1.461
	no video	10	64.00	4.876	1.542

Independent Samples Test

		Levene's Test for Equality of Variances		t-test for Equality of Means						95% Confidence Interval of the Difference	
		F	Sig.	t	df	Sig. (2-tailed)	Mean Difference	Std. Error Difference	Lower	Upper
Att to Computers A	Equal variances assumed	.169	.686	3.767	18	.001	8.000	2.124	3.538	12.462
	Equal variances not assumed			3.767	17.947	.001	8.000	2.124	3.537	12.463

The second table presents the results of the independent *t*-test analysis (again, we have shaded the information which is relevant). Now, what does it all mean?

Recall that one of the important assumptions underlying the *t*-test is that the spread of the data should be roughly equal for the two groups (so-called, homogeneity of variance). As part of the *t*-test analysis, SPSS provides a statistic to confirm whether the groups are homogeneous or not. (Note that this is one of those rare occasions when you do not want a statistic to be significant – that is, you do not want the variability of the two groups to differ.)

The two columns headed 'Levene's Test for Equality of Variances' provides this information. Forget what *F* actually means at this stage, you need only be concerned with the column headed 'Sig.' (.686). Like all statistical analyses, this 'sub-analysis' begins by assuming that there is no difference between the variabilities of the two groups. The statistic compares these variabilities and the value of .686 refers to the probability that the result could have been produced assuming the null hypothesis were true. Here, that probability is 68.6% or 686 changes in 1000, indicating that it is much too likely that the null hypothesis could have produced this result. Therefore, we fail to reject the null hypothesis and conclude that there is no significant difference between the variabilities of the two groups. Therefore, *the assumption of homogeneity holds*. This tells us that we can look at the row headed 'Equal variances assumed' and ignore the other row.

Here, we see that *t* = 3.77 (confirming our earlier calculation), with 18 degrees of freedom and a probability of .001 to 3 decimal places. Thus we conclude that, assuming H_0 is true (that there is no difference between the means for *video* and *no video*), the likelihood that we could have obtained this result is .001 (or .1%, or 1 in 1000). It is, therefore, highly unlikely that this result could have been obtained under the null hypothesis, and sufficiently unlikely (< 0.05) that we can reject H_0 as the explanation of the data. Thus, we reject H_0 and conclude that there is a statistically significant difference between the *video* and *no video* conditions.

The summary statistics tell us that, on average, those who had seen the video had more positive attitude towards computers than those who had not.

Before reading on...

Repeat the steps above for the second data set (B).

... now read on

You should have obtained the following output – note that, this time, the probability of obtaining the result, assuming H_0 is true is .084, greater than .05 and, therefore, too likely to allow is to reject H_0 as an explanation for the result. Hence, we conclude that there is no statistically significant difference between the *video* and *no video* conditions.

Group Statistics

	Video Condition	N	Mean	Std. Deviation	Std. Error Mean
Att to Computers B	video	10	72.00	9.068	2.867
	no video	10	64.00	10.446	3.303

Independent Samples Test

		Levene's Test for Equality of Variances		t-test for Equality of Means						
									95% Confidence Interval of the Difference	
		F	Sig.	t	df	Sig. (2-tailed)	Mean Difference	Std. Error Difference	Lower	Upper
Att to Computers B	Equal variances assumed	.350	.561	1.829	18	.084	8.000	4.374	−1.190	17.190
	Equal variances not assumed			1.829	17.651	0.084	8.000	4.374	−1.203	17.203

Mann-Whitney *U* test as an alternative

An alternative statistical test for independent groups is based on ranking the data. This is an ideal option when there are concerns about violation of the assumptions of the *t*-test, particularly multiple violations.

Consider the two data sets originally introduced on p. 110. For each data set, the combined scores for *video* and *no video* can be ranked, yielding the diagrams shown in Figure 7.19 (this figure originally appeared as Figure 7.12 on p. 112).

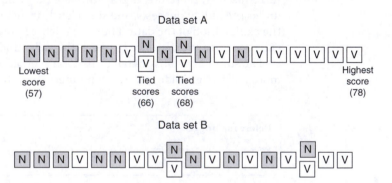

Figure 7.19 Combined rankings of *Attitude to Computers*: Contrasting data sets

As is also clear graphically in Figure 7.11 on p. 111, there is a marked contrast between the two data sets. In data set A, there is relatively little overlap – the lower scores are predominantly for *no video* and the higher scores for *video*. In data set B, however, there is substantially more overlap.

The *U* statistic, developed by statisticians Henry Mann and Ransom Whitney, is a measure of the degree of intermingling in the combined rank ordering. One way to define this statistic is as shown in Figure 7.20. Consider the first sequence of Vs and Ns above.

How often in this sequence does a V come before an N? The first V in the sequence comes before 5 Ns, so we count 5 for that. The next V ties with one N (we call that .5) and comes before 4 other Ns, giving a contribution of 4.5. The next V contributes

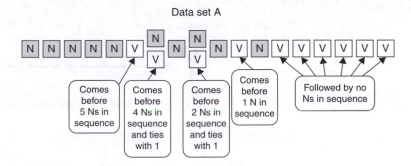

Figure 7.20 Diagrammatic illustration of Mann-Whitney U

2.5, and the next 1. The remaining 6 Vs are followed by no Ns in the sequence, so contribute nothing. Adding them all together we get:

$$5 + 4.5 + 2.5 + 1 = \textbf{13}$$

Repeating the process for the second sequence, we get:

$$7 + 5 + 5 + 4.5 + 3 + 2 + 1 + 0.5 = \textbf{28}$$

If we do it the other way round, and ask how many times an N comes before a V, we get 87 and 72 as the respective totals. (Note that $13 + 87 = 28 + 72 = 100 = n_1 \times n_2$, and this relationship will always hold.) When this process is carried out, the U statistic is the *smaller* of the two numbers obtained – in this case $U = 13$ for data set A, and $U = 28$ for data set B.

For 10 Vs and 10 Ns, consider the *possible* sequences. The extreme cases are where there is no overlap at all:

V V V V V V V V V V N N N N N N N N N N

or

N N N N N N N N N N V V V V V V V V V V

and in both cases, $U = 0$ (think this through, given the definition of U). Thus, a value of $U = 0$ represents the strongest evidence that one could get from two groups of 10 using the U statistic that there is a difference in the population between the groups. On the other hand, a maximal intermingling of Vs and Ns might look something like this:

V N V N V N V N V N N V N V N V N V N V

giving the greatest possible value $U = 50$, and representing no evidence whatsoever of a difference between the groups. The closer U is to 0, the stronger the evidence, as is summed up graphically in Figure 7.21. *Note that this is an unusual example of a statistic where the smaller its value, the stronger the effect.*

The usual question then arises. How close to zero does U need to be to be statistically significant? Here we simply state that the sampling distribution for U for any values of n_1 and n_2 can be worked out (note that n_1 and n_2 don't need to be equal), and the computer will tell you about the statistical significance, or lack of it. For $n_1 = n_2 = 10$, the critical value is 23 (that is, any value of U less than or equal to 23 is statistically significant), so we can augment the diagram as shown in Figure 7.22.

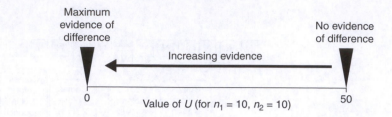

Value of U (for n_1 = 10, n_2 = 10)

Figure 7.21 Value of U and strength of evidence

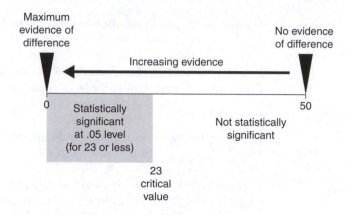

Figure 7.22 Value of U and strength of evidence – critical value and statistical significance

One further technical point needs to be covered. When n_1 and n_2 are large, the U statistic can be converted into a different statistic, z. For the z statistic, the *critical* cut-off value for statistical significance at the p =.05 level is *always* ±1.96, but the software that you use may well give you the precise p that corresponds to your z value.

> **Reporting U**
>
> (For data set A): The difference between the *video* and *no video* condition was significant: U = 13, N_1 = 10, N_2 = 10, p = .005 (or $p < .05$).
>
> (For data set B): The difference between the *video* and *no video* conditions was not significant: U = 28, N_1 = 10, N_2 = 10, p = .096 (or $p > .05$, or NS).

Making sense of SPSS

 ### Coding data and calculating Mann-Whitney U

Note: The version of this statistic in SPSS 18 is radically different from previous versions. We suggest that you do not use this more recent version. Instead, as illustrated below, choose the 'Legacy' version of the test. We recommend you also consult Brace et al. (2009), pp. 143–145, who provide further information.

1. Creating a data file

Since Mann-Whitney U is an alternative to independent t, we use the same data set as in the independent t example. Simply locate the data file if you saved it, or repeat the steps in the last SPSS example. We remind you of the golden rule that *each individual participant (case) occupies a single row of their own in the data file.* Bear in mind also that we took a short cut by coding the scores for both data sets A and B.

Open the data file which will appear as follows:

2. Calculating Mann-Whitney U

The version of Mann-Whitney U we require is located in **Analyze > Nonparametric Tests > Legacy Dialogs > 2 Independent Samples ...**

A dialogue screen entitled *Two-Independent-Samples Tests* will appear. Move *Att to Computers A* to the box labeled **Test Variable List:** (remember that *Att to Computers B* effectively does not exist for your purposes), and *condition* to the **Grouping Variable:** box. Click on **Define Groups ...** and assign the numerical values **1** and **2** for *condition* as in the independent t example above'.

Click **Continue** followed by **OK**.

The following results will be displayed in the **SPSS Statistics Viewer**.

This gives us the value of U, the associated p value (.005) and more besides. Somewhat misleadingly (certainly for readers of this book), Wilcoxon W is presented, which should be ignored altogether. The z statistic discussed previously, to which U approximates for larger samples, is also given. You may be relieved to know that the value labelled **Exact Sig. [2*(1-tailed Sig.)]** should also be ignored.

Test Statistics[a]

	Att to Computers A
Mann-Whitney U	13.000
Wilcoxon W	68.000
Z	−2.799
Asymp. Sig. (2-tailed)	.005
Exact Sig. [2*(1-tailed Sig.)]	.004[b]

[a]Grouping variable: Video condition
[b]Not corrected for ties.

Before reading on…

Repeat the steps above for the second data set (B).

… now read on

You should have obtained the following output for data set B – note that, as was the case for independent t, the result for data set B indicates that there is no significant difference between *video* and *no video*, therefore, we fail to reject H_0 (referred to here as 'retain H_0').

Test Statistics[a]

	Att to Computers B
Mann-Whitney U	28.000
Wilcoxon W	83.000
Z	−1.664
Asymp. Sig. (2-tailed)	.096
Exact Sig. [2*(1-tailed Sig.)]	.105[b]

[a]Grouping variable: Video condition
[b]Not corrected for ties.

For those who wish to dig a little deeper: choosing between t and U

We have said that the Mann-Whitney U test is an alternative to the t-test, the key point being that the t-test is based on the assumptions that the samples are drawn from populations in which the dependent variable is distributed in accordance with normal distributions of similar variabilities. The Mann-Whitney U test does not depend on these assumptions.

Since we never will have the data for whole populations, we cannot tell whether or not they are normally distributed (or a good approximation). However, if the data for the samples shows marked signs of *non-normality*, then it is safer to use the Mann-Whitney U test instead. The implications can be illustrated by referring back to the example of reaction times for squash players and chess players analysed in Chapter 4 (see p. 56). For convenience, the data are presented again in Figure 7.23.

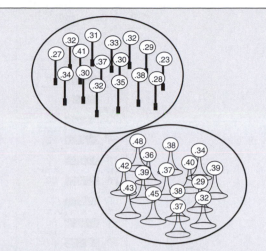

Figure 7.23 *Quick on the draw*: Reaction times (seconds) for squash and chess players

The distributions of RTs for each group look reasonably like the normal distribution (see graphical representations on p. 57, especially Figure 4.12). If we carry out t and U tests for these data the results are as follows:

$t = 3.87$ $p = .0006$
$U = 38.5$ (z equivalent $= -3.229$) $p = .0012$

Consider the effect of adding the two outliers considered previously (see p. 58). Recall that the previous difference in RT between squash and chess players disappeared when these outliers were included. Note, however, how the distribution of RTs for the squash players is decidedly non-normal. If we repeat the tests with the amended data, the results are:

$t = 1.45$ $p = .158$
$U = 68.5$ (z equivalent $= -2.409$) $p = .016$

Now the t-test does not produce a statistically significant result, but the U test still does. The U test is much less strongly affected by the addition of the two outliers than is the t-test. The reason for this is that the t-test, because of the way it is defined, is non-resistant (that is, heavily affected by outliers), whereas the Mann-Whitney U test, being based on ranks, is resistant – much less affected by the outliers.

The general rule is if you have theoretical or empirical reasons for suspecting radical departures from normality in the distribution of the dependent variable, then it is better to use the Mann-Whitney U test. Unfortunately, there are no clear guidelines for making this decision.

Comparison within paired data

Recall from Chapter 4 that, in some circumstances, it is possible to make comparisons by testing just one group of participants, but doing so under two conditions – this type of experimental design is known as a **repeated measures** (or **within subjects) design** (since we have repeated measures for each participant and comparisons involve poking at the change within each participant).

Let your fingers do the talking

Paralleling our discussion of tests of difference between independent groups, we introduce two data sets to suggest why the difference between means for the two related conditions will not on its own work as a statistic for testing for statistical

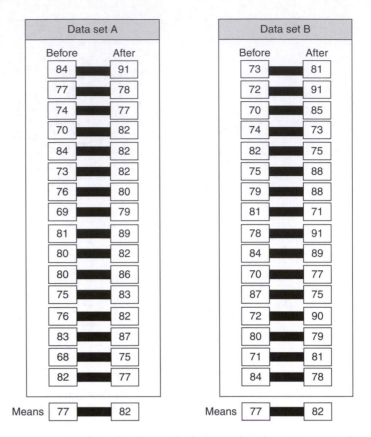

Figure 7.24 Typing speed (wpm) *before* and *after a tea break* – contrasting data sets

significance. Figure 7.24 shows two data sets which, for the sake of concreteness, represent two possible outcomes for mean typing speed (in words per minute) measured for the same people both before and after a tea break. In both cases, the mean typing speed before tea break is 77 and 82 after tea break.

Before reading on…

Have a good look at the two data sets. Sketch some graphical representations of them. You should be able to see a clear contrast.

… now read on

Representing the data graphically shows up a marked difference (see Figure 7.25). In data set A, the related line chart shows a consistent increase in typing speed after the tea break, with only two exceptions to the pattern. In data set B, the results are more mixed in this respect.

Further insight can be gained by adding columns to the data to show participants' before–after changes, as in Figure 7.26. In each case the *after* measure is subtracted from the *before* measure (leading to positive or negative results, depending on which is the larger). The mean difference (m_d), as you can see, is 5 in both cases. What becomes clear from looking at the differences is that they are much more widely spread for the second data set than for the first. This can be measured, for example, by working out the standard deviation for the difference (s) in each case.

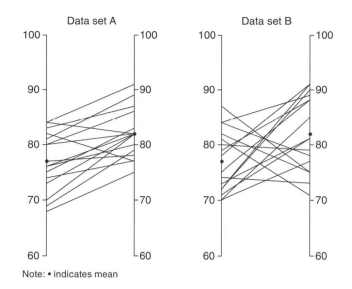

Note: • indicates mean

Figure 7.25 Contrasting related line charts

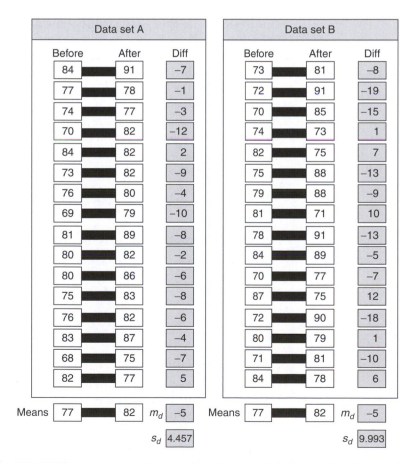

Figure 7.26 Differences in participants' typing speed *before* and *after tea break* – contrasting data sets

If you think about it, you'll see that this is not unconnected to the contrast already mentioned – 14 out of 16 in data set A showing improved performance after the tea break, as opposed to 10 out of 16 in data set B.

A similar argument to that used with the independent groups example leads us to reject the simple difference between the means (or mean difference, which is the same – see Figure 7.26) as a statistic. It's not just the size of the mean difference that needs to be taken into account, but also the spread of the differences and, linked to that, how they are distributed between positive and negative values.

The paired *t*-test

The argument presented above is by way of introducing the standard statistic for comparisons between paired data sets. It is called the **paired *t*-test** (or **correlated *t*-test,** or **within-subjects *t*-test**). As noted above, although we have two conditions (two levels of the independent variable), the data are based on a single group of participants. The logic of the *t*-test in this case is to consider the magnitude of the change (or difference) in participants' scores between the two conditions. Accordingly, the *t* formula for paired data takes the general form:

$$t = \frac{m_d}{\textit{Measure of spread of differences}}$$

So, in essence, we have got rid of the original data and replaced them with a single set of differences between the two conditions, and the formula encapsulates m_d as the average 'spread' of the participants **between** the two conditions relative to the overall spread **within** these differences. (Initially, this may take a little reflection to grasp fully, but the trick is to think about *change* between conditions and forget about the actual data).

Assumptions underlying the paired *t*-test

Data are **interval or ratio-scaled.**
Variables are roughly **normally distributed.**
Homogeneity of variance (actually, since the groups are equal in size – they are the same participants – violations of this assumption are ignored, and no test of homogeneity is required).

For those who wish to dig a little deeper: a simplified paired *t* formula

Incidentally, the reason why the paired formula is also called *t* is that it has the same sampling distribution as the independent *t*-test. (Subscripts are sometimes used to differentiate the two uses of the statistic, t_{ind} for independent groups *t*-test, and t_{paired} for paired *t*-test.)

A *simplified approximation* to the precise formula for *t* is the following:

$$t = \frac{m_d}{s_d} \times \sqrt{N}$$

The formula takes into consideration:

1. Average overall change *between* the two conditions, as measured by m_d
2. Variation *within* the set of changes, as measured by their standard deviation (sd)
3. Total number of pairs, given as N.

The degrees of freedom for the paired *t*-test is 1 less than the number of pairs, namely $N - 1$. Analogously to the formula for degrees of freedom for the independent *t*-test, the formula $N - 1$ reflects the fact that, in calculating the standard deviation of the differences, only $N - 1$ of the deviations from the mean are free to vary.

The criterion for significance or non-significance (or *critical t* value) is similar to that used in the case of the independent *t*-test. Again, a rough rule of thumb is that the value of *t* must be more extreme than ±2 to be significant. The precise critical value varies with N (and hence, *df*) as indicated in the same 'mini-table' as before (p. 118).

For the data sets used in the example, the values of *t* are:

$$t = \frac{-5}{4.475} \times \sqrt{16} = -4.49 \qquad t = \frac{-5}{9.993} \times \sqrt{16} = -2.00$$

The critical value is 2.13 for N = 16 (*df* = 15). Thus, you can see that for data set A, the difference is clearly statistically significant, whereas for data set B, it is not.

Reporting paired *t*

(For data set A): A paired *t*-test showed that the difference between the *before* and *after* conditions was significant: $t = 4.49$, $df = 15$, $p < .001$ (or $p < .05$). You should also describe the nature (direction and magnitude of the difference).

(For data set B): A paired *t*-test showed that the difference between the *before* and *after* conditions was not significant: $t = 2.00$, $df = 15$, $p = .064$ (or $p > .05$, or NS).

Making sense of SPSS

Coding data and calculating paired *t*

Note: We recommend you also consult Brace et al. (2009), pp. 136–139, who present further information.

1. Creating a data file

We continue to remind you of the golden rule that *each individual participant (case) occupies a single row of their own in the data file*. For data set A there are 16 different participants, so there will be 16 rows in the data table. Each participant produces two scores, one in each condition, so we will have two columns, one for each condition. Unlike independent *t*, there is no need to code participants' group membership. Since the design is repeated measures, SPSS 'knows' that the first column refers to the first condition and the second column the second condition. *So, the final data table will have 16 rows and two columns.*

Launch SPSS and bring up the data window as you were shown in Chapter 3 (p. 44). Once again, we will take a shortcut and code data set B as well. When analysing data set A, simply ignore the fact that the data set B columns are there at all.

Click **Variable View**. Here we have two variables, one for *before* and the other for *after*. Complete the details in the **Variable View** window, as below.

Now click on **Data View** to reveal the blank data table again. You will see four columns entitled *beforeA*, *afterA*, *beforeB* and *afterB* (with a blank column in between the two data sets for ease of inspection). So, in effect, we have two separate data files in one, each with two columns. The first data set has *beforeA* and *afterA*, and the second has *beforeB* and *afterB*.

The data are entered as indicated below. Remember to save the data giving the file an appropriate name.

2. Calculating paired *t*

The specific routine for paired *t* is located in **Analyze > Compare Means > Paired Samples T Test...** (Again, don't ask us why *t* is written as capital T – we don't know either!).

The following dialogue box will appear. As far as you are concerned there are only two variables in the left-hand window (*beforeA* and *afterA*). Highlight *beforeA* and, using the arrow, move it across to the right-hand box labelled **Paired Variables:**. Now, do the same for *afterA*.

Click **OK**.

The **SPSS Statistics Viewer** will display the result of the paired t analysis as below. (It has been necessary to compress the larger table in order to fit it on the page – you will see a more elongated table which you will have to scroll across.)

Again, do not be intimidated by the detail presented here – you only require some of it. Let's step through the output. The first table simply presents some descriptive statistics for your two related conditions (we have shaded the information that is relevant to you). This is useful because, if the analysis suggests that there is a statistically significant difference between the groups, the summary statistics will allow you to see the nature of this difference.

Paired Samples Statistics

		Mean	N	Std. Deviation	Std. Error Mean
Pair 1	Before tea break	77.00	16	5.279	1.320
	After tea break	82.00	16	4.472	1.118

The more important table below presents the results of the paired t-test analysis (again, we have shaded the information which is relevant). Now, what does it all mean?

Paired Samples Test

		Paired Differences							
					95% Confidence Interval of the Difference				
		Mean	Std. Deviation	Std. Error Mean	Lower	Upper	t	df	Sig. (2-tailed)
Pair 1	Before tea break – After tea break	−5.000	4.457	1.114	−7.375	−2.625	−4.487	15	0.000

Here, we see that the mean difference score (md) is −5.0 and the SD of the differences is 4.46, confirming our earlier calculations. We also see that $t = -4.49$, with $df = 15$ and an associated probability of .000 (actually, this is a further common inconvenience of SPSS – the p value is not .000, it is .000 something, and has to be at least .0004 because it has not been rounded up – you can either use .0004 or .001). Thus we conclude that, assuming H_0 is true (that having a tea break has no effect on typing speed), the likelihood that we could have obtained this result is .001 (or .1%, or 1 in 1000). It is, therefore, highly unlikely that this result could have been obtained under the null hypothesis and sufficiently unlikely ($< .05$) that we can reject H_0 as the explanation of the data. Thus, we reject H_0 and conclude that there is a statistically significant change in typing speed *after* a tea break, compared to *before*.

The summary statistics tell us that, on average, this significant change reflects a speeding up.

Before reading on...

Repeat the steps above for the second data set (B).

... **now read on**

You should have obtained the following output – note that, this time, the probability of obtaining the result assuming H_0 is true is .064, greater than .05 and, therefore, too likely to allow is to reject H_0 as an explanation for the result. Hence, we conclude that there is no statistically significant change in typing speed after a tea break.

Paired Samples Statistics

		Mean	N	Std. Deviation	Std. Error Mean
Pair 1	Before tea break	77.00	16	5.574	1.393
	After tea break	82.00	16	6.870	1.718

Paired Samples Test

		Paired Differences							
					95% Confidence Interval of the Difference				
		Mean	Std. Deviation	Std. Error Mean	Lower	Upper	t	df	Sig. (2-tailed)
Pair 1	Before tea break – After tea break	−5.000	9.993	2.498	−10.325	.325	−2.001	15	.064

Sign test as a simple alternative

There is a very simple alternative test for paired data. It is based on counting the number of pairs for which the first score is higher and the number for which the second score is higher (if there are any ties, they are ignored). For data set A in the example there are 2 cases where the *before* tea break performance is better, and 14 where the *after* tea break performance is better. The corresponding figures for data set B are 6 and 10.

In fact, the sampling distribution for this statistic has been discussed already in Chapter 6 (see Fig. 6.8 on p. 86). The null hypothesis for the sign test is that, for each individual, the difference is as likely to go one way as the other. The situation, therefore, is exactly analogous to tossing sixteen coins and counting the number of heads. It was shown in Chapter 6 that an imbalance in this situation as great as 13:3 in either direction represents a statistically significant result, but any lesser imbalance is not statistically significant. Hence, by the sign test, data set A yields a statistically significant result, whereas data set B does not.

For larger N, the statistic can be converted to a value of z, which can then be compared with the critical value ±1.96 (as with the Mann-Whitney U test). Again we assume that the software you use will do this. For this particular example, the sign test is not a particularly good choice, and either t_{paired} or the rank-based test we are about to deal with is better.

Wilcoxon matched pairs signed-ranks test as an alternative

As you might expect, the same assumptions underlie paired t as independent t. Those are that data are interval- or ratio-scaled, data are approximately normally distributed, and the variability of the sample data are roughly equal (although, statistically, this assumption is assessed differently for paired t due to the fact that it is difference scores that are analysed – the technicalities need not concern you).

Just as the Mann-Whitney U test is a rank-based alternative to t_{ind}, the Wilcoxon Matched Pairs Signed-Ranks test (yes, devised by Frank Wilcoxon) is a rank-based alternative to t_{paired}. To see how it works, look again at the illustrative data sets, with the differences calculated.

Whereas the sign test merely takes into account whether the differences are positive or negative, the Wilcoxon Matched Pairs test also takes into account the size of the differences. This is done by initially treating all of the difference scores as a single set regardless of whether they are positive or negative. These are then ranked from smallest to largest. Figure 7.27 shows the result for data set A. The statistic for this test, denoted by (capital) W, is the sum of the ranks associated with the *less* frequent sign (in this case positive). For data set A, $W = 9.5$, as shown.

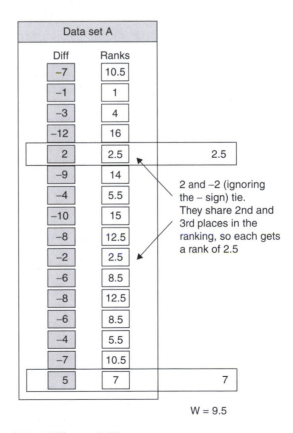

Figure 7.27 Calculating Wilcoxon's W

Before reading on...

To check that you follow the procedure correctly, calculate W for data set B.

... now read on

It should be clear that W will equal zero if, *and only if,* all the differences are in one direction (all positive or all negative). This would constitute the strongest evidence on the basis of this test for a difference between the two conditions. Due to the way it is defined, W is by nature non-negative. The larger it is, the less strong the evidence of a difference in the population between the scores for the two conditions. *Like Mann-Whitney, this is another unusual example where, the larger the statistic, the less strong the effect.*

Again, the critical values for small N can be calculated exactly, while for large N, the value of W can be converted into a value of z to test for statistical significance.

In the case of our example, with N = 16, the critical value is 14. Hence, as you might expect, data set A yields a statistically significant result, while data set B (you should have calculated W to be 33) does not.

Reporting W

(For data set A): The difference between the *before* and *after* conditions was significant: $W = 9.5$, $N = 16$, $p = .002$ (or $p < .05$). You should also describe the direction of this difference. Incidentally, if you were quoting the z statistic instead (here $z = 3.027$ as you will see in the SPSS calculation below), you should note that the value is more extreme than the cut-off for significance of 1.96, as previously mentioned (p. 126), so this is consistent with your significant p value. It's always reassuring when everything hangs together!

(For data set B): There was no significant difference between the *before* and *after* conditions: $W = 33$, $N = 16$, $p = .070$ (or $p > .05$, or NS). Note too here that the z equivalent is 1.811, a less extreme value than the 1.96 required for significance.

Making sense of SPSS

Coding data and calculating the Sign Test and Wilcoxon's W

Note: The version of this statistic in SPSS 18 is radically different from previous versions. We suggest that you do not use this more recent version. Instead, as illustrated below, choose the 'Legacy' version of the test. We recommend you also consult Brace et al. (2009), pp. 146–149, who provide further information.

1. Creating a data file

Since Wilcoxon's W is an alternative to paired t, we analyse the same data set as in the paired t example. Simply locate the data file if you saved it, or repeat the steps in the last SPSS example. We remind you of the golden rule that *each individual participant (case) occupies a single row of their own in the data file.* Bear in mind also that we took a short cut by coding the scores for both data sets A and B.

Open the data file. The **Data View** will appear as follows:

2. Calculating the Sign Test and Wilcoxon's *W*

The specific routine we require for Wilcoxon's *W* is located in **Analyze > Nonparametric Tests > Legacy Dialogs > 2 Related Samples ...**

A dialogue screen entitled **Two-Related-Samples Tests** will appear. Move the two variables for data set A, *Before tea break* and *After tea break*, under **Variable 1** and **Variable 2** respectively in the **Test Pairs:** box. **Wilcoxon** is already checked by default. Also check **Sign** to calculate a Sign Test.

Click **OK**.

The **SPSS Statistics Viewer** displays the results of both the Sign Test and Wilcoxon's *W*. For the Sign Test, the result is as below. As previously noted, there are 2 cases in one direction and 14 in the other. The probability that such a result would be obtained assuming H_0 were true is .004, or 4 chances in 1000 ($< .05$), so we reject H_0 as an explanation for the result.

Frequencies

		N
After tea break – Before tea break	Negative Differences[a]	2
	Positive Differences[b]	14
	Ties[c]	0
	Total	16

[a]After tea break < Before tea break
[b]After tea break > Before tea break
[c]After tea break = Before tea break

Test Statistics[a]

	After tea break – Before tea break
Exact Sig. (2-tailed)	.004[b]

[a] Sign test
[b] Binomial distribution used.

For Wilcoxon's W, the results are presented as follows. Note the similarities with the Sign Test. The smaller sum of ranks is 9.50 which gives us W (in fact, SPSS uses the larger rank for W which is potentially confusing – ignore this and choose the smaller). As for Mann-Whitney U, this is one of the rare statistics where the smaller the value of the statistic, the greater the effect. Here, the probability of obtaining such a result under H_0 is .005, which is much smaller than .05. Again, we reject H_0 as an explanation for the result. Note too, that the z statistic is 3.027, which represents an extreme result of more than three standard deviations.

Ranks

		N	Mean Rank	Sum of Ranks
After tea break – Before tea break	Negative Ranks	2[a]	4.75	9.50
	Positive Ranks	14[b]	9.04	126.50
	Ties	0[c]		
	Total	16		

[a]After tea break < Before tea break
[b]After tea break > Before tea break
[c]After tea break = Before tea break

Test Statistics[a]

	After tea break – Before tea break
Z	−3.027[b]
Asymp. Sig. (2-tailed)	.002

[a] Wilcoxon Signed-Ranks Test
[b] Based on negative ranks.

Before reading on ...

Repeat these steps above for the second data set (B).

... now read on

You should have obtained the following output – note that, as was the case for independent *t*, the results for data set B indicates that there is no significant difference *before* and *after* tea break; therefore, we fail to reject H$_0$.

Sign Test:

Frequencies

		N
After tea break – Before tea break	Negative Differences[a]	6
	Positive Differences[b]	10
	Ties[c]	0
	Total	16

Test Statistics[b]

	After tea break – Before tea break
Exact Sig. (2-tailed)	.454[a]

Wilcoxon's *W*:

Ranks

		N	Mean Rank	Sum of Ranks
After tea break – Before tea break	Negative Ranks	6[a]	5.50	33.00
	Positive Ranks	10[b]	10.30	103.00
	Ties	0[c]		
	Total	16		

Test Statistics[b]

	After tea break – Before tea break
Z	−1.811[a]
Asymp. Sig. (2-tailed)	.070

Choosing between paired *t* and Wilcoxon's *W*

As with the tests for comparing independent groups, the choice of tests for paired data hinges on the conditions necessary for the test to be appropriate. t_{paired} is based on the assumption that the differences between the paired scores are normally distributed in the population. If there is indication from the data that this assumption is not reasonable, the Wilcoxon *W* is a more careful choice to make. As with the previous contrast between t_{ind} and Mann-Whitney *U*, t_{paired} is a less resistant test than *W*. But again there are no clear guidelines for making the choice.

Making links: Another case of paired data: Matched Pairs Design

For the repeated measures design we have been discussing, the data are paired by virtue of the fact that each pair of scores is produced by a single individual. Here, we consider another type of experimental design – the **matched pairs design** – which also results in paired data, but for a different reason, which we illustrate with an example.

Boys' and girls' mathematical abilities

Suppose a researcher wished to test whether 9-year-old boys and girls differ in mathematical ability as measured by some test. Data bearing on this question could be collected by measuring samples of 9-year-olds and comparing their scores using an independent groups *t*-test. However, the researcher may be worried that mathematical ability is highly related to attitudes to mathematics, and that the samples of boys and girls might differ markedly in this respect, thus complicating the interpretation of any difference that might be found between the scores for the two groups. One way to avoid this possibility is to test initial samples of boys and girls for attitude to mathematics (there are standardized psychometric tests that do this) and then, from these samples, choose **matched pairs**; that is, boy–girl pairs of the same, or very similar, measured attitudes to mathematics. The resulting data could then be analysed using a paired *t*-test – paired, because the data are paired by virtue of the matching process. A matched pairs design may be represented schematically, as in Figure 7.28. For analysis purposes, the data are then treated as if the paired scores were produced by the same individuals.

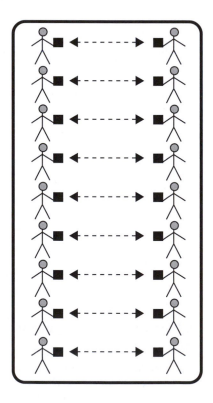

Figure 7.28 Matched pairs design

Chapter review

In this chapter, the general procedure for carrying out statistical tests based on the null hypothesis and testing for statistical significance has been worked through for a number of common experimental designs and corresponding data concerned with comparisons. Specifically, tests have been introduced for the following:

- Comparing proportions of responses from different groups.
  Example: *Do the proportions of students preferring various courses differ between two faculties?*
- Comparing two groups' measurements on some variable.
  Example: *Is attitude towards computers more positive in a group of females shown a promotional video, compared to a group not shown the video?*
- Comparing performances of one group of people under different conditions.
  Example: *Do people type more efficiently after a tea break than before?*

For independent groups and paired data comparisons, more resistant rank-based alternatives to t_{ind} and t_{paired} tests were described.
SPSS procedures for calculating these statistics were also described.

Statistical tests: Correlating

In this chapter

... the workings of more statistics are explained. Whereas the last chapter was about tests for making *comparisons* between two sets of data for different groups of people or paired measurements for a single group of people, this chapter deals with ways of measuring the strength of *relationships* between variables. These methods extend the descriptive analyses of relationships between variables introduced in Chapter 5.

Quantifying strength of relationship

In Chapter 5, the use of scattergrams to show the relationship between pairs of variables was illustrated by several examples. Further, it was shown how an initial rough idea of the nature of the relationship could be obtained by dividing the scattergram into quadrants by vertical and horizontal lines through the mean value for the respective variables.

As a reminder, three of the examples are reproduced in Figure 8.1. The first shows the relationship between height and weight for a sample of sixty male psychology students. The majority of points lie in the A and C quadrants, reflecting a **positive correlation**; that is, (as you would expect) the general pattern is that the taller people are, the heavier they are. The second example shows the relationship between head size and measured IQ. In this case, the points are distributed relatively evenly among the four quadrants, reflecting no strong relationship (where brains are concerned, size is not everything, according to these data). The third example (a work of fiction) shows the relationship between number of parties attended and exam performance. Here the majority of points lie in the B and D quadrants, reflecting a pattern whereby (in general, with some exceptions) the more parties attended, the less good the exam performance, and vice versa. Such a pattern is called a **negative correlation**.

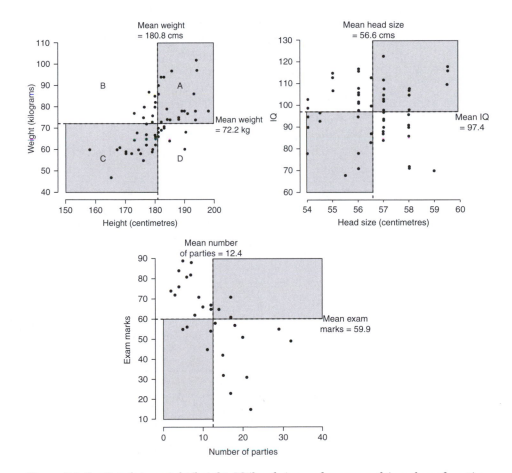

Figure 8.1 Scatterplots: weight/height, IQ/head size, and exam mark/number of parties

Assigning a numerical value to correlation

Now we take the quadrant analysis a step further to introduce a single number which – in a very *specific* sense, to be defined – measures the strength of the relationship between two variables for which data have been collected for a group of participants. A number of this sort is called a **correlation coefficient**. A simpler example with just 10 points is used to introduce the formula and work through the calculation.

The formula for this correlation coefficient, the conventional symbol for which is r, is as follows:

$$r = \frac{\sum(X - \overline{X})(Y - \overline{Y})}{\sqrt{\sum(X - \overline{X})^2 \sum(Y - \overline{Y})^2}}$$

While you may consider that this looks a little daunting, it is easy enough to interpret when you know how. Concentrate for now on the top line:

$$\sum(X - \overline{X})(Y - \overline{Y})$$

The capital Greek letter sigma (Σ) indicates summation (that is, adding up). The symbolic expression as a whole tells you to work out $(X - \overline{X})(Y - \overline{Y})$ for each data pair, and add all the results together. $X - \overline{X}$ is the value of X, for any individual, relative to the mean of all the X values. It can be positive or negative, depending on whether the X value is, respectively, greater or less than the mean. For example, if you got 65 in a statistics test and the mean for the class was 57, then you would have scored 8 above the mean ($65 - 57 = 8$). If you got 53, that would be 4 below the mean, which can be symbolized as -4 (since $53 - 57 = -4$).

Similarly, $Y - \overline{Y}$ means the value of Y, for any individual, relative to the mean value of Y for all cases. The technical term for either $X - \overline{X}$ or $Y - \overline{Y}$ is **deviation from the mean**. The calculation of the top line can be carried out systematically, as indicated in Figure 8.2.

These are the steps in the calculation (descriptions overleaf):

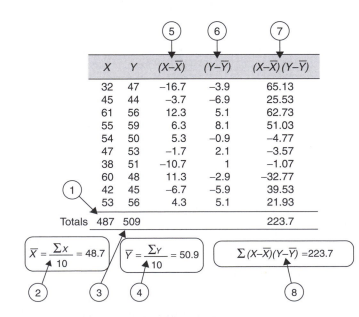

	X	Y	(X–X̄)	(Y–Ȳ)	(X–X̄)(Y–Ȳ)
	32	47	−16.7	−3.9	65.13
	45	44	−3.7	−6.9	25.53
	61	56	12.3	5.1	62.73
	55	59	6.3	8.1	51.03
	54	50	5.3	−0.9	−4.77
	47	53	−1.7	2.1	−3.57
	38	51	−10.7	1	−1.07
	60	48	11.3	−2.9	−32.77
	42	45	−6.7	−5.9	39.53
	53	56	4.3	5.1	21.93
Totals	487	509			223.7

$$\overline{X} = \frac{\Sigma X}{10} = 48.7 \qquad \overline{Y} = \frac{\Sigma Y}{10} = 50.9 \qquad \Sigma(X-\overline{X})(Y-\overline{Y}) = 223.7$$

Figure 8.2 Calculation of top line of formula for r

1 Add the X values together: the sum comes to 487.
2 Dividing by 10 gives $\bar{X} = 48.7$.
3 Add the Y values together: the sum comes to 509.
4 Dividing by 10 gives $\bar{Y} = 50.9$.
5 Calculate $X - \bar{X}$ for each case; some are positive, some are negative.
6 Calculate $Y - \bar{Y}$ for each case; some are positive, some are negative.
7 Multiply each value of $X - \bar{X}$ by the corresponding $Y - \bar{Y}$ to give $(X - \bar{X})(Y - \bar{Y})$.
8 Add up the values obtained in Step 7, which comes to 223.7.

Before reading on...

What relationship can you see between the quadrant a given point is in and the corresponding values of $(X - \bar{X})$ and $(Y - \bar{Y})$?

... now read on

What we hope you have noticed is that points in quadrants A and C contribute positively to the sum, while points in quadrants B and D contribute negatively. In the case of quadrant A, both deviations from the mean are positive – points in this quadrant represent individuals above the respective means for both variables. In quadrant C are individuals with two negative deviations from the mean – multiplying two negative numbers gives a positive result (why this is so is a fascinating topic in itself, but not one we can take on in this book). In quadrants B and D, one deviation is positive and the other negative, so the result of multiplying them is negative.

Apart from the sign (positive or negative), the size of each contribution depends on how far the point lies away from each of the means; if it is close to one or both means, the product of $X - \bar{X}$ and $Y - \bar{Y}$ will be relatively small. If the total contributions from quadrants A and C outweigh those from quadrants B and D (as in this example) then the sum will be positive; conversely, if the total contributions from quadrants B and D outweigh those from quadrants A and C, then the sum will be negative. If they balanced exactly, the sum would be zero.

Now for the bottom line in the formula for r:

$$\sqrt{\sum(X - \bar{X})^2 \sum(Y - \bar{Y})^2}$$

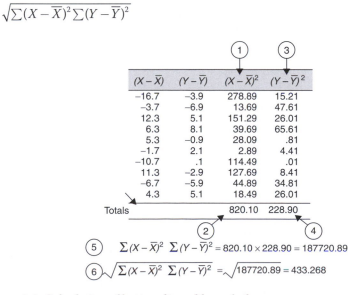

Figure 8.3 Calculation of bottom line of formula for r

Figure 8.3 illustrates the step-by-step method for calculating r, starting from the values of $X - \bar{X}$ and $Y - \bar{Y}$ already determined:

1 Square each value of $X - \bar{X}$. (Note that squaring always yields a positive result, regardless of whether the number squared is positive or negative.)
2 Add the results together to get $\Sigma(X - \bar{X})^2 = 820.10$.
3 Square each value of $Y - \bar{Y}$.
4 Add the results together to get $\Sigma(Y - \bar{Y})^2 = 228.90$.
5 Multiply $\Sigma(X - \bar{X})^2$ and $\Sigma(Y - \bar{Y})^2$.
6 Take the square root (positive) of the answer.

We can now find r:

$$r = \frac{\Sigma(X - \bar{X})(Y - \bar{Y})}{\sqrt{\Sigma(X - \bar{X})^2 \Sigma(Y - \bar{Y})^2}} = \frac{223.7}{433.268} = .516$$

The bottom line of the formula accomplishes a couple of useful things: (i) because of the way the mathematics works out, it acts as a kind of scaling factor, so that r is forced to lie between −1 and +1 (of which more in a minute); and (ii) it means that r is not affected by changes of the units used to measure the variables. For example, in the relationship between height and weight, if height were measured in inches instead of centimetres, and weight in pounds instead of kilograms, the value of r would not be changed. Since r is intended to be a measure of the strength of the relationship between height and weight, it should be clear intuitively that keeping the same value of r in these circumstances is highly desirable.

As just mentioned, because of the way it is defined, r is constrained to lie between −1 and +1. In extreme cases, $r = \pm 1$ if, *and only if*, the points in the scattergram lie exactly on a straight line (+1 for a perfect positive relationship, −1 for a perfect negative relationship). For real data, it's virtually certain that this degree of exact relationship will never occur, but a more or less good approximation to it will be found when variables are correlated. In general, r may be thought of *specifically* as a measure of 'straightline-ness' (linearity, to use a more technical term). The closer the points in a scattergram approximate to a straight line, the closer r will be to +1 (positive correlation) or −1 (negative correlation).

Before reading on...

To check that you have followed the procedure correctly, calculate r by hand for these data. Just five points have been used to lessen the amount of calculation for you.

X	7	12	5	14	8
Y	11	9	6	15	10

... now read on

You will find the answer at the end of this section. A couple of comments are in order as to why, for this statistic, we have worked through the steps of the calculation in detail, whereas in general we use computer software, making calculation unnecessary. One reason is that the calculations, in this case, should help to give you insight into the way the formula fits together to do the job required. Another is to give at least one example where you can check the answer on the computer and see for yourself that the formula leads to the same result – just to show that the computer is not some black box, but offers a way of carrying out a sequence of well-defined arithmetical procedures. An SPSS example is presented later in this chapter.

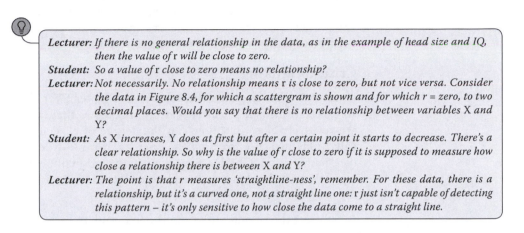

Lecturer: If there is no general relationship in the data, as in the example of head size and IQ, then the value of r will be close to zero.
Student: So a value of r close to zero means no relationship?
Lecturer: Not necessarily. No relationship means r is close to zero, but not vice versa. Consider the data in Figure 8.4, for which a scattergram is shown and for which r = zero, to two decimal places. Would you say that there is no relationship between variables X and Y?
Student: As X increases, Y does at first but after a certain point it starts to decrease. There's a clear relationship. So why is the value of r close to zero if it is supposed to measure how close a relationship there is between X and Y?
Lecturer: The point is that r measures 'straightline-ness', remember. For these data, there is a relationship, but it's a curved one, not a straight line one: r just isn't capable of detecting this pattern – it's only sensitive to how close the data come to a straight line.

The full title of *r* is the *Pearson product-moment correlation coefficient.* It was devised, as you might guess, by a statistician called (Karl) Pearson. 'Product-moment' is merely a technical way of describing the way in which the multiplication of $X - \overline{X}$ and $Y - \overline{Y}$ is used in its calculation.

(Answer to the *Before you read on...* calculation from the previous page: *r* = .74)

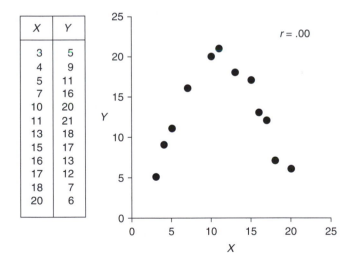

X	Y
3	5
4	9
5	11
7	16
10	20
11	21
13	18
15	17
16	13
17	12
18	7
20	6

Figure 8.4 Example of *r* = 0 – no relationship?

Assumptions underlying the Pearson product-moment correlation coefficient

Data are **at least ordinal scaled**, although a categorical variable with two levels (dichotomous) is suitable.
The distribution of pairs of scores in the population, from which the pairs of scores in the sample are drawn, is **normally distributed**.

A rank-based alternative

The product-moment correlation coefficient is just one of many alternative measures of correlation. Each measure reflects a different way of looking at the strength of a correlation, is used in different circumstances, and has different characteristics. For our purposes, we need to consider just one more correlation coefficient, the calculation of which is based on ranking procedures.

Critical thinking

Figure 8.5 again presents the data from Chapter 5 for three critics' rankings of 10 classic films (see p. 72). A scattergram shows that the judgements of A and B are relatively close, but how can the degree of closeness be expressed numerically? One measure is called the **Spearman rank-order correlation coefficient** (yes, named after (Charles) Spearman) conventionally symbolized by ρ (the Greek equivalent of r, and pronounced 'roe'). Figure 8.6 illustrates the steps in calculating ρ.

1 Subtract the second rank from the first rank in each case to find the difference, d.
2 Square these differences.
3 Add the squared differences, which comes to 24.
4 Calculate ρ using the formula shown (where N is the number of cases – 10 in this example).

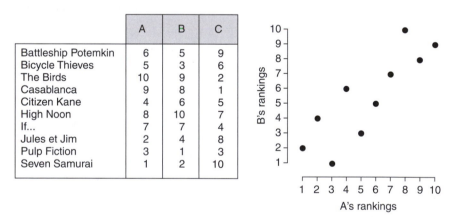

	A	B	C
Battleship Potemkin	6	5	9
Bicycle Thieves	5	3	6
The Birds	10	9	2
Casablanca	9	8	1
Citizen Kane	4	6	5
High Noon	8	10	7
If...	7	7	4
Jules et Jim	2	4	8
Pulp Fiction	3	1	3
Seven Samurai	1	2	10

Figure 8.5 Classic film rankings and scatterplot for A/B

> **Before reading on...**
>
> To check that you have followed the procedure correctly, calculate ρ for the rankings of A and C. (You can check your answer at the end of this section.)
>
> **... now read on**

Clearly, the sum of the squared differences reflects the overall level of agreement between the rankings. In the extreme case where the rankings agree exactly, Σd^2 will equal zero (make sure you understand why this is so). The greater the overall disagreement between the rankings, the larger Σd^2 will be. The formula for r ensures that, in the case where $\Sigma d^2 = 0$, Spearman $\rho = 1$ (again, make sure you see why this

A	B	d	d^2
6	5	1	1
5	3	2	4
10	9	1	1
9	8	1	1
4	6	−2	4
8	10	−2	4
7	7	0	0
2	4	−2	4
3	1	2	4
1	2	−1	1

Total $(\Sigma d^2) = 24$

$$\rho = 1 - \frac{6\Sigma d^2}{N^3 - N} = 1 - \frac{144}{990} = .85$$

Figure 8.6 Calculating ρ

X	Y	Rank X	Rank Y
3	5	1	1
4	9	2	4
5	11	3	5
7	16	4	8
10	20	5	11
11	21	6	12
13	18	7	10
15	17	8	9
16	13	9	7
17	12	10	6
18	7	11	3
20	6	12	2

Figure 8.7 Data for $r = 0$ – ranked

is the case). Moreover, if the opposite extreme occurs (that is, one set of rankings *exactly reverses* the other), then (as some algebra will show) $\Sigma d^2 = (N^3 - N)/3$ so that $\rho = -1$ (follow that through, too). As with Pearson's product-moment correlation, if there is very little relationship between the rankings, ρ will be close to zero – but, as we saw in Figure 8.4, *the converse does not necessarily hold*.

The rank-order correlation coefficient can be used with any variables where the data are ranked. If the original data are measurements on some scale, they can be converted to ranks first, and the same steps as shown above can then be applied to calculate ρ. For example, for the data on p. 149, the original 'raw' data for X and Y and the corresponding ranks are as shown in Figure 8.7 (ranking has been done here from lowest to highest, but highest to lowest would do equally well, as long as the choice is the same for both variables).

The value of ρ for these data is −.01, to 2 decimal places (you might like to check that by doing the calculations for yourself), illustrating the point that a value of ρ close to zero does not signal automatically the lack of a relationship between the variables. What ρ measures specifically is agreement between rankings, so it is not alert to the U-shaped relationship that is obvious to the naked eye when the data are scattergrammed.

(Answer to the *Before you read on...* calculation from p. 151: $\rho = -.61$)

Comparing r and ρ

As was emphasized above, r and ρ measure somewhat different aspects of correlation that will not always lead to similar values for the correlation coefficients. To illustrate this, consider the three data sets in Figure 8.8. The summary statistics for all three are the same. However, when the scatterplots are drawn (Figure 8.9), striking differences become obvious. Data set 1 shows a strong linear relationship with the points scattered reasonably close to a straight line, while data set 2 shows an even stronger linear relationship for all the points – with one exception that doesn't conform to the trend of the rest. As we saw before, such an anomalous point is called an **outlier**. Data set 3 is even more strikingly different. Here all the points except the outlier show a negative relationship, and the outlier is very far away. Yet the product-moment correlation for all the data sets is .76 – how can this be?

The product-moment correlation of .76 for data set 1 is clear enough, reflecting the strong linear relationship apparent in the scattergram. For data set 2, the correlation would be much higher than .76 were it not for the effect of the outlier. In the case of data set 3, the outlier dominates the calculation of r, raising it to .76. Here there is in fact a negative correlation between the remaining points after the outlier is removed.

This example shows how important it is *not to rely on summary statistics alone when analysing data*. In former times, when computer packages tended to be limited

	Data set 1			Data set 2			Data set 3	
	X	Y		X	Y		X	Y
	5	5		5	7		8	11
	7	4		7	6		9	10
	8	9		8	7		10	12
	9	6		9	8		10	9
	11	14		11	10		11	13
	12	18		12	10		11	10
	14	9		14	12		12	9
	15	10		15	11		13	14
	17	14		17	26		13	11
	18	19		18	14		15	7
	19	20		19	16		16	8
	20	14		20	15		27	28
Mean	12.9	11.8		12.9	11.8		12.9	11.8
s.d.	5.0	5.5		5.0	5.5		5.0	5.5
r		.76			.76			.76

Figure 8.8 Data sets with identical summary statistics

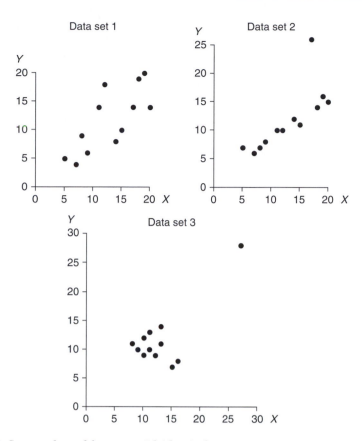

Figure 8.9 Scatterplots of data sets with identical summary statistics

to print-outs giving numerical values of summary and inferential statistics, it was easily possible to misinterpret data by relying only on these statistics. With advances in computer software, however, there is no longer any excuse for not taking the time to examine data graphically, since a package of any quality will make this possible in a matter of seconds. In particular, we would suggest as a general rule: *Never calculate a correlation coefficient without also plotting a scattergram.*

Now consider the rank-order correlation coefficients for the same three data sets. For data set 1, ρ =.79, close to the value for r. For 'well-behaved' data such as these, r and ρ will, in general, yield fairly similar values.

Before reading on...

Make a 'guesstimate' of the rank-order correlation coefficients for data sets 2 and 3.

... now read on

The rank-order correlation coefficient, ρ, for data set 2 is .93, much higher than the corresponding r. The damping effect of the outlier on the overall outcome is limited. Thus, the rank-order correlation coefficient, like other statistics based on ranking procedures, is resistant (that is, not overly affected by outliers); the product-moment correlation coefficient, as has been demonstrated, is non-resistant.

The rank-order correlation coefficient for data set 3 is −.01 (compare this with.76!). Again, the ranking process yields a statistic resistant to the distortion of the outlier. For both data sets 2 and 3, the rank-order correlation coefficient better summarizes the overall pattern, not allowing the anomalous point to dominate the statistic. For this reason, where one or more obvious outliers exist, it is generally better to use ρ than r.

An alternative strategy is to drop the outliers from the data. Careful examination of the anomalous case, and possible reasons for the anomaly, may produce acceptable grounds for doing this. If this course is followed here, we find for data set 2 that $r = .97$ and $\rho = .96$. For data set 3, $r = −.38$ and $\rho = −.32$. Note the huge effect on r of removing the outlier, and the comparatively mild effect on ρ. The various values are summarized in Figure 8.10.

		Data set 1	Data set 2	Data set 3
Full data	r	.76	.76	.76
	ρ	.79	.93	−.01
Without outlier	r		.97	−.38
	ρ		.96	−.32

Figure 8.10 r and ρ data for data sets with identical summary statistics

Testing for significance

As with other statistics, r and ρ can be tested for statistical significance. The null hypothesis for r is that *no linear relationship (positive or negative) exists between the variables* (note the specific reference to *linear* relationship, as already discussed). Similarly, the null hypothesis for r is that *no general pattern of agreement (positive) or disagreement (negative) between the rankings exists*. In both cases, a value of 0 represents no evidence of a relationship, and the further away from 0 towards either +1 or −1, the stronger the evidence of a relationship, summarized graphically in Figure 8.11.

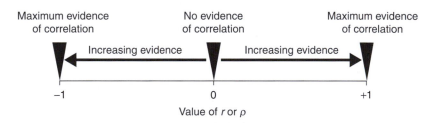

Figure 8.11 Value of r or ρ and strength of evidence

As usual, a procedure is needed to decide how far from zero r needs to be to be significant. Again, we use a simulation to throw some light on this question. The scatterplot in Figure 8.12 represents a population of 100 cases, with $r = \rho = 0$; that is, for this population the null hypothesis for both statistics is true. What we do now is to pick 10 points at random from this population, shown as black dots in Figure 8.12. For these 10 points, $r = .06$ and $\rho = .20$. Now we select a different random sample of 10, repeat the process, and so on. The results of 20 such samplings are shown in the

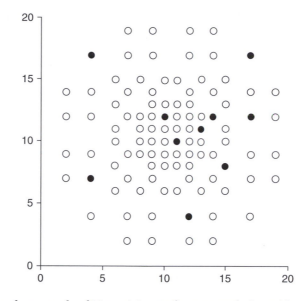

Figure 8.12 Random sample of 10 participants from a population with *r* and *ρ* = 0

form of histograms for the values of *r* and *ρ* obtained (Figure 8.13). The differences in the histograms reflect the differences in the values of *r* and *ρ*. Notice that

- the values are roughly symmetrical about zero (in the case of the values for *r*, the histogram is, in fact, exactly symmetrical 'by chance'); and
- quite high correlations can be obtained by chance.

Now we repeat the simulation, but with samples of 40 participants this time. Figure 8.14 presents the corresponding histograms for 20 samples. Notice that the values cluster much more closely around zero (the same scale was maintained for the histograms to make this obvious). Values beyond ±.2 are relatively unlikely.

As with other statistics, the exact sampling distributions for *r* and for *ρ* can be worked out mathematically. In particular, it can be shown that, if the null hypothesis is true for *r*, and the number of cases, *N* = 10, then the probability of *r* being as far away from 0 as ±.63 is .05. This statement translates into saying that a value of *r* (with *N* = 10) greater than .63 or less than −.63 is statistically significant at the .05 level.

The corresponding critical values for *ρ* are ±.65 (just slightly different). For *N* = 40, the critical values are ±.31 for both *r* and *ρ* (see Figure 8.15). The marked difference between *N* = 10 and *N* = 40 confirms the pattern indicated by the simulation – for a small number of cases, there is a much higher chance of a sample 'just by chance' producing a high positive or negative correlation, even though the correlation for the population is zero. The larger the number of cases, the lower this chance becomes, so that a less extreme value of *r* or *ρ* is required to reach statistical significance.

In practice, we assume you will be using a statistical package that will tell you if the result is statistically significant or not. It is likely, in fact, that an exact probability will be reported – for example, for *N* = 40 and *r* = .324, the associated probability is. 041 (to 3 decimal places). As this *p* value is less than .05, the result is statistically significant at the .05 level.

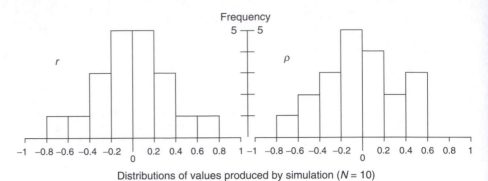

Figure 8.13 Histogram of 20 random samples of 10 participants from a population with *r* and *ρ* = 0

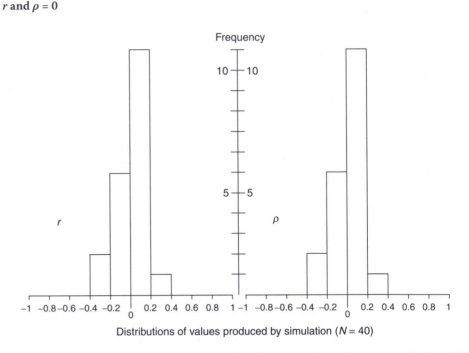

Figure 8.14 Histogram of 20 random samples of 40 participants from a population with *r* and *ρ* = 0

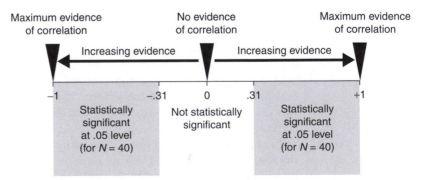

Figure 8.15 Value of *r* and *ρ*, and strength of evidence – critical value and statistical significance (*N* = 40)

Making sense of SPSS

Coding data and calculating Pearson *r* and Spearman's *ρ*

Note: We recommend you also consult Brace et al. (2009), pp. 162–169 who present further information on this topic.

1. Creating a data file

In this example, we use the data for variables *X* and *Y* from Figure 8.2 to calculate both correlation coefficients. We continue to remind you of the golden rule that *each individual participant (case) occupies a single row of their own in the data file*. In Figure 8.2, there are 10 pairs of scores representing 10 cases, each producing a score for both variables *X* and *Y*.

Launch SPSS and bring up the data window as you were shown in Chapter 3 (p. 44). Click **Variable View**. Complete the details as below.

Now click on **Data View** to reveal the blank data table again. You will see two columns labeled *X* and *Y*. The data are entered as indicated below. Remember to save the data giving the file an appropriate name.

2. Calculating Pearson's r and Spearman's ρ

The specific routine for Pearson's r is located in **Analyze > Correlate > Bivariate ...**

The following dialogue box will appear. You will see that **Pearson** is already selected by default. You also need to select **Spearman** to compute ρ.

Now, highlight X and, using the arrow, move it across to the right-hand box labeled **Variables:**. Now, do the same for Y.

Click **OK**.

The **SPSS Statistics Viewer** will display two tables, one for the result of the Pearson r and the other for Spearman's ρ. Both tables present both the X/Y and the Y/X correlations which is unnecessary, since they are the same thing. Also, the leading diagonals (of each variable correlated with itself) are redundant. So the only information to note from the first table is that there is a Pearson's correlation between X and Y of .516, and a Spearman's correlation of .541 between X and Y. The probability values associated with each are .127 and .106 respectively, indicating that, assuming H_0 to be true, the probability of obtaining either correlation is greater than our cut-off of .05. It is thus too likely that the null hypothesis could have produced either result, so, in both cases, we fail to reject H_0 and conclude that there is no significant correlation between the two variables.

Correlations

		X	Y
X	Pearson Correlation	1	.516
	Sig. (2-tailed)		.127
	N	10	10
Y	Pearson Correlation	.516	1
	Sig. (2-tailed)	.127	
	N	10	10

Correlations

			X	Y
Spearman's rho	X	Correlation Coefficient	1.000	.541
		Sig. (2-tailed)	.	.106
		N	10	10
	Y	Correlation Coefficient	.541	1.000
		Sig. (2-tailed)	.106	.
		N	10	10

Reporting r and ρ

Pearson r

Using Brace et al.'s (2009) convention, we would say that the correlation between X and Y was not significant ($r = .516$, $N = 10$, $p = .127$, two-tailed).

Spearman ρ

Similarly, we would say that the correlation between X and Y was not significant ($\rho = .541$, N = 10, $p = 106$, two-tailed).

Correlation and causation

In many situations where some variable X *causes* another variable, Y, it follows that the more of X, the more of Y (or in some cases, the direction will be reversed – the more of X, the less of Y – as in the proverbial 'more haste, less speed'). For example, it seems pretty clear that pollution is likely to be a cause of lung disease. This is reflected in data showing that if the level of pollution and the prevalence of lung disease are measured for many different cities, then the values of those two variables will be correlated.

The converse does not necessarily follow. For example, when data began to emerge showing tobacco consumption and lung cancer to be correlated, this did not constitute *logical proof* that smoking causes lung cancer. Apologists for the tobacco industry could argue validly that smokers differ from non-smokers in many ways. For example, it is a logical possibility, however implausible, that smokers generally differ in their personalities in ways that make them more likely to get lung cancer. Or, it may be that smoking is more associated with living in cities, where pollution is higher. Thus, a number of possible alternative explanations could be found for the correlation other than a direct causative link between smoking and lung cancer. On the other hand, it was perfectly reasonable for people concerned about health to argue that the observed correlation is certainly consistent with a causative

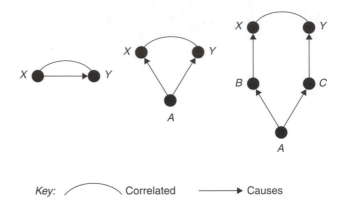

Key: ⌒ Correlated   ⟶ Causes

Figure 8.16 Correlation, causation and latent variables

explanation or, to put it more strongly, suggestive of a causative explanation. In the case of tobacco smoking, the suggestiveness of the correlations was a major motivating factor behind the medical research that identified the underlying causes of lung cancer and proved that tobacco is a factor.

The situation is radically different when the experiment has *direct control*. For example, if animals are tested with a chemical, the experimenter can *randomly assign* animals to different levels of the chemical. If the incidence of a disease rises systematically with the dosage level, this is strong direct evidence that the chemical causes the disease.

Figure 8.16 illustrates an important contrast between situations where a correlation results from X causing Y, and situations where X and Y both have the same underlying (or *latent*) cause (let's call it A). For example, among a sample of people there will clearly be a high correlation between the size of their hands and the size of their feet. Here the variable underlying both of these is general size. In other cases, more complex chains of causation may be hypothesized. For example, it might be speculated that an underlying cause, A, may cause B and C, which in turn cause X and Y respectively, hence accounting for a correlation between X and Y.

What can be stated validly is that, if an experimenter hypothesizes some link between X and Y in a causative chain, collects data and finds that X and Y are indeed correlated, this may be taken as *some degree* of evidence in support of the hypothesis.

Example: Burt's data on juvenile delinquency

In the 1920s, Sir Cyril Burt studied 'juvenile delinquency' in London. As part of his analysis he compiled a table showing, for each of the 29 boroughs in London, the incidence of juvenile delinquency, and various measures of social conditions, part of which is reproduced in Figure 8.17.

The precise definition of the variables in the table is as follows:

Juvenile delinquency

The number of reported cases per 10,000 of the total number of children on the school rolls during 1922 and 1923.

Poverty

Calculated on the basis of an earlier survey by an experimenter called Charles Booth.

Borough	Juvenile delinquency (per 10000)	Poverty (Booth's measure)	Poor relief (per 1000)	Percentage overcrowding
Finsbury	42	37	22	34
Holborn	36	49	16	20
Shoreditch	28	42	51	32
Bermondsey	23	44	46	23
St. Pancras	21	30	20	22
Southwark	18	49	32	24
Stepney	17	38	20	29
Battersea	16	38	43	12
Deptford	16	40	40	13
St. Marylebone	15	27	8	18
Westminster	15	35	5	10
Paddington	14	22	15	15
Bethnal Green	14	45	25	28
Islington	14	31	26	19
Hammersmith	13	34	17	14
Lambeth	12	26	21	13
Poplar	12	36	83	21
Kensington	12	25	10	17
Chelsea	12	25	13	14
Greenwich	11	37	16	14
Camberwell	10	29	34	13
Fulham	9	25	14	13
Woolwich	9	25	27	8
Hackney	8	24	18	12
Lewisham	7	18	23	5
City of London	5	32	4	7
Wandsworth	4	27	8	7
Hampstead	2	14	3	7
Stoke Newington	0	19	8	8

Figure 8.17 Burt's data on 'juvenile delinquency', poverty, poor relief and overcrowding

Poor relief

Number per 1000 in receipt of domiciliary relief.

Overcrowding

Percentage of total population living in conditions classified as overcrowded.

(In passing, since all the boroughs of London were included, it could be pointed out that these data are for the whole population (of boroughs), not a sample. However, it could be considered as a sample (though not a random sample, of course) from a larger population of city areas. The analysis of correlation which follows is not affected, in any case.)

To analyse the data in the table, the scatterplots, product-moment correlations, and rank-order correlations are first produced (see Figure 8.18). The six scattergrams

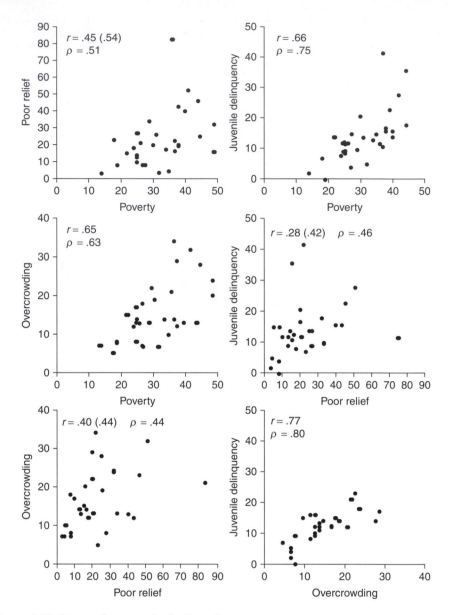

Figure 8.18 Scatterplots, *r* and *ρ* for Burt data

(representing all possible pairings of the four variables) are arranged in two groups of three. The first column shows the three correlations among Poverty, Poor Relief, and Overcrowding. Each of these may plausibly be considered as a reflection of an underlying variable, namely bad social conditions. The relationship between any two of them is, in a sense, symmetrical (analogous to the relationship between two siblings). It is arbitrary as to which variable is plotted on the horizontal, and which on the vertical, axis.

The second column of three scattergrams represents the correlations of Juvenile Delinquency with each of the three indices of poverty in turn. Here we may at least postulate that Poverty, Poor Relief and Overcrowding are contributory factors in

Juvenile Delinquency (it wouldn't make sense to postulate the converse). So the relationships in this case are asymmetrical (like the relationship between a parent and a child, by way of analogy). Conventionally, we plot the possible causal variable on the horizontal axis.

The scatterplots involving Poor Relief show up obvious outliers, and we can trace these to the anomalously high Poor Relief of 83% in the borough of Poplar. The correlation coefficients are given with the scatterplots (figures in brackets are for the values of *r* with the outlier removed). Note, in particular, how the rank-order correlation coefficient is much higher for Poor Relief/Juvenile Delinquency; the product-moment correlation is much reduced by the outlier, as is indicated by the effect of recalculating it without the outlier.

Burt's (1925) comments on these data are worth quoting:

> The highest coefficient of all is that for the correlation between juvenile delinquency and overcrowding, namely .77. Allowing for the gross shortcomings, inevitable in estimates so crude, so vague, and in some cases so largely out of date, these several figures are remarkably consistent one with another. They indicate plainly that it is in the poor, overcrowded, insanitary households... that juvenile delinquency is most rife.
>
> But throughout I must insist that, however extensive and however exact, a mere comparison of tabulated figures must never take the place of concrete studies, or of an intensive firsthand scrutiny of the concrete chain of causation, as it operates in particular cases. Here as elsewhere, in gauging the effect of any natural agency, we can put little faith in arm-chair deductions: we must watch that agency at work. (*The Young Delinquent*. London: University of London press, p. 78)

This is an eloquent statement of the principle that, however suggestive correlations may be of causal patterns, they are not by themselves conclusive. He also reminds us that, while general patterns are, of course, important – and the focus of most research in experimental psychology – each individual case is different. Elsewhere in his book, Burt emphasizes the multiplicity of factors underlying any such complex social phenomenon, and argues that hereditary and environmental explanations are complementary (this, of course, represents one of the deepest questions in psychology).

Fitting a straight line

The two correlation coefficients we have considered each measure, in their own way, of the strength of the relationship between two variables. A further quantification of the relationship is to fit a straight line to the data.

By way of introduction to this idea, consider a case where, by definition, an exact straight-line relationship exists, namely temperature measured in Centigrade versus temperature measured in Fahrenheit. Figure 8.19 presents a table and graph showing some such data. The straight line through the points represents the total relationship. Moreover, it can be expressed alternatively in algebraic terms in the equation:

$$F = 32 + 1.8C$$

(where F is the temperature in Fahrenheit and C is the temperature in Centigrade). Given any temperature in Centigrade, this formula can be used to work out the corresponding temperature in Fahrenheit.

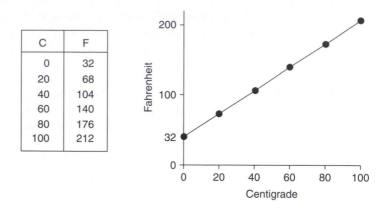

Figure 8.19 Relationship between fahrenheit and centigrade temperatures

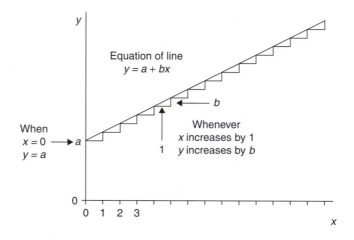

Figure 8.20 Slope, intercept and general equation of straight line

The general equation for any straight line is:

$y = a + bx$

In this equation, a is the value of y when $x = 0$ (see Figure 8.20): it is called the **intercept**, because in graphical terms, it is where the line cuts the y-axis; b is the amount y increases by for each unit increase in x – it is called the **slope** (because it determines the slope of the line once the scales for the two axes have been fixed).

By way of an analogy, suppose you hire a car and the charge is £25 initial payment + £60 per day. Then the cost, c, in pounds for n days is given by the formula:

$c = 25 + 60n$

Here the initial payment of £25 is like the intercept. The daily payment of £60 is like the slope – for every extra day, the cost increases by another £60.

With psychological data, of course, you just won't get the exact relationship between variables as exists by definition in the Centigrade/Fahrenheit and car-hire examples. Nevertheless, a straight line can be fitted which reflects any trend in the data. To illustrate how this works, consider a very small data set for two variables, labelled X and Y in Figure 8.21.

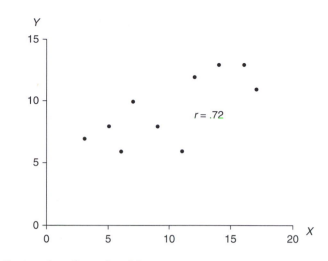

Figure 8.21 Scatterplot of correlated data

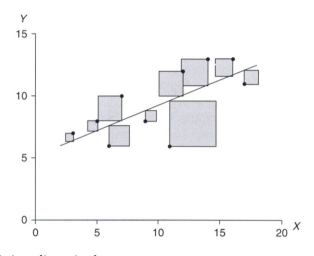

Figure 8.22 Fitting a line using least squares

The scatterplot shows a fairly strong relationship. It would be possible to fit a straight line 'by eye'; that is, to draw a straight line that best fits the points subjectively. However, it is easy to be more precise. One standard method works by the following line of reasoning. Suppose a particular line is drawn – how could you measure how well it fits the points? A commonly used measure is to take the vertical distance each point lies away from the line, square that, and add them all together. This total, then, is an overall measure of how well the line fits. The **best fit**, by this method of measuring goodness of fit, is clearly the line that makes this value as small as possible. This is called the **regression line**, based on the criterion of so-called **least squares**, i.e. minimizing the sum of the squared vertical distances of the points from the line. Figure 8.22 shows a way of describing schematically the sum of squared vertical distances of the points from a particular line – the squared distances are represented, literally, as squares.

The equation for the best fit regression line can be worked out exactly. Its slope is given by:

$$b = \frac{\sum(X - \overline{X})(Y - \overline{Y})}{\sum(X - \overline{X})^2}$$

and its intercept by:

$$a = \overline{Y} - b\overline{X}$$

For the example, this gives the equation

$$Y' = 5.23 + .42X$$

Note our notation here. Y is used to indicate the *actual data* values for that variable. We are using Y' to give the equation of the *straight line* that fits the points on the scattergram, as shown in Figure 8.23.

Squaring r

Pearson's r is a useful statistic in itself and, in later chapters, we discuss further uses for it. Here, we introduce you to a particular property of r which is widely used in psychology research. That is, if we simply take r and square it, we obtain a well known measure known as the **coefficient of determination** and abbreviated to r^2. This statistic tells you the *proportion of all the variation in the data shared by the two variables*, sometimes expressed as the *proportion of variance in one variable accounted for by the other*.

In Figure 8.21, we see an r of .72. Squaring this value we obtain an r^2 of .52, which tells us that 0.52, or 52%, of the variance is shared by the variables X and Y. In the extreme case of a perfect correlation ($r = 1.00$), r^2 also equals 1.00, indicating that the two variables share 100% of the variation in the data.

The coefficient of determination provides a useful perspective from which to consider the importance of a result. In particular, although a correlation of, say, 0.3 may not seem altogether negligible, the associated r^2 value of .09 indicates that only 9% of the variance is explained by the relationship between the two variables. While in some contexts, namely with large or very large samples, this may be a reasonable result, it is far from impressive, especially with more modest sample sizes.

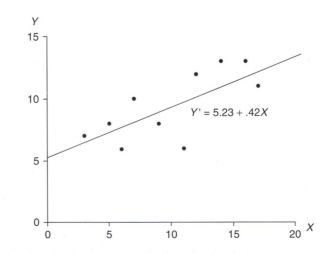

Figure 8.23 Equation of line: Slope and intercept calculated from formulae

For those who wish to dig a little deeper

Let's look a little more closely at the idea of the proportion of variance explained by (in this case) the correlation between X and Y. Figure 8.24 shows two measures of variability associated with the scatterplot in Figure 8.21 and the subsequent figures.

The graph on the left shows the total variance in the scores around the mean for Y, which happens to be 9.40, shown by the horizontal line. This is otherwise known as the total variance or the total sum of squares (SS_{total}). The graph on the right is from Figure 8.22 and shows the variability, or error, around the regression line, otherwise known as the error sum of squares (SS_{error}) associated with the best fit line. Now, if we subtract SS_{error} from SS_{total}, it makes sense that the variance left over is the variance associated with the regression line, that is, the systematic variance explained by the relationship between X and Y.

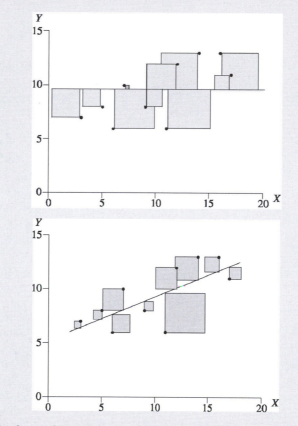

Figure 8.24 Total sum of squares (top) and error sum of squares (bottom)

Rather than simply giving this value of $SS_{total} - SS_{error}$ as the actual *amount* of variance, it makes more sense to express it as a *proportion* of the total variance in the data, simply by dividing it by the total variance, that is, SS_{total}. So, we have hit upon an important formula for this crucial concept of the proportion of variance explained. Moreover, the formula extends far beyond this case of correlation.

Thus, the proportion of variance explained is given by:

$$\frac{SS_{total} - SS_{error}}{SS_{total}}$$

Interestingly, and although it is beyond the scope of this text, it can be shown that r^2 yields the same value as that produced by this formula.

An example of regression lines: Analysis of Burt data

As a further example, we apply regression analysis to some of the Burt data already considered. The least-squares regression lines for the relationships between Poverty, Poor Relief and Overcrowding, respectively, and Juvenile Delinquency, are as shown in Figure 8.25.

In the case of Poor Relief, it seems clear that the outlier (Poplar) is having a very distorting effect on the regression line. As with the product-moment correlation coefficient, the least-squares method of calculating a line is highly non-resistant; that is, liable to be affected strongly by outliers. One response would be to recalculate

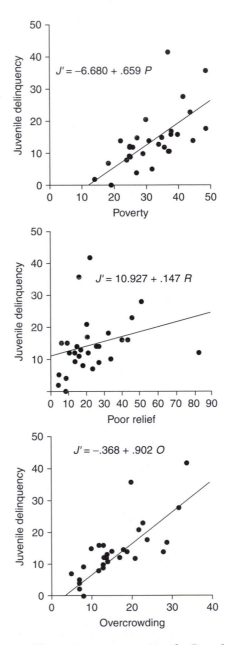

Figure 8.25 Scatterplots and least-squares regressions for Burt data

the regression line with the outlier omitted, and this leads to a line that appears to summarize more adequately the general trend (Figure 8.26).

Another possible response is to use a rank-based procedure to calculate a line of best fit that is resistant. Figure 8.27 shows how to work out the Tukey line (named after its inventor, John Tukey) for these data:

1 Divide the data vertically into three roughly numerically equal sub-groups – in this case, sub-groups of 10, 9, 10 would be reasonable.

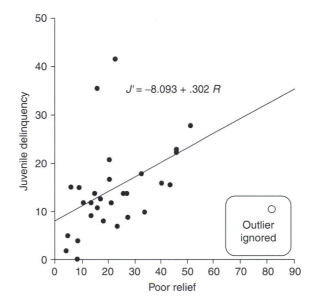

Figure 8.26 Regression recalculated with outlier removed

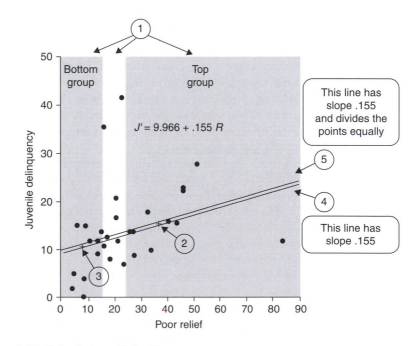

Figure 8.27 Calculating a Tukey line

2 For the top sub-group, calculate the median of the values for each variable. For Poor Relief this comes to 37, and for Juvenile Delinquency, 15. Plot these two values as the point (37, 15).

3 Repeat this process for the bottom third of the data, yielding the point (8, 10.5).

4 The line joining these two points determines the slope of the Tukey line. The slope of the line joining two points (x_1, y_1) and (x_2, y_2) in general is $(y_2 - y_1)/(x_2 - x_1)$, so in this case it comes to $b = 4.5/29 = .155$

5 In geometrical terms, what is done now is to keep the slope constant, and adjust the line up or down till half of the points lie above it and half below (with 29 points, in fact, it will pass through 1 point and have 14 above and 14 below). In numerical terms, this is achieved by working out $Y - bX$ for each point, and taking the median of these values, which in this case is 9.966. This median defines the intercept, a, so the Tukey line is as shown.

Unfortunately, many pieces of software do not offer this option and, as you can see, it is takes some calculation to work it out. We include it in line with our general policy of stressing resistant statistics.

Testing for significance of regression

The null hypothesis in this context is that there is *no linear relationship between the variables*. Testing for statistical significance in this case is, in fact, exactly equivalent to testing for the statistical significance of the product-moment correlation coefficient.

For example, in the Burt example above, the product-moment correlation (r) for Juvenile Delinquency and Poor Relief is .42 with the outlier removed, which for $n = 28$ is highly statistically significant (the critical value is.31). By contrast, the product-moment correlation with the outlier included is only .28, which is not statistically significant.

Chapter review

In this chapter, two correlation coefficients have been defined as measures of specific aspects of the relationship between two variables. The product-moment correlation coefficient is a measure of how closely the data conform to a straight-line relationship, whereas the rank-order correlation coefficient is a measure of the level of agreement between the two sets of scores when they are ranked. Neither coefficient is equipped to pick up all forms of systematic relationship between two variables – a U-shaped relationship being a case in point. The rank-order correlation is resistant by comparison with the product-moment coefficient, and is often to be preferred when there are one or more outliers.

These correlation coefficients were illustrated by a number of examples, including data by Burt linking amount of Juvenile Delinquency to indices of unfavourable social conditions. A distinction was made between symmetrical situations in which the variables may be considered as simply related, and asymmetrical situations, in which one variable may be considered as, at least possibly, causing the other. The importance of analysing the relationship between correlation and causation logically was stressed.

A second quantitative approach is to calculate a line that summarizes any linear trend in the data. The most common such line is based on minimizing the sum of squares of the vertical distances between the points and the line. This is also non-resistant, and can be affected strongly by outliers, so a rank-based alternative was also introduced.

We also introduced the coefficient of determination, r^2, as a measure of the proportion of variance in one variable which is explained by the other.

Experimentation in psychology

In this chapter

... through dialogues and the elaboration of earlier examples, ideas about the experimental method introduced in Chapter 1 are extended. Three main experimental designs are discussed: independent groups, repeated measures and matched pairs. Key concepts relating to statistical inference are explored, and linkages between experimental design and choice of statistical test are made explicit.

Putting a little more meat on the bones

In the preceding chapters, we have presented many important statistical and methodological concepts. Here, we pull these ideas together. By integrating various concepts, the inextricable links between research design and statistical methods are made explicit.

Inevitably, this chapter will involve cross-referencing to earlier material. In order to reduce the amount of scuttling back and forth, we reiterate the essential details of the various examples as appropriate.

Recap: The empirical process

Figure 9.1 summarizes the elements of the empirical approach first introduced in Chapter 1 (see p. 9). Recall that the researcher defines a topic, identifies specific hypotheses and then designs a study to generate data intended to cast light on these hypotheses. Following statistical analysis of the data, findings are interpreted, disseminated and integrated into existing knowledge.

In this chapter, we focus on the approach known as the experimental method, first discussed in Chapter 1 (see p. 10). As we explained there, the essence of experimental studies is the control, or manipulation, of so-called **independent variables**, a characteristic that allows causal relationships between variables to be investigated.

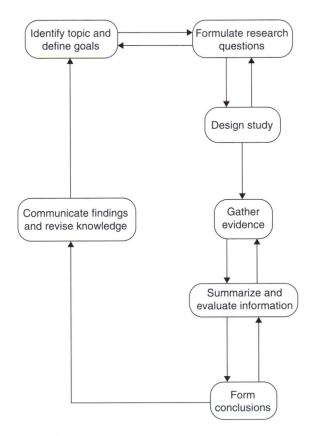

Figure 9.1 The empirical process

Experimental designs

For the sake of clarity, and consistent with our approach, we recap and draw together the ideas about experimental design introduced in earlier chapters. In keeping with our philosophy, we consider at this point only the basic forms of experimental design.

Designs for comparing two sets of scores

In Chapter 7 you were introduced to statistical tests for *comparing* scores, based on either two separate groups of participants, or on testing the same individuals on two occasions. Let's look in a little more detail at the design of the experiments from which such data originate.

Independent groups: Quick on the draw

Recall that in Chapter 4 we considered how to investigate whether squash players have faster reaction times than chess players (see p. 55). An important feature of this example is that the two groups are totally separate (for simplicity, we assume that the people in the samples *either* play squash *or* chess, but not both). As we saw, it is possible to use a variety of graphical displays to provide visual evidence of a difference between the two groups. For obvious reasons, this type of design is known as **independent groups** (or **between groups**, or **unrelated groups**).

> *Lecturer:* What are the main variables in this example?
> *Student:* Let's see, one variable is whether someone is a squash player or a chess player.
> *Lecturer:* That's right, but do you know what type of variable it is?
> *Student:* Er... an independent variable with two levels – squash and chess?
> *Lecturer:* It certainly has two levels and it's an independent variable of sorts – but what more can you say about it?
> *Student:* Ah, yes, it's a subject variable, because it's not under the direct control of the experimenter. So, when participants come along to be tested, they are already designated as squash players or chess players – that's one of their characteristics.
> *Lecturer:* Good. Now, is there another variable?
> *Student:* Yes, the dependent variable is the participants' reaction time.
> *Lecturer:* Well done!

More on independent groups: Changing computer attitude

Chapter 7 presents another independent groups design, in which one group of ten females is shown a video intended to foster a positive attitude towards computers, while a separate group of ten females is not shown the video.

> **Before reading on...**
>
> Look back at this example. Name the independent and dependent variables.
>
> **... now read on**

In this example, the independent variable, let's call it *condition*, is manipulated at two levels – *video/no video*, and participants are assigned randomly to one of the two treatments. The *video* group may be referred to as an **experimental group**, while the *no video* group is one example of a **control group**.

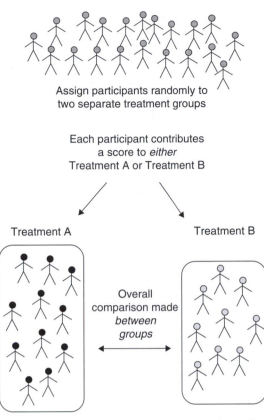

Assign participants randomly to
two separate treatment groups

Each participant contributes
a score to *either*
Treatment A or Treatment B

Treatment A

Treatment B

Overall
comparison made
between
groups

Note: Groups do not need to be exactly equal in size, but random
assignment should ensure roughly equal group sizes

Figure 9.2 Independent (or between, or unrelated) groups design

The precise nature of the control condition is an important matter in itself. For example, instead of a *no video* control, we could opt for a control treatment in which participants are shown a neutral video (for example, about natural history) of the same duration. You may consider this to be a more appropriate control, since it is more similar to the experimental task than the *no video* control.

The dependent variable is the measure of *Attitude to Computers*. As you saw in Chapter 7, the effect of watching the video on the dependent variable is assessed by comparing the *overall* (mean) performance of the two groups. Put another way, the comparison is made *between* groups (hence, the term *between groups design*). A schematic representation of the between groups design is given in Figure 9.2.

Paired data: Let your fingers do the talking

Chapter 7 presents an example of a **repeated measures** (or **within-subjects**, or **related samples**) design, in which the typing speed of a single group of sixteen typists is measured on two occasions – before and after a tea-break (see p. 129).

Before reading on...

What are the independent and dependent variables in this example?

... now read on

Here the independent variable (let's call it *tea-break*) has two levels – *before* and *after* – and the dependent variable is *typing speed*, in words per minute. It is worth reiterating that, whereas in the independent groups example, the twenty participants are assigned to *either* one treatment *or* the other, in this repeated measures example, the typists participate in *both* levels of the independent variable.

The resulting paired data give rise to a different logic for comparing the two sets of scores. This time, rather than emphasizing overall differences between treatments, our repeated measures example assesses the effect of the independent variable in terms of the *difference* or *change* in each typist's performance between the two treatments. That is, the effect of the independent variable is assessed *within* individual subjects (hence the term *within-subjects design*). Figure 9.3 presents a schematic representation of the repeated measures design.

Matched pairs: Boys' and girls' mathematical abilities

In Chapter 7, we presented another case of paired data, although in that instance the design also involved separate groups of participants. You might rightly regard it as a hybrid between independent groups and repeated measures. Recall that, in this example of a **matched pairs design**, initial samples of boys and girls are *pre-tested* for attitudes to mathematics and then a sub-sample of boy–girl pairs with matched

Assign participants to
both treatment groups

Each participant contributes a score
to *both* Treatment A and Treatment B

Treatment A   Treatment B

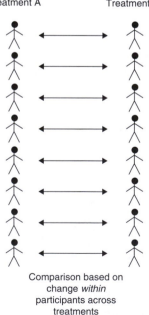

Comparison based on
change *within*
participants across
treatments

Figure 9.3 Repeated measures (or within-subjects, or unrelated samples) design

attitudes scores are chosen. Here the independent variable is gender at two levels; the dependent variable is mathematical ability; and the **matching variable** is attitudes to mathematics. Obviously, since gender is a subject variable, participants cannot be assigned randomly to the levels of the independent variable! A schematic representation of the matched pairs design is shown in Figure 9.4.

It is important to note that, in spite of there being two separate groups, the fact that participants are paired up or 'yoked' (and hence so are their scores) means that the groups are not independent. For this reason, matched pairs designs are classified along with repeated measures designs, and the resulting data are treated in the same way as other paired data.

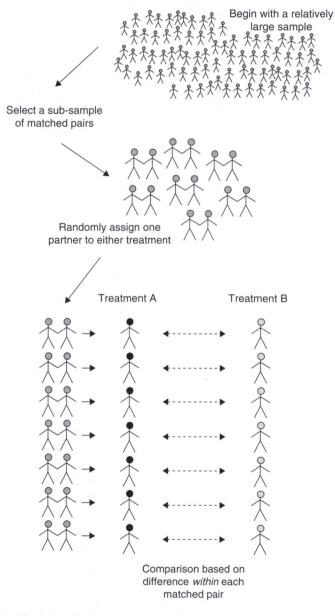

Begin with a relatively large sample

Select a sub-sample of matched pairs

Randomly assign one partner to either treatment

Treatment A   Treatment B

Comparison based on difference *within* each matched pair

Figure 9.4 Matched pairs design

Pros and cons of the various designs

Let's revisit some of the above examples.

Changing computer attitudes (again)

> **Lecturer:** *Think about our example, in which one group of females is shown a video and another group isn't, and then both groups' Attitude to Computers are measured.*
>
> **Student:** *I remember, the independent groups design.*
>
> **Lecturer:** *That's right. Suppose that, overall, those in the* video *condition have more positive attitude to computers than the* no video *group. How confident can you be that the difference is caused by the video?*
>
> **Student:** *Depending on the size of the difference, pretty confident. The independent variable was manipulated by the experimenter, so I can infer a causal relationship.*
>
> **Lecturer:** *Are there any issues that might cause you to hesitate?*
>
> **Student:** *I suppose if I discovered that the* no video *group just happened to have a few radical technophobes and, by chance, the* video *group contained five members of the Bill Gates fan club, I might think twice.*
>
> **Lecturer:** *What do you think the chances are of something like that happening?*
>
> **Student:** *OK. Well, assuming the samples were big enough and the experimenter assigned participants randomly to treatments, then it shouldn't be a problem.*
>
> **Lecturer:** *Are two groups of ten females big enough?*
>
> **Student:** *I'm not sure – maybe. It's quite possible the groups weren't equivalent to start with, even if they were randomly selected, and one or two 'extreme' individuals in either group could tip the balance in either direction.*
>
> **Lecturer:** *Food for thought, eh?*

Let your fingers do the talking (again)

Let's look again at the *tea-break* example. Clearly, there is no problem with non-equivalent groups. Not only are the groups equivalent – they are identical, with each typist acting as her or his own control. So, supposing typing speed is faster after a tea-break, can we be more confident this time that the difference results from the independent variable?

> **Before reading on...**
>
> Think about this question and jot down your thoughts.
>
> **... now read on**

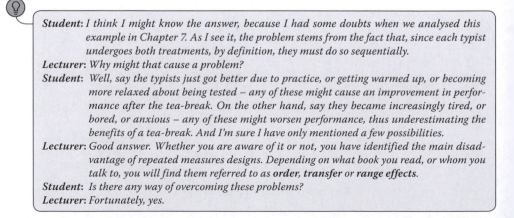

> **Student:** *I think I might know the answer, because I had some doubts when we analysed this example in Chapter 7. As I see it, the problem stems from the fact that, since each typist undergoes both treatments, by definition, they must do so sequentially.*
>
> **Lecturer:** *Why might that cause a problem?*
>
> **Student:** *Well, say the typists just got better due to practice, or getting warmed up, or becoming more relaxed about being tested – any of these might cause an improvement in performance after the tea-break. On the other hand, say they became increasingly tired, or bored, or anxious – any of these might worsen performance, thus underestimating the benefits of a tea-break. And I'm sure I have only mentioned a few possibilities.*
>
> **Lecturer:** *Good answer. Whether you are aware of it or not, you have identified the main disadvantage of repeated measures designs. Depending on what book you read, or whom you talk to, you will find them referred to as* **order, transfer** *or* **range effects.**
>
> **Student:** *Is there any way of overcoming these problems?*
>
> **Lecturer:** *Fortunately, yes.*

Coping with transfer

There are two broad approaches to dealing with order effects in repeated measures designs. One is to find some way to minimize **transfer** from the first condition to the second. The other, more common, approach is to **alternate** or **counterbalance** the order of conditions across participants.

In fact, everyday life is full of examples of alternating conditions. Sport is a particularly rich vein, given the obvious need to ensure that one competitor does not have an advantage over another. In tennis, players swap sides every two games throughout a match. In chess, players take turns between white and black. In sports such as soccer, ice hockey, field hockey, basketball and rugby, teams change ends at half-time, or at the end of each quarter. Similarly, in knock-out competitions, the result of a tie may be taken over two legs – home and away.

The instinct to balance any possible advantage of one competitor over another is ever-present, even when we cannot necessarily identify the precise nature of any advantage. Beyond the sporting arena, we find other everyday examples. You may be familiar with the advice to turn houseplants regularly through 180 degrees to ensure even growth. We are also told that swapping the front and rear tyres on your car every 6000 miles will promote even wear across the life of the tyres.

> **Before reading on...**
>
> Try to identify some more real-life examples of alternating treatments of conditions. Jot these down for later discussion with friends or your tutor.
>
> **... now read on**

Let your fingers do the talking (again)

Back to our *tea-break* study. In this case, one option for dealing with order effects is to try to minimize the impact of transfer from *before* to *after*.

> **Before reading on...**
>
> Spend some time thinking about how you could cope with order effects in this example. Jot down your thoughts for later comparison.
>
> **... now read on**

Let's see how you got on. One method of dealing with the problem would be to increase the time interval between conditions, so that order effects are minimized. For example, the *before* condition could be done on one day (with no *after* testing) and the *after* condition done the next (with no *before* testing). That way, many (but not all) of the order effects would be reduced. Incidentally, this approach would also allow half of the participants to do *after* on the first day, followed by *before* on the next, and vice versa.

> **Before reading on...**
>
> Which of the following might be minimized by this method:
> - practice;
> - anxiety;
> - boredom;
> - memory of the content of the test;
> - fatigue; or
> - getting warmed up?
>
> Any others you can think of?
>
> **... now read on**

Alternating treatments

Fortunately, unlike the *tea-break* example, most repeated measures designs do not require treatments to be carried out in a rigid sequence. For example, suppose we are interested in comparing memory for written and spoken words. We could carry out a repeated measures experiment by exposing participants to two sets of words – one written, the other spoken, and testing memory for each. Half of the group would be randomly selected to take *written* followed by *spoken*, while the remainder would do the opposite. Figure 9.5 shows this approach more generally – a simple example of the **Latin Square Design**.

> **Student:** *Cool, so when the data are aggregated for the whole group, any transfer from the first to the second condition will be balanced by an equivalent transfer in the opposite direction.*
> **Lecturer:** *Correct, although the assumption that transfer is symmetrical, that is, that one direction cancels out the other, is precisely that – an assumption.*
> **Student:** *Also, even if transfer does cancel out across the whole group, for any individual participant, the transfer effects remain.*
> **Lecturer:** *Indeed, so if you want to look at a single participant, or a very small group, alternating treatments might not be suitable.*
> **Student:** *Then what?*
> **Lecturer:** *Let's see.*

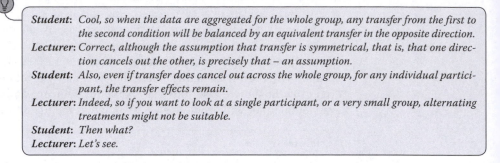

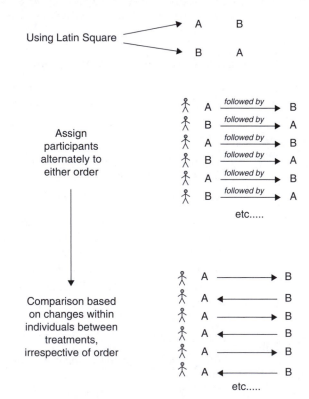

Figure 9.5 Latin Square Design

Counterbalancing: A-B-B-A

Another method of alternating treatments, known as counterbalancing, is to ask participants to perform the first treatment, followed by the second, followed by the second again, followed by the first (see Figure 9.6). So, in the case of our memory example, participants would take (say) *written* first, *spoken* second, *spoken* third and *written* fourth.

Averages are then obtained for each participant's two *written* scores and two *spoken* scores. The logic here is that any order effects are balanced out because participants do one treatment first and last, and the other treatment second and third. An assumption here is that such transfer applies *evenly* across the four conditions, for example, in the case of a gradual build up of fatigue or reduction of anxiety. Again, this assumption may not always hold.

All participants undergo
both treatments *twice*, in
the following sequence:

A *followed by* B *followed by* B *followed by* A

Each participant's two
A & B scores are averaged

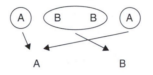

A   B

In the ususal way for repeated
measures, comparison is based on
differences in A & B scores
within each participant

A ⟷ B
A ⟷ B
A ⟷ B
A ⟷ B

etc....

Figure 9.6 Counterbalancing

The advantage of this method is that the order effects are controlled for each participant, so it is not necessary to average over an entire group to see the benefit. This is particularly useful if the number of participants is limited. However, the disadvantage is that each participant has to perform a total of four conditions, which may be problematic if the tasks are lengthy.

Boys' and girls' mathematical abilities

Recall the matched pairs example from Chapter 7, in which girl–boy pairs, matched for attitudes to mathematics, are compared on mathematical ability (see p. 142).

Student: This design looks as if it offers the best of both worlds. I can't imagine why psychologists don't use it all the time.
Lecturer: Why do you like it so much?
Student: Well, although you have two separate groups, because participants have been matched and paired up, you also have related scores.
Lecturer: So?
Student: The independent groups ensure that there can be no transfer between conditions – participants are only tested once. Since participants are pre-tested and carefully matched, although the paired scores are not from the same individual, they might as well be.
Lecturer: Do you think it's as cut and dried as that?
Student: Well... yes. Don't you?
Lecturer: Often it is pretty cut and dried, but it is important to be aware that the experimenter has to assume that the chosen pre-test is a valid means of matching participants; that is, it must take account of all variables likely to affect performance in the experiment. It should also be borne in mind that the pre-testing of participants is logistically more demanding than independent groups or repeated measures, and may even be impractical.
Student: Ah, so that's why psychologists don't use it all the time!

Summing up: Design, validity and insidious variables

It should be clear to you by now that, in designing experiments, considerable care must be taken to ensure that the findings can be interpreted unambiguously, a property known as **internal validity**. In our discussion of the anatomy of the three main experimental designs, we have identified various threats to internal validity. In the case of independent groups designs, we saw that results may be unclear because of non-equivalent groups. Repeated measures designs, on the other hand, are prone to order and transfer effects, while the internal validity of matched pairs designs may be threatened by the use of an inappropriate matching variable.

The empirical arena is full of **extraneous variables** that affect a participant's behaviour. The majority of these exert a relatively minor, and random, influence, so are simply ignored as so-called **nuisance variables**. Some extraneous variables, however, are more insidious, biasing data systematically and otherwise threatening internal validity. Researchers have developed an impressive armoury of methodological devices to deal with these **confounding variables**, many of which are found in this book. The concept of confounding is crucial to understanding experimental research. In essence, confounding variables prevent the researcher from drawing unambiguous conclusions from the manipulation of an independent variable. In order to avoid confounding, all participants must be treated identically *except for the specific manipulation of the independent variable*, if not, the experimenter will not be able to decide whether differences between participants scores are due to the manipulation, or to the confounding variable, or both. Rather than review methods for dealing with confounding in isolation, we discuss them as an integral part of the statistical techniques they support.

Statistical inference

In preceding chapters, you will have encountered the idea that, in all but the rarest cases, psychological research involves the use of one or more samples of participants drawn from one or more target populations. The role of statistical tests is to allow us to generalize findings from these samples to their respective populations. Generally, since textbooks have tended to use somewhat arcane, though in most cases technically correct, language to explain this idea, students could be forgiven for struggling to grasp the nub of the issue.

From sample to population: The story so far

Chapter 6 used the example of Big-Endians (B) and Little-Endians (L) from *Gulliver's Travels* to illustrate a popular approach to statistical inference involving the *null hypothesis* (see p. 93). In this example, the null hypothesis is that Bs and Ls are represented equally in the population. The essence of the approach is to take a sample of the population and count the numbers of Bs and Ls. The likelihood of this result having occurred, assuming equal numbers of Bs and Ls, is then evaluated.

This is a somewhat indirect approach to the precise question of how many Bs and Ls there are in the population. As we pointed out in Chapter 6, our result does *not* tell us how likely it is that there are equal numbers of Bs and Ls. Rather, for the sake of argument, we *assume* equal numbers in the population (that is, that the null hypothesis is true). After counting the number of Bs and Ls in the sample, we then ask, 'What is the likelihood of obtaining such a result, assuming that the null hypothesis is true'.

By convention, if the imbalance between Bs and Ls in the sample is such that the likelihood of it having occurred under the null hypothesis is 5% (.05) or less, we declare the result to be statistically significant, and we decide to *reject* the null hypothesis. On the other hand, if the result is less extreme, such that the likelihood of it occurring under the null hypothesis is greater than this cut-off of .05, we *fail to reject* the null hypothesis. This cut-off point of .05 is known as the **level of significance**, a term introduced in Chapter 6 (see p. 102). More of this later.

Errors in statistical inference

Self-evidently, in any situation where decisions are taken on the basis of probability, there is a risk – albeit possibly a very small one – of that decision being wrong. Take the example of a jury in a court of law entrusted with the task of reaching a verdict in the absence of total certainty. In such situations, there are two possible decisions – innocent or guilty – and two possible states of reality – innocence or guilt. Of course, in most legal systems, jurisprudence dictates that a defendant is innocent until found to be guilty beyond all reasonable doubt. Figure 9.7 illustrates the relationship between decision and reality, as well as four possible scenarios.

While the outcomes shown in Figure 9.7 may seem obvious, for reasons that will become clear it is worth taking a little time to consider them. Depending on the reality of the situation, namely the guilt or innocence of the defendant, the jury risks making one of two possible errors – either wrongly to convict an innocent person, or wrongly to acquit a guilty person. Bear in mind that the jury are not privy to the reality of the situation. Presuming the defendant to be innocent, they must evaluate the facts of the case and decide whether the evidence casts *reasonable doubt* on this presumption of innocence. The question, 'How reasonable should *reasonable* be?' also arises. Which outcome is worse – letting a guilty person walk free, or sending an innocent person to jail? Indeed, in some legal systems, the consequence of a wrong conviction may be even more profound.

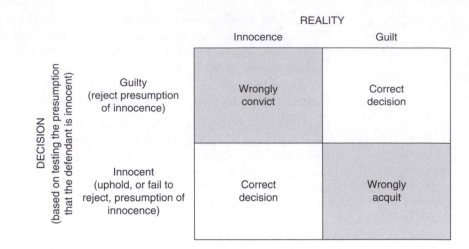

Figure 9.7 **Reaching a verdict: Four possible outcomes**

> **Before reading on...**
>
> Spend some time thinking about these points. Do you notice any parallels with statistical inference in psychology experiments? Jot down your thoughts for later reflection.
>
> **... now read on**

This example is a useful analogy for statistical inference in experiments. The presumption that *the defendant is innocent* may be thought of as the null hypothesis. The examination of the facts by the jury is akin to analysis of the data. The jury's consideration of the likelihood of the events occurring, assuming the defendant is innocent, is similar to deciding whether the results of an experiment are significant or not. Only *strong* doubt that the defendant's innocence (H_0) is consistent with the facts of the case (data analysis) would lead the jury to reject the presumption of innocence – effectively to reject the null hypothesis. If, on the other hand, the jury considered it possible that the events could have occurred, given a presumption of innocence, there would not be grounds to reject the null hypothesis.

Figure 9.8 summarizes outcomes in relation to experimental reality and corresponding decisions about the null hypothesis (H_0). As in the jury example, we see that there are two possible types of error in making statistical inferences. First, the researcher could wrongly *reject* the null hypothesis *when it was true* (cf. 'wrongly convict an innocent person'), or they could wrongly *fail to reject* the null hypothesis *when it was false* (cf. 'wrongly acquit a guilty person'). Note from Figure 9.8 that these decision errors are called **Type I** and **Type II** errors, respectively.

Statistical significance, reasonable doubt and Type I errors

It should be clear by now that the process of statistical inference involves a gamble. In any experiment, the essence of this approach to statistical analysis of the data is to calculate *the likelihood of obtaining our result, assuming the null hypothesis to be true.* Since the result of this calculation is in the form of a probability, we must then

REALITY

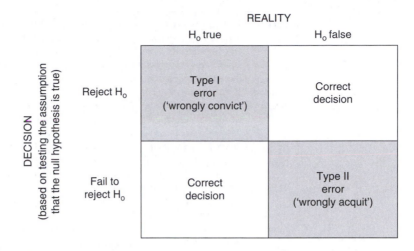

Figure 9.8 Type I and II errors

decide whether or not the evidence is strong enough to allow us to reject the null hypothesis.

While in the jury example, level of confidence is expressed in terms of strong doubt, statistical inference is based on setting firm levels of *risk* in taking decisions. Earlier in this chapter, we referred to the so-called *.05 level of significance* used widely in psychological research. This cut-off value of .05 (or 5%) is the probability value corresponding to the *likelihood of obtaining a result equal to, or more extreme than our result, assuming the null hypothesis is true.*

Student: *So, basically, if the probability of obtaining a result as extreme as ours – assuming the null hypothesis to be true – is .05 or less, we consider it doubtful that the null hypothesis could have produced this result?*

Lecturer: *Correct. If you like, we have set a 5 per cent likelihood as a cut-off for strong doubt, which we call the level of significance.*

Student: *But sometimes we'll be wrong in rejecting the null hypothesis.*

Lecturer: *Indeed. After all, it's a game of chance like any other, and that's the risk we take.*

Student: *So you're saying that 'significant at the 5 per cent level' means that, even for a null hypothesis that is in fact true, there is a small chance that the result will be interpreted as statistically significant.*

Lecturer: *Right.*

Student: *Ah, I've seen a link that hadn't occurred to me before – the level of significance is the risk of making this mistake.*

Lecturer: *Exactly. In fact, many statistics texts define level of significance as the probability of wrongly rejecting a true null hypothesis, or words to that effect.*

Student: *Hang on, I think I see another link. Isn't this type of mistake called a* Type I *error?*

Lecturer: *Correct.*

Student: *So, doing some joined-up thinking, isn't level of significance actually the probability of making a Type I error?*

Lecturer: *Excellent! You will often see level of significance abbreviated to the Greek letter* α *– pronounced 'al-fa' – in textbooks and computer-based statistical packages.*

Student: *I'm sure I've also seen it referred to as* p *in some text books.*

Lecturer: *Actually,* α *and* p *are not exactly the same, although they are very closely related. Both represent the level of significance; that is, the probability of wrongly rejecting a true null hypothesis.*

Student: *So what's the difference?*

Lecturer: *Well, α is a **predefined** cut-off point, such as .05. So, when you carry out a statistical test, you compare your result with a so-called* critical value *of the statistic representing your predefined level of significance. Your decision to reject the null hypothesis or not would depend on whether your result is greater or less (depending on the test) than the corresponding critical value.*

Student: *What is p then?*

Lecturer: *Unlike α, p is not a predefined cut-off. As we saw in Chapter 7, it is the **precise** significance associated with your result. Since statistical packages like SPSS came along, it has been possible to calculate exact p values, rather than simply asking whether a result is above or below a cut-off point, such as .05. So, when a statistical test is calculated on a computer, you obtain a p value – such as .004, or .3318, or even .0000 to 4 decimal places – and you simply look to see whether this value is equal to or less than .05, say.*

Student: *Ah, so you don't need to compare the actual value of the statistic with its corresponding critical value – you just need to look at the p value. That's definitely a handier way to do it, thanks to the good old computer.*

Lecturer: *But remember, ultimately both approaches tell you the same thing, that is, whether or not you should reject the null hypothesis.*

Before reading on...

You may find it useful to look again at Chapter 7 (pp. 102, 116–19). Make sure you understand the points raised in the above dialogue and how they relate to those in Chapter 7.

... now read on

Student: *Mind you, a cut-off of .05 might be an acceptable level of risk in some psychology studies, but I'm not sure I would always want to risk making wrong decisions 5 per cent of the time. Also, if I were researching a cure for cancer, or trying to send a rocket to the moon, I would want to be much more confident than that.*

Lecturer: *Indeed. Remember that .05 is a cut-off that we deem to be an acceptable level of risk for general purposes. However, we are free to set any value of α that we wish. In fact, an alternative to α = .05 adopted in many psychology experiments is to set an α value of .01.*

Student: *So in these cases, the probability of a Type I error is reduced to 1 per cent?*

Lecturer: *Right. And in the case of research of the sort you mentioned, with critical consequences, we can reduce the probability of a Type I error as much as we like by setting very small α values, like .005, .001, .0001, and so on.*

Student: *Cool! But why don't we make the α value as small as we possibly can, so that we virtually never make a Type I error?*

Lecturer: *There is an important trade-off in doing this, as we shall see.*

Before reading on...

Read this dialogue again in conjunction with Figure 9.8. Make sure you can see the various linkages. Can you think what 'trade-off' the lecturer is talking about? Jot down your thoughts.

... now read on

Statistical power, reasonable confidence and Type II errors

While reducing the risk of a Type I error may be a laudable objective, this is only one side of a two-sided coin. Consider what happens when a researcher sets lower and lower significance levels. (In a sense, reducing the probability of wrongly rejecting the null hypothesis is achieved at the cost of making it less likely that you will

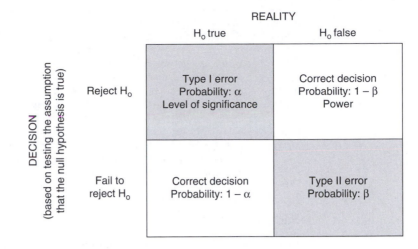

Figure 9.9 Decision errors, significance and power

reject the null hypothesis *at all*, whether it is true or false in reality.) While the risk of a Type I error may have been reduced, the corresponding reluctance to reject the null hypothesis increases the risk of retaining a null hypothesis that is, in reality, untrue – in other words, the probability of a Type II error.

In research, it is just as desirable to avoid Type II errors as it is to minimize Type I errors. The notion of statistical **power** is closely linked to that of Type II error. Power refers to the *probability that a researcher will reject the null hypothesis when it should be rejected*. Figure 9.9 summarizes the various relationships between power, Type II errors and statistical significance. By convention, the probability of a Type II error is denoted by the Greek letter β (pronounced 'bee-ta'), and statistical power by $1 - \beta$.

Student: So, by setting a very small level of significance, the chance of you failing to take seriously a 'real' result is decreased; that is, you reduce power.

Lecturer: Correct. However, it's more a matter of where to set the balance between Type I and Type II errors, as in the question posed earlier in this section, namely, Which is worse – acquitting a guilty person, or convicting an innocent one?

Student: I suppose it depends on the circumstances. If I were a clinical psychologist assessing the effectiveness of a new treatment with potentially harmful side-effects, I'd want to be pretty sure that it worked before cutting loose on my patients; so I would try to minimize the risk of a Type I error. In other circumstances, I may wish to be more speculative and accept a lower standard for statistical significance.

Lecturer: In thinking about this, you might find the following analogy useful. Suppose an astronomer has two telescopes – one quite weak but pretty reliable, the other very powerful but more prone to producing artefacts. Now, this astronomer thinks she may have discovered a new star. If so, she has calculated that it will appear in a particular part of the sky on a given evening. Which telescope would you suggest she uses?

Student: Well, ultimately, it depends on the reality of the situation; but she can't know this in advance.

Lecturer: Take me through the hypothetical scenario that, in reality, there is no new star.

Student: Right, say she assumes there is no star (that is, the null hypothesis is true), and in reality there isn't one. If she used the powerful telescope and saw something, she would reject the null hypothesis, but she would have made a Type I error, since it was an aberration. If she used the weaker telescope, she wouldn't see anything, and she'd be right not to reject the null hypothesis.

> *Lecturer*: Now, say there is a new star.
> *Student*: Well, she should still begin with the assumption that there isn't one. Now, if she used the powerful telescope, she would almost certainly see the new star – even if it were quite faint – and she would correctly reject the null hypothesis. On the other hand, if she used this weaker instrument and did not see anything – especially if the star were faint – she would conclude that there was no new star, thus making a Type II error.
> *Lecturer*: I hope you see statistical tests are like telescopes. Some are powerful and others less so. Powerful statistical tests have a greater ability than their more conservative counterparts to find an effect where one exists – even a weak effect. By the same token, they also increase the risk of a false-positive; that is, 'detecting' an effect where one does not exist. Less powerful methods reduce the risk of such false-positives, but are more likely to miss out, as it were.

Factors affecting power

Increasingly, it is recommended that you assess the likelihood that your experiment will detect an effect, if one exists, *before* carrying out the research. Power calculations are becoming more prevalent in published research, although they are still far from commonplace. As it happens, SPSS does not offer power calculations. Open source and strictly non-commercial software called G*Power 3 is a useful program for such calculations and can be readily downloaded from www.psycho.uni-duesseldorf.de/aap/projects/gpower/.

It is important at this stage that you have a conceptual grasp of the principles underlying its calculation. Several factors are known to affect statistical power, and these should be addressed when designing a study, whether experimental or observational.

Significance level

As we have already seen, the 'cut-off' α value chosen by the experimenter can have a major effect on statistical power. In short, the more stringent the level of significance, the less the power.

Effect size

It may go without saying that, if an effect exists, then the stronger that effect, the better your chances of detecting it. Thus, in assessing power, you need to get a handle on the magnitude of the effect. This information may be available in previously published research, or it may be calculated, or indeed estimated. There are several approaches to calculating **effect size**, although many of those textbooks that mention the topic tend to portray it as something of a black art. More recently, effect size has been proposed as important supplementary information to statistical significance as a way of assessing the importance of a result. We deal with this in some detail in the next chapter and thereafter.

Sample size

In preceding chapters, we have considered some of the implications of sample size for statistical tests. Overall, we conclude that larger samples provide better estimates of population values than smaller samples, and are less subject to the effects of outliers and other potentially harmful influences. In the context of statistical power, the larger the sample, the greater the power, which is especially important if an effect is moderate.

Choice of statistical test

As a rule of thumb, the so-called *parametric* tests, such as the *t*-test and Pearson *r*, are more powerful than their rank-based (*non-parametric*) equivalents. One obvious reason for this is the fact that the former use actual scores in the calculation of the statistic, and so are more sensitive to patterns within the data. On the flip side, they are more prone to distortion from extreme data, so may give an erroneous result.

Choice of experimental design

Repeated measures designs tend to be more powerful than equivalent independent groups designs, because of the emphasis they place on changes *within* the same individuals (tested under two conditions), rather than on overall differences *between* separate groups.

To sum up

It is advisable to consider these factors when designing a study. All other things being equal, identify a research question that previous research suggests may offer a reasonably strong effect; choose a repeated measures design; recruit as large a sample as possible; don't set your *α* value any higher than necessary; and, provided assumptions are met, analyse the data using parametric statistics. If only it were that simple!

Choosing the right statistical test

Saturday, 10.00 am

Salesman: Good day, Madam, can I be of assistance?
Client: I'd like to buy a car, but I'm having trouble making up my mind.
Salesman: I see. Perhaps I can be of some help.
*   What do you do for a living? (Investment broker)*
*   Do you have a spending figure in mind? (Flexible)*
*   Can I ask if you will be sharing the car with any other drivers? (My partner)*
*   Do you have any children? (No)*
*   How much driving do you do? (Lots)*
*   What's your favourite colour of car? (Yellow)*
*   What are you looking for in a car? (Sporty, fast, chic)*
*   Perhaps I can interest you in our latest German sports cars brochure. Step this way, Madam.*

Saturday, 10.25 am

Salesman: Good day, Madam, can I be of assistance?
Client: I'd like to buy a car, but I'm having trouble making up my mind.
Salesman: I see. Perhaps I can be of some help.
*   What do you do for a living? (Parent)*
*   Do you have spending figure in mind? (Not exactly, but limited)*
*   Do you have any children? (Five)*

> *How much driving do you do?* (Shops and schools mostly)
> *What's your favourite colour of car* (Anything that's not rusted)
> *What are you looking for in a car?* (Cheap, space for 2 adults, 5 kids, 2 dogs and can tow a caravan)
> *Ah, yes. I think there may be something out the back. Step this way, Madam. I don't know if you've heard, but converted second-hand buses are all the rage these days.*

We hear you ask, 'What has this got to do with choosing statistical tests?' Well, when choosing a new car, we find there are lots of different, models, types, colours, prices – many more than there are statistical tests in fact. Cars all do roughly the same thing – they get you from A to B. Some differences between models are major, some are merely subtle nuances, and others are technical. In spite of the choice being difficult at times, few people would argue that there should be fewer models of car from which to choose.

Contrast this with statistical tests. Students often claim to find the number and variety of statistical tests confusing: 'How do I decide which one to choose on any given occasion?' they ask. 'Why can't there just be one or two tests?' Sound familiar?

We agree that there do appear to be a lot of statistical tests and it's not always easy to choose between them. Try to think of it as a bit like choosing a car. Just as different cars suit different circumstances, in deciding upon a suitable statistical test, you have to take into account a number of factors.

What do we know so far?

In the first eight chapters of this book, we introduced and discussed all the ideas and concepts needed to inform your choice of statistical technique for simple experimental designs, be it for summarizing, displaying or analysing data. In Chapter 2 we presented a series of examples of methods used by psychologists to measure behaviour, and went on to consider the properties of the data generated by these methods. We discussed the characteristics of performance measures (dependent variables) in terms of their *levels of measurement* (nominal, ordinal, interval or ratio). We also considered variables under experimental control (independent variables).

In Chapter 3, we discussed different methods for summarizing and displaying single data sets, depending on the properties of the variable and the summary information required. We then elaborated these ideas in Chapters 4 and 5 to include comparisons, and relationships between two variables. Chapters 7 and 8 further extended this approach to include statistical methods for comparing and relating data.

Recall that, in Chapter 3, we discussed how the properties of our variable influence our choice of method for summarizing and displaying the data. For example, we showed that, when data contain outliers, the more *robust* or *resistant* median is a more sensible measure of average than the mean, and the semi-interquartile range a better indication of spread than standard deviation.

Chapter 4 discussed various methods of comparing groups of data. In the first two examples – *Hint, hint* (see p. 51) and *A question of taste* (see p. 52) – we saw that the dependent variables took the form of categories; that is, success/failure and favourite psychology module. The appropriate method for summarizing these nominal variables is to cross-tabulate the frequency or percentage of each response against the independent variable (*hint/no hint*, and *Arts/Science*). The resulting contingency tables clearly showed the extent to which responses were associated with (or *contingent* upon) the independent variable. So, in determining how data should be summarized, the property of the dependent variable is an important consideration.

The remaining examples in Chapter 4 used data in the form of numbers, rather than categories. We saw data displayed in terms of averages and spread. Importantly, these examples also illustrated how the *design* of a study determines the best methods of organizing and displaying results. Thus, in the independent groups example (*Quick on the draw*), the *overall* averages and variabilities of the two groups provided the basis for summarizing the data. On the other hand, in the repeated measures example (*Coffee time*), data were compared in terms of the *change* or difference in each individual's performance between the two conditions and the variability of these difference scores.

Before reading on...

Look over the examples in Chapter 4. If necessary, reread the comments above until you are satisfied that you understand the issues.

... now read on

Taking Chapters 4 and 5 together, you can see that, not only was the choice of method for organizing data influenced by the properties of the dependent variable and the experimental design, but also by the *question* to be asked of the data. Compare the *Coffee time* example at the end of Chapter 4 with any of the examples in Chapter 5. All these examples may be described as repeated measures design, in so far as the same participants are tested under two conditions. So, how does the *Coffee time* example differ from the others?

Student: *Is it because the independent variable in* Coffee time *is controlled by the experimenter, while all the others are subject variables?*

Lecturer: *No, but I can see what you're driving at. In any case, in the* Consistency *example in Chapter 5, the two Attitude to Computers tests were chosen, or controlled, by the experimenter.*

Student: *Ah, I missed that. I'm afraid I'm stumped.*

Lecturer: *Well, what do we want to know in the* Coffee time *example?*

Student: *Whether there is a difference in each participant's performance between the two treatments – coffee and no coffee.*

Lecturer: *Good. Now look at the examples in Chapter 5. What are we interested in this time?*

Student: *Ah, right, in all the examples there are two measures, and we want to know if participants who score highly on one measure also score highly on the other, and vice versa. Or, in some cases, like the* Party time *example, we want to know if those who score high on one measure score correspondingly low on the other measure, and vice versa.*

Lecturer: *Correct. It is a little long-winded. Can you put it more succinctly?*

Student: *Um... we want to know if there is a relationship between the two variables.*

Lecturer: *Good. So you see, this time, it's not just the design of the study that determines how we should examine the data, though that is important, but the* question *we are asking. Often the distinction is fairly clear, but not always. For example, in the* Height and weight *example, it makes no sense to ask whether people's heights differ from their weights – the only sensible question is whether they are related.*

Student: *Ah, but in the* Critical thinking *example, it makes sense to ask whether A's and B's judgements are related* and *whether they are different.*

Lecturer: *That's why you need to keep your wits about you.*

> *Student*: *Also, in the* Coffee time *example, are we not actually asking if there is a relationship between coffee-drinking and reaction time?*
> *Lecturer*: *Indeed. Remember that the term 'relationship' can be ambiguous. Think of it this way; in the* Coffee time *example, we are interested in a relationship between the independent variable – with only two levels, remember – and the dependent variable, reaction time. We examine this relationship by comparing performance across the two conditions. In the other examples, we are also interested in relationships, but this time between two measures, such as height and weight.*
> *Student*: *Ah, so in the Chapter 5 examples there are no independent variables as such, unlike the* Coffee time *study.*
> *Lecturer*: *Just so. Such studies are known as* **correlational designs**.

Summing up: Choosing the right test

> *Salesman*: *Good day Madam, can I be of assistance?*
> *Client*:   *I'd like to buy a statistical test, but I'm having trouble making up my mind.*
> *Salesman*: *I see. Perhaps I can be of some help.*
>   *What sort of scores do you have?* (Reaction times)
>   *What question do you wish to ...*

We hope you have been persuaded that choosing the appropriate statistical test is much more straightforward than you might at first have thought. Remember, it's a bit like buying a car – more straightforward than that, maybe! Just ask yourself a few basic questions. Figure 9.10 presents a schematic representation of the various statistical tests you have encountered so far. We recommend that you keep this flow chart handy and, as you encounter a test, use it to see where that test fits into the overall scheme.

As well as showing you the statistical landscape, the flow chart also helps you decide what statistical methods to use, and when. Simply begin at the top and work your way down. Note the three main branching points, shown as three 'layers' in the diagram.

1. What type of scores do I have?
    The big issue at this point is whether your dependent variable is in the form of categories (that is, a *nominal* variable), or a numerical scale (that is, an ordinal, interval or ratio variable). If the data are nominal, then the appropriate statistical methods are cross-tabulation and χ^2. You need go no further. On the other hand, if your scores are at least an ordinal scale, you need to ask two more questions.
2. What question do I want to answer?
    This question relates to the last student/lecturer dialogue. Here, you are asking about the type of question posed in your hypothesis, the important choice being *comparison* or *correlation*. As the lecturer in the dialogue points out, the answer is usually pretty obvious, but occasionally the distinction may be subtle and you need to exercise caution.

    For hypotheses concerned with a relationship between two sets of scores, the data should be organized and displayed as in Chapter 5, and the appropriate statistical test is some form of correlation coefficient. As we saw in Chapter 8, you have a choice between Pearson *r* and Spearman ρ, depending on your data. Again,

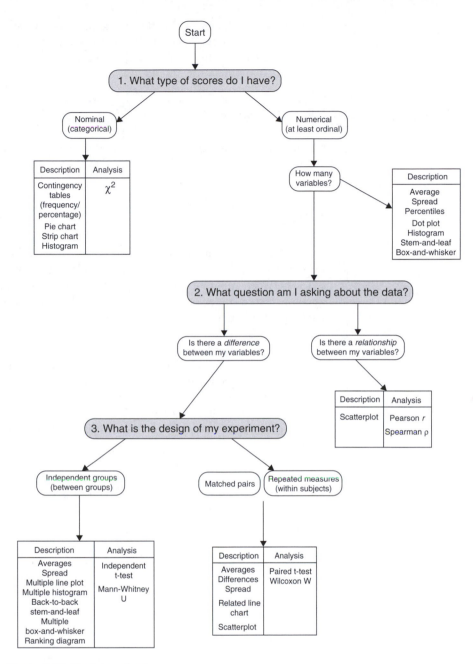

Figure 9.10 Decision chart

you need go no further. On the other hand, if your hypothesis is concerned with a difference between two sets of scores, you need to go down the route of comparison. In order to determine the appropriate form of comparison, you need to answer the next question.

3. What is the design of my study?

This question is asking how participants were assigned to the two conditions in your experiment. If each individual participated in only one of the two treatments (that is, independent samples), and there was no matching, your data should be displayed as shown in Chapter 4 (see pp. 55–59) and you should choose one of the tests in Chapter 7 (see pp. 109–129). Alternatively, if individuals contribute to both treatments (that is, repeated measures), or if participants are paired up (that is, matched pairs), you should take the 'related' part of the comparison branch.

Before reading on…

Spend some time studying Figure 9.9 and refer to the comments above. Try to ensure that you know why you should choose one branch of the chart rather than another.

… now read on

Chapter review

Using examples from Chapters 4 and 7, the anatomy of three basic experimental designs was explored. These were independent groups, in which comparisons are made between separate groups of participants; repeated measures, where a single group is tested under both experimental conditions; and matched pairs, in which participants are first pre-tested and then paired up on the basis of matching pre-test performances.

The relative merits and demerits of these designs were explored in respect of threats to their internal validity, most notably non-equivalent groups (in the case of independent groups designs) and transfer effects (in relation to repeated measures designs). Methods for coping with these threats to validity were also discussed. Concepts of statistical inference, first introduced in Chapter 6, were extended, and level of significance, Type I and Type II errors, and statistical power were elaborated.

Finally, advice on how to choose the right statistical test was given, and a decision chart showing the relationship between the various tests was presented. For ease of access, this is repeated on the inside front cover.

Other ways of assessing the importance of results

In this chapter

... relevant sections of Chapters 7 and 8 are revisited to allow consideration of further ways of making sense of data and statistical analysis. The use of confidence intervals is considered as an alternative, or as a supplement, to statistical significance, and effect size and statistical power are discussed. Graphical representation and interpretation of confidence intervals is also considered.

An alternative to significance: Confidence intervals

The term 'statistical significance' is much more specific than many people realize. It refers *solely* to the **null hypothesis approach** to statistical inference which we introduced in Chapter 6 (p. 93). All of our statistical examples so far have been based on this approach and you should by now be familiar with the underlying rationale:

- Begin by assuming the null hypothesis is true.

Then:

- Ask "how likely is it that I could have obtained my result (or an even more extreme result), *given the null hypothesis is true*"?
- The less likely it is that H_0 produced the result, the more evidence against H_0.
- Specifically, if the likelihood is .05 (5%) or less, then we reject H_0 as an explanation for the data.
- We conclude that there is a statistically significant result.

This approach to judging the significance of data has been dominant throughout the history of psychology and many other disciplines. Despite its ubiquity, it would be a mistake to assume that the approach is problem free. Indeed, more recently, null hypothesis testing has been subject to criticism. In particular, the slavish adherence to .05 and .01 as cut-off values in judging statistical significance has increasingly been criticized as rigid, formulaic and of limited value. Some have gone so far as to describe it as invalid.

> **Student:** *Are you saying that everything we have learned so far about statistical analysis is invalid?*
> **Lecturer:** *No, not quite! I suppose the best way to think about it is that the concept of statistical significance has limitations. But the null hypothesis approach has been around for well over a century and it will be around for many years to come.*
> **Student:** *So why are we considering an alternative?*
> **Lecturer:** *Well, first, because there is an alternative; indeed there are several useful ways of making sense of data and these are being used increasingly in published journal articles. So, it is a good idea to know about them.*
> **Student:** *Do these other methods tell us something different about our data than null hypothesis testing? If so, that's pretty worrying. Which approach should we use?*
> **Lecturer:** *That would be worrying. However, it's not that these other methods are telling us something different in the contradictory sense. As you might expect, if data are statistically significant, we would expect that to be reflected in other approaches to analysis.*
> **Student:** *So what's the point?*
> **Lecturer:** *Well, there are some unusual occasions when there is a mismatch between the outcomes of different analyses. But, more importantly, various methods present the results from different perspectives, so they tell you something slightly different. For example, some methods make it easier to compare different journal articles more directly than is possible with H_0 testing.*

Confidence intervals

Recall that the term *inferential statistics* gets its name from the fact that we collect a sample of data from our population of interest and use the results from this sample to draw conclusions, that is, to make inferences about the population as a whole. A popular approach in psychology is to calculate the sample mean and to use this as a specific estimate of the population mean, often referred to as a **point estimate**. It is of course unlikely that this estimate will equal the true population mean. As we saw in Chapter 6, if we were to draw several samples of the same size from a population, the summary statistics for each are likely to differ from the others and, in relatively rare cases, may differ markedly from the others. Given this **sample variation**, the question arises as to how **representative** a particular sample is of the **parent population**.

Lecturer: Can you suggest how we might go about quantifying how representative a sample may be of its parent population?

Student: Wow, haven't a clue! I can see how the summary statistics we calculate tell us about the characteristics of a sample, but I can't imagine how I would go about assessing how representative the sample is of a population as a whole.

Lecturer: OK, let's think about it systematically. What do we mean by **representative** here?

Student: Well, I suppose the main issue would be whether or not the average for a sample accurately reflects the average for the population.

Lecturer: Good so far. It is the case that the representativeness of a sample is assessed in terms of the similarity of its average – usually the mean – to that of the population. OK, so how would we express such similarity?

Student: Hmm, well, we could work out the difference between our sample mean and the population mean – the bigger the difference, the less representative.

Lecturer: OK, not bad, but there is a snag here. We don't actually know the population mean. Remember, we are relying entirely on the sample data to say something about the population.

Student: Right. That kind of limits our options. How about if we say that our population mean will be 'at or around' our sample mean?

Lecturer: Excellent! Actually, in practice, what we do is to define 'at or around' by creating a range, or **interval**, around the sample mean that has a high probability of capturing the population mean.

Student: I suppose, the wider we make this range, the more confident we can be that it would contain the population mean, the narrower the range, the less confident we would be.

Lecturer: Precisely, although we would not want the range to be so wide that it ceases to be useful. Incidentally, there is a technical term for this range – a **confidence interval**.

As the lecturer and student discussed above, a confidence interval is a range estimated from your sample data (known as an **interval estimate**) which can be assumed to capture the population mean *most of the time*. Note that we say most of the time, not always. Just as in the case of statistical significance, where we can be wrong on some (5% or fewer) occasions, we can also fail altogether to capture the population mean in our estimated range on some occasions.

As noted above, the bigger the range we set, the more likely it is that we will have captured the population mean, and if we were to make the interval infinitely wide, we would be certain to capture it, although the range would be pretty useless in telling us much about the population. So obviously, we have to strike a balance and try to set a range that allows us to be as confident as we reasonably can be that we have captured the population mean – hence the term *confidence interval*. It might not surprise you that the level of confidence is, by convention, 95% or 99% (analogous to .05 and .01 levels of significance) depending upon how stringent we wish to be.

Thus, the confidence referred to in confidence interval is the percentage of time that we will be successful in capturing the population mean within our estimated range. So, for a 95% confidence interval, the estimated range of the dependent variable will contain the population mean 95% of the time, and 5% of the time it will not.

For those who wish to dig a little deeper

Alert

In our description of confidence intervals above, we have touched upon, some would say we have committed, a common error. Indeed, for this reason, we have been careful to use the term 'capture' when referring to the population mean, although we accept that this will not satisfy those who correctly argue that, strictly speaking, our description is erroneous. Let's consider the issue in a little more depth.

When we use sample data to estimate a population mean, almost by definition, we do so because we usually do not know the true value of the population mean. However, in the real world, this true mean exists and is fixed, whether or not we know it. It can be argued therefore that, for any given sample data, the associated confidence interval either does or does not contain the true mean, that is, with a probability of 1 (does contain the population mean) or 0 (does not). Strictly, therefore, it is not correct to think in terms of a confidence interval with a specified probability (say .95) of including the population mean.

In order to clarify what we may mean by the phrase '*95% confident that our interval contains the population mean*', consider the following example. Let's suppose that, in the real world, the true mean *Attitude to Computer* score for the entire population of students is 58.25. Suppose also that we have collected *Attitude to Computers* scores for 20 different samples of 6 students and that we have calculated the mean and 95% confidence interval for each sample (the method for calculating a confidence interval is described later in this chapter). The resulting 20 confidence intervals may look something like those in Figure 10.1 which also shows the population mean.

Lecturer: What do you notice about the confidence intervals in Figure 10.1?
Student: Well, they all cluster around the population mean, but they do not do so exactly. Each is to the right or left to a greater or lesser extent.
Lecturer: Correct, and that is as expected. Each interval is centred on its own sample mean. Anything else?
Student: The actual intervals are different in width – some are much wider than others. Why is that?
Lecturer: That's because the data in each sample vary to a greater or lesser extent. Samples with greater variability lead to wider confidence intervals due to the greater uncertainty inherent in more variable data sets – for these sets we need a wider interval to achieve the same level of confidence as for less variable sets. What else do you see?
Student: Oh yes, all but one of the intervals contains the population mean. The third sample from the top does not coincide with the true mean.
Lecturer: Correct! The limits of the third sample do not capture the population mean. So, for 20 samples, one does not contain the true mean and nineteen do. Is there another way to say that?
Student: How about – 5% of intervals do not contain the population mean and 95% do?
Lecturer: Well done – and this is consistent with the fact that these are 95% confidence intervals.
Student: So, when we say that there is a probability that a given interval will capture the population mean, we are indicating that, if we were to collect lots and lots of intervals, 95% of the intervals would capture the true mean and 5% would not?
Lecturer: Precisely, and this is a very important clarification.

It may be helpful to think about Figure 10.1 as follows. Imagine you are at a fairground and one of the games involves tossing rings at a vertical peg. To win, the ring has to fall over the peg and encircle it. Imagine also that you are handed 20 pegs of different sizes, one after the other. As it happens, you are very good at the game and you manage to encircle the peg nineteen times, only missing the peg once. This is an analogy for the statistical exercise represented in Figure 10.1, where the experimenter 'tosses' 20 confidence intervals of different sizes at the population mean.

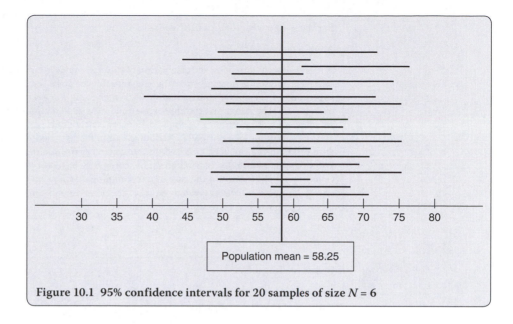

Population mean = 58.25

Figure 10.1 95% confidence intervals for 20 samples of size *N* = 6

Calculating a confidence interval

In order to construct a confidence interval, we need briefly to remind ourselves about the *standard error of the mean* introduced in Chapter 6 (p. 90). Recall that when we think about the spread of data within a sample, we are considering the variability of individual data and we quantify this variability using the standard deviation. Here, however, we are concerned, *not* with the individual data, but instead with the mean of these data. Specifically, we wish to know something about how the means of lots of similar random samples from the same population would be expected to 'behave'.

As we saw in Chapter 6, we can construct a distribution of these sample means, known as a *sampling distribution*. A useful property of such a distribution is that we can use the standard deviation of our single sample to work out the spread of sample means (the *standard error*, or SE, for short) within the sampling distribution. In Chapter 6, we did this for the twenty-seven *Attitude to Computers* scores by dividing the standard deviation for the sample by the square root of the sample size, as follows:

$$SE = \frac{sd}{\sqrt{N}} = \frac{7.85}{\sqrt{27}} = \frac{7.85}{5.196} = \mathbf{1.51}$$

Having obtained the spread of mean scores in the sampling distribution (standard error), we can now use this measure to calculate the confidence interval for the population mean. This is the same calculation that we carried out in Chapter 6 (p. 91). There we noted that the standard error was simply another standard deviation and, therefore, we know that 95% of the sample means lie within the range ±1.96 standard errors around our sample mean. Given a sample mean of 57.3 and our standard error of 1.51, the 95% confidence interval will be 57.3 ± 1.96 × 1.51, giving the interval 54.34 to 60.26. So, based on our sample of 27 students, we can conclude with 95% confidence that the mean *Attitude to Computers* score for all students is captured by the interval 54.34 to 60.26.

For those who wish to dig a little deeper

Alert (a technical caveat)

We have slightly simplified the calculation of the confidence interval by assuming that the sampling distribution is normally distributed. Actually, for large samples, the normal distribution approximates the actual (*t*) distribution extremely well. For relatively small samples, such as ours, it should be noted that the approximation is less good, although, in practice, for all but the smallest samples (less than 15–20) the difference is negligible.

The assumption of a normally distributed sampling distribution allows us to use ±1.96 standard errors in the calculation, based on our general definition of standard deviation where we know that, in a normally distributed set of scores, 95% of scores lie within 1.96 standard deviations around the mean. (In the case of our sampling distribution of means, strictly, this is only true if our mean of means is *exactly* equal to the population mean of means. In general, though, it is acceptable to use ±1.96 standard errors.)

Before reading on...

Now calculate the 99% confidence interval for the 27 *Attitude to Computers* scores. What do you notice about this interval compared to the 95% interval?

... now read on

We hope that you will have realized that, as for all measures of standard deviation (in this case, standard error), 99% of the means will lie in the range ±2.58 standard errors (to 2 decimal places) around our sample mean. Hence, the 99% confidence interval will be 57.3 ± 2.58 × 1.51, giving the interval 53.40 to 61.20. Inevitably, the greater confidence of capturing the population mean has come at the cost of a less precise interval (7.80) than previously (5.92). Since the sample data are attitudes towards computing, this is probably no big deal, but, if the study were concerned with the efficacy of a cancer treatment, then the drop in accuracy may have real consequences.

Student: I have to say, a lot of this reminds me of the stuff we did earlier about statistical significance – I mean, with all the talk of 95% and 99% confidence, and the probability that we will be correct in estimating that the population mean will lie within a particular range. Sounds a lot like .05 and .01 to me.

Lecturer: In many ways that's a fair comment. There is indeed some overlap between the two.

Student: So why is it necessary to introduce a different way of looking at data? Are there any advantages of approaching it this way? It just seems to be adding to the confusion.

Lecturer: Trust me, there are good reasons for you to know about confidence intervals. One advantage relates to our basic need to make sense of our data. If nothing else it reminds us that our sample mean is merely an estimate of the population mean and that there is a degree of error involved, sometimes quite substantial error.

Student: OK, but we can be aware of this when we test the null hypothesis, since significance levels are about the probability of making an error.

Lecturer: Yes, that's true, but a significance test does not give you any information about the likely value of the population mean. I admit that the case for an alternative approach is perhaps not very convincing so far, since our discussion has been restricted to a single sample. When we come to consider confidence intervals associated with comparisons between two or more samples, you will see further advantages.

Making sense of SPSS

Calculating confidence intervals for a single sample

Note: We recommend you also consult Brace et al. (2009), pp. 64–67 who present further information on this topic.

At this point, we introduce a further SPSS routine, **Explore…**, that provides confidence intervals as well as the summary statistics we obtained previously. (We have already commented that a potentially confusing feature of SPSS, especially for students learning about statistics, is that the same statistics may be obtained using different routines.)

We pick up this example at the point of obtaining the summary statistics. If you need to be reminded of the process for coding data, look back at Chapter 3 (pp. 35–38).

Click on **Analyze** in the top menu bar and drag down to select **Descriptive Statistics > Explore…**

The following dialogue box will appear. Simply move *Attitude to Computers* from the box on the left to the **Dependent List:** box by highlighting it and clicking on the arrow. Also, for this exercise, select **Statistics** in the **Display** box near the bottom.

Next, click on the **Statistics…** button near the top right hand corner of the window to reveal the following dialogue window:

Here you will see that the **Descriptives** option is already selected. You can also select the desired level of confidence for your interval – the default is 95%. You can experiment with different confidence levels yourself. Here, we keep 95% confidence. Ignore the other options. Click **Continue**.

Click **OK**.

The table below will appear in the **SPSS Statistics Viewer**. Note that the standard error is 1.510 as calculated above. You will also see the descriptive statistics obtained in Chapter 3, as well as several others (don't worry about the measures Skewness, Kurtosis or 5% Trimmed Mean), including the upper and lower values of the 95% confidence interval (54.19 and 60.40). You will notice that these are very slightly different from those which we calculated by hand. This is because SPSS uses the t distribution rather than the normal distribution as we have done (remember, for larger samples, the two distributions are effectively identical. The t distribution is more exact for samples less than 100 or so, but the difference is very small (for our sample of 27, the SE is multiplied by 2.06 rather than 1.96). Don't worry about this technical detail – our aim is that you understand the concept of confidence intervals without additional complexities that may get in the way.

Descriptives

			Statistic	Std. Error
Attitude to Computers	Mean		57.30	1.510
	95% Confidence Interval for Mean	Lower Bound	54.19	
		Upper Bound	60.40	
	5% Trimmed Mean		57.30	
	Median		57.00	
	Variance		61.601	
	Std. Deviation		7.849	
	Minimum		43	
	Maximum		71	
	Range		28	
	Interquartile Range		13	
	Skewness		.059	.448
	Kurtosis		−.918	.872

Confidence in various statistical procedures

In this section, we take the idea of confidence intervals further by considering their use in statistical analysis of more than a single data sample. The use of confidence intervals is most commonly reported for statistics that compare differences between treatments and is less frequently reported for correlation. Here, we confine our attention to comparison tests whose confidence intervals are more intuitive to calculate. Although it is entirely appropriate to calculate such intervals for correlation, the procedure is less transparent and, in our opinion, may impede understanding of the general concept.

It is generally impractical to calculate confidence intervals by hand, so we assume you have access to a software package in order to obtain relevant confidence intervals. Here, we use SPSS to illustrate their use in statistical analysis. In order to do this, we revisit the statistical procedures presented in Chapter 7. Where possible, we consider how confidence intervals can offer a different way of determining the importance of a result. Note, that not all comparison tests can be viewed from the perspective of confidence intervals, at least not usefully for your purposes. In these cases (χ^2 and other rank-based comparison tests), the analyses have not been included.

Chapter 7 revisited: Comparing

Comparison between independent groups: Video/no video

In Chapter 7 (pp. 119–124) we showed how to use SPSS to carry out an independent t-test to compare *Attitude to Computers* scores for *video* and *no video* conditions. Recall that two sets of data were analysed, A and B, one producing a significant and the other a non-significant result.

> **Before reading on...**
>
> If you need reminded of the details, look back at this example.
>
> **... now read on**

The tables presenting the results of the independent t-test for data set A are shown again in Figure 10.2. In the first table, you will see that the mean score for the *video* condition is 72.00, compared to 64.00 for *no video*, a difference of 8.00. As you should be aware by now, the independent t-test assesses the magnitude of the difference between the means of the two conditions in relation to the overall variability within each condition. In the resulting table, note that, on the right hand side, lower and upper values are given for the 95% confidence interval of the **difference between means**.

Conceptually, this confidence interval is somewhat different from the single sample example described above. Here, rather than providing an estimate of a population mean, the logic here is based on what might be expected if we were to carry independent t-tests on lots of similar sets of two unrelated samples. If we were to do this in practice, for each set, the difference between the two samples would be calculated and a sampling distribution of these differences would be constructed. As in the single sample example, upper and lower confidence limits would then be calculated using the overall mean of the differences and the standard error of the differences. Fortunately, it is possible to derive the confidence interval theoretically, the technicalities of which need not concern you.

Group Statistics		N	Mean	Std. Deviation	Std. Error Mean
	Video condition				
Att to Computers A	video	10	72.00	4.619	1.461
	no video	10	64.00	4.876	1.542

Independent Samples Test

		Levene's Test for Equality of Variances		t-test for Equality of Means						
									95% Confidence Interval of the Difference	
		F	Sig.	t	df	Sig. (2-tailed)	Mean Difference	Std. Error Difference	Lower	Upper
Att to Computers A	Equal variances assumed	.169	.686	3.767	18	.001	8.000	2.124	3.538	12.462
	Equal variances not assumed			3.767	17.947	.001	8.000	2.124	3.537	12.463

Figure 10.2 Data set A: SPSS summary of independent *t*-test for *video/no video* example

---

Before reading on...

Look at the confidence interval in the table (equal variances assumed, since Levene's test is not significant). Reflect on what the values mean. What does the confidence interval tell us about the importance of the result? Compare your reasoning to that of the student in the dialogue below.

... now read on

Lecturer: As you can see in the results table, the confidence interval for the difference between means is 3.538 to 12.462. What does this say to you?

Student: Well, the first thing that strikes me is that that's a pretty wide interval – from about three and a half to twelve and a half. And the 99% confidence interval would be even wider.

Lecturer: Fair point. The difference between our two independent samples was 8.0, so the interval is roughly 4.5 above and below our obtained sample difference. Now, what does this interval tell us?

Student: I think it tells us that we can be 95% confident that the true difference between the two treatments lies between 3.538 and 12.462. Beyond that, I'm not sure what it means. I realize that the t-test itself was statistically significant with p = .001, but I can't map that onto the confidence interval if you see what I mean.

Lecturer: Yes, I see. Although confidence intervals in themselves do not directly address statistical significance, they should allow us to say something about the importance of the data consistent with the statistical significance of the result.

Student: I'm afraid I'm a bit stumped in making a connection between the two.

Lecturer: OK, let's take it step-by-step. Consider if, in reality, there was absolutely no effect of showing a video on attitude to computers. What would you expect the true difference between the video and no video two means to be?

Student: Zero?

Lecturer: Correct. Now, look at the confidence limits for the true difference between the means. What do you notice?

Student: Ah, got it! Our confidence interval does not contain the value zero. So we can be 95% confident that the true value is greater than zero.

Lecturer: Precisely! More generally, if the confidence limits are either both positive or both negative – because, remember, t values can be negative if you arbitrarily subtract the large mean from the small mean – then we may infer that the result is 'significant', since neither interval includes zero. However, if one limit is negative and the other positive, then the confidence interval includes zero, so the true value of the difference might be zero.

Figure 10.3 confirms this conclusion regarding the presence of zero within a confidence interval of differences between the mean. Here, despite identical mean scores to data set A, the analysis of data set B shows a non-significant result with $p = .084$. As noted in Chapter 7, the lack of significance is due to the greater variability of scores within each condition. This time, the confidence interval for the difference between means goes from -1.190 to 17.190, giving a much wider interval than before of 16.00. More importantly, one of the limits of the interval is negative and the other positive, indicating that the confidence interval contains zero. Thus, this time, the true value of the difference might be zero.

Graphing confidence intervals

It is common, and is rapidly becoming an absolute expectation, for graphical representations of data, such as those in the example above, to include some visual indication of the variability or 'error' in the data. Commonly used graphs such a bar charts or line graphs are increasingly expected to display so-called **error bars** based on one of several common measures of error. One such measure is the 95% confidence interval; others are the standard deviation and the standard error of the mean.

Interestingly, in spite of the increasing importance placed on the use of error bars in graphs by journal reviewers and editors, it has been reported that few consumers of published research can actually interpret their meaning. Take, for example, the bar charts in Figure 10.4. These show the mean scores for the *video* and *no video* conditions for data sets A and B from the example above. The error bars represent the 95% confidence intervals for each condition. (Bear in mind that these are the separate confidence intervals for the means of the two conditions as distinct from the confidence interval for the difference between the means reported in the independent *t*-test in the example above.)

For convenience, we have included a dotted arrow on each graph to indicate the extent of overlap between the two error bars. It should be clear that, for data set A, there is no overlap between the error bars while, for data set B, there is clear overlap.

Group Satistics					
	Video Condition	**N**	**Mean**	**Std. Deviation**	**Std. Error Mean**
Att to Computers B	video	10	72.00	9.068	2.867
	no video	10	64.00	10.446	3.303

Independent Samples Test										
		Levene's Test for Equality of Variances		**t-test for Equality of Means**						
									95% Confidence Interval of the Difference	
		F	**Sig.**	**t**	**df**	**Sig. (2-tailed)**	**Mean Difference**	**Std. Error Difference**	**Lower**	**Upper**
Att to Computers B	Equal variances assumed	.350	.561	1.829	18	.084	8.000	4.374	−1.190	17.190
	Equal variances not assumed			1.829	17.651	.084	8.000	4.374	−1.203	17.203

Figure 10.3 Data set B: SPSS summary of independent *t*-test for *video/no video* example

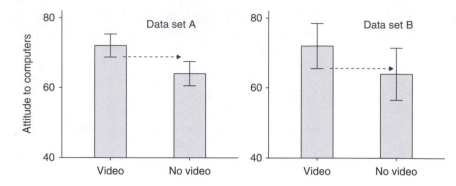

Figure 10.4 Data sets A and B: Bar charts and 95% confidence intervals for *video/no video* example

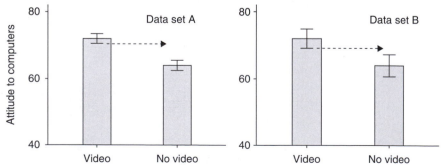

Student: Ah, so that's what the error bars show! If they do not overlap, then the result is significant; if they do, the result is not significant.

Lecturer: That is certainly the case here. However, it is not quite as simple as that. First, bear in mind that there are different types of error bar and you need to be clear which type you are looking at on any occasion.

Student: Right, the error bars here are the 95% confidence intervals. So the rule applies for this type?

Lecturer: No, not always, although it is the case here.

Student: Oh dear! Not as straightforward as I thought.

Lecturer: Look at the graphs in Figure 10.5. This time, instead of 95% confidence intervals, the error bars show standard errors. What do you notice?

Student: Wow! This time, the error bars do not overlap for either data set. This suggests that the means differ significantly for both data sets, except we know that the difference for data set B is non-significant.

Lecturer: It should be clear, therefore, that we need some rules of thumb for interpreting error bars. Without going into the technical details, the following rules of thumb apply:

> For 95% confidence intervals, the bars can overlap by as much as 25% of the total length of the bars in order for the means to remain significantly different. In Figure 10.4, for data set B, the overlap is greater than 25% of the bar length, so the difference between means is not significant.
>
> For standard errors, if the bars abut exactly or overlap to any extent, then the means do not differ significantly. Also, the means do differ significantly if the standard error bars are separated by a minimum of half of the length of the bars. In Figure 10.5, for data set B, although the bars do not overlap, the separation is less than half of the bar length, so, again, the difference between means is not significant.

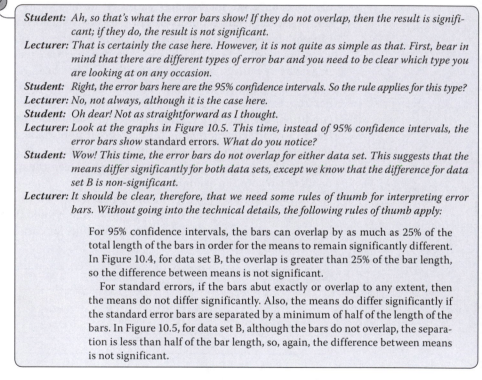

Figure 10.5 Data sets A and B: Bar charts and standard error bars for *video/no video* example

Comparison within paired data: Let your fingers do the talking

Chapter 7 (pp. 133–136) presented an SPSS analysis of two data sets, A and B, using the paired *t*-test. In this example, the typing speed (in words per minute, wpm) of participants was measured before and after a tea-break. Again, data set A produced a statistically significant result while data set B did not.

> **Before reading on...**
>
> If you need reminded of the details, look back at this example.
>
> ... **now read on**

Figures 10.6 and 10.7 show the outcome of these analyses for data sets A and B respectively. As in the independent groups example, the mean difference between the two conditions is the same (5.00 wpm), while the variability is greater in data set B. For data set A (Figure 10.3), the confidence interval for the difference reflects the statistical significance of the result, with both upper and lower limits negative, indicating that zero is not captured within the confidence interval. Thus, there is a 95% chance that the true difference between the two treatments is between −7.375 and −2.625 (the minus sign indicating that participants produced more words per minute after a tea-break).

In contrast, data set B, which produced a non-significant result, has confidence limits of −10.325 and 0.325 (one negative and one positive), an interval which does capture zero, although only just. Again, this is consistent with the marginal nature of the result, which just fails to reach significance. Note too that, in order to achieve

Paired Samples Test

		Paired Differences							
					95% Confidence Interval of the Difference				Sig. (2-tailed)
		Mean	Std. Deviation	Std. Error Mean	Lower	Upper	t	df	
Pair 1	Before tea-break − After tea-break	−5.000	4.457	1.114	−7.375	−2.625	−4.487	15	.000

Figure 10.6 Data set A: SPSS summary of paired *t*-test for *before/after tea-break* example

Paired Samples Test

		Paired Differences							
					95% Confidence Interval of the Difference				Sig. (2-tailed)
		Mean	Std. Deviation	Std. Error Mean	Lower	Upper	t	df	
Pair 1	Before tea-break − After tea-break	−5.000	9.993	2.498	−10.325	.325	−2.001	15	.064

Figure 10.7 Data set B: SPSS summary of paired *t*-test for *before/after tea-break* example

the same level of confidence (95%), the width of the interval has to be much greater than for data set A (10.65 vs 4.75).

Alert

Do not plot confidence intervals or other error bars when graphing means of paired data

Although plotting error bars is useful for comparing means of unrelated data, such as in the *video/no video* example earlier in this chapter, they are much trickier for paired data. Figure 10.8 illustrates the problem using typing speed for 7 data pairs. Each participant's performance is represented by a black line joining their score in the *before* condition with that in the *after*. In the left hand graph, the trend from *before* to *after* is the same for all participants (and, in fact the difference between means is statistically significant). In the right hand graph, the trend is highly variable across participants (and the difference is not at all statistically significant). In both cases, however, the means and error bars (95% confidence intervals) are identical.

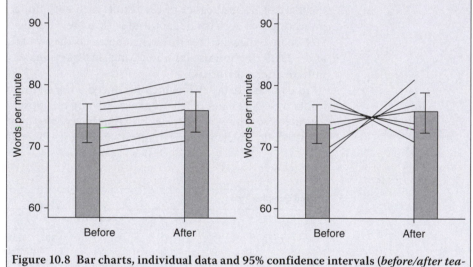

Figure 10.8 Bar charts, individual data and 95% confidence intervals (*before/after tea-break, N = 7*)

Effect size

The concept of *effect size* was introduced briefly in Chapter 9 as one of the factors influencing *statistical power*. Not surprisingly, then, effect size and statistical power are closely related and both provide important contexts for interpreting statistical significance. The use of effect size alongside statistical significance has burgeoned in published psychological research over the last few years, although effect size is often reported formulaically, something for which the reporting of statistical significance has been criticized. A further problem, or so it seems to us, is that, to date, coverage in textbooks has been patchy and at times vague, not to say inconsistent.

Student: Blimey, just when I think I might have cracked confidence intervals, along comes another way of thinking about data. Why do we need a measure called effect size *and what does it offer that significance does not?*

Lecturer: Well, you probably already know some of the answer. Think about what statistical significance tells us, or more importantly, does not tell us.

Student: I think we touched on this earlier in this chapter. I suppose the main issue is that statistical significance is merely a cut-off for rejecting H_0 as an explanation for a result. If p is less than .05, we reject H_0, if it is greater, we fail to reject it. It doesn't really tell us more than that.

Lecturer: Correct, and that is at the root of the problem. Many people who carry out statistical tests, including some experienced researchers, merely scan their analysis for the 'sacred' p value and ignore everything else. It is important to make sense of data and statistics in the fullest sense.

Student: And do effect sizes help us do this?

Lecturer: Yes they do. Let me put it like this. Say a researcher is interested in whether a new drug helps alleviate severe anxiety. A p value will indicate whether the new drug is significantly better than an older drug, or a placebo, or psychotherapy, etc. But it will not indicate how much *better*. This would be a major issue if, for example, the new drug cost vastly more than the old one.

Student: Well, if it's significantly better, does that not mean that it's much better?

Lecturer: Not necessarily. Remember some of the things you already know about what influences whether a result is significant or not – try listing them.

Student: Well, I know that, if the sample size is bigger, then some statistical values do not have to be very big to be significant. I've also seen that, depending on the variability within samples, the same difference between means can produce a result that is either significant or not. Oh, and some statistical tests are more likely to give you a significant result than others, for example parametric rather than rank-based tests. Yes, and some tests can be distorted by outliers and give a significant result, especially if the sample size is small.

Lecturer: That's plenty to be going on with! The important point is that there are so many things that can influence whether a result reaches statistical significance or not, that you can conclude little without looking at the result more closely. Effect size is one way of getting a handle on how impressive or not a result is.

Measuring effect size

You may already have gathered that there is not a single measure of effect size. As with other statistics, the choice will depend on the nature of the data, its structure and the research question you wish to answer. Measures of effect size need not be complex, and most are not. In fact, in certain circumstances, they may be very rudimentary, such as the simple difference between two means when comparing two samples. For example, if it were reported that boys and girls differed in verbal intelligence by 9.5 IQ points, to a qualified psychologist, this difference would be readily interpretable in terms of the strength of the effect, given what is known about IQ scores. On the other hand, a simple difference would not be as meaningful if the dependent variable were measured on a more arbitrary scale, so, for example, a raw difference between male and female students on *Attitude to Computers* of, say, 6.8 would not convey much about the size of the effect. Below, as in the previous section, we revisit the statistical tests reported in Chapter 7, and in this case Chapter 8. Where possible, we obtain appropriate measures of effect size and consider how these may offer a different perspective to a result.

Chapter 7 revisited: Comparing

Comparing proportions and A question of taste

In Chapter 7 (pp. 100–109), we considered two examples of how to analyse data consisting of two nominal variables. The first example was a simple 2 × 2 cross-tabulation of gender (male, female) and computer experience (yes, no). The second was a larger 2 × 4 contingency table comparing arts and science students on their preference for one of four courses (psycholinguistics, social, stats, HCI). For each example, we used χ^2 to analyse the strength of the imbalance between the groups in terms of their response to either computer experience or favourite course.

Before reading on...

If you need reminded of the details, look back at these examples.

... now read on

For the first example, we obtained a χ^2 value of 5.255, which exceeded the critical value of χ^2 at the .05 level of significance. Subsequent SPSS analysis revealed an exact *p* value of .022, suggesting that the probability of the null hypothesis having produced this result was 2.2%. The analysis therefore indicated that there was a significant difference between males and females in their experience of computers prior to entering university.

Although this result was significant, however, we do not know whether the effect is large enough to cause concern. There are several options for assessing the effect size of contingency data such as these, namely, the Phi statistic (Φ), Cramer's *V* (yes, named after (Harald) Cramer, a famous Swedish statistician) and the Contingency coefficient. All three are quite closely related and, often, the choice is arbitrary. Generally, Cramer's *V* is preferable to the Contingency coefficient, which is really best suited to 2 × 2 contingency data. So, all in all, Cramer's *V* is probably the best bet. As with many statistics, these are provided by a variety of software packages. In Figure 10.9, we present those produced by SPSS and the method for obtaining them is shown below for those who wish to know this.

The three measures presented in Figure 10.9 are basically correlations, a special case of Pearson's *r* to be precise. All three measures are very close (two are identical), which is a relief, since they are all measuring the same effect. It would appear that the effect size is small, in spite of its statistical significance. As with *r*, we can also obtain a measure of the proportion of variation attributable to the relationship by squaring any of the statistics. Here, Φ^2 is .03, indicating that 3% of the variation can be attributed to the association between gender and computer experience. In practical terms, then, not too much to be concerned about, we would suggest!

Symmetric Measures		Value	Approx. Sig.
Nominal by nominal	Phi	−.181	.022
	Cramer's V	.181	.022
	Contingency coefficient	.178	.022
N of valid cases		159	

Figure 10.9 *Comparing proportions*: **Measures of effect size**

Making links

Student: I'm a little bit confused. Here we have a result that is statistically significant but has a small effect size, accounting for only 3% of the variance. Is this not contradictory?

Lecturer: I know what you mean, but it would only be contradictory if there were a very solid link between effect size and statistical significance. Although they are often consistent, they do not have to be, and this is an example of that.

Student: So why is it inconsistent in this case?

Lecturer: The answer most probably lies in the statistical power *associated with this analysis.* Recall from Chapter 9 that one of the major factors in determining power is the sample size – the larger the sample, the more powerful. In this example there were 159 participants in the 2 × 2 contingency table, which is pretty large.

Student: So, if we had a much smaller number of participants, we might not have obtained a significant result with the same effect size?

Lecturer: Correct. So here, the sample size has increased the chances of detecting a significant result, despite the small effect size.

Student: Cool!

Making sense of SPSS

Obtaining measures of effect size when comparing proportions

Look back at the SPSS procedure for these examples (pp. 103–108). Here, we need only add the method for obtaining the measures of effect size.

At the point where the **Crosstabs** dialogue box is obtained and the **Statistics ...** button is clicked (p. 105), select **Contingency coefficient** and **Phi and Cramer's V** in the box labeled **Nominal** as shown (in Chapter 7, you had been instructed only to select 'Chi-square').

The table shown in Figure 10.9 above will appear for the *Comparing proportions* example.

For *A question of taste*, Figure 10.10 shows the effect sizes. Here, Φ and V are .389, which can be considered a moderate effect size, and, by squaring the statistic we

Symmetric Measures		Value	Approx. Sig.
Nominal by nominal	Phi	.389	.001
	Cramer's V	.389	.001
	Contingency coefficient	.362	.001
N of valid cases		116	

Figure 10.10 *A question of taste*: **Measures of effect size**

obtain .151, indicating that 15.1% of the variation is attributable to the association between *faculty* and *favourite course*.

We have some degree of inconsistency, although not nearly as much as in the last example. Again, the result of a highly significant result (*p* = .001), despite a moderate effect size, was very likely due to the enhanced statistical power resulting from a decent sample size of 116.

Comparison between independent groups: Video / no video

We return to the *video / no video* example introduced in Chapter 7 and revisited above. Recall again that two sets of data were analysed, A and B, one producing a significant, and the other a non-significant, result.

> **Before reading on...**
>
> If you need reminded of the details, look back at this example.
>
> **... now read on**

Figure 10.11 shows again the SPSS summary tables for the *t*-test carried out on data set A. Here, we see that the difference between the means of the two conditions is 8.00, the confidence interval for the population mean difference is 3.538 to 12.462, and the result is statistically significant with *p* = .001. *However, we still do not know if this result has any practical importance.* Is a mean difference of 8.00 in *Attitude to Computers* small or large? In order to answer this question, we need to obtain an appropriate measure of effect size. In fact, there are several statistics suitable for assessing the effect size of the difference between two means. Here, we consider the two most commonly used. The first, Cohen's *d* (named after American psychologist and statistical pioneer (Jacob) Cohen), will not surprise you, the second, Pearson's *r*, may.

Cohen's *d*

As you can see from Figure 10.11, there is no default measure of effect size provided in the SPSS summary. Somewhat astonishingly, there is no option to select it either, so we have to calculate effect size by hand. Fortunately, the calculation of Cohen's *d* is very straightforward, so let's jump in right away with the formula, beginning with the conceptual formula:

$$d = \frac{\text{difference between sample means}}{\text{standard deviation of two samples combined}}$$

> *Student:* This looks very like the independent t formula we saw in Chapter 7 on page 112.
> *Lecturer:* You are right that there is a strong overlap between the two, but there is a crucial difference. Can you see it?
> *Student:* Ah, the bottom line of the formula is different, for the t-test, the variability measure is based on the standard error of the difference between means, whereas, for Cohen's d, it is simply a combination of the standard deviations for each sample.
> *Lecturer:* Well done – remember, the t-test is based on a sampling distribution of difference of random samples from a population based on the null hypothesis. Cohen's d is simply a one-off calculation based on our particular sample data.
> *Student:* OK, so how does it tell us about the effect size?
> *Lecturer:* Read on and find out!

Group Statistics

	Video Condition	N	Mean	Std. Deviation	Std. Error Mean
Att to Computers A	video	10	72.00	4.619	1.461
	no video	10	64.00	4.876	1.542

Independent Samples Test

		Levene's Test for Equality of Variances		t-test for Equality of Means					95% Confidence Interval of the Difference	
		F	Sig.	t	df	Sig. (2-tailed)	Mean Difference	Std. Error Difference	Lower	Upper
Att to Computers A	Equal variances assumed	.169	.686	3.767	18	.001	8.000	2.124	3.538	12.462
	Equal variances not assumed			3.767	17.947	.001	8.000	2.124	3.537	12.463

Figure 10.11 Data set A: SPSS independent *t*-test group statistics for *video/no video* example

The corresponding computational formula is given below. Note that, in the bottom line of the formula, the two standard deviations have been combined by simply averaging them. Again, this formula is suitable only if the number of participants in each sample is relatively similar – for large discrepancies in sample size, combining standard deviations is more complicated. That said, notice that the definition of d does not explicitly depend upon N. Indeed, the non-reliance on N is something that is common to all measures of effect size, and it is this property which allows us to compare the strength of effects in different studies with different sample sizes.

$$d = \frac{\text{mean}_{video} - \text{mean}_{no\text{-}video}}{\left(\text{sd}_{video} + \text{sd}_{no\text{-}video}\right) \div 2}$$

For our example, the calculation is straightforward since all of the information required is given in the Group statistics in Figure 10.11. This table is part of the SPSS summary of the independent *t*-test presented in Chapter 7 (p. 122). Thus:

$$d = \frac{72.00 - 64.00}{\left(4.619 + 4.876\right) \div 2} = \frac{8}{4.748} = 1.68$$

The value of 1.68 for Cohen's d tells us that the difference between the two means is of the order of 1.7 standard deviations, which is considered a very large effect size according to the following guidelines of Cohen regarding the magnitude of d:

$d = 0.2$ – 'small' effect
$d = 0.5$ – 'medium' effect
$d = 0.8$ – 'large' effect

These values may seem somewhat arbitrary to you, and you would be correct, but they are widely used. The judgment of a large effect size (to say the least) is consistent with the result of the *t*-test, which revealed a highly statistically significant difference between the conditions ($p < .001$).

Group Statistics					
	Video Condition	N	Mean	Std. Deviation	Std. Error Mean
Att to Computers B	video	10	72.00	9.068	2.867
	no video	10	64.00	10.446	3.303

Figure 10.12 Data set B: SPSS independent *t*-test Group Statistics for *video/no video* example

For data set B, Figure 10.12 presents the SPSS Group Statistics. As for data set A, Cohen's *d* is calculated as follows:

$$d = \frac{72.00 - 64.00}{(9.068 + 10.446) \div 2} = \frac{8}{9.757} = 0.82$$

Using Cohen's guidelines, this represents a large effect size, in spite of the fact that the statistical analysis was non-significant, although only just (p = .084).

Making links

This is another case where the statistical non-significance and the estimate of a large effect size are somewhat at odds, the latter suggesting a more important result than indicated by the independent *t*-test. This time, a likely candidate is the relatively limited statistical power associated with the analysis as a result of the modest sample sizes (N = 10 in each group).

Pearson's *r* as a measure of effect size for comparisons

As you saw in Chapter 8, this second measure is *r*, a correlation coefficient. As you are about to see, there is a close link between *t* and *r*, and converting between one and the other is very simple.

Making (another) link

Recall that, in earlier chapters, we have discussed how the terms 'comparison' and 'relationship' are actually quite blurred. So, as in our *video / no video* example here, although we are asking whether there is a *difference* between our two conditions, it is not unusual to hear some people express this idea as whether there is a *relationship* between the treatment participants receive (*video* or *no video*) and their *Attitude to Computers* scores. Either way of expressing the idea is acceptable, although, for students learning about different statistical tests, we tend to encourage them to make a strong distinction between the comparisons and relationships. Indeed, by and large, we continue to emphasize this distinction in the book, although it is necessary to blur the distinction on occasions. This is one such occasion.

As an alternative to *t*, let's instead think about how we might use correlation to explore the difference between our two samples. Here, this involves correlating a *dichotomous* variable (*video / no video*) with a numerical variable, *Attitude to Computers*. Obviously, the dichotomous variable has to be assigned numerical values to make this possible, which is why we did so when coding the data into SPSS (see p. 120). Although strictly there is a specially modified correlation (known as the point biserial correlation) for use with one dichotomous and one scale variable, it is perfectly appropriate simply to calculate Pearson's *r*, which, as it turns out, produces an identical value to the point biserial in such cases.

Figure 10.13 presents the result of using SPSS to calculate Pearson's *r* for both data sets (A and B) in the *video / no video* example. Recall that, previously, when

Correlations		Video Condition	Att to Computers A	Att to Computers B
Video Condition	Pearson correlation	1	−.664**	−.396
	Sig. (2-tailed)		.001	.084
	N	20	20	20
Att to Computers A	Pearson correlation	−.664**	1	.296
	Sig. (2-tailed)	.001		.206
	N	20	20	20
Att to Computers B	Pearson correlation	−.396	.296	1
	Sig. (2-tailed)	.084	.206	
	N	20	20	20
** Correlation is significant at the 0.01 level (2-tailed).				

Figure 10.13 SPSS summary of Pearson's *r* for *video/no video* example (Data sets A and B)

independent *t*-tests were carried out, data set A produced a significant difference between the two conditions, while data set B did not. The table contains quite a lot of redundant and repeated information, however, picking through the results, it can be seen that, consistent with the *t*-test results, the correlation between condition and scores in data set A is significant, while that for data set B is not. More interestingly, the magnitude of the correlations can be taken as a measure of effect size. Pearson's *r* is often considered to be a more desirable measure than Cohen's *d* due to its statistical transparency – most people have an intuitive feel for what the magnitude of a correlation coefficient means. Cohen also suggested the following guidelines for *r* when used as a measure of effect size:

$r = 0.1$ – 'weak' effect
$r = 0.3$ – 'moderate' effect
$r = 0.5$ – 'strong' effect

In our example, *r* for data set A is .66, suggesting a strong effect size, and, for data set B, the value is .40, indicating an effect size somewhere between moderate and strong. Reassuringly, these results are broadly in line with those obtained previously for the Cohen's *d* calculations. Actually, it is not necessary to calculate *r* in such cases, since there is a direct correspondence between *r* and *d*. Cohen's *d* can be readily converted into *r*, and vice versa, using the table presented in Figure 10.14.

Revisiting Mann-Whitney *U* test as an alternative

It is possible to obtain a measure of effect size if you have carried out a Mann-Whitney *U* test on the data, rather than an independent *t*-test. Figure 10.15 presents a summary of the SPSS calculations for both data sets, as seen in Chapter 7 (p. 128). In order to calculate effect size, we convert the *z* statistic to *r* for each data set. The method is very straightforward – simply divide *z* by $\sqrt{N}$, where *N* equals the total number of participants (in our example, 20). Thus,

$$\text{For data set A: } r = \frac{z}{\sqrt{N}} = \frac{2.799}{\sqrt{20}} = \frac{2.799}{4.472} = \textbf{.63}$$

$$\text{For data set B: } r = \frac{1.664}{4.472} = \textbf{.37}$$

Note the broad similarity of these effect sizes to the previous calculations of *r*, in spite of their being based on a different statistical procedure.

r	d	r	d	r	d	r	d	r	d	r	d
.00	0.00	.17	0.35	.34	0.72	.51	1.19	.68	1.85	.85	3.23
.01	0.02	.18	0.37	.35	0.75	.52	1.22	.69	1.91	.86	3.37
.02	0.04	.19	0.39	.36	0.77	.53	1.25	.70	1.96	.87	3.53
.03	0.06	.20	0.41	.37	0.80	.54	1.28	.71	2.02	.88	3.71
.04	0.08	.21	0.43	.38	0.82	.55	1.32	.72	2.08	.89	3.90
.05	0.10	.22	0.45	.39	0.85	.56	1.35	.73	2.14	.90	4.13
.06	0.12	.23	0.47	.40	0.87	.57	1.39	.74	2.20	.91	4.39
.07	0.14	.24	0.49	.41	0.90	.58	1.42	.75	2.27	.92	4.69
.08	0.16	.25	0.52	.42	0.93	.59	1.46	.76	2.34	.93	5.06
.09	0.18	.26	0.54	.43	0.95	.60	1.50	.77	2.41	.94	5.51
.10	0.20	.27	0.56	.44	0.98	.61	1.54	.78	2.49	.95	6.08
.11	0.22	.28	0.58	.45	1.01	.62	1.58	.79	2.58	.96	6.86
.12	0.24	.29	0.61	.46	1.04	.63	1.62	.80	2.67	.97	7.98
.13	0.26	.30	0.63	.47	1.06	.64	1.67	.81	2.76	.98	9.85
.14	0.28	.31	0.65	.48	1.09	.65	1.71	.82	2.87	.99	14.04
.15	0.30	.32	0.68	.49	1.12	.66	1.76	.83	2.98		
.16	0.32	.33	0.70	.50	1.15	.67	1.81	.84	3.10		

Figure 10.14 Corresponding Cohen's _d_ and Pearson's _r_ values as measures of effect size (Cohen's guideline values for small/weak, medium/moderate and large/strong effect sizes are shaded in increasing intensity)

Test Statistics[a]		
	Att to Computers A	Att to Computers B
Mann-Whitney U	13.000	28.000
Wilcoxon W	68.000	83.000
Z	−2.799	−1.664
Asymp. Sig. (2-tailed)	.005	.096
Exact Sig. [2*(1-tailed Sig.)]	.004[b]	.105[b]
[a]Grouping variable: Video condition.		
[b]Not corrected for ties.		

Figure 10.15 SPSS summary of Mann-Whitney _U_ tests for _video/no video_ example (Data sets A and B)

Comparison within paired data: Let your fingers do the talking

We return to the paired _t_-test example from Chapter 7 (pp. 129–136) and revisited above (p. 207). Recall that the typing speed (in words per minute, wpm) of participants was measured before and after a tea-break. Again, there were two data sets, data set A which produced a statistically significant result and data set B which did not.

As with the independent _t_-test example above, SPSS does not provide a measure of effect size for the related _t_-test, neither by default, nor as an option, so we must calculate it. The good news is that the method is identical to that for independent _t_, so, the formula below for calculating Cohen's _d_ is used.

$$d = \frac{\text{mean}_{\text{before}} - \text{mean}_{\text{after}}}{(\text{sd}_{\text{before}} + \text{sd}_{\text{after}})/2}$$

Figures 10.16 and 10.17 present the paired samples statistics for data sets A and B respectively from the paired t-tests presented for the tea-break example in Chapter 7. These tables contain all of the information needed to calculate d, as follows:

$$\text{For data set A: } d = \frac{77.00 - 82.00}{(5.279 + 4.472) \div 2} = \frac{-5}{4.876} = -1.03$$

$$\text{For data set B: } d = \frac{77.00 - 82.00}{(5.574 + 6.870) \div 2} = \frac{-5}{6.222} = -0.80$$

Note that, consistent with the paired t-test for data set A which produced a highly significant result with $p < .001$ (p. 135), d is well in excess of the cut-off for a large effect. By contrast, the non-significant result for data set B ($p = .064$), although only just, is contradicted by a large effect size estimate. Again, here we have an example (data set B), where the statistical significance of the difference and the effect size are somewhat at odds, with the difference not *statistically* significant, but the effect size indicating that the difference is of 'large' *practical* significance. Here, the likely candidate for this discrepancy is the relatively low power associated with the analysis due to the relatively modest 16 participants.

Using the table in Figure 10.14, it is possible to obtain the equivalent values of Pearson's r for the two data sets. These are 0.46 for data set A and 0.37 for data set B, corresponding to strong (nearly) and moderate-to-strong effect sizes, respectively, based on Cohen's guidelines for r.

Paired Samples Statistics

		Mean	N	Std. Deviation	Std. Error Mean
Pair 1	Before tea-break	77.00	16	5.279	1.320
	After tea-break	82.00	16	4.472	1.118

Figure 10.16 Data set A: SPSS paired samples statistics for *before/after tea-break* example

Paired Samples Statistics

		Mean	N	Std. Deviation	Std. Error Mean
Pair 1	Before tea-break	77.00	16	5.574	1.393
	After tea-break	82.00	16	6.870	1.718

Figure 10.17 Data set B: SPSS paired samples statistics for *before/after tea-break* example

Revisiting Wilcoxon *W* test as an alternative

As with the Mann-Whitney U test for independent samples, it is possible to obtain an estimate of effect size for related samples if you have carried out a Wilcoxon signed-ranks test on the data, rather than a paired t-test. Figure 10.18 presents a summary of the SPSS calculations for both data sets A and B, as seen in Chapter 7 (pp. 140–141). Again, the z statistic presented in the SPSS summary is used, and we

Test Statistics[a]	After tea-break – Before tea-break A	After tea-break – Before tea-break B
Z	−3.027[b]	−1.811[a]
Asymp. Sig. (2-tailed)	.002	.070

[a]Wilcoxon signed ranks test.
[b]Based on negative ranks.

Figure 10.18 SPSS summary of Wilcoxon *W* tests for *before/after tea-break* example (Data sets A and B)

convert z to r for each data set by dividing by $\sqrt{N}$, where N equals the total number of observations – note, *not* participant pairs (in our example, 32). Thus,

For data set A: $r = \dfrac{z}{\sqrt{N}} = \dfrac{3.027}{\sqrt{32}} = \dfrac{3.027}{5.657} = 0.54$

For data set B: $r = \dfrac{1.811}{5.657} = 0.32$

These results suggest a strong effect of tea-break for data set A and a moderate effect for data set B. The point is the same, however, namely that a result that was found to be statistically non-significant ($p = .064$) has an associated moderate effect size.

Chapter 8 revisited: Correlating

In Chapter 8 (pp. 146–148), we considered how to calculate Pearson's r and Spearman's ρ for variables X and Y, comprising pairs of scores from 10 participants. Later in that chapter (pp. 157–159) we showed how to use SPSS to obtain these statistics.

Before reading on...

If you need reminded of the details, look back at this example.

... now read on

Figure 10.19 presents the results of the SPSS analysis. Recall that the magnitudes of r (.516) and ρ (.541) were quite similar and neither was found to be statistically significant ($p = .127$ and .106 respectively). Now, let's see how much more we can say about the importance, or otherwise of, these results. The issues are presented by means of a dialogue.

Correlations		*X*	*Y*
X	Pearson correlation	1	.516
	Sig. (2-tailed)	–	.127
	N	10	10
Y	Pearson correlation	.516	1
	Sig. (2-tailed)	.127	–
	N	10	10

Figure 10.19 Continued overleaf

Correlations			X	Y
Spearman's rho	X	Correlation coefficient	1.000	.541
		Sig. (2-tailed)	.	.106
		N	10	10
	Y	Correlation coefficient	.541	1.000
		Sig. (2-tailed)	.106	.
		N	10	10

Figure 10.19 SPSS summary of Pearson's r and Spearman's ρ for variables X and Y

Effect size in correlation

Student: *Dead easy – isn't it? We've already seen that* r *is a measure of effect size that can be applied across the board – even to tests of comparison.*

Lecturer: *You would think so, wouldn't you? Actually, you are strictly correct, but you will find a pretty muddled or evasive account of effect size in correlation in some textbooks.*

Student: *Why did I think it might not be entirely plain sailing! Actually, a faint alarm bell was ringing, because I notice that the* r *value for the X/Y correlation of .516 suggests a strong effect, but the associated* p *value is .127, much too large to allow us to reject* H_0.

Lecturer: *Well reasoned. Let's think about it. Take the result for X and Y which is based on 10 data pairs. Suppose, in an extreme case, I had a scatter plot of X against Y with only two points, that is, only two pairs of scores. What could you say about the relationship between X and Y.*

Student: *Hmm – I suppose there is only one line that can possibly fit the two points.*

Lecturer: *Correct – in fact, any line can be uniquely defined by two points on it. So, what would you expect the correlation between X and Y to be based on these two points?*

Student: *Well, if there is an exact fit for the line, would the correlation be perfect – a correlation of 1?*

Lecturer: *Spot on! It is the case that a correlation based on two pairs of scores, that is, two participants will always give a correlation of 1.00. Now, what if we introduce a third participant?*

Student: *Eh, if the three points lie on a straight line...*

Lecturer: *Suppose they don't remember in our example X and Y correlate about .5.*

Student: *If they don't, then the correlation will be less than 1, depending on how good a linear shape the three points make.*

Lecturer: *OK, now what if I introduce a fourth point?*

Student: *Well, I suppose the possibilities become even greater – the correlation could take on any value.*

Lecturer: *Now, what if I had ten points on the scatter?*

Student: *Well, that's the same sample size as in our example, so maybe the correlation would not be far from .5?*

Lecturer: *Correct, assuming appropriate sampling and a fair wind! But, if we were to carry on in this way, introducing more and more values, we would in fact find that, all other things being equal, the correlation coefficient would get smaller and smaller, to the point that, if we had thousands of values, the* r *would become very small, even with the same strength of relationship in the population.*

Student: *So, the correlation coefficient is affected directly by sample size?*

We hope you can see from the above dialogue that, especially for small sample sizes, high correlations can occur by chance, as in our example of 10 participants, where we obtained a correlation of .516, but the probability that null hypothesis could have produced this result was .127, or 12.7% – far too big to allow us to reject H_0. Conversely, with large sample sizes, even a very small r value can be highly significant. These cases are a clear example of where a very small effect size (r) can be statistically significant due to the high power associated with a large sample size, and vice versa.

Making links: r^2

In Chapter 8 (p. 166), we introduced the *coefficient of determination* as another means of judging the importance of a correlation. This provides useful additional information about the correlation and, although prone to the impact of sample size just as r is, it provides a further perspective on your result. Thus, in our example, we would summarize the result as suggested above, namely, $r = .516$ with 8 degrees of freedom and an associated p value of .127, indicating no significant relationship between X and Y. However, as seen in Chapter 8, r^2 was .27, indicating that 27% of the variance was shared by the two variables. Hence, although not statistically significant, this added perspective may prompt you to consider that the result has some importance.

The coefficient of determination also gives an additional perspective to Cohen's guidelines regarding the interpretation of r as a measure of effect size. His suggested value of $r = 0.1$ for a weak effect gives an r^2 of 0.01, or 1% of the total variance shared by the two variables. For a moderate effect ($r = 0.3$), 9% of the variance is explained, and, for a strong effect ($r = 0.5$), 25% is accounted for.

Making links: Why this chapter?

In 1999, the American Psychological Association (APA) Task Force on Statistical Inference proposed guidelines on the use of statistics in research. Among other things, the Task Force (incidentally, one of whose members was Jacob Cohen) was charged with elucidating "some of the controversial issues surrounding applications of statistics including significance testing and its alternatives" (*American Psychologist*, Vol 54(8), p. 594). The Task Force's recommendations were extensive and included recommendations for researchers to use the simplest statistics possible; always to provide a measure of effect size when reporting a p value; to provide confidence intervals; and, to use graphical representation where possible, including error bars on graphs.

Given these recommendations of the APA, we hope you appreciate the reasons for dealing with the issues in this chapter in such detail. In later chapters, we shall routinely consider confidence intervals and effect sizes alongside statistical significance.

Chapter review

In this chapter, relevant sections of Chapters 7 and 8 were revisited and the examples were explored by considering 95% confidence intervals and effect sizes as additional perspectives to statistical significance as ways of making sense of data.

Confidence intervals were discussed, both for the mean of a singel sample of scores and in terms of the difference between two samples.

Graphical interpretation of confidence interval bars and standard error bars was explored, noting that their meaning was seldom understood even by experienced researchers. The pitfall of using error bars when graphing related means was emphasized.

For both correlation and comparison, apparent inconsistencies between the results of statistical tests and corresponding effect sizes were discussed in terms of the level of statistical power associated with these analyses.

Part II

Making sense of 'bigger' designs

Seeing patterns in data: Comparing more than two groups

In this chapter

... we extend the methods of organizing, summarizing and displaying data to reveal patterns that were dealt with in Chapter 4. Whereas that chapter was restricted to comparisons between two groups of data, here we consider comparisons between more than two groups. By these methods, we can investigate empirically questions such as the following:

- Do students from Arts, Science and Economics faculties differ in their attitude to computers?
- Do regular coffee and decaffeinated coffee affect speed of reaction relative to a (third) control condition?

The distinction, introduced in Chapter 4 and elaborated in Chapter 9, between three experimental designs, namely independent groups, repeated measures and matched pairs, is extended to comparisons between more than two groups.

Examples of comparisons

Technophilia/technophobia

Ways of measuring how people react to computers were discussed in Chapter 2 (see p. 21) and *Attitude to Computers* was used in several examples in Chapters 4 and 7. Figure 11.1 shows some real data collected from a class of first-year psychology students, each enrolled in one of three faculties.

```
ARTS N = 101

54 47 44 56 53    41 61 56 52 58    43 50 55 58 53    53 54 46 44 48
54 54 57 47 54    52 56 55 52 48    48 43 39 56 55    54 67 51 45 61
52 55 41 47 47    43 61 47 57 59    60 43 54 66 52    67 44 59 52 50
44 50 58 54 50    68 56 45 58 52    42 67 57 45 47    50 46 56 56 44
52 53 45 51 49    34 58 59 60 56    54 61 61 59 49    45 53 50 60 44 41


SCIENCE N = 39

46 43 45 56 53    42 65 51 55 63    49 47 45 63 52    61 40 56 58 52
59 69 43 61 48    39 51 55 64 55    56 52 60 39 52    66 48 46 46


ECONOMICS N = 33

41 49 57 56 53    52 45 50 64 49    45 58 70 47 48    43 66 58 59 44
65 53 53 52 50    49 71 57 53 64    39 56 58
```

Figure 11.1 *Technophilia/technophobia: Attitude to Computers* **scores for three faculties (real data)**

Summary statistics can be calculated for each of the faculties as follows:

	Arts	Science	Economics
Median	53	52	53
Semi-interquartile range	4.75	6.50	4.75
Mean	52.17	52.59	53.76
Standard deviation	6.78	8.00	8.08

> **Before reading on...**
>
> Study the table of summary statistics. What do they suggest?
>
> **... now read on**

The most salient feature of the summary statistics is that they are very similar for all three faculties. Note also that the means and medians are extremely close together. (And remember the rule of thumb from Chapter 3, that standard deviation is likely to be roughly 1.5 times semi-interquartile range – pretty good approximation isn't it?)

The information on means and standard deviations is often shown graphically. In Figure 11.2 the points represent the means, and the lines stretch to 1 standard deviation above and below the mean in each case.

The data can be summarized more fully using extensions of various graphical devices introduced in Chapter 4. Multiple histograms could be used, but are not particularly easy to interpret. Back-to-back stem-and-leaf plots obviously won't work for more than two groups. One of the best methods is to use multiple box-and-whisker plots. Figure 11.3 confirms the impression from the summary statistics: the

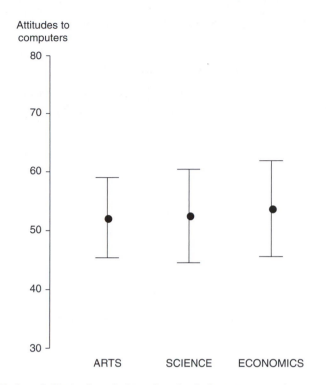

Figure 11.2 *Technophilia/technophobia*: Standard deviations and mean *Attitude to Computers* scores and standard deviations by faculty

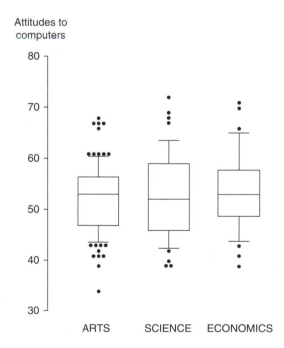

Figure 11.3 *Technophilia/technophobia*: Box-and-whisker plots of *Attitude to Computers* scores by faculty

distributions of attitude to computer scores are very similar across the samples from the three faculties.

Quick on the draw

In Chapter 4 data were presented on the reaction times of samples of chess and squash players. Figure 11.4 extends the data to include further samples of bridge players and fencers. (Fencers, in particular, might be expected to have fast reaction times.)

Another graphical method that can be used effectively with a relatively small data set is *multiple line plots* (see Figure 11.5).

Before reading on...

What does the graph in Figure 11.5 suggest?

... now read on

It looks as if fencers and squash players have faster reaction times, with fencers somewhat faster on average. Chess and bridge players have longer reaction times, about the same overall.

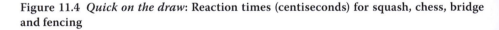

SQUASH *N* = 16

27 32 34 41 31 30 32 37 33 30
35 32 38 29 28 23

CHESS *N* = 15

42 43 48 36 39 45 37 38 38 37 40 34 29 32 39

BRIDGE *N* = 14

35 38 33 46 29 34 49 35 41 36 37 37 43 31

FENCING *N* = 15

29 32 30 25 36 35 28 27 20 33 35 31 28 36 31

Figure 11.4 *Quick on the draw*: **Reaction times (centiseconds) for squash, chess, bridge and fencing**

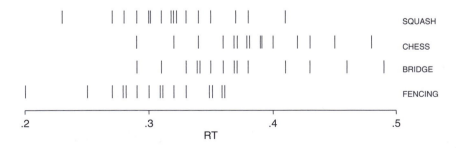

Figure 11.5 Multiple line plots of squash, chess, bridge and fencing scores

> **Before reading on...**
>
> Use the line plots in Figure 11.5 to find the median for each group, and to estimate the semi-interquartile range, mean, and standard deviation (for the last, you can use the rule of thumb that about two-thirds of the data lie within 1 standard deviation above or below the mean). Use SPSS or another suitable statistical package to check the medians and your estimates of the other summary statistics. For answers, see *Making sense of SPSS* below.
>
> **... now read on**

One more method for exploring the data, again an extension of an approach introduced in Chapter 4, is to combine all the data in a single ranking. In Figure 11.6, the raw data are listed on top, running from 20 to 49 centiseconds, and the ranks (from highest to lowest) underneath, running from 1 to 60. Different symbols are used to represent individuals from the four samples. Thus the longest reaction time was for one of the bridge players, the next longest for one of the chess players, and so on. When ties occur, the ranks are calculated as indicated in Figure 11.6. The preponderance of black figures to the left, and white figures to the right, reflects very clearly the pattern that squash players and fencers in the samples have faster reaction times than bridge and chess players.

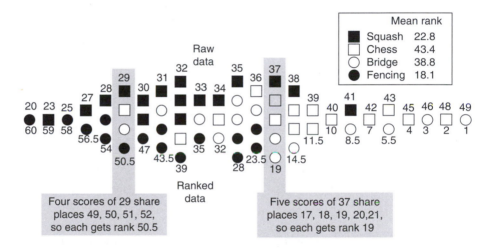

Figure 11.6 *Quick on the draw*: **Combined ranking of squash, chess, bridge and fencing scores**

Coffee time

In Chapter 4, an example dealt with the effects of coffee on reaction time. In the experimental design described there, the same participants were tested under both conditions – the control condition (without coffee) and the experimental condition (with coffee). This is an example of a *repeated measures design*. The design can be extended to more than two groups. Here we add another experimental condition – decaffeinated coffee – and the data to be considered are as shown in Figure 11.7.

The fact that this is a repeated measures design, so that each linked set of three data come from the same participant, is represented here by the stick figures in the diagram. The means for the three conditions, given at the bottom, show that, for this sample, reaction times were only slightly faster for the decaffeinated condition, but

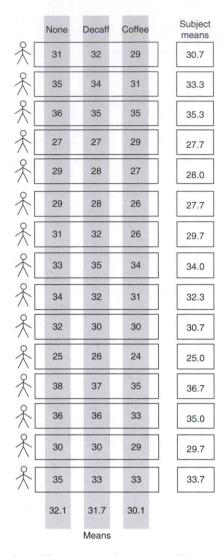

	None	Decaff	Coffee	Subject means
	31	32	29	30.7
	35	34	31	33.3
	36	35	35	35.3
	27	27	29	27.7
	29	28	27	28.0
	29	28	26	27.7
	31	32	26	29.7
	33	35	34	34.0
	34	32	31	32.3
	32	30	30	30.7
	25	26	24	25.0
	38	37	35	36.7
	36	36	33	35.0
	30	30	29	29.7
	35	33	33	33.7
Means	32.1	31.7	30.1	

Figure 11.7 *Coffee time* data: Three repeated measures (RT centiseconds)

the coffee condition shows a larger effect of 2 centiseconds faster, on average. The mean for each participant can also be calculated, as indicated. These means can be used to compare participants for overall speed of reaction, and show that such speed varies considerably between participants within the sample – from a mean of 25.0 to a mean of 36.7 – an aspect whose relevance will be considered later.

A ranking process can be carried out on the data. Here the three data for each participant are ranked (from highest to lowest) as indicated in Figure 11.8.

Having done this participant-by-participant ranking, the mean rank for each condition can be calculated. The mean rank for the decaffeinated condition is slightly higher than that for the control condition; but the mean rank for the coffee condition is considerably higher. The mostly salient pattern is that for the majority (13 out of 15) the reaction time is either lowest (that is, fastest) or equal lowest in the coffee condition, but there is relatively little difference overall for the control and decaffeinated conditions.

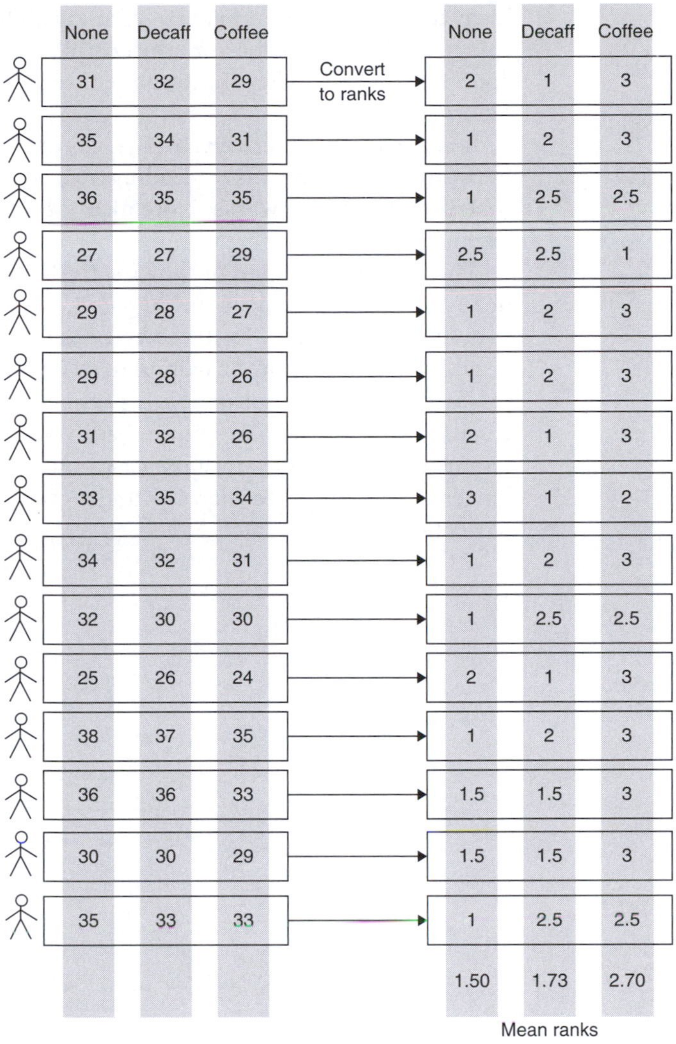

Figure 11.8 *Coffee time* data ranked

Maze running

This example illustrates the third major type of experimental design, the *matched subjects design*. It concerns the effects of certain drugs, labelled A, B, and C, on the maze-running performance of rats (as measured by the number of seconds taken to get through the maze), relative to a control condition with no drug. If a repeated measures design were used – that is, each rat ran the maze under each condition – there would be complications, since it is likely that the rat's performance would improve with practice, or be subject to other order effects. As we saw in the previous chapter, there are ways to get round that difficulty in repeated measures designs, but here we consider a different approach, also discussed in Chapter 9. Rats are used in groups of four, with each group of four coming from the same litter. One member of each group of four is tested under each of the conditions. Because they come from the same litter, the rats within each group are related genetically and hence likely to be more similar in maze-running ability than rats from different litters, and this matching allows for a more controlled comparison between the experimental conditions. The data for the number of seconds taken to run the maze are shown in Figure 11.9.

It appears that, relative to the Control condition, drugs A and B enhance performance on the maze, leading to faster times on average, whereas drug C makes performance worse. Note also the wide variation in overall litter-by-litter performance.

The graphical method of showing the data as in Figure 11.10, again an extension of an approach introduced in Chapter 4, can be effective, particularly with smallish data sets. While Figure 11.10 shows the data clearly, in order to get the most from the graphical display it may be helpful to modify it slightly, as in Figure 11.11. Although precisely the same information is presented in both figures, note how the general trends within the data are more readily apparent from the rearranged display. As Figure 11.11 illustrates, in most cases the litter member treated with drug C took longer to run the maze than the undrugged litter member (seven out of ten cases, with one tie).

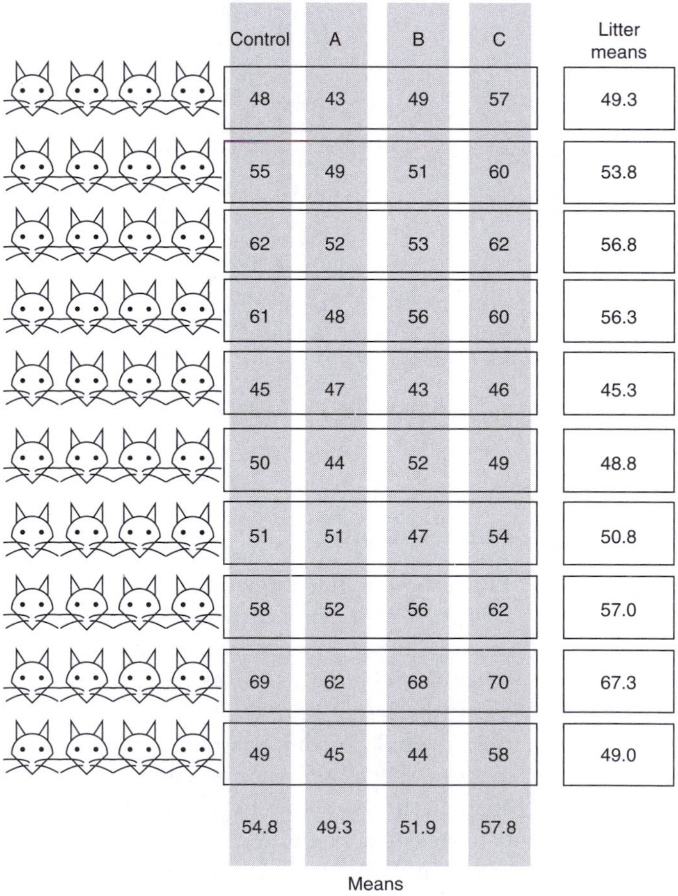

	Control	A	B	C	Litter means
	48	43	49	57	49.3
	55	49	51	60	53.8
	62	52	53	62	56.8
	61	48	56	60	56.3
	45	47	43	46	45.3
	50	44	52	49	48.8
	51	51	47	54	50.8
	58	52	56	62	57.0
	69	62	68	70	67.3
	49	45	44	58	49.0
	54.8	49.3	51.9	57.8	

Means

Figure 11.9 *Maze-running* data (seconds): 'Matched rats' design

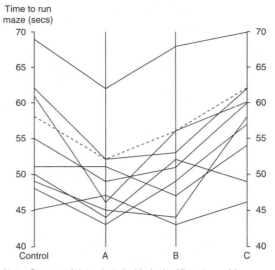

Note: One set of date plotted with dashed lines to avoid
confusion because of overlap.

Figure 11.10 Graphical display of *Maze-running* data

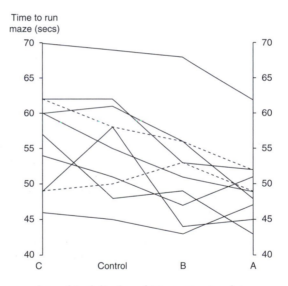

Figure 11.11 Rearranged graphical display of *Maze-running* data

Beyond graphical analysis

The examples have illustrated how data may be displayed in forms that bring out the
salient characteristics. Thus, from looking at the graphs, the data appear to provide
some evidence that

- students in different faculties do not differ in their attitude to computers;
- squash players and fencers have faster reaction times than bridge and chess
  players;

- decaffeinated coffee has no marked effect on reaction time but regular coffee does; and
- Drugs A and B improve maze-running, but C makes it worse.

However, these conclusions are tentative. They are based on samples, whereas the questions we are interested in are more general. To provide a sharper analysis of the data, and the implications for the populations from which the samples are drawn, we need statistical tests, which are covered in the next chapter.

Making sense of SPSS

Creating data files and obtaining summary statistics and graphical summaries for more than two groups

1. Creating the data files

In Chapter 3 (pp. 35–38), we showed how to create SPSS data files in some detail. Here, we present data files for the four examples introduced in this chapter coded using the same methods.

> **Before reading on...**
>
> If necessary, look again at Chapter 3 to remind yourself of the important points in creating a data file, in particular, the difference between coding independent groups and repeated measures data.
>
> **... now read on**

We remind you of the golden rule for coding any data in SPSS – that *each individual participant (case) occupies a single row of their own in the data file*. This is known as a *casewise* data structure.

Technophilia/technophobia

Let's first take the *Technophilia/Technophobia* example. Here, we have a single independent variable (*faculty*) with three levels (science, arts, economics). The design is independent (unrelated) groups, so each of the 173 participants produces only a single score. We know that there will be 173 rows in the data file and two columns – one to code which faculty each participant is in and the other for the participant's score.

When you have created the data file, the **Data View** should look as below (cases 95–110 shown). Remember to save your data.

	faculty	att_comp
95	1	56
96	1	60
97	1	48
98	1	61
99	1	50
100	1	44
101	1	44
102	2	46
103	2	59
104	2	43
105	2	69
106	2	45
107	2	43
108	2	56
109	2	61
110	2	53

Quick on the draw

The second example concerns the reaction times of four groups of participant. Again, there is one independent variable (group) with four levels (squash, chess, bridge, fencing), and the design is independent (or unrelated) groups. Here, we have a total of 60 participants, so there will be 60 rows in the data matrix and, as in the previous example, we require two columns, one to code participants' group membership and the other to record their score.

When you have created the data file, the **Data View** should look as below (cases 31–46 shown). Remember again to save your data.

	group	reaction_time
31	2	39
32	3	35
33	3	38
34	3	33
35	3	46
36	3	29
37	3	34
38	3	49
39	3	35
40	3	41
41	3	36
42	3	37
43	3	37
44	3	43
45	3	31
46	4	29

Coffee time

The third example presents reaction times of 15 participants, each tested under three conditions. Here, as in the previous two examples, we have one independent variable (condition) with three levels (no coffee, decaffeinated coffee, regular coffee). This time, the design is repeated measures, since each participant receives all three conditions. Therefore, the data file will have 15 rows (one for each participant) and three columns of scores, since participants produced three scores each. We do not require any coding column, since there is no independent groups variable.

When you have created this data file, the **Data View** should look as below. Remember again to save your data.

	none	decaff	coffee
1	31	32	29
2	35	34	31
3	36	35	35
4	27	27	29
5	29	28	27
6	29	28	26
7	31	32	26
8	33	35	34
9	34	32	31
10	32	30	30
11	25	26	24
12	38	37	35
13	36	36	33
14	30	30	29
15	35	33	33

Maze running

The final example concerns a matched subjects design, in which sets of four matched rats are assigned to one of four drug conditions and their times to run through a maze are measured. In all, there are 10 sets of matched rats. Since they have been matched, each set of four is treated as if it were a single participant, so, for analysis purposes, we have a repeated measures design with 10 participants. Here again, we have one independent variable (drug) with four levels (control, drug A, drug B, drug C). As in the previous example, we do not have an independent groups variable, so the data file will consist of 10 rows and four score columns.

When you have created this data file, the **Data View** should look as below. Remember again to save your data.

	control	A	B	C
1	48	43	49	57
2	55	49	51	60
3	62	52	53	62
4	61	48	56	60
5	45	47	43	46
6	50	44	52	49
7	51	51	47	54
8	58	52	56	62
9	69	62	68	70
10	49	45	44	58

2. Calculating summary statistics and drawing graphical summaries

Here, we use appropriate SPSS routines to obtain summaries, statistical and graphical, of the four data sets coded above. As we proceed, you will notice that some of the graphical techniques presented in this chapter are simply not available in SPSS. Where possible, we improvise and, otherwise, we present the graphs that are available.

Technophilia/technophobia

Recall that, in Chapter 3, we used the **Descriptives ...** and **Frequencies ...** subroutines of **Analyse > Descriptive Statistics** to obtain summary statistics. However, neither of these routines allows us to break down the summary statistics by the levels of our independent variable (here, *faculty*) which is obviously necessary. In order to do so, we use the **Explore ...** subroutine under the same menu. This routine will also allow us to obtain some graphical summaries as well, although we need to suppress most of them, since they are far from succinct (try them out for yourself if you want to see what we mean).

First, select **Analyse > Descriptive Statistics > Explore ...**

The dialogue window below will appear. Move your dependent variable (*attitude to computers*) to the box labeled **Dependent List:** and your independent variable (*faculty*) to the one labeled **Factor List:** as shown. Note that, under **Display**, the

Both button is selected by default – this will give you both statistical and graphical summaries.

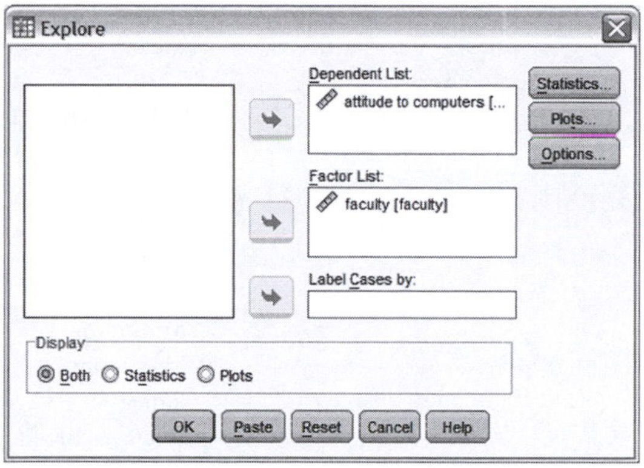

It is not necessary to click on the **Statistics...** button, as the default options are fine. As suggested above, however, you do need to click on the **Plots...** button in order to ensure you obtain only the succinct graphical summaries. In particular, ensure that neither **Stem-and-leaf** (which is selected by default) nor **Histogram** are selected in the **Descriptive** box. Leave the **Boxplots** box as it is, since we only have one dependent variable, so we do not need to tell SPSS how to cluster the boxplot.

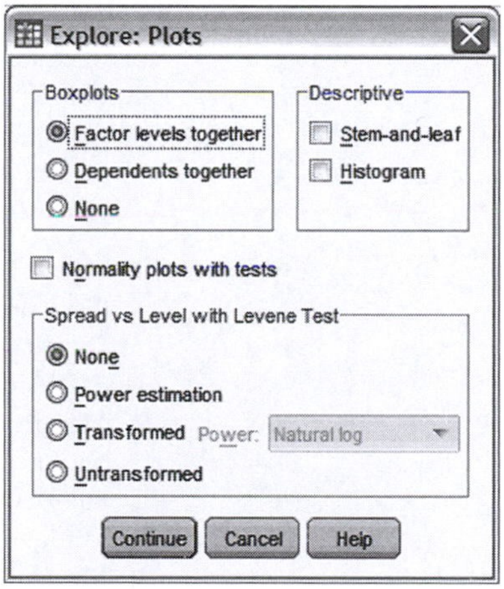

An **SPSS Statistics Viewer** window will appear containing the summary shown below. Note that, when you have three levels of an independent variable, the summary statistics table gets quite long. The only graphical summary produced is the boxplot, which is an excellent option is this case.

You will notice that this boxplot is not identical to that shown in Figure 11.3. This is merely because the whiskers have been defined differently, so the outliers in Figure 11.3 are contained within the wider intervals represented by the whiskers below. Our whiskers define the range from the 10th to the 90th percentiles, whereas, the range defined by SPSS is altogether more obscure and too technical to mention here.

Descriptives

	faculty			Statistic	Std. Error
attitude to computers	arts	Mean		52.17	.675
		95% Confidence Interval for Mean	Lower Bound	50.83	
			Upper Bound	53.51	
		5% Trimmed Mean		52.07	
		Median		53.00	
		Variance		46.001	
		Std. Deviation		6.782	
		Minimum		34	
		Maximum		68	
		Range		34	
		Interquartile Range		10	
		Skewness		.037	.240
		Kurtosis		−.194	.476
	science	Mean		52.59	1.281
		95% Confidence Interval for Mean	Lower Bound	50.00	
			Upper Bound	55.18	
		5% Trimmed Mean		52.51	
		Median		52.00	
		Variance		63.985	
		Std. Deviation		7.999	
		Minimum		39	
		Maximum		69	
		Range		30	
		Interquartile Range		13	
		Skewness		.138	.378
		Kurtosis		−.826	.741
	economics	Mean		53.76	1.406
		95% Confidence Interval for Mean	Lower Bound	50.89	
			Upper Bound	56.62	
		5% Trimmed Mean		53.60	
		Median		53.00	
		Variance		65.252	
		Std. Deviation		8.078	
		Minimum		39	
		Maximum		71	
		Range		32	
		Interquartile Range		10	
		Skewness		.349	.409
		Kurtosis		−.348	.798

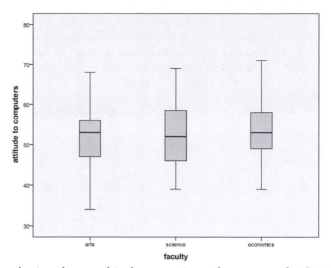

In order to obtain other graphical summaries we have to use the **Graphs > Legacy Dialogs** menu which offers the options shown in the window below.

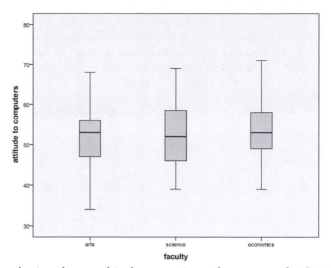

In order to obtain the graph in Figure 11.2, select **Error Bar...** and ensure that **Simple** and **Summaries of groups of cases** are selected as below.

Click **Define**

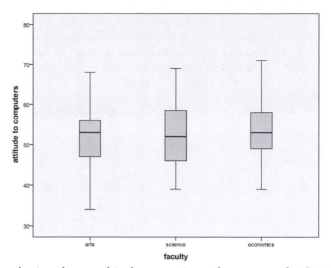

In the following dialogue window, assign the variables as shown. Here, the default option for the error bars is the **Confidence interval for the mean**, set at 95%. This is a perfectly good option, however, in Figure 11.2, the errors bars represent one standard deviation above and below the mean, which is another good option. As shown, select **Standard deviation** from the drop down menu and change the value in the **Multiplier:** box to **1**.

Click **OK**.

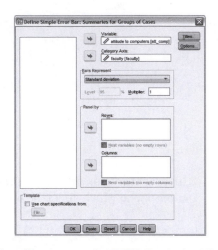

The following graph will appear in the **SPSS Statistics Viewer** window. Note the reassuring similarity to Figure 11.2 (the actual graph produced by SPSS has a different scale on the Y axis, so we have adjusted this to bring it into line).

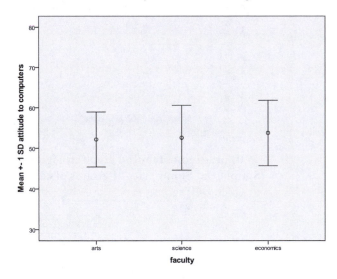

Quick on the draw

In the *Before reading on …* task on page 228, you were invited to find the median for each group, and to estimate the semi-interquartile range, mean and standard deviation, then to check these out using a computer package. Here we use SPSS to do so and, again, because we require the summary statistics to be broken down by group, as above, we use **Explore…** to do so.

The results are shown below (note an even longer summary table due to the four levels of the independent variable). The boxplot also shows the comparisons between the four groups.

Descriptives

	group			Statistic	Std. Error
Reaction time (c.sec)	squash	Mean		32.00	1.111
		95% Confidence	Lower Bound	29.63	
		Interval for Mean	Upper Bound	34.37	
		5% Trimmed Mean		32.00	
		Median		32.00	
		Variance		19.733	
		Std. Deviation		4.442	
		Minimum		23	
		Maximum		41	
		Range		18	
		Interquartile Range		6	
		Skewness		.125	.564
		Kurtosis		.420	1.091
	chess	Mean		38.47	1.257
		95% Confidence	Lower Bound	35.77	
		Interval for Mean	Upper Bound	41.16	
		5% Trimmed Mean		38.46	
		Median		38.00	
		Variance		23.695	
		Std. Deviation		4.868	
		Minimum		29	
		Maximum		48	
		Range		19	
		Interquartile Range		6	
		Skewness		.041	.580
		Kurtosis		.319	1.121
	bridge	Mean		37.43	1.500
		95% Confidence	Lower Bound	34.19	
		Interval for Mean	Upper Bound	40.67	
		5% Trimmed Mean		37.25	
		Median		36.50	
		Variance		31.495	
		Std. Deviation		5.612	
		Minimum		29	
		Maximum		49	
		Range		20	
		Interquartile Range		8	
		Skewness		.698	.597
		Kurtosis		.083	1.154
	Fencing	Mean		30.40	1.150
		95% Confidence	Lower Bound	27.93	
		Interval for Mean	Upper Bound	32.87	
		5% Trimmed Mean		30.67	
		Median		31.00	
		Variance		19.829	
		Std. Deviation		4.453	
		Minimum		20	
		Maximum		36	
		Range		16	
		Interquartile Range		7	
		Skewness		−.732	.580
		Kurtosis		.610	1.121

> **Before reading on...**
>
> Only the previous page we see that the medians for the four groups are 32, 38, 36.5 and 31 (how did you do?).
>
> Also check out the actual values of the semi-interquartile ranges, means and SD's and compare these to your estimates. Reflect on any discrepancies.
>
> Check these summary statistics against the boxplot – you should be able to find the medians and SIQRs. Also, look back at the original data to see the two outliers in the chess group – these even lie outside the wider whiskers produced by SPSS.
>
> **... now read on**

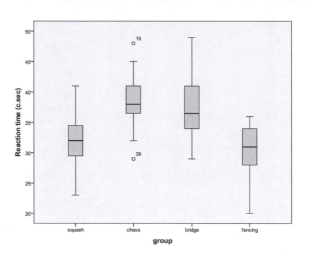

Coffee time

For this example, we do not present summary statistics, since the method for doing this using **Explore...** has been shown above. More importantly, we do not provide any of the usual graphical summaries (boxplot, error bars, etc) due to the pitfalls in interpreting such graphs when applied to related means. Note that SPSS is not good at providing graphical summaries that do justice to repeated measures designs. The only graphs that are not potentially completely misleading are bar charts without error bars or a line graph, again without error bars. It is not possible to obtain either from the **Explore...** routine.

Instead, using **Graphs > Legacy Dialogs > Line...**, we can obtain the following line graph. Bear in mind that the means shown here are of limited value due to the fact that changes within individuals are not shown.

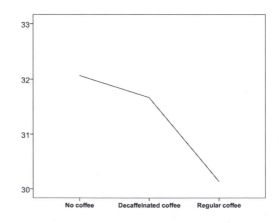

For those who wish to dig a little deeper

After much fudging, we have used SPSS to produce the following graphical summary which is more suitable for repeated measures. It is too fiddly for most readers to consider producing, so, unless you are very daring, you need not read the details below.

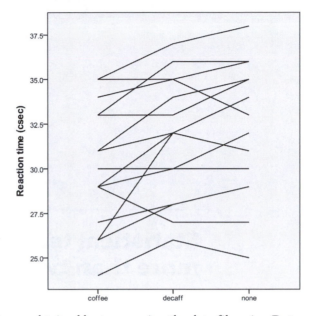

This graph was obtained by transposing the data file using **Data > Transpose …**, then using **Graphs > Legacy Dialogs > Line …** (**Multiple / Summaries of separate variables**).

Maze running

Again, we suggest that you use **Explore …** to obtain summary statistics and check these against those given in the example above. We also suggest that you use **Graphs > Legacy Dialogs > Line …** to obtain a line graph or bar chart. If you are very daring, you can attempt to use SPSS to obtain Figure 11.10 and/or 11.11.

Chapter review

This chapter has extended summary statistics and graphical methods to comparisons involving more than two groups. Similarly, we have considered graphical techniques appropriate to the different experimental designs: independent groups, repeated measures, and matched groups.

We noted that, in general, within-subjects designs (repeated measures and matched pairs) are not well served in terms of readily available graphical methods.

Statistical tests: Comparing more than two groups

In this chapter

... we extend the tests covered in Chapter 7 to similar tests designed to compare more than two sets of data, building on the descriptive foundations laid in Chapter 11.

Extending from two to more than two groups

As you saw in Chapter 7, for two independent groups, the independent (unpaired) t-test is a test of the null hypothesis that the samples come from populations with identical normal distributions. A rank-based alternative is the Mann-Whitney U test. For repeated measures or matched pairs designs, the paired (correlated) t-test is a test of the null hypothesis that the differences between pairs of data come from a population normally distributed with mean zero. The Wilcoxon signed ranks test, W, is the corresponding rank-based test.

To show how all of these tests can be extended beyond two groups of data, we begin with two simple examples.

Before reading on...

The above is a fairly dense summary of the ideas in Chapter 7 concerning the comparison of unpaired and paired data sets, including the appropriate null hypotheses and rank-based alternatives. If you feel the need to refresh your memory of any of these ideas, now is the time to do so. Before continuing with this chapter, you should grasp the difference in approach between the unpaired and paired t-tests, particularly in respect of the null hypotheses, and the reasons for this.

... now read on

Example 1: Independent groups

General knowledge

For the purposes of explaining the general approach to comparing more than two independent groups, simple data have been made up for this example. To give an imaginable context, the 'cover story' is that samples of French, Irish and American students have been given a list of 35 capital cities – Rome, Paris, Dublin and so on – and asked to identify the corresponding countries. The (fictitious) data are their totals of correct responses. To keep the example simple, the numbers are small (only 8 in each sample), much smaller than a serious study of this nature would use. Further, for simplicity, the numbers have been arranged so that the means come out as whole numbers. Moreover, to enable some important points to be made, we have presented two contrasting versions of data, as shown in Figure 12.1.

Note that the means are the same for the two data sets. Accordingly, if we tried to use these data to evaluate the evidence for a difference in knowledge of world capitals among French, Irish and American students *only* on the basis of the differences between means in the samples, both data sets would lead us to the same conclusion. Yet, if we display the data graphically, a difference becomes obvious.

Looking at the data set A in Figure 12.2, the scores for the American students look quite different from the other two samples, but in data set B, there is considerably more overlap, and the difference is much less obvious. The underlying distinction between the two data sets is that the data within each sample are much more spread out in data set B than in A. Just as with the independent t-test, it is necessary to take into account, not just the variation **between groups** – reflected in the differences between the group means – but also the variation **within groups**, that is, how spread out the data are within each of the samples.

French	Irish	US
22	21	16
18	25	20
21	27	18
23	25	18
19	23	15
19	20	14
24	26	19
22	25	16
21	24	17
	Means	

French	Irish	US
16	23	18
27	28	14
26	16	25
19	27	27
14	18	11
25	31	12
26	26	15
15	23	14
21	24	17
	Means	

Data set A   Data set B

Figure 12.1 *General knowledge* scores: **Contrasting data sets**

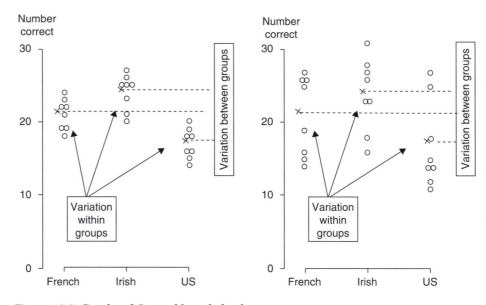

Figure 12.2 Graphs of *General knowledge* **data**

A statistical approach called **Analysis of Variance** (**ANOVA** for short, pronounced 'ann-oh-vah') uses this basic idea: the relationship of variation between groups to variation within groups. In fact, as noted in Chapter 7, p. 115, ANOVA is a generalization or extension of the *t*-test.

Making links

Student: *I'm a bit confused. You say this test called 'analysis of variance' can be thought of as a generalization of the t-test?*

Statistician: *That's right, the t-test is limited to cases where there are two means to be compared, while ANOVA can be used to compare more than two means.*

Student: *But the t-test analyses the difference between means, whereas ANOVA analyses variation.*

Statistician: *Ah, I see where you're coming from. In fact, ANOVA does analyse the differences between the means of sets of scores.*

Student: *Then why is it called analysis of variance? Why not analysis of means, or analysis of differences?*

Statistician: *I suppose it could be, but analysis of variance is a pretty good description of what the test, or more precisely the 'family' of tests, does.*

Student: *I've still not fully got my head around it. Why is it called analysis of variance?*

Before reading on...

Spend a little time thinking about the discussion so far between the student and statistician. Why do *you* think it might be called analysis of variance?

... **now read on**

Statistician: *OK, but you already know the answer – you just haven't made the connection. Let's think about an independent t-test for a moment. Do you remember the basic rationale of that test?*

Student: *I think so. Basically, you calculate the difference between the two means and you divide it by some measure of the overall variability in the data. The bigger the difference in means compared to the variability, the bigger the t value and the more significant the difference. The larger the overall variability in the data compared to the difference between the means, the smaller the t value.*

Statistician: *That's pretty good. Now think about three sets of data. How would you calculate the difference between these means?*

Student: *Well, this time you have to compare three means, so you would subtract the first two, then subtract the second and third, then maybe subtract the first and third. But I'm not sure how you would summarize these three differences.*

Statistician: *Right, it could get pretty cumbersome. Imagine what you would have to do if there were five or six means, or more.*

Student: *So, what we need is a single overall measure of the differences between all the means.*

Statistician: *Right again, you're nearly there. Now, can you think of a measure that corresponds to the differences between several scores?*

Student: *Ah, I think I see now – if a set of scores, in this case three means, differs a lot, we would say that they* vary *a lot.*

Statistician: *Correct! So a good way of expressing the differences between three or more means is to use a measure of variation.*

Student: *Something akin to* variance, *for example.*

Statistician: *See, I said you already knew the answer.*

Student: *So, in the case of a t-test, the difference between the two means can also be thought of as the variation between the two groups?*

Statistician: *That's certainly one way of thinking about it.*

Student: *So, can you do an ANOVA on just two sets of data instead of a t-test?*

Statistician: *Absolutely.*

ANOVA terminology

Some further terminology needs to be introduced at this point. In ANOVA, independent variables are referred to as **factors**. In this chapter, we are concerned only with ANOVA involving a single factor; that is, **one-factor** or **one-way** ANOVA. Chapters 13 and 14 deal with designs involving more than one factor. The different values that the factor can take are called **levels**. If an independent groups design is used, it is called a **between groups** factor (since comparisons *between* separate groups are being made). If a repeated measures or matched groups design is used, it is called a **within-subjects** factor (since comparisons are being made *within* the same subjects, or *within* members of matched groups).

To return to our example, we have one independent variable (*nationality*) and participants are assigned to only one level, depending on their nationality. Hence, we have an independent groups design and, therefore, we carry out an ANOVA procedure for *one independent variable* (or *factor*) made up of *independent groups* (known as a **One-Way Independent Groups**, or a **One-Way Between Groups** ANOVA).

Assumptions underlying one-way between groups ANOVA

As with statistics we have considered earlier, before carrying out an ANOVA, we should be aware of the basic assumptions underlying the use of the test. These are that:

Data consist of **interval or ratio** scale variables
Data are approximately **normally distributed**
Data within groups have roughly equal spread (**homogeneity of variance**)

Making links

You should notice that these are very similar to the assumptions underlying the *t*-test, which makes sense, since, as noted above, the *t*-test is a special case of ANOVA.

In keeping with our general approach throughout this book, we do not present a calculation of ANOVA. Our expectation is that you will have access to software that will do the analysis for you (the SPSS calculation is given below). If an ANOVA is carried out for data set A in our example, the **ANOVA summary table** will appear as in Figure 12.3.

Source of Variation lists the so-called *systematic* and *non-systematic* sources of variation alluded to above (p. 245). Essentially, the total variability in the data is chopped up into the variation that can be explained by our experimental manipulation, and all the uncontrolled variability arising from a variety of unspecified causes. The former is often referred to as *between* groups (here denoted by 'Groups') and the latter *within* groups, here labelled 'Error'. Why 'error' precisely? For complex historical reasons, this is the term that has been adopted conventionally, though the rationale for its use is by no means clear. We have simply to ask you to accept it

Source of Variation	Sum of Squares	df	Mean Square	F	p
Groups	197.333	2	98.667	19.923	.0000
Error	104.000	21	4.952		
Total	301.333	23			

Figure 12.3 *General knowledge*: ANOVA summary table for data set A

as a piece of conventional terminology. A useful way to think about it is that it represents the unsystematic variation, attributable to individual differences within the population and other random influences, that remains after the systematic sources of variation have been taken out (here the only systematic source is differences between groups).

Sum of Squares (or **SS**) is a particular measure of variability for each source of variation, in the first case, the systematic variation between groups, in the second, error variation (in the sense explained above). As its name suggests, the SS (Total), which represents the overall variation in the data, is equal to the sum of the SS (Groups) and SS (Error). In other words, in this example, the entire variability in the data is explained by one or other of these sources of variation.

df stands for *Degrees of Freedom*, as usual. Again, a technical understanding of this term is beyond what we aim to cover in this book. Suffice it to say that, for each calculation (in this case the Sums of Squares) the corresponding degrees of freedom represents roughly, but not exactly, the number of data points involved in that calculation (to be precise, the number of data points minus one, in this case). So, since 3 group means are used to calculate SS (Groups), the corresponding *df* is $3 - 1 = 2$. Using precisely the same reasoning for SS (Total), the corresponding *df* is $24 - 1 = 23$. The *df* for Error is calculated indirectly, that is, whatever is left over from the total *df* when the systematic *df* has been allocated; here there is only *df* (Groups), hence, *df* (Error) $= 23 - 2 = 21$.

Mean Square (or **MS**) is a modified measure of variation found by dividing each Sum of Squares by its corresponding *df*. This helps to 'modulate' each measure of variation, since the SS (Group) is calculated using only three values, while SS for Error and Total use many more. So the latter two will tend to be disproportionately larger simply by virtue of the fact that they were calculated using a greater number of scores to begin with. Converting all of the SS 'into the same money', so to speak, allows us to weigh each source of variation directly against the others, rather than comparing apples and oranges, as it were.

F is the actual statistic for the test, as described above, that is, the ratio of the systematic and non-systematic Mean Squares (MS), in this case MS (Group) and MS (Error). Some points about the *F* statistic:

- There is a separate value of *F* for each separate systematic source of variation (here, we only have one systematic source).
- Because of the way it is calculated, it is always positive.
- The larger the value of *F*, the stronger the evidence from the data that there is a difference between the populations; and
- As a rule of thumb, *F* needs to reach a value of approximately 4 to be statistically significant (the exact value depends on the *df* associated with the two Mean Squares).

p (or level of significance). As with other statistics considered previously, the *p* value needs to be equal to or less than .05 for the result to be 'statistically significant at the .05 level'.

For data set A in our example, you can see that *F* is large and the corresponding *p* value is very small; in fact, so small that it is .0000 rounded to 4 decimal places (this doesn't mean that it is zero – for example .00003 is .0000 if rounded off). This result indicates that the null hypothesis – that French, Irish and American students are equally knowledgeable about world capitals – can be rejected.

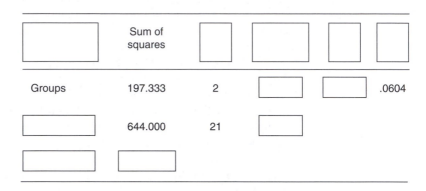

Figure 12.4 1-Factor independent groups ANOVA – summary table with blanks

Now let's consider the ANOVA summary table for data set B (see Figure 12.5). You should recognize it as Figure 12.4 with the blanks filled in.

Here you can see that the variability measures (SS and especially MS) for Groups are the same as for data set A, reflecting the fact that the means are identical for both data sets. However, now the SS (Error) and MS (Error) are considerably bigger, as is the SS (Total), reflecting the greater spread of data within the groups. As a consequence, the *F* ratio is much smaller and, in fact, not large enough to reach statistical significance at the .05 level, as indicated by the *p* value of .0604 (greater than .05).

Source of variation	Sum of squares	df	Mean squares	F	p
Groups	197.333	2	98.667	3.217	.0604
Error	644.000	21	30.667		
Total	841.333	23			

Figure 12.5 *General knowledge* – ANOVA summary table for data set B

If these data had been obtained in an experiment, therefore, the conclusion would have been to *fail to reject* the null hypothesis.

Student: So, for data set A, the ANOVA summary table tells us that the groups differ significantly in their knowledge of world capitals, but for data set B, the groups don't differ significantly?

Lecturer: Correct. More formally, we would say that there is a significant **main effect** of Groups for data set A.

Student: And no significant main effect of Groups for data set B?

Lecturer: Right, and remember, the means for the three groups are identical in each data set.

Student: But, in data set A, the variability due to the systematic source of variance (that is, Groups), is sufficiently large compared to the variability of non-systematic sources (that is, Error), to allow us to reject the null hypothesis?

Lecturer: Correct, but not so for data set B.

Student: Done and dusted, as they say!

Lecturer: Not so fast – we've not quite finished. Given that we have obtained a significant main effect of Groups, what can we conclude?

Student: Eh, that the three groups differ significantly from each other in their knowledge of world cities?

Lecturer: Possibly, but a significant main effect gives rise to several possibilities. All an ANOVA tells you is that, somewhere *across the levels of your independent variable,* there is a difference. It may be that all three means differ significantly. Equally, it may be that mean 1 differs from means 2 and 3, but the latter two don't differ from each other. Or means 2 and 3 may differ, but neither differs from mean 1, and so on.

Student: Oh, so just because you have a significant main effect, you can't assume that all your means differ significantly?

Lecturer: Correct, you have to do more digging to identify the precise nature of the differences.

Student: How do you do that then?

Lecturer: The process of digging around is known as **post hoc** testing. We shall come back to this later.

Other ways of interpreting the importance of the data

In Chapter 10, we considered the possibility that statistical significance – based on a consideration of the likelihood of obtaining a result under the assumption that the null hypothesis is true – may not be "the be all and end all" for judging the importance of a result. In particular, we looked at two other aspects, namely, confidence intervals and estimates of effect size.

Confidence intervals in ANOVA

In Chapter 10, we considered confidence intervals for a single data set and for various statistical methods. In the case of the *t*-test, we saw that SPSS provided a 95% confidence interval for the difference between the means scores of the two groups. If zero fell into this interval, we could not reject the null hypothesis, since there was a possibility that the population mean could be zero.

Before reading on...

Look back at Chapter 10 and make sure that you are familiar with the use of confidence intervals when comparing two means.

... now read on

In the case of ANOVA, the use of confidence intervals is more restricted. SPSS does not provide an analogous confidence interval to the t-test that can embrace the overall magnitude of the differences across several means and, in any case, such an interval would be difficult to interpret in a straightforward manner. In fact, SPSS does not provide any confidence interval for ANOVA by default. Instead, optionally, you can obtain confidence intervals for the mean of each group or condition. We show how to do this in the *Making sense of SPSS* example below and consider what the resultant confidence intervals tell us.

Effect size in ANOVA

In general, discussion of effect size in ANOVA in textbooks is inconsistent and, in some cases, driven by what is available in SPSS.

> **Lecturer:** *Before we go any further, let's look informally at the idea of effect size in ANOVA. In assessing the significance of a result, what does ANOVA use to quantify the difference between groups or conditions?*
>
> **Student:** *It uses the variability of the mean scores to indicate the magnitude of the differences across the means and then it sets this against another measure of variability to do with general error variation.*
>
> **Lecturer:** *Good. Now, can you think of any way of measuring effect size based on this approach?*
>
> **Student:** *Hmm, one effect size measure that resonates here is the idea of the proportion of the variance explained, that was r², but there is no r² here.*
>
> **Lecturer:** *Good! In fact, you are closer to an r² than you think, but let's not get bogged down in symbols here. How might you assess the proportion of the total variance explained by the difference between our means?*
>
> **Student:** *Well, the total sum of squares is given in the table, and this is an index of the overall variation in the data.*
>
> **Lecturer:** *Yes, go on.*
>
> **Student:** *So, if we take the sum of squares for our means and divide by the total sum of squares, would that give us the proportion of the total variation explained by our means?*
>
> **Lecturer:** *Indeed it would!*

There is just such a measure for ANOVA – sometimes you will see it abbreviated to r^2, just as in correlation. More usually, it is abbreviated to η^2 (**eta squared**). In fact, SPSS does not provide this measure, nor does it automatically provide any measure of effect size for ANOVA. Optionally, it provides a measure known as **partial eta squared**. *We suggest you do not choose this option.* Partial eta squared (η_p^2) is a difficult statistic to interpret and should *not* be used to describe any effect as 'small', 'medium' or 'large'. Eta squared is much more straightforward to interpret, but has to be calculated by hand from the ANOVA summary table (see *Making sense of SPSS* below). Fortunately, it is very easy to do (which rather begs the question as to why it is not available in SPSS).

For those who wish to dig a little deeper

There has been recent concern about the misreporting of η^2 and η_p^2 in the literature, usually the latter is wrongly reported as the former. Both indicate the proportion of the overall variance accounted for by the factor of interest. Eta squared is the preferred measure – it simply gives the proportion of total variance explained by the effect in question (in our example, there is only one effect – the difference between the conditions). Straightforwardly, all of the η^2 values add up to 1, reflecting the fact that 100% of the variance has been divided up between the various sources.

Partial Eta Squared, on the other hand, is an adjusted measure that, as the name suggests, takes account of interrelationships between the various systematic effects in the analysis, giving the proportion of the variance explained by the effect after these other effects have been partialled out. Invariably, η_p^2 is greater, sometimes much greater, than η^2 and the total of the η_p^2 values exceeds, sometimes greatly, 1 – hence the difficulty of interpretation. One exception is the case of one-way between groups ANOVA, where there is only one systematic effect, so η^2 and η_p^2 are equal.

Although η^2 is the preferred measure of the two, it is still known as a 'biased' estimate, since it is calculated purely on the basis of the sample data and does not estimate the likely strength of the effect in the population. The closely related measure, ω^2, does estimate the population effect size. However, it is a little more complicated to compute and we suggest that you stick with η^2 which is entirely satisfactory for your purposes.

A rank-based alternative: Kruskal-Wallis *H*

As with all tests considered in this book thus far, there is an alternative based on ranking procedures. This has, in fact, been anticipated in Chapter 11, and we pick up the example again here.

Quick on the draw: Ranked

Here again is the figure from Chapter 11 (see p. 229) showing the combined data for reaction times of squash players, chess players, bridge players and fencers (see Figure 12.6). There is one difference, however; in Chapter 11 they were ranked 1 to 60 from highest to lowest. Here, instead, they have been ranked 1 to 60 from lowest to highest. Why? Simply because that is what computer programs do conventionally. (Note that when the order of ranking is reversed, a convenient way of calculating the new ranking in each case is to subtract the old rank from 61 – try it.)

For each of the four groups, the mean rank can be calculated as indicated. These means differ quite a bit, reflecting in particular that reaction times for squash

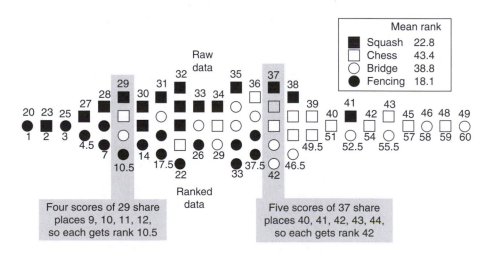

Figure 12.6 *Quick on the draw*: **Combined ranking of squash, chess, bridge and fencing scores**

players and fencers are generally faster than those for chess and bridge players, as was discussed earlier.

To test whether these differences in mean ranks are statistically significant, a test called the **Kruskal-Wallis** One-Way ANOVA is used (you've guessed it, devised by statisticians (William) Kruskal and (Allen) Wallis). In line with our general philosophy, we expect you to use software to determine the value of the statistic associated with the test, and whether or not it is high enough to reach statistical significance. In fact, the appropriate statistic is distributed as the chi-squared (χ^2) statistic, with degrees of freedom 1 less than the number of groups (so 3 in this case). For our example, the result is:

$$\chi^2 = 22.2, df = 3, N = 60, p = .0001$$

Making sense of SPSS

Coding data and calculating a one-way ANOVA for independent groups and the rank-based equivalent, Kruskal-Wallis

Note: We recommend you also consult Brace et al. (2009), pp. 211–215, 248–251 and 256–258 who provide further information.

1. Creating the data file

We remind you of the golden rule that *each individual participant (case) occupies a single row of their own in the data file*. In the two *General knowledge* data sets above, we have eight participants in each of three separate nationality groups – 24 cases in total. Therefore, the data file will have 24 rows. Each participant only produces one score, so we will have one column of scores. We also need a coding column, that is, a column that tells SPSS which nationality each case belongs to. *So, the final data table will have 24 rows and two columns.*

Create the data file as you were shown in the independent *t* example (Chapter 7, p. 119). Your **Data View** should resemble that shown below (cases 4 to 19 visible here). Note again that we have taken a short cut and coded the scores for data sets A and B in the one file. (Remember that, for the analysis of data set A, the second column of scores does not exist, and vice versa.) Note too that we have coded 1 = French, 2 = Irish, 3 = US for the *nationality* variable.

Remember to save the data giving the file an appropriate name.

	nationality	gknowledgeA	gknowledgeB
4	1	23	19
5	1	19	14
6	1	19	25
7	1	24	26
8	1	22	15
9	2	21	23
10	2	25	28
11	2	27	16
12	2	25	27
13	2	23	18
14	2	20	31
15	2	26	26
16	2	25	23
17	3	16	18
18	3	20	14
19	3	18	25

Data View Variable View

2. Calculating One-Way Independent (Between) Groups ANOVA

The specific routine for this analysis is located in **Analyze > General Linear Model > Univariate…** – somewhat opaque, we grant you. **General Linear Model** refers to a family of statistics of which ANOVA is one. **Univariate…** refers to the fact that each participant produces a single score (since the independent variable consists of unrelated groups).

The dialogue box below will appear. Move *Nationality* into the box labeled **Fixed Factor(s):** (as we have seen, the term *factor* is used in ANOVA to mean *independent variable* – don't concern yourself with the term *fixed*). Move *Data set A scores* into the box marked **Dependent variable:** (remember data set B does not exist for the purposes of this analysis).

Before proceeding with the analysis, let's take the opportunity to choose some further statistics – relevant to the *homogeneity* assumption of ANOVA and to *confidence intervals*. There is also an effect size option which gives η_p^2, so we do not recommend that you select it.

Click on the **Options…** button. The dialogue box below will appear. As you can see, there are lots of options, but we are only interested two. Check the **Homogeneity tests** box.

Also, as discussed above, in order to obtain confidence intervals for the means of the three groups, highlight *nationality* and move it across to the box labeled **Display Means for:**. Click **Continue**.

Then click **OK**.

The **SPSS Statistics Viewer** will display the results tables shown overleaf. Again, somewhat characteristic of SPSS, there is *much* more than you require here, so don't be put off. We have highlighted the relevant information.

The first table labeled 'Between-Subjects Factors' merely summarizes the independent variable and the number of participants in each level.

The table labeled 'Levene's Test of Equality of Error Variances' tells us whether the variabilities of the three groups are approximately equal (homogeneity). Recall that this statistic (Levene's test) was provided automatically for independent *t*, but has to be chosen here. The *p* value associated with the statistic is .860, very large and much larger than .05 – which is good, because it indicates that the variabilities of the three groups do not differ significantly, hence, the assumption of homogeneity holds.

The third table labeled 'Tests of Between-Subjects Effects' is the ANOVA summary table. Look back at Figure 12.3 and compare the highlighted results with that table. The unhighlighted results are not necessary for your purposes. The *Corrected Model* combines all of the systematic effects into a single model and, since there is only one effect, is redundant here. The *Intercept* tells you the extent to which the data differ from zero which is of no interest to you.

The summary table shows a highly significant *main effect* of nationality, indicating that *some or all* of the nations differ in their knowledge of capital cities. The probability of obtaining such a result under the null hypothesis is < .0004 (say) – extremely unlikely by any standards.

At this point, it is useful to calculate the associated effect size. As discussed above, the preferred statistic is eta squared (η^2), which is obtained by dividing the sum of squares for the factor ($SS_{nationality}$) by the total sum of squares (SS_{total}), thus:

$$\eta^2 = \frac{SS_{nationality}}{SS_{total}} = \frac{197.333}{301.333} = \mathbf{0.655}$$

This indicates that 65.5% of the total variance is accounted for by the difference between the means of the three nationalities. Since, as we have discussed above, η^2 is directly equivalent to r^2, if we take the square root of η^2, we obtain a measure of effect size, equivalent to *r*. Hence,

$$r = \sqrt{.655} = \mathbf{0.81}$$

Given Cohen's guideline of $r = 0.5$ for a strong effect, this is indeed a *very* strong, or large, effect size.

The final table labeled 'Nationality' presents means and 95% confidence intervals for the three levels of our independent variable (factor). So, based on the sample mean of 21.0 for the French group, we can say that there is a 95% probability that the mean for the *population* of similar French participants will lie between 19.36 and 22.64, and so on for the other two groups.

Between-Subjects Factors

		Value Label	N
Nationality	1	French	8
	2	Irish	8
	3	US	8

Levene's Test of Equality of Error Variances[a]
Dependent Variable: Data set A scores

F	df1	df2	Sig.
.152	2	21	.860

Tests the null hypothesis that the error variance of the dependent variable is equal across groups.
[a]Design: Intercept + nationality

Tests of Between-Subjects Effects
Dependent Variable: Data set A scores

Source	Type III Sum of Squares	df	Mean Square	F	Sig.
Corrected Model	197.333[a]	2	98.667	19.923	.000
Intercept	10250.667	1	10250.667	2069.846	.000
Nationality	197.333	2	98.667	19.923	.000
Error	104.000	21	4.952		
Total	10552.000	24			
Corrected Total	301.333	23			

[a]R Squared =.655 (adjusted R squared =.622)

Nationality
Dependent variable: Data set A scores

			95% Confidence Interval	
Nationality	Mean	Std. Error	Lower Bound	Upper Bound
French	21.000	.787	19.364	22.636
Irish	24.000	.787	22.364	25.636
US	17.000	.787	15.364	18.636

Before reading on...

Repeat the above steps for data set B and summarize the results.

... now read on

You should have obtained the following ANOVA output. Note here that, unlike the first data set, the p value is greater than our cut-off of .05 (only just, but greater nonetheless), so we fail to reject the null hypothesis, and conclude that there is no significant difference between any of the three nationalities in their knowledge of capital cities.

You should also have calculated η^2 as .235, indicating that 23.5% of the total variance is explained by the difference between our groups. Taking the square root as before, an r of 0.48 is very close to Cohen's guideline of 0.5, so the effect size for data set B is also large. Hence, although strictly non-significant, the result is not unimportant, underscoring the marginal p value. Also note the greater uncertainty regarding the population means – confidence intervals are much wider than for data set A, reflecting the greater error variability within the groups.

Between-Subjects Factors

		Value Label	N
Nationality	1	French	8
	2	Irish	8
	3	US	8

Levene's Test of Equality of Error Variances[a]
Dependent Variable:Data set B scores

F	df1	df2	Sig.
.336	2	21	.719

Tests the null hypothesis that the error variance of the dependent variable is equal across groups.
[a]Design: Intercept + nationality

Tests of Between-Subjects Effects
Dependent Variable:Data set B scores

Source	Type III Sum of Squares	df	Mean Square	F	Sig.
Corrected Model	197.333[a]	2	98.667	3.217	.060
Intercept	10250.667	1	10250.667	334.261	.000
Nationality	197.333	2	98.667	3.217	.060
Error	644.000	21	30.667		
Total	11092.000	24			
Corrected Total	841.333	23			

[a]R Squared =.655 (Adjusted R Squared =.622)

Nationality
Dependent Variable:Data set B scores

			95% Confidence Interval	
Nationality	Mean	Std. Error	Lower Bound	Upper Bound
French	21.000	1.958	16.928	25.072
Irish	24.000	1.958	19.928	28.072
US	17.000	1.958	12.928	21.072

3. Calculating Kruskal-Wallis

Above, we used the *Quick on the draw* example to illustrate the rank-based test for several unrelated means, Kruskal-Wallis *H*. For the SPSS calculation, you will need the data file for this example which was coded in Chapter 11 (p. 235). Load this data file.

The specific routine for this analysis is located in **Analyze > Nonparametric Tests > Legacy Dialogs > K Independent Samples…** (K simply refers to a number greater than 2, here $K = 3$).

In the dialogue window, move *Group* into the **Grouping Variable:** box, then click on **Define Range…** and enter 1 and 4 (this is a range and captures the 1, 2, 3 and 4 levels of *Group*). Move *Reaction time* into the **Test Variable List:** box. **Kruskal-Wallis H** is already selected by default.

Click **OK**.

The **SPSS Statistics Viewer** presents the results as below. The first table gives the mean ranks for the four groups and the second table shows the χ^2 approximation, *df* and *p* (Asymp .Sig) which should be stated as < .001, < .0004, or some such.

Ranks

	group	N	Mean Rank
Reaction time (c.sec)	squash	16	22.78
	chess	15	43.43
	bridge	14	38.79
	fencing	15	18.07
	Total	60	

Test Statistics[a,b]

	Reaction time (c.sec)
Chi-square	22.180
df	3
Asymp. Sig.	.000

[a]Kruskal Wallis Test
[b]Grouping Variable: group

Reporting the results of a one-way between groups ANOVA

There is no absolutely rigid convention and different journal articles will contain slightly different information depending on editorial policy. Consistent with Brace et al. (2009), we recommend the following for a summary of the ANOVA:

Data set A: There was a significant main effect of nationality ($F(2,21) = 19.92$, $p < .001$, $\eta^2 = .655$)

Data set B: The main effect of nationality was not significant ($F(2,21) = 3.22$, $p = .06$, $\eta^2 = .235$)

... and for Kruskal-Wallis

For reaction time there was a significant effect of nationality: $\chi^2(3, N = 60) = 22.18$, $p < .001$

Making links: *t*-test and ANOVA – Key idea

Let's go back to the independent *t*-test example of the effect of *video / no video* on *Attitude to Computers* scores. Below, instead of a *t*-test, we have used SPSS to carry out a one-way unrelated ANOVA on data set A. The ANOVA results and the corresponding *t*-test results from Chapter 7 are given below.

Before reading on...

If you wish, carry out this ANOVA yourself using SPSS and check that you obtain the same results.

... now read on

ANOVA:

Levene's Test of Equality of Error Variances[a]
Dependent Variable: Att to Computers A

F	df1	df2	Sig.
.169	1	18	.686

Tests of Between-Subjects Effects
Dependent Variable:Att to Computers A

Source	Type III Sum of Squares	df	Mean Square	F	Sig.	Partial Eta Squared
Corrected Model	320.000[a]	1	320.000	14.187	.001	.441
Intercept	92480.000	1	92480.000	4100.099	.000	.996
condition	320.000	1	320.000	14.187	.001	.441
Error	406.000	18	22.556			
Total	93206.000	20				
Corrected Total	726.000	19				

Video Condition
Dependent Variable: Att to Computers A

Video Condition	Mean	Std. Error	95% Confidence Interval	
			Lower Bound	Upper Bound
video	72.000	1.502	68.845	75.155
no video	64.000	1.502	60.845	67.155

t-TEST:

Group Statistics

	Video Condition	N	Mean	Std. Deviation	Std. Error Mean
Att to Computers A	video	10	72.00	4.619	1.461
	no video	10	64.00	4.876	1.542

Independent Samples Test

		Levene's Test for Equality of Variances		t-test for Equality of Means					95% Confidence Interval of the Difference	
		F	Sig	t	df	Sig. (2-tailed)	Mean Difference	Std. Error Difference	Lower	Upper
Att to Computers A	Equal variances assumed	.169	.686	3.767	18	.001	8.000	2.124	3.538	12.462
	Equal variances not assumed			3.767	17.947	.001	8.000	2.124	3.537	12.463

Lecturer: *OK, what do you notice about the results of the two tests?*

Student: *Well, the first thing that jumps out is the Levene's test for homogeneity – the values are identical in both the t-test and the ANOVA tables.*

Lecturer: *That's not surprising, since it's the identical homogeneity test in both cases. It would have been very worrying if the values had been different. Anything else?*

Student: *Looking at the means and standard errors, something confuses me. Obviously the means are the same, but the standard errors are not. How can that be?*

Lecturer: *Well, look closely at the two standard errors given in the t-test summary – 1.461 and 1.542. Now look at the values given in the ANOVA result.*

Student: They're both the same – 1.502. There's a contradiction here.

Lecturer: What do you get if you average 1.461 and 1.542?

Student: Ah – 1.502! So, in the ANOVA, the standard errors have been pooled – like when we calculated Cohen's d.

Lecturer: Correct. Don't worry about the technicalities as to why this has been done – as long as you realize that there is no inconsistency between the two analyses, that's fine. Now, what else do you notice?

Student: I notice that the p values are the same for both statistics – .001. But the two statistics have no similarity – t is 3.767 and F is 14.187.

Lecturer: Come on – look more closely.

Student: Sorry, I'm stumped.

Lecturer: What do you get if you square 3.767?

Student: Blimey – 14.19! It's equal to F, to 2 decimal places.

Lecturer: Good. You have just hit on the relationship between t and F, demonstrating that t is a special case of F. The relationship is given by $F = t^2$.

Example 2: Repeated measures

Fading memories

Again, we use some fictitious, simplified data to show how to analyse more than two groups where the data are related – either because a *repeated measures design* has been used (for example, *Coffee Time* on p. 230 in Chapter 11) or a *matched groups design* (for example, *Maze-running* on p. 232 in Chapter 11). The cover story is that 8 participants learn a list of 30 words, and each individual is tested 3 times for recall of these words – 1 day, 2 days and 3 days later, giving data as shown in Figure 12.7.

| | Original data | | | Participant | Relative to means | | |
| | Days | | | | Days | | |
	1	2	3	Means	1	2	3
P1	24	22	14	20	4	2	−6
P2	13	14	6	11	2	3	−5
P3	17	12	10	13	4	−1	−3
P4	12	15	9	12	0	3	−3
P5	20	18	13	17	3	1	−4
P6	19	17	12	16	3	1	−4
P7	19	14	9	14	5	0	−5
P8	12	8	7	9	3	−1	−2

Figure 12.7 *Fading memories* data: Repeated measures

Before reading on...

Spend some time considering the data in Figure 12.7. Can you detect any additional systematic source of variation (or information) that was not available in the previous example? (*Hint*: Note the contrast between the design of this example and the previous one.)

... **now read on**

How did you do? We hope you managed to distinguish *three* sources of variation in this example – two systematic and one non-systematic. There is, of course, the variation *between conditions*, reflected in the means – 17 for 1 day; 15 for 2 days; 10 for 3 days. However, in contrast to the previous example, we can also 'track' individual participants across the three conditions and look at their changes in performance. This gives us an additional systematic source of variation, called *between-subjects* variation. *(Note: In keeping with current thinking, where possible, we prefer to use the term 'participant' rather than 'subject'. However, to avoid undue confusion, we continue to use 'subject' when it is intended as a technical term.)*

We can calculate a mean of the three scores for each participant as indicated, which constitutes a baseline for that individual. The overall variation in these means is essentially a measure of the magnitude of individual differences in reaction time among the sample. This is a systematic source of variability – *between subjects* – which we can separate out from the other systematic source – the change in participants' performance *between conditions*. This latter source is calculated in a slightly subtle manner using each individual's baseline performance. Each participant's data are recalculated relative to his/her mean, with the results shown (see also Figure 12.8). So, we have in fact got rid of the actual performance of each participant and, instead, we consider participants' *relative* changes over day.

The third source of variation is, of course, is *Error*, that is, any variability in the data not explained by the two systematic sources. In this case, the error variation is the variation in these new *relative* scores. Now the ANOVA summary table appears as in Figure 12.9.

Before reading on...

Look back at Figure 12.3 the previous example for independent groups. Spend some time comparing the two summary tables and reflecting on the similarities and differences between them.

... **now read on**

You will have noticed an extra line in Figure 12.9. This is to take account of the additional systematic information available in the repeated measures design – individual differences *between subjects*. Although it is perfectly possible to do so, it is usually unnecessary to report an *F* ratio for this additional systematic source of variation, since it would only tell you whether there were overall differences between participants, which would not be particularly earth shattering. The *F* ratio for our independent variable is found by dividing the Mean Square for *Day* by the Mean Square for *Error*. For these data, *F* is statistically significant, as can be seen, indicating a significant *main effect* of *Day*.

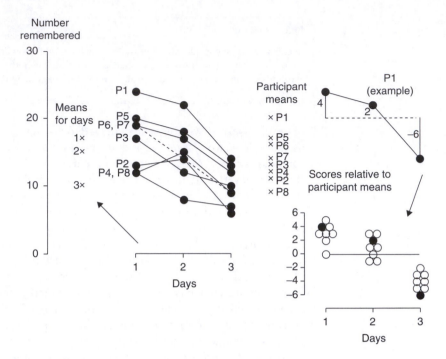

Figure 12.8 *Fading memories* – graphs of original recall scores and participants' recall relative to their baselines

Source of Variation	Sum of Squares	df	Mean Square	F	p
Subjects	264.000	7			
Day	208.000	2	104.000	31.652	.0000
Error	46.000	14	3.286		
Total	518.000	23			

Figure 12.9 ANOVA summary table for *Fading memories*

> **Assumptions underlying one-way within-subjects ANOVA**
>
> Data consist of **interval or ratio** scale variables
> Data are approximately **normally distributed**
> Data within conditions have roughly equal spread (**homogeneity of variance**)

A rank-based alternative: Friedman's test

This was anticipated in Chapter 11, and we pick up the example again here.

Coffee time: Ranked

Here again is the figure from Chapter 11 (see p. 231) showing the reaction times under three conditions ranked participant-by-participant (see Figure 12.10). Again, the difference is that the order of rankings has been reversed to go from lowest to highest, because of computer software conventions. The mean ranks for the three conditions differ considerably – in particular, there is a marked tendency for the *coffee* condition to produce the lowest (fastest) reaction time.

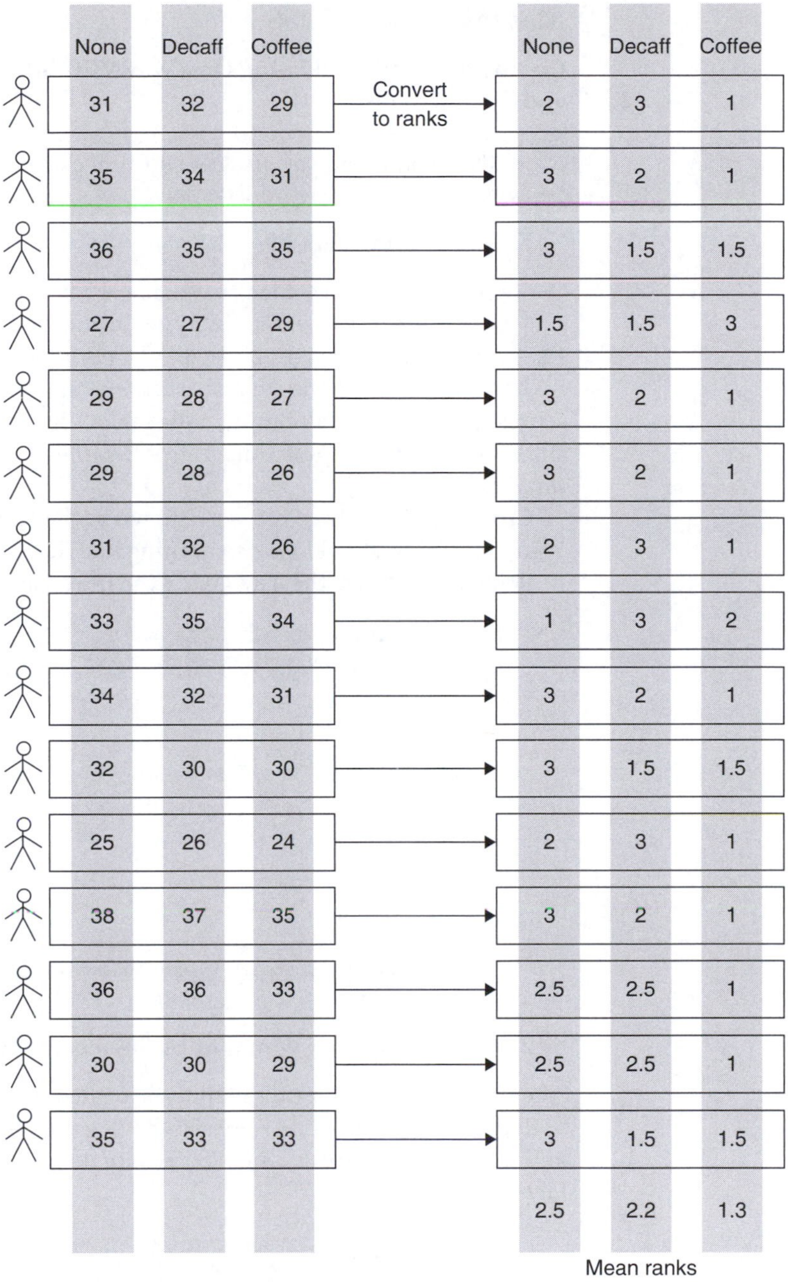

Figure 12.10 *Coffee time* data ranked

To test whether these differences are marked enough to achieve statistical significance, the appropriate test is called the **Friedman** test (yes, developed by the famous
economist Milton Friedman). Again, it results in a statistic that has the chi-square
(χ^2) distribution (with degrees of freedom 1 less than the number of conditions), the
result for this example being:

$$\chi^2 = 13.0, df = 2, p = .0015$$

Making sense of SPSS

Coding data and calculating One-Way Within-Subjects ANOVA and Friedman test

Note: We recommend you also consult Brace et al. (2009), pp. 222–227 and pp. 259–260 who provide further information.

1. Creating the data file

We remind you of the golden rule that *each individual participant (case) occupies a single row of their own in the data file.* In the *Fading Memories* example above (see Figure 12.7), we have eight participants, each tested on three occasions. Therefore, we have eight rows in the data table representing eight cases and each case has three scores each requiring a column in the table. There is no need for any coding variable, since we only have repeated measures. *So, the final data table will have 8 rows and three columns.*

Create the data file as you were shown in the paired *t* example (Chapter 7, p. 133). Your **Data View** should look something like that below.

Remember to save the data giving the file an appropriate name.

![SPSS Data View window showing a data table with columns day1, day2, day3 and eight rows of data.]

2. Calculating One-Way Within-Subjects ANOVA

The specific routine for this analysis is located in **Analyze > General Linear Model > Repeated Measures…**. Here, we have a single repeated measures factor (*day*) and **Repeated Measures…** in SPSS is shorthand for *at least one repeated measures factor.*

![SPSS window showing the Analyze menu expanded with General Linear Model selected, and a submenu showing Univariate, Multivariate, Repeated Measures, and Variance Components.]

The dialogue box below will appear. We need to give SPSS the details of the repeated measures factor(s) in our experiment (here we have only *one* factor). Thus, in the **Within-Subject Factor Name:** box, replace *factor1* with *day* and enter *3* in the **Number of Levels:** box. Click the **Add** button to place these details in the box immediately below. We now have to tell SPSS which scores refer to which levels of the independent variable.

Click **Define**.

In the **Repeated Measures** dialogue box below, move each level of the independent variable in turn (*day1*, *day2*, *day3*) across to the box now labeled **Within-Subjects Variables (day):**. This procedure simply tells SPSS which column in the data table refers to which level of the factor (it's straightforward here, but not always so) – a bit like the function of a coding variable in independent groups data.

Click on the **Options...** button and, in the dialogue window as below, choose **Homogeneity tests**. Also move days into the box labeled **Display Means for:**. Click **Continue**.

Then click **OK**.

The **SPSS Statistics Viewer** will display the results of the analysis. (Note, we have had to compress some of the tables to fit onto the page.) This time, there is a truly daunting amount of information and, again you do not need most of it. SPSS output for ANOVAs involving repeated measures is one of the most unsatisfactory features, in our opinion, especially for students learning statistics.

OK, don't panic – let's just extract what we need and forget the rest. Before doing so, look back at Figure 12.9 to remind yourself what the ANOVA summary table should contain. You will see just three 'Sources' – two systematic and one non-systematic. *Subjects* (this is the extra between-subjects element which repeated measures gives us – the variability associated with each participant's mean performance across the three days – individual differences between participants); *day* (this is our factor of interest); and *Error* (this is the non-systematic variability within-subjects).

Now, for reasons best known to others, SPSS does not present a neat ANOVA summary table containing these three elements. Instead, you have to find the relevant information and compile the table yourself.

The first table headed 'Mauchly's Test of Sphericity' (bit of a mouthful, we know) tells us about the homogeneity assumption – again, if it is *not* significant, that's good. Here $p = .849$ which is vastly greater than our cut-off of .05, so there are no significant differences in the variabilities of our three sets of scores. This makes compiling our ANOVA summary table straightforward. All you need are the shaded bits, for which the homogeneity assumption (referred to here as sphericity) holds. Simply ignore the rest.

We use the second and third tables to compile our ANOVA summary table. Look back at Figure 12.9 to see the structure of the summary table. The first line of the summary table, our additional between-subjects source, is highlighted in the table headed 'Tests of Between-Subjects Effects'. Unhelpfully, this source is labeled 'Error', *not* so for our purposes. You can include the Mean Square value as well as the Sum of Squares if you wish – we have chosen not to do so. The second and third lines of the summary are highlighted in the table headed 'Tests of Within-Subjects Effects'. These refer to the systematic effect of *day* and the associated *error*. The final line of the summary table, representing the total sum of squares, is not available from the SPSS output, so we must calculate it by adding up the sum of squares (and *df*) for the three sources above.

Note here the similarity of the values in the SPSS output to those in Figure 12.9. Here, we have a significant main effect of day, suggesting that some or all of the means scores differ significantly. At this point we also calculate η^2 by dividing SS_{day} by SS_{total}, thus:

$$\eta^2 = \frac{SS_{day}}{SS_{total}} = \frac{208.00}{518.00} = 0.40$$

This indicates that 40% of the total variance is accounted for by our factor *day*. Taking the square root of 0.40, we obtain a measure of effect size of 0.63, a strong effect according to Cohen's guidelines for *r*.

The table headed 'day' gives the 95% confidence intervals for populations treated identically to our sample. Just as when graphing confidence intervals (see Chapter 10, p. 208), these values must be treated with extreme caution or, better still, ignored. It is simply not possible to conclude anything about the changes in each participant across the three days which is the basis of our analysis.

Mauchly's Test of Sphericity[a]
Measure:MEASURE_1

Within-Subjects Effect	Mauchly's W	Approx. Chi-Square	df	Sig.	Epsilon[b]		
					Greenhouse-Geisser	Huynh-Feldt	Lower-Bound
day	.947	.326	2	.849	.950	1.000	.500

Tests the null hypothesis that the error covariance matrix of the orthonormalized transformed dependent variables is proportional to an identity matrix.

[a] Design: Intercept.

[b] May be used to adjust the degrees of freedom for the averaged tests of significance. Corrected tests are displayed in the Tests of Within-Subjects Effects table.

Within-Subjects Design: day

Tests of Within-Subjects Effects
Measure:MEASURE_1

Source		Type III Sum of Squares	df	Mean Square	F	Sig.
Day	Sphericity Assumed	208.000	2	104.000	31.652	.000
	Greenhouse-Geisser	208.000	1.899	109.505	31.652	.000
	Huynh-Feldt	208.000	2.000	104.000	31.652	.000
	Lower-bound	208.000	1.000	208.000	31.652	.001
Error(day)	Sphericity Assumed	46.000	14	3.286		
	Greenhouse-Geisser	46.000	13.296	3.460		
	Huynh-Feldt	46.000	14.000	3.286		
	Lower-bound	46.000	7.000	6.571		

Tests of Between-Subjects Effects
Measure: MEASURE_1
Transformed Variable: Average

Source	Type III Sum of Squares	df	Mean Square	F	Sig.
Intercept	4704.000	1	4704.000	124.727	.000
Error	264.000	7	37.714		

Day
Measure:MEASURE_1

Day	Mean	Std. Error	95% Confidence Interval	
			Lower Bound	Upper Bound
1	17.000	1.535	13.370	20.630
2	15.000	1.476	11.510	18.490
3	10.000	1.000	7.635	12.365

3. Calculating Friedman

Above, we used the *Coffee Time* example to illustrate the rank-based method for comparing several means, the Friedman test. In order to carry out the test, we need the *Coffee Time* data file created in Chapter 11 (p. 236). Load this data file.

The specific routine for this analysis is located in **Analyze** > **Nonparametric Tests** > **Legacy Dialogs** > **K Related Samples...** (again, K refers to a number greater than 2, here K = 3).

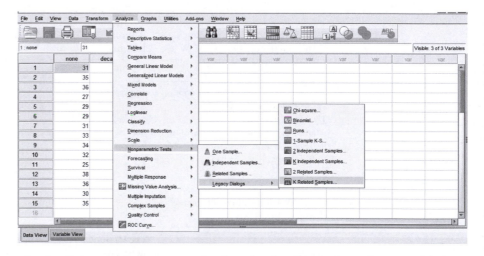

In the dialogue window, move the three levels of the independent variable (none, decaff, coffee) into the box labeled **Test Variables:**. Under **Test Type**, **Friedman** is already selected by default.

Click **OK**.

The **SPSS Statistics Viewer** presents the results as below. The first table gives the mean ranks for the three conditions and the second table shows the χ^2 approximation, *df* and *p* (labeled Asymp. Sig.) which should be stated as =.002.

Ranks

	Mean Rank
No coffee	2.50
Decaffeinated coffee	2.20
Regular coffee	1.30

Test statistics[a]

N	15
Chi-square	13.000
df	2
Asymp. Sig.	.002

[a]Friedman Test

Reporting the results of a one-way within-subjects ANOVA

Again, there is no rigid convention and different journal articles will contain slightly different information depending on editorial policy. Consistent with Brace et al. (2009), we recommend the following for a summary of the repeated measures ANOVA:

There was a significant main effect of day ($F(2,14) = 31.65, p < .0001, \eta^2 = .40$)

... And for Friedman

Typing speed varied significantly across the three conditions: $\chi^2(2, N = 15) = 13.00, p < .001$

When to use the rank-based alternatives

There are no hard-and-fast rules as to when the rank-based alternatives are preferable to one-factor ANOVA. They are resistant to the effects of outliers, so one indication that they may be better is the existence in the data of prominent outliers – but there are no firm guidelines on exactly how outlying the outliers need to be to trigger the use of the rank-based alternatives. They are also preferable if there is an indication, either from the distribution of the samples, or on general grounds, that the distribution of the dependent variable in the population departs markedly from the normal distribution.

There are other, more obvious, circumstances where the rank-based tests are the only possible ones to use; namely, when the original data are themselves ranks. One example of each type will serve to illustrate this point.

A possible scenario is that you want to compare the mathematics performance of three groups of children within a class – those with a computer at home, those with a calculator, and those with neither – and that the data on mathematics performance available to you is a ranking by the teacher of all the pupils in the class. Then a Kruskal-Wallis test would be appropriate. (It must be said that these circumstances – where a lot of people are ranked on some variable, rather than measured in some way – are not likely to occur very often.)

It is more common for repeated measures to take the form of rankings, in particular when a number of objects are rated by several individuals. For example, students might each be asked to rank four psychology courses – Psycholinguistics, Social Psychology, Statistics, Human–Computer Interaction – from most liked (1) to least liked (4). A Friedman test would be the appropriate way to analyse such data.

Settling differences: Post hoc tests

As the last student/statistician dialogue revealed, an *F* ratio that reaches statistical significance allows us to reject the null hypothesis. This implies *some* difference between the groups (for a between factor ANOVA) or the conditions (for a within-factors ANOVA). However, it does not pinpoint the *precise* difference or differences, and a follow-up test is necessary to do that. (Note that this complication does not arise with *t*-tests – if you think about it, you will realize why.)

Drilling down: Multiple comparisons

General knowledge

Consider data set A from our *General knowledge* example again, with the data shown graphically in Figure 12.11. Earlier in this chapter, the ANOVA summary table (Figure 12.3) showed a statistically significant *F* ratio for *Groups*, pointing to a difference between French, Irish and American students. However, there are three specific comparisons underlying our significant result:

French v. Irish;
French v. American; and
Irish v. American.

Which of these is statistically significant?

There are many different methods available for comparing pairs of means 'after-the-event' or *post hoc*. These so-called **unplanned comparisons** are available in SPSS with three restrictions, as noted by Brace et al. (2009). First, only comparisons for independent variables with three or more levels are available (since the main effect is sufficient for variables with only two levels – think about it). Second, comparisons

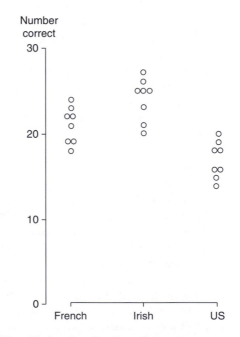

Figure 12.11 *General knowledge*: **Graph of first data set**

Multiple Comparisons

Data set A scores
Tukey HSD

(I) Nationality	(J) Nationality	Mean Difference (I – J)	Std. Error	Sig.	95% Confidence Interval Lower Bound	Upper Bound
French	Irish	−3.00*	1.113	.035	−5.80	−.20
French	US	4.00*	1.113	.005	1.20	6.80
Irish	French	3.00*	1.113	.035	.20	5.80
Irish	US	7.00*	1.113	.000	4.20	9.80
US	French	−4.00*	1.113	.005	−6.80	−1.20
US	Irish	−7.00*	1.113	.000	−9.80	−4.20

Based on observed means.
The error term is Mean Square (Error) = 4.952.

*The mean difference is significant at the .05 level.

Figure 12.12 Data set A: SPSS summary of Tukey's HSD tests (*General knowledge*)

are only readily available for between groups, that is unrelated groups, independent variables (although, as we shall see, there are ways and means of obtaining such comparisons for within-subjects factors). Third, comparisons should only be used if the ANOVA indicates a significant effect.

SPSS offers no fewer than 18 options for *post hoc* comparisons. All essentially do the same thing. Some, however, are suited to equal group sizes, while others cope with unbalanced sample sizes. Some require homogeneity of sample variances, while others do not. Some are more cautious or conservative in asserting a difference between means. Here we consider just one (Brace et al. (2009) consider a different one), which goes by the catchy title of **Tukey's Honestly Significant Difference (HSD) test**. Applying this test to our data using a standard statistical package produces a summary of so-called *paired comparisons*. While the form of presentation may vary from one package to another, each will present the same information, namely a summary of comparisons of all possible pairs of means. Figure 12.12 presents the format used by SPSS.

As you can see from the table, there is far more information than you need. SPSS provides both permutations of each paired comparison, that is, Irish v French and French v Irish, and so on. This is clearly unnecessary and you simply need to pick out one of the comparisons. For each paired comparison, the table presents the difference between the means of the two groups being compared, the associated *p* value (labeled Sig.), and the confidence interval of the difference between the means. Hence, looking at the comparison, between the French and Irish groups, the difference between the groups (French minus Irish) is −3.00, the sign indicating that the Irish mean is greater than the French. This difference is statistically significant (*p* = .035), and there is a 95% chance that the population mean difference between these groups lies between 5.80 and 0.20.

In fact, we can see from the table that, for data set A, all three comparisons are statistically significant, especially the difference between Irish and American, with a mean difference of 7.00 and an associated *p* value < .001. Note also from the table, that none of the confidence intervals contains zero at the 95% level of confidence.

Applying the same test to data set B produces the table shown in Figure 12.13.

					95% Confidence Interval	
		Mean Difference			Lower	Upper
(I) Nationality	(J) Nationality	(I − J)	Std. Error	Sig.	Bound	Bound
French	Irish	−3.00	2.769	.534	−9.98	3.98
	US	4.00	2.769	.337	−2.98	10.98
Irish	French	3.00	2.769	.534	−3.98	9.98
	US	7.00*	2.769	.049	.02	13.98
US	French	−4.00	2.769	.337	−10.98	2.98
	Irish	−7.00*	2.769	.049	−13.98	−.02

Multiple Comparisons

Data set B scores
Tukey HSD

Based on observed means.
The error term is Mean Square (Error) = 30.667.

*The mean difference is significant at the .05 level.

Figure 12.13 Data set B: Results of Tukey's HSD tests (*General knowledge*)

> **Before reading on...**
>
> Interpret the table in Figure 12.13.
>
> ... now read on<

We hope you noticed that, this time, although the same mean differences were obtained, only one paired comparison was significant, that between the Irish and American groups and, at that, p = .049 – just significant and no more. The lack of significance is, of course due to the greater overall variability of scores, as indicated by the larger value for the pooled standard error (2.769 compared to 1.113 for data set A). Apart from this one comparison, no other p value is even close to the .05 cut-off for significance. Also note that all confidence intervals, except for the Irish/ American comparison contain zero and, even that comparison comes very close, with a population mean difference lying between 0.02 and 13.98 at the 95% confidence level.

Making sense of SPSS

Obtaining multiple paired comparisons for unrelated groups

Note: We recommend you also consult Brace et al. (2009), pp. 249–251 who provide further information.

General knowledge

The method described here is merely a modification of the one-way between groups ANOVA that we illustrated in the *Making sense of SPSS* example earlier in this chapter (pp. 254–257). Specifically, when you obtain the **Univariate** window below, click on the **Post Hoc...** button.

The dialogue window will appear as below. This window presents the myriad options for *post hoc* tests alluded to above. Move your factor *nationality* into the box headed **Post Hoc Tests for:**, as shown, and tick **Tukey**. The table in Figure 12.12 will appear.

Related groups: Fading memories

Drilling down into data following a within-subjects ANOVA requires a little more ingenuity. SPSS user guides, including Brace et al. (2009) will inform you that *post hoc* multiple comparisons are not available for repeated measures factors and, strictly, they are correct. However, it is possible to obtain several types of *post hoc* test for related data. Figure 12.14 shows the results of one such method, Bonferri adjusted pairwise comparisons, for our *Fading memories* example.

Interestingly, the results indicate that there is no significant difference in recall between days 1 and 2 ($p = .257$), but that there is a significant difference between days 2 and 3 ($p = .002$) and, obviously, between days 1 and 3 ($p < .001$). Thus, according to the pairwise comparisons, it would appear that the highly significant ($p < .001$) main effect of *day* reported in the one-way within-subjects ANOVA is driven by the difference between day 3 and days 1 and 2. This illustrates the need to explore significant main effects.

Pairwise Comparisons						
Measure:MEASURE_1						
(I) day	(J) day	Mean Difference (I–J)	Std. Error	Sig.[a]	95% Confidence Interval for Difference[a]	
					Lower Bound	Upper Bound
1	2	2.000	1.000	.257	−1.128	5.128
	3	7.000*	.824	.000	4.424	9.576
2	1	−2.000	1.000	.257	−5.128	1.128
	3	5.000*	.886	.002	2.228	7.772
3	1	−7.000*	.824	.000	−9.576	−4.424
	2	−5.000*	.886	.002	−7.772	−2.228
Based on estimated marginal means						
[a] Adjustment for multiple comparisons: Bonferroni.						
*The mean difference is significant at the.05 level.						

Figure 12.14 *Fading memories*: **Bonferroni adjusted pairwise comparisons for** *day*

Making sense of SPSS

Obtaining multiple paired comparisons for related samples

Fading memories

Again, this is a modification of the method for one-way within-subjects ANOVA shown above (pp. 266–270). When you obtain the **Repeated Measures** window below, if you were to click on the **Post Hoc...** button, you would be presented with the completely inert dialogue window shown alongside, with no option to select *post hoc* tests (the factor *day* does not even appear in the **Factor(s):** box).

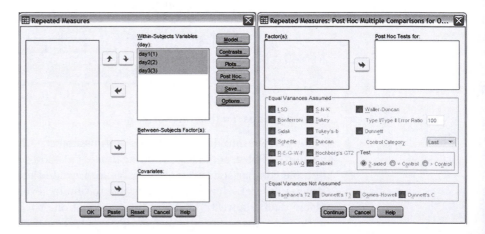

All is not lost, however! Instead, choose **Options...** in the **Repeated Measures** window (recall that **Options...** was previously chosen in the *Making sense of SPSS* example (p. 267) in order to select **Homogeneity tests**). As shown in the **Repeated Measures: Options** dialogue window below, ensure that *day* has been moved into the **Display Means for:** box (note, this had been done previously on p. 268 to obtain confidence intervals). Now, tick **Compare main effects**, select **Bonferroni** from the drop down menu, and click **Continue** followed by **OK**.

(Note, it is also possible choose the slightly less conservative **Sidak** option rather than **Bonferroni**. The third option **LSD(none)**, is not generally recommended, especially if lots of comparisons are required. Here, **LSD(none)** is identical to carrying out three paired *t*-tests.)

The resulting multiple comparisons table is as shown in Figure 12.14.

Trend-setting: Fading memories

The levels of a factor in ANOVA often are values of a category variable – for example, faculty, nationality or experimental treatment. Since the ordering of the levels is arbitrary in these cases, it is sufficient to use multiple comparisons to discover what differs from what.

In some cases, however, the levels of a factor may have a natural order. A clear example is *Fading memories*, in which the levels are the number of days elapsed (1, 2 or 3) since the items were committed to memory. In such cases, we are usually interested in more than merely whether one level of a factor differs from any other. Instead, we may wish to know whether there is a general **trend** across the levels of our factor. In order to examine this question, we carry out **planned comparisons**, in contrast to the unplanned comparisons in the previous section. Hence, rather than simply comparing everything with everything, we specify the particular direction and, in this case, order of differences between conditions.

As might be expected, the graphical analysis of the memory data does show a clear trend – the longer the time elapsed, the more forgetting takes place (Figure 12.15). Indeed, the data can roughly be fitted by a straight line, as indicated. In such a case, a sub-part of the variation associated with the systematic source *day* can be identified as relating specifically to a linear trend, and this can be expressed separately. In terms of the ANOVA summary table, this may be indicated as shown in Figure 12.16. The linear trend is associated with 1 *df*, and an *F* ratio can be calculated. In this case, it will be seen that the linear trend accounts for a high proportion of the variance in experimental conditions, and the corresponding *F* ratio is very high, confirming the impression of a strong linear trend given by the graph.

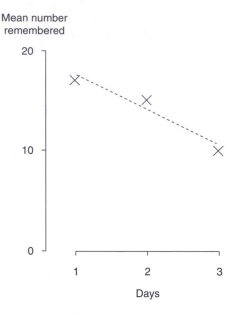

Figure 12.15 *Fading memories*: Trend across days

Source of Variation	Sum of Squares	df	Mean Square	F	p
Subjects	264.000	7			
Day	208.000	2	104.000	31.652	.0000
Linear trend	*196.000*	*1*	*196.000*	*72.211*	*.0000*
Error	*19.000*	*7*	*2.714*		
Error	46.000	14	3.286		
Total	518.000	23			

Figure 12.16 *Fading memories*: ANOVA summary table including linear trend test

> **Alert**
>
> Care must be exercised when specifying a linear trend, or any other trend, in data. This is only valid if you can be sure that the intervals between the levels of your ordered independent variable are equal. Here, self-evidently, the variable *day* gives such equal intervals, so the observation of a linear trend is appropriate.

In our *Making sense of SPSS* example above (p. 269), we used the relevant values from the ANOVA summary table to calculate the proportion of the total variance accounted for by the main effect of *day*, thus: $\eta^2 = SS_{day}/SS_{total} = 208.00/518.00 = 0.40$ and, by taking the square root, we obtained a large effect size of ($r = 0.63$).

Similarly, we can calculate η^2 and the effect size for the linear trend associated with *day*:

$$\eta^2 = \frac{SS_{linear}}{SS_{total}} = \frac{196.00}{518.00} = \mathbf{0.38}$$

giving a large effect size of $r = 0.62$. Thus, virtually all of the variation explained by the main effect *day* is accounted for by the linear trend across days.

Making sense of SPSS

Planned comparisons: linear trend analysis

Fading memories

This is a further modification of the method for one-way within-subjects ANOVA shown above (pp. 266–270). Let's start again with the **Repeated Measures** window below.

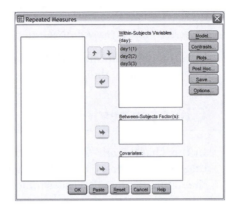

Choose **Contrasts....** As shown in the **Repeated Measures: Contrasts** dialogue window below, ensure that Polynomial is showing in the drop down menu (this should be the default option). Click **Continue** followed by **OK**.

Among the resulting ANOVA tables is the one shown below, labelled Tests of Within-Subjects Contrasts. The two highlighted lines are those included in the ANOVA summary table in Figure 12.16.

Tests of Within-Subjects Contrasts
Measure:MEASURE_1

Source	day	Type III Sum of Squares	df	Mean Square	F	Sig.
day	Linear	196.000	1	196.000	72.211	.000
	Quadratic	12.000	1	12.000	3.111	.121
Error(day)	Linear	19.000	7	2.714		
	Quadratic	27.000	7	3.857		

Post hoc tests following Kruskal-Wallis and Friedman

So far, we have focused on drilling down into data following one-way ANOVA. Of course, if one of the rank-based alternatives were used, it is still possible to carry out post hoc analysis, although these have to be done somewhat laboriously.

In the case of Kruskal-Wallis, a succession of Mann-Whitney U tests can be carried out in the manner shown in Chapter 7, as in the *General knowledge* example, to compare the various pairings of the three nationalities.

For Friedman, Wilcoxon W tests would be carried out, as in our *Fading memories* example, to compare the various pairings of the three days.

Practice makes you-know-what

We strongly recommend that you use some of the data sets provided in Chapter 11 to reinforce your ability to carry out and interpret the tests covered here.

Chapter review

In this chapter, *one-factor* (also known as *one-way*) ANOVA has been introduced, together with rank-based alternative tests and follow-up (*post hoc*) tests to pinpoint the nature of any differences indicated by a statistically significant result. The relationships between the tests for two samples – either independent or related – and those for more than two samples are summarized in Figure 12.17.

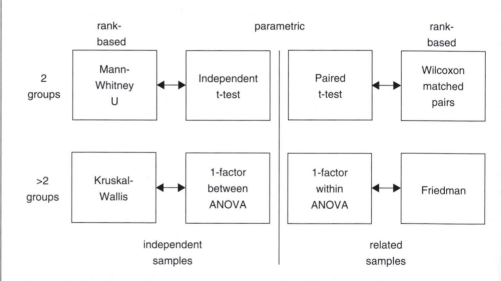

Figure 12.17 Relationship between parametric and rank-based tests for comparing groups

Seeing patterns in data: Comparisons involving more than one independent variable

In this chapter

... comparisons within more complex experimental designs are illustrated through summary statistics and graphs. Whereas Chapters 4 and 11 described comparisons based on a *single independent variable* with two or more levels, this chapter extends these ideas to comparisons involving *two factors* (independent variables). As in the earlier chapters, factors may be *between* (groups) or *within* (subjects), so there are three cases to be considered:

- both factors between;
- 1 between and 1 within factor; and
- both factors within.

Illustrative examples

Technophilia/technophobia

We have previously considered differences between faculties in terms of *Attitude to Computers*. It might also be of interest to test whether there is any evidence of a gender difference. It would be possible to test this using a single *t*-test for all the faculties combined, or possibly three separate *t*-tests to compare females and males within each of the three faculties. However, a more powerful method is to consider faculty and gender *together* as two independent variables (or factors) within a single analysis.

In this example, there are two factors, namely *faculty* and *gender*. They are both *between groups* factors, since no student can belong to more than one faculty or to more than one gender. *Faculty* has three levels – arts, science and economics; *gender* has two levels – female and male. This type of design is known formally as a **2-factor (or 2-way) independent groups design**.

Figure 13.1 displays the six combinations of two genders in three faculties. In each *cell*, the data are illustrated (not given in full), and the number of cases and mean are given for each cell. As well as these means, overall means can be worked out for:

- all males, all females; and
- all arts students, all science students, all economics students, as indicated.

Having calculated the means for each *gender/faculty* combination, they can be displayed effectively using the sort of graph shown in Figure 13.2. From this graph (as from the original table showing means) it can be seen that there is very little variation in the mean *Attitude to Computers* scores, either among faculties, or between genders. It looks very much as if these data provide essentially no evidence of any systematic differences attributable to either *gender* or *faculty*.

	ARTS	SCIENCE	ECONOMICS	
Male	*n* = 33	*n* = 17	*n* = 9	*n* = 59
	67 56 52 58 45 45 44 57	60 66 55 52 52 39 40 56	41 64 39 58 56 49 50 53	All males
	mean 53.3	mean 54.0	mean 52.0	mean 53.1
Female	*n* = 68	*n* = 22	*n* = 24	*n* = 114
	42 54 67 55 45 56 61 51	46 64 56 46 48 61 52 58	63 56 53 57 52 50 45 49	All females
	mean 51.6	mean 51.5	mean 54.4	mean 52.5
	n = 101	*n* = 39	*n* = 33	
	All Arts	All Science	All Econ.	
	mean 52.5	mean 52.8	mean 53.2	

Figure 13.1 *Technophilia/technophobia*: **Computer attitude by faculty and gender – partial data for illustration**

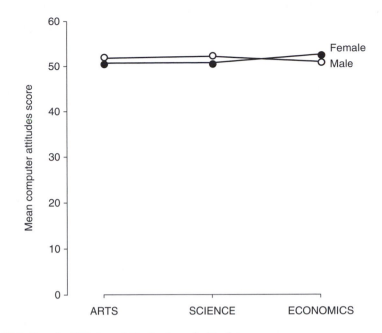

Figure 13.2 Graph of *Technophilia/technophobia* data

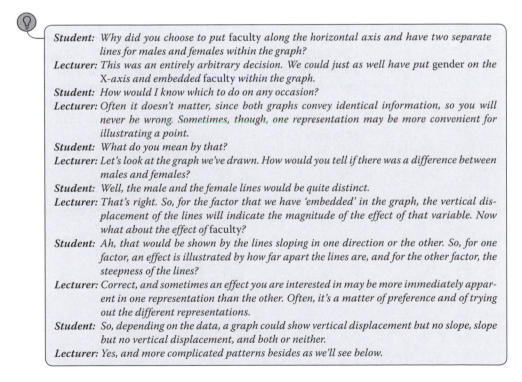

Student: Why did you choose to put faculty *along the horizontal axis and have two separate lines for males and females within the graph?*

Lecturer: This was an entirely arbitrary decision. We could just as well have put gender *on the X-axis and embedded* faculty *within the graph.*

Student: How would I know which to do on any occasion?

Lecturer: Often it doesn't matter, since both graphs convey identical information, so you will never be wrong. Sometimes, though, one representation may be more convenient for illustrating a point.

Student: What do you mean by that?

Lecturer: Let's look at the graph we've drawn. How would you tell if there was a difference between males and females?

Student: Well, the male and the female lines would be quite distinct.

Lecturer: That's right. So, for the factor that we have 'embedded' in the graph, the vertical displacement of the lines will indicate the magnitude of the effect of that variable. Now what about the effect of faculty?

Student: Ah, that would be shown by the lines sloping in one direction or the other. So, for one factor, an effect is illustrated by how far apart the lines are, and for the other factor, the steepness of the lines?

Lecturer: Correct, and sometimes an effect you are interested in may be more immediately apparent in one representation than the other. Often, it's a matter of preference and of trying out the different representations.

Student: So, depending on the data, a graph could show vertical displacement but no slope, slope but no vertical displacement, and both or neither.

Lecturer: Yes, and more complicated patterns besides as we'll see below.

Couch potatoes

Figure 13.3 shows some data on the average number of hours (to the nearest hour) children spent watching TV. The data are broken down by the socioeconomic status (SES) of the father and the age of the child. For each combination of *SES/age*, data for six children are listed in the row. The mean for each group of six children is shown in the final column.

SES	Age	Hours TV per week	Means
AB	6	17 22 13 21 15 19	17.8
	10	21 19 15 18 22 14	18.2
	14	11 19 17 12 23 15	16.2
C1	6	25 14 18 20 18 18	18.8
	10	27 23 10 18 24 23	20.8
	14	17 22 15 21 26 19	20.0
C2	6	26 22 18 19 15 19	19.8
	10	19 25 29 14 25 16	21.3
	14	24 11 24 27 22 23	21.8
DE	6	19 16 28 23 17 24	21.2
	10	21 17 31 19 25 25	23.0
	14	13 35 26 21 17 22	22.3

Figure 13.3 *Couch potato* data

Before reading on...

How many factors are there in this study, and what type is each? How many levels are there of each factor?

... now read on

We hope you identified the following anatomy of the study. There are two factors; father's *SES* at four levels (AB, C1, C2, DE), and *age* of child at three levels (6, 10, 14 years). Since participants are assigned to only one level of *SES* and one level of *age*, both factors are between groups (also referred to as independent or unrelated groups). This too is a **2-factor (or 2-way) independent groups design**.

Again, the simplest way to look at the patterns in the data is to graph the means as in Figure 13.4.

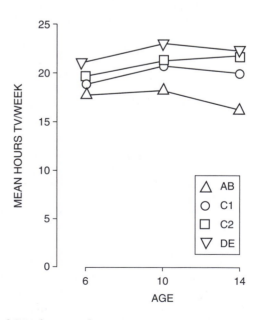

Figure 13.4 Graph of *Couch potato* data

Before reading on...

What patterns do you see in this graph? Jot down your thoughts.

... **now read on**

The apparent patterns are visible:

- A clear relationship between *SES* and amount of TV watching. As *SES* goes progressively from AB to DE the average amount of viewing consistently increases; and
- not much indication of change with *age* – slightly lower figures for the 6-year-olds.

As an exercise, you might like to replot the graph with *SES* along the *X*-axis and separate lines for the three ages.

Making sense of SPSS

Couch potato: Creating the data file and obtaining graphical summaries

1. Creating the data file

In Chapter 3 (pp. 35–38), we showed how to create SPSS data files in some detail. Here, we present the data file for *Couch potato* using the same methods.

Before reading on...

If necessary, look again at Chapter 3 to remind yourself of the important points in creating a data file, in particular, the difference between coding independent groups and repeated measures data.

... **now read on**

We remind you that the golden rule for coding any data in SPSS is that *each individual participant (case) occupies a single row of their own in the data file.* This is known as a *casewise* data structure.

As noted above, in this *Couch potato* example, we have two independent variables: *SES* with four levels (AB, C1, C2, DE) and *age* with three levels (6, 10, 14). The design is entirely between groups, so each of the participants produces only a single score. Since there are 6 participants in each of the 12 separate subgroups, we know that there will be a total of 72 rows in the data file and three columns – one to code *SES*, one to code *age*, and the other for the participant's score.

When you have created the data file, the **Data View** should look as below (cases 5–20 shown). Remember to save your data.

2. Graphical summaries

Unfortunately, SPSS is poor at generating summary statistics and we avoid doing so here. The problem is that, as Figure 13.4 implies, we need to obtain summaries for the 12 separate subgroups. However, the SPSS **Explore...** routine will only give a summary of one variable averaged across the other and vice versa. In the next chapter, you will see how to obtain such statistics from within a statistical analysis.

The same is true of the graphical summaries available in **Explore...**. However, we have another option available, namely the **Graphs** menu. Let's draw a line graph like that in Figure 13.4. Select **Graphs > Legacy Dialogs > Line...**. In the resulting dialogue window (see below), select **Multiple** and leave the default **Summaries for groups of cases** selected. Click **Define**.

The dialogue window below will appear. First, select the option **Other statistic (e.g., mean)**, then move the dependent variable (**Hours of TV watched per week**) into the **Variable:** box which has become active. For consistency with Figure 13.4, move the independent variable 'Age of child' to the **Category axis:** box and 'Father's socio-economic status' to the box labeled **Define lines by:**. Note, as implied in the Student/Lecturer dialogue on page 283, the allocation to these latter two boxes is arbitrary.

Click **OK**.

The line graph will appear as below (following a few cosmetic 'tweaks'). Note that this is very similar to Figure 13.4, except that, by default, the origin is set at 16 rather than zero, thus amplifying the magnitude of the effects.

SES

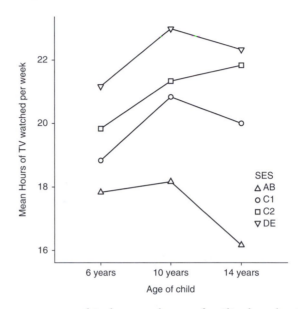

Let's choose one more graphical type – the now familiar boxplot. This time select **Graphs** > **Legacy Dialogs** > **Boxplot…**. From the resulting dialogue screen below, select **Clustered** and **Summaries for groups of cases**.
Click **Define**.

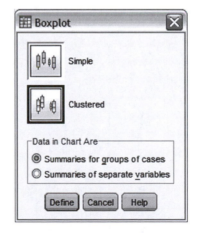

In the dialogue window below, assign the dependent and independent variables as shown. (Again, the allocation to **Category Axis:** and **Define Clusters by:** is arbitrary).
Click **OK**.

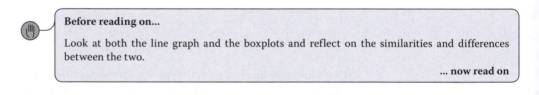

The boxplot diagram below will appear (again, following a few cosmetic 'tweaks')..

Before reading on...

Look at both the line graph and the boxplots and reflect on the similarities and differences between the two.

... now read on

Father's SES
AB

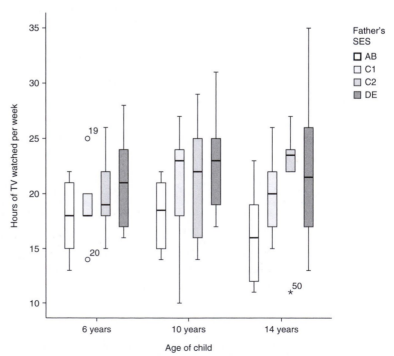

Fading memories

In a modification of the *Fading memories* example introduced in Chapter 12, participants were again asked to memorize a list of 30 words, and, this time, each participant was tested for the number correctly recalled 1 day, 2 days, 3 days and 4 days later. Also, an additional experimental condition was included, whereby half the participants were taught a mnemonic strategy beforehand (experimental group) and the other half were not (control group). There were seven participants in each group. Data are presented in Figure 13.5.

Before reading on...

Identify the factors and say which type each one is. How many levels for each factor?

... **now read on**

In this case, there are two factors – experimental condition (memory strategy) is a *between groups* factor with two levels (no mnemonic, mnemonic), and number of days elapsed is a *within-subjects* factor with four levels (1, 2, 3, 4 days). This type of design is known formally as a **2-factor (or 2-way) mixed design** (*mixed* because one factor is between and the other within). Plotting the means leads to the graph in Figure 13.6.

Before reading on...

What are the salient points in the graph in Figure 13.6? Jot down your thoughts.

... **now read on**

		Day		
	1	2	3	4
No strategy training	20	13	8	5
	23	18	13	11
	19	15	12	7
	25	19	14	13
	20	17	16	11
	16	9	5	4
	24	15	11	7
Means	21.0	15.1	11.3	8.3
Strategy training	28	26	22	23
	24	21	20	20
	27	27	22	21
	27	23	21	19
	26	23	18	19
	22	20	19	20
	22	18	17	17
Means	25.1	22.6	19.9	19.9

Figure 13.5 *Fading memories*: **Recall scores by strategy and day**

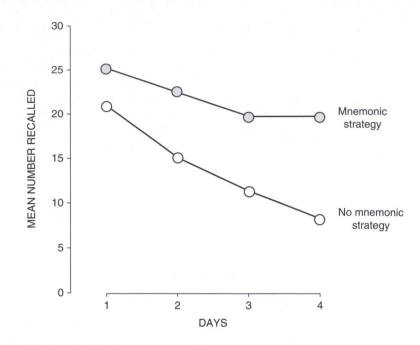

Figure 13.6 Graph of *Fading memories* data

It appears from the graph that

- memory deteriorates over the four days, *irrespective of the memory strategy* – this is called a *main effect* of *day*;
- the mnemonic strategy has a beneficial effect in aiding recall, *irrespective of the number of days* – this time a *main effect* of *strategy*; and, moreover,
- the rate of forgetting, as shown by the slope of the line, is less slow for the experimental (mnemonic) group than for the control (no mnemonic) group.

When the pattern across one factor (here *day*) differs for different levels of the other factor (*strategy*), this is called an **interaction**. In this example, then, it appears that there is a ***day* × *strategy* interaction**, as well as a main effect for *day* and a main effect for *strategy*. The concept of interaction is among the most important that you will learn about in this chapter and the next.

More about interaction: Key concept

Before proceeding, let's take a closer look at the concept of interaction. Already at this stage of having considered some designs with more than one factor, it may have occurred to you that, as soon as you move beyond a single factor situation, various possibilities arise. The seemingly innocuous act of introducing an additional factor, as in the above examples, creates an order of complexity greater than when only a single factor is involved.

> *Student:* *This idea of* interaction *has suddenly appeared out of the blue. I'm a bit confused.*
> *Lecturer:* *OK, let's look back at the graph in Figure 13.6. It's not blatantly obvious – we'll see a much clearer example a little later – but it is apparent that the eight means make quite an interesting shape. Why don't you describe it for me.*

> *Student:* Well, we have separate lines for the two strategy conditions and both of these show a gradual decrease in memory score across the four days, but the decrease tails off for the mnemonic group.
>
> *Lecturer:* So what are you saying about the pattern of means across the four days for the two strategies?
>
> *Student:* They're a bit different.
>
> *Lecturer:* Correct. If I were to put it a little more technically, I would say that the effect of day was different for the two strategies. Can we think about it in any other way?
>
> *Student:* Hmm, not sure.
>
> *Lecturer:* Well, instead of looking at the shape of the two lines across day, how about looking at the differences between the two strategies at each of the four days.
>
> *Student:* Oh right, so now we are looking at the differences between the strategies at each level of day? Well, on day 1, the difference is about 5 words remembered and this changes at each day until, by day 4, the difference is about 12 words.
>
> *Lecturer:* Precisely. We see a **difference in the differences** across the levels of day.
>
> *Student:* A difference in the differences! That's a pretty eccentric expression.
>
> *Lecturer:* Yes it is, but it's a good way of remembering what an interaction is.
>
> *Student:* So an interaction means that the effect in one factor is different for the different levels of the other factor.
>
> *Lecturer:* Not so memorable, but spot on!

So, as discussed by our student and lecturer, the effect of *day* is different for the two levels of *strategy*. Or, the effect of *strategy* is different for the four levels of *day*. That is, there is an interaction between our two factors, a ***day* × *strategy*** **interaction**. Needless to say, at this stage, we cannot say how large or *strong* the interaction is, but it's certainly noticeable.

> *Lecturer:* What would you expect the graph to have looked like if there had not been an interaction?
>
> *Student:* Eh, the pattern of both lines would have been the same?
>
> *Lecturer:* Or the difference between the strategies would have been the same for each of the four days.
>
> *Student:* Right – two sides of the same coin.
>
> *Lecturer:* Very well put, I'll use that myself in future! But, what would this mean in practice?
>
> *Student:* Think I'm on a roll here – if the differences were the same for the four days, the lines would be parallel.
>
> *Lecturer:* You are on a roll – that's exactly right. If the lines on a graph are **parallel**, there is **no interaction**. If they are **not parallel**, there is **an interaction**. The **strength** of the interaction will be indicated by the extent of the **non-parallelness** of the lines, to coin a phrase.

Read over the dialogue carefully until you are sure that you grasp the important points. We shall return to this more formally in the next chapter when considering how to decide whether an interaction is sufficiently strong to be statistically significant. In multifactor designs (here, we consider only two-factor), it is not just the main effects that have to be assessed for significance, but the interactions (two-factor designs only have only one interaction).

Fame and recognition

In this experiment male (*n* = 8) and female (*n* = 9) students were shown 60 photographs – 20 of fashion models, 20 of footballers, and 20 of pop stars – and asked to identify them. The dependent variable is the correct number (see Figure 13.7). This is another example with 1 between groups factor and 1 within-subjects factor – a *2-factor mixed design*. Here the between factor is *gender* (with two levels, female and male) and the within factor is *category* of photograph (with three levels, models, footballers, pop stars). If you look at the total scores out of 60, you can see from the table that the means for males (30.6) and females (30.9), *irrespective of category*, are essentially the same; we can express this by saying that there appears to be no main effect of *gender*. Similarly, the overall means for *category* of photograph, *irrespective of gender*, are very close (10.1, 10.3 and 10.3, respectively). So it might appear that there are no interesting effects in these data. That this would be a wrong conclusion is evident when the data are graphed, as in Figure 13.8 (you may have noticed it from the table).

This is the much clearer example of an interaction we referred to above. Here there is a very strong **gender × category interaction**, even though neither factor produces an effect when considered in isolation (main effect). It is clear that the lines are anything but parallel and, at least on visual inspection, the strength of the interaction could well be significant, if only we knew how to decide this (all in good time!). The interaction arises because the males are much better at identifying footballers, and females at identifying models – in terms of the total scores for males and females, these differences cancel out.

	Models	Footballers	Pop Stars	Total
	7	15	11	33
	4	12	5	21
	5	17	9	31
Male	11	18	14	43
	8	15	8	31
	8	16	13	37
	3	14	11	28
	4	16	6	26
Means	6.1	15.1	9.3	30.6
	10	3	11	24
	17	10	14	41
	17	11	17	45
	15	5	11	31
Female	18	5	10	33
	11	4	9	24
	12	2	9	23
	15	7	12	34
	12	3	8	23
Means	14.1	5.6	11.2	30.9
Overall means	10.1	10.3	10.3	

Figure 13.7 *Fame and recognition*: Identification scores by *gender* and *type* of photograph

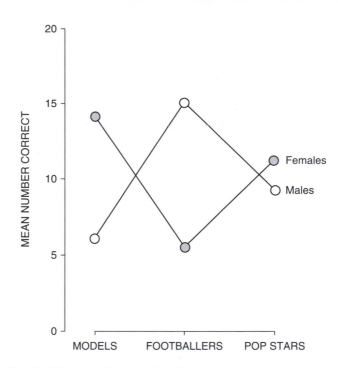

Figure 13.8 Graph of *Fame and recognition* data

Making sense of SPSS

Two-factor mixed designs: Creating data files and obtaining graphical summaries

1. Creating the data files

In Chapter 3 (pp. 35–38), we showed how to create SPSS data files in some detail.

> **Before reading on...**
>
> If necessary, look back at Chapter 3 to remind yourself of the important points in creating a data file, in particular, the difference between coding independent groups and repeated measures data.
>
> **... now read on**

Again, we remind you of the golden rule for coding any data in SPSS – that *each individual participant (case) occupies a single row of their own in the data file*. This is known as a *casewise* data structure.

Fading memories

As noted above, in the *Fading memories* example, we have two independent variables: *day* with four levels (1, 2, 3, 4) and *strategy* with two levels (mnemonic, no mnemonic). In this mixed design, *day* is the within-subjects factor and *strategy* the between groups. So each of the participants produces four scores – one for each day. Since there are 7 participants in each of the 2 strategies, we know that there will be a total of 14 rows in the data file, and 5 columns – one to code *strategy*, and one for each of the four scores for each participant.

When you have created the data file, the **Data View** should look as below. Remember to save your data.

	strategy	day1	day2	day3	day4
1	1	20	13	8	5
2	1	23	18	13	11
3	1	19	15	12	7
4	1	25	19	14	13
5	1	20	17	16	11
6	1	16	9	5	4
7	1	24	15	11	7
8	2	28	26	22	23
9	2	24	21	20	20
10	2	27	27	22	21
11	2	27	23	21	19
12	2	26	23	18	19
13	2	22	20	19	20
14	2	22	18	17	17

Fame and recognition

Recall that, in this mixed example, we again have two independent variables: *category* of photograph with three levels (models, footballers, pop stars) and *gender* with two levels (male, female). *Category* is the within-subjects factor and *gender* the between groups. So each participant produces three scores – one for each *category* of photograph. Since there is a total of 17 participants (8 male, 9 female), we know that there will be a total of 17 rows in the data file, and four columns – one to code *gender*, and one for each of the three scores for each participant.

When you have created the data file, the **Data View** should look as below. Remember to save your data.

	gender	models	footballers	pop_stars
1	1	7	15	11
2	1	4	12	5
3	1	5	17	9
4	1	11	18	14
5	1	8	15	8
6	1	8	16	13
7	1	3	14	11
8	1	4	16	6
9	2	10	3	11
10	2	17	10	14
11	2	17	11	17
12	2	15	5	11
13	2	18	5	10
14	2	11	4	9
15	2	12	2	9
16	2	15	7	12
17	2	12	3	8

2. Graphical summaries

Remarkably, although your data files are correctly structured, it is not possible to use the **Graphs** menu to obtain line graphs like those in Figures 13.6 and 13.8. This must be done from inside the appropriate statistical application, as we shall demonstrate in the next chapter.

Hot and bothered

To complete the picture, here are some data from an experiment involving two within-subjects factors: a **2-factor (or 2-way) repeated measures design**. Eight experienced typists are tested for their typing speed (words per minute) under three levels of noise (low, moderate, high) combined with three ambient temperatures (50°F, 55°F, 60°F), yielding nine combinations, as indicated in Figure 13.9. The graph in Figure 13.10 has *temperature* plotted on the horizontal axis and separate lines for the three levels of *noise*. (Recall the Student /Lecturer dialogue earlier in this chapter. What if you plot level of noise on the horizontal axis and a separate line for each temperature? Is one arrangement better than the other?)

From the graph, it would appear that

- performance deteriorates as *noise* level increases, *irrespective of temperature*;
- performance is better at 55°F than either colder or hotter, *irrespective of noise level*; and

Noise	Low			Moderate			High		
Temp.	**50°**	**55°**	**60°**	**50°**	**55°**	**60°**	**50°**	**55°**	**60°**
S1	90	94	89	85	90	87	77	85	77
S2	78	86	80	76	85	73	68	77	69
S3	88	90	89	82	88	87	80	80	83
S4	86	93	90	82	85	86	72	78	72
S5	76	84	76	75	80	71	66	72	66
S6	79	85	81	73	81	73	69	73	71
S7	83	90	85	78	84	79	71	80	71
S8	80	85	83	77	81	78	71	72	68
Means	82.5	88.4	84.1	78.5	84.3	79.3	71.8	77.1	72.1

Note: Temperature in degrees Fahrenheit

Figure 13.9 *Hot and bothered*: Typing speed (wpm) by *noise* and *temperature*

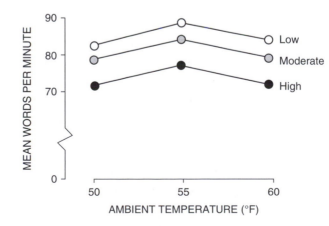

Figure 13.10 Graph of *Hot and bothered* data

• the pattern across temperatures is the same for each level of *noise*, which we can express by saying that there is no sign of a *noise × temperature interaction*. This is indicated by the visibly parallel nature of the lines on the graph, suggesting no "differences in the differences" in either factor across the levels of the other.

Pictures in the mind

In a well-known experiment on perception, participants are presented with simple figures, such as the letter 'F', with the following variations as shown in Figure 13.11:

• The figure is normal, or reversed; and/or
• it is rotated through varying angles.

The task is to decide, as quickly as possible, if the letter is normal or reversed, and the dependent variable is the time (in milliseconds) to make this decision.

If each participant is tested with all 12 variations, the design has 2 *within-subjects* factors, with two (normal, reversed) and six (0°, 60°, 120°, 180°, 240°, 300°) levels. Again, this is known as a *2-factor repeated measures design*. Figure 13.12 presents

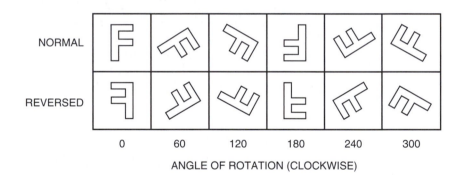

Figure 13.11 *Pictures in the mind*: Six angles of rotation and two figure types (normal and reversed)

Normal						Reversed					
Angle of Rotation (Clockwise)						Angle of Rotation (Clockwise)					
0	60	120	180	240	300	0	60	120	180	240	300
552	621	789	1067	780	630	609	670	835	1124	828	678
533	601	760	1048	771	598	579	648	812	1097	822	644
565	611	777	1061	773	615	615	666	828	1112	823	665
521	578	734	1021	740	584	566	631	789	1078	788	631
589	649	801	1091	798	646	638	697	852	1141	841	699
547	599	749	1027	752	607	599	644	796	1072	798	652
551	610	768	1053	769	613	601	659	819	1102	817	662
MEANS						MEANS					

Figure 13.12 *Pictures in the mind*: Response time (msec.) by *angle* and *type*

some representative data for such an experiment with 6 participants – the resultant graph is shown in Figure 13.13.

Clearly, as the angle increases to 180°, the time to determine whether the figure is reversed or not increases. Thereafter it decreases, symmetrically. Since a clockwise rotation of 240° is equivalent to an anticlockwise rotation of 120°, and clockwise 300° is the same as anticlockwise 60°, this symmetry indicates that it is the size of the angle that determines the time, regardless of whether the rotation is clockwise or anticlockwise. So there is clearly a *main effect* for *angle* of rotation; that is, *irrespective of type*. The data are consistent with an explanation that the decision as to whether the figure is reversed or not is made by first mentally rotating it (at constant speed) into its vertical orientation and then checking whether the rotated image is normal or reversed.

Second, the reversed figures consistently take longer (by about 50 milliseconds) than the normal figures. This small increment in decision time for reversed figures is *irrespective of the angle of orientation*, that is, a *main effect* of *type*.

The pattern of response times for normal and reversed figures looks pretty independent of the angle of rotation (and vice versa), indicating *no interaction* between the

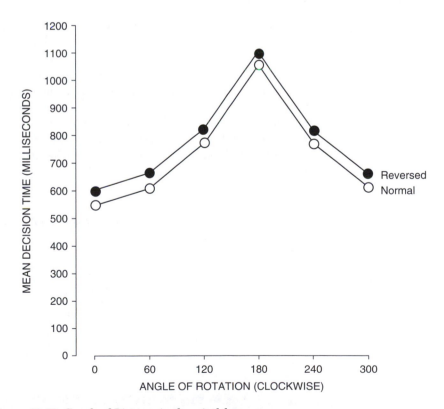

Figure 13.13 Graph of *Pictures in the mind* data

two factors. In fact, you will rarely see lines more parallel than those in Figure 13.13. Here, we can say that there are (virtually) no 'differences in the differences' between normal and reversed figures, or, put another way, no 'difference in the differences' across angles for the two types of figure – two ways of describing the same non-interaction.

Making sense of SPSS

Two-factor repeated measures designs: Creating data files and obtaining graphical summaries

1. Creating the data files

In Chapter 3 (pp. 35–38), we showed how to create SPSS data files in some detail.

> **Before reading on...**
>
> If necessary, look back at Chapter 3 to remind yourself of the important points in creating a data file, in particular, the difference between coding independent groups and repeated measures data.
>
> **... now read on**

Again, we remind you of the golden rule for coding any data in SPSS – that *each individual participant (case) occupies a single row of their own in the data file*. This is known as a *casewise* data structure.

Hot and bothered

As noted above, in the *Hot and bothered* example, we have two independent variables: *noise* with three levels (low, moderate, high) and *temperature* with three levels (50°F, 55°F, 60°F). Since this is a fully repeated measures design, by definition, both factors are within-subjects. So each of the participants produces a total of nine scores – one for each combination of noise level and ambient temperature. Since there are 8 participants, we know that there will be a total of 8 rows in the data file, and nine columns – one for each of the nine scores produced by each participant. Note, since there are no between groups factors, we do not require any coding columns.

When you have created the data file, the **Data View** should look as below. Remember to save your data.

	low_50	low_55	low_60	moderate_50	moderate_55	moderate_60	high_50	high_55	high60	var	var
1	90	94	89	85	90	87	77	85	77		
2	78	86	80	76	85	73	68	77	69		
3	88	90	89	82	88	87	80	80	83		
4	86	93	90	82	85	86	72	78	72		
5	76	84	76	75	80	71	66	72	66		
6	79	85	81	73	81	73	69	73	71		
7	83	90	85	78	84	79	71	80	71		
8	80	85	83	77	81	78	71	72	68		

> **Alert**
>
> You will see that we have 'nested' *temperature* under *noise*, that is, we exhaust the low noise level before moving on to the moderate, and so on. This is, of course, arbitrary – we could have arranged the data as: 50_low, 50_moderate, 50_high, 55_low, 55_moderate, … and so on. Although it is arbitrary, when you have opted for one order or the other, it is essential that you stick with this throughout any analysis.

Pictures in the mind

Recall that, in this repeated measures example, we again have two independent variables: *type* with two levels (normal, reversed) and *angle* with six levels (0°, 60°, 120°, 180°, 240°, 300°). Again, since this is a fully repeated measures design, by definition, both factors are within-subjects. So each of the participants produces a total of 12 scores – one for each combination of *type* and *angle*. Since there are 6 participants, we know that there will be a total of 6 rows in the data file, and 12 columns – one for each of the 12 scores produced by each participant. Again, note that, since there are no between groups factors, we do not require any coding columns.

When you have created the data file, the **Data View** should look as below. Remember to save your data.

> **Alert**
>
> Note here that we have 'nested' *angle* under *type*, that is, we exhaust normal before moving on to the reversed. Again, this is arbitrary – we could have arranged the data as: 0_normal, 0_reversed, 60_normal, 60_reversed, 120_normal, … and so on. Although it is arbitrary, when you have opted for one order or the other, it is essential that you stick with this throughout any analysis.

File   Edit   View   Data   Transform   Analyze   Graphs   Utilities   Add-ons   Window   Help

1 : normal_0   552   Visible: 12 of 12 Variables

	normal_0	normal_60	normal_120	normal_180	normal_240	normal_300	reversed_0	reversed_60	reversed_120	reversed_180	reversed_240	reversed_300
1	552	621	789	1067	780	630	609	670	835	1124	828	678
2	533	601	760	1048	771	598	579	648	812	1097	822	644
3	565	611	777	1061	773	615	615	666	828	1112	823	665
4	521	578	734	1021	740	584	566	631	789	1078	788	631
5	589	649	801	1091	798	646	638	697	852	1141	841	699
6	547	599	749	1027	752	607	599	644	796	1072	798	652
7												
8												
9												
10												
11												
12												
13												
14												
15												
16												
17												
18												

Data View   Variable View

2. Graphical summaries

As with the two-factor mixed examples, although your data files are correctly structured, it is not possible to use the **Graphs** menu to obtain line graphs like those in Figures 13.10 and 13.14. This must be done from inside the appropriate statistical application, as we shall demonstrate in the next chapter.

Beyond graphical analysis

In line with our approach, this chapter has introduced examples of data for 2-factor experimental designs. However, the graphical analysis of such data, while it may be indicative of patterns in the data, needs to be followed by statistical tests, and these are the subject of the next chapter.

Chapter review

In this chapter, three types of 2-factor design

- 2 between (all independent groups);
- 1 between, 1 within (2-factor mixed); and
- 2 within (all repeated measures)

have each been illustrated by two examples, with analysis through calculation of means, and graphically.

Statistical tests: Comparing more than one independent variable

In this chapter

... the examples examined descriptively and graphically in Chapter 13 are revisited, using Analysis of Variance (ANOVA) to test for which differences are statistically significant. Various follow-up tests designed to pinpoint more precisely the nature of statistical significance are also explained.

Two-factor between groups designs

Technophilia/technophobia

Here, again, is the graph of the data introduced in Chapter 13 (pp. 282–283) for *Attitude to Computers* among students in relation to *faculty* and *gender* (see Figure 14.1). As discussed in Chapter 13, this is an example of a **two-factor design**, with *faculty* and *gender* as our factors. Since there are two factors, the data are analysed using a version of ANOVA known as **two-factor**, or **two-way**, ANOVA. Moreover, since both factors are examples of unrelated, or *between groups*, variables, the analysis is a **two-way between groups ANOVA**. The summary table for this analysis is given in Figure 14.2.

Here, there are four sources of variation:

- Differences between faculties – reflected in the graph, and in the faculty means (very small differences, so variation is small);
- Differences between genders – reflected in the graph, and in the gender means (again, very small differences, so variation again small);
- Interaction between faculties and gender (little indication of an interaction in the graph); and
- 'Error' variation – the 'background variation' resulting simply from individual differences.

The first three are *systematic* sources of variation, while the fourth is *non-systematic*. Although this example may appear more complex than the one-factor ANOVAs discussed in Chapter 12, the basic approach and rationale is identical. For each systematic source of variation, an *F* ratio is obtained by dividing the Mean Square (MS) for that effect by the MS (Error). As can be seen, each of these *F* ratios is small and, correspondingly, the *p* values are well above .05, so none of the three is statistically significant, confirming what the graph suggests strongly – that there is no indication from these data that attitude to computers depends on either *faculty* or *gender*, or the *interaction* between these two factors.

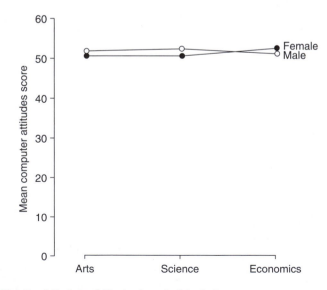

Figure 14.1 Graph of *Technophilia/technophobia* data

Source of Variation	Sum of Squares	df	Mean Square	F	p
Faculty	11.451	2	5.545	0.107	.8988
Gender	10.890	1	10.890	0.203	.6528
F × G interaction	108.065	2	54.032	1.008	.3673
Error	8954.946	167	53.622		
Total	9182.486	172	53.387		

Gender Means	
Male	53.1
Female	52.5

Faculty Means	
Arts	52.5
Science	52.8
Economics	53.2

Figure 14.2 ANOVA summary table for *Technophilia/technophobia* example

---

Key idea

Recall that, in the last chapter, the issue of how to decide whether an interaction was statistically significant was raised. As seen in the ANOVA summary table above, we simply treat the interaction term as another systematic source of variation – just like a main effect, if you like. In terms of the total variation in the data, we now chop it up into three systematic chunks and an error chunk. So, in the same way that SSs, MSs, F and p are calculated for the main effects, we calculate these statistical values for the interaction.

Before reading on...

In order to help consolidate your knowledge of how F ratios are obtained, fill in the blanks in Figure 14.3. Bear in mind that the relationships between the various elements in the summary table are identical to the one-way case in Chapter 12, the only difference being that there are three systematic sources of variation, rather than one. You can check your calculations later in this chapter.

... now read on

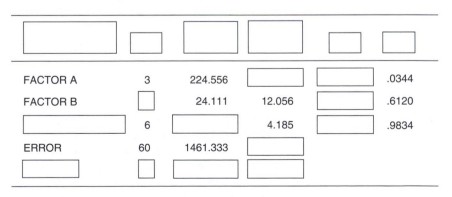

	df				p
FACTOR A	3	224.556			.0344
FACTOR B		24.111	12.056		.6120
	6		4.185		.9834
ERROR	60	1461.333			

Figure 14.3 2-factor unrelated ANOVA: 'Blank' summary table

Confidence intervals

Figure 14.4 presents SPSS calculations of 95% confidence intervals for the means of each main effect and for the six '**interaction means**', as they are known (see *Making sense of SPSS* below for how to obtain these). Note the virtual total overlap in each set of confidence intervals, emphasizing the absence of any significant effects as seen in the ANOVA summary table.

1. Faculty

Dependent Variable: Attitude to Computers

Faculty	Mean	Std. Error	95% Confidence Interval	
			Lower Bound	Upper Bound
arts	52.468	.777	50.935	54.002
science	52.750	1.182	50.416	55.084
economics	53.208	1.431	50.383	56.034

2. Gender

Dependent Variable: Attitude to Computers

Gender	Mean	Std. Error	95% Confidence Interval	
			Lower Bound	Upper Bound
male	53.111	1.092	50.955	55.268
female	52.507	.779	50.969	54.044

3. Faculty * Gender

Dependent Variable: Attitude to Computers

Faculty	Gender	Mean	Std. Error	95% Confidence Interval	
				Lower Bound	Upper Bound
arts	male	53.333	1.275	50.817	55.850
	female	51.603	.888	49.850	53.356
science	male	54.000	1.776	50.494	57.506
	female	51.500	1.561	48.418	54.582
economics	male	52.000	2.441	47.181	56.819
	female	54.417	1.495	51.466	57.368

Figure 14.4 *Technophilia/technophobia*: **Means, SEs and 95% confidence intervals**

Post hoc tests

Strictly, of course, we should not carry out *post hoc* tests on these results, since none of the effects was significant; however, we do so to help consolidate some ideas about unplanned tests. Figure 14.5 presents SPSS calculations of Tukey's Honestly Significant Difference (HSD) test for *faculty* (as noted in Chapter 12, page 272, SPSS does not carry out *post hoc* tests for fewer than three levels of a factor, since the main effect suffices). These comparisons confirm the outcomes of both the ANOVA and the calculation of confidence intervals above, with no comparisons approaching significance.

Multiple Comparisons						
Attitude to Computers Tukey HSD						
(I) Faculty	(J) Faculty	Mean Difference (I − J)	Std. Error	Sig.	95% Confidence Interval Lower Bound	Upper Bound
arts	science	−.42	1.381	.950	−3.69	2.84
	economics	−1.59	1.468	.526	−5.06	1.88
science	arts	.42	1.381	.950	−2.84	3.69
	economics	−1.17	1.732	.779	−5.26	2.93
economics	arts	1.59	1.468	.526	−1.88	5.06
	science	1.17	1.732	.779	−2.93	5.26

Based on observed means.
The error term is Mean Square(Error) = 53.622.

Figure 14.5 *Technophilia/technophobia*: **Tukey HSD results for** *faculty*

Effect sizes

Using the appropriate sums of squares from the ANOVA summary table in Figure 14.2, we can calculate the proportion of the total variance accounted for by each of the systematic effects, as follows:

$$\text{For }faculty\text{: }\eta^2 = \frac{SS_{faculty}}{SS_{total}} = \frac{11.45}{9182.49} = .001$$

$$\text{For }gender\text{: }\eta^2 = \frac{SS_{gender}}{SS_{total}} = \frac{10.89}{9182.49} = .001$$

$$\text{For }faculty \times gender\text{: }\eta^2 = \frac{SS_{faculty \times gender}}{SS_{total}} = \frac{108.07}{9182.49} = .012$$

As the η^2 values indicate, neither *faculty* nor *gender* explains more than a tiny proportion of the total variance. Strictly speaking, the η^2 value for the interaction represents a small effect (see the corresponding value of *r* below). Incidentally, SS (Error) explains 97.5% of the total variance (see if you can work this out using the appropriate values from Figure 14.2).

In terms of *r* as a measure of effect size, taking the square root of the three η^2 values, we obtain .03, .03 and .11 for *faculty*, *gender* and *faculty* × *gender*, respectively. Note that the latter value equates to a weak effect based on Cohen's guidelines for effect sizes based on *r* (see p. 215).

Couch potato

Figure 14.6 presents a graph of the data for the amount of TV viewing by children of different ages, related to father's socioeconomic status (*SES*). Note that the data are plotted differently from in Chapter 13. This time, *SES* is on the category (*X*) axis and *age* is indicated by separate lines on the graph. We remind you that, as above, this example has *two between groups* factors.

SES

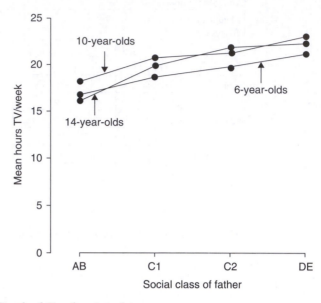

Figure 14.6 Graph of *Couch potato* data

> **Before reading on...**
>
> Look back at the corresponding graph in Chapter 13 (Figure 13.4, p. 284). Remember, both versions contain the same mean scores and convey identical information. Study these graphs and consider how each version allows you to view the same data from different perspectives. What effects are more apparent in each version?
>
> **... now read on**

The ANOVA summary table for these data is shown in Figure 14.7. You should recognize it as Figure 14.3 with the blanks filled in.

> **Before reading on...**
>
> Compare the values in the summary table with your own. Check any calculations that do not tally.
>
> **... now read on**

Source of Variation	Sum of Squares	df	Mean Square	F	p
SES	224.556	3	74.852	3.073	.0344
Age	24.111	2	12.056	0.495	.6120
S × A interaction	25.111	6	4.185	0.172	.9834
Error	1461.333	60	24.356		
Total	1735.111	71	24.438		

SES Means			Age Means	
AB	17.39		6	19.42
C1	19.89		10	20.83
C2	21.00		14	20.08
DE	22.17			

Figure 14.7 ANOVA summary table and means for *Couch potato* example

Student: *Are my eyes deceiving me? The graph seems to show an interaction between the two factors. You can see that the 14-year-olds in the AB group are out of place, so the line is not parallel with the others at this point. Yet the ANOVA summary table suggests that the interaction is not even close to significant.*

Lecturer: *Well spotted, and you are correct in your observation. However, ANOVA gives an overall assessment of the interaction across all levels of both factors. So, while this is undoubtedly an aberration, the magnitude of the displacement of this group is relatively small and it only occurs at the AB level, so it is insufficient to influence the overall pattern of results.*

Confidence intervals

Figure 14.8 presents SPSS calculations of 95% confidence intervals for the means of each main effect and for the 12 interaction means (see *Making sense of SPSS*

1. SES

Dependent Variable: Hours of TV watched per week

SES	Mean	Std. Error	95% Confidence Interval Lower Bound	95% Confidence Interval Upper Bound
AB	17.389	1.163	15.062	19.716
C1	19.889	1.163	17.562	22.216
C2	21.000	1.163	18.673	23.327
DE	22.167	1.163	19.840	24.493

2. Age

Dependent Variable: Hours of TV watched per week

Age	Mean	Std. Error	95% Confidence Interval Lower Bound	95% Confidence Interval Upper Bound
6 years	19.417	1.007	17.402	21.432
10 years	20.833	1.007	18.818	22.848
14 years	20.083	1.007	18.068	22.098

3. SES * Age

Dependent Variable: Hours of TV watched per week

SES	Age	Mean	Std. Error	95% Confidence Interval Lower Bound	95% Confidence Interval Upper Bound
AB	6 years	17.833	2.015	13.803	21.863
	10 years	18.167	2.015	14.137	22.197
	14 years	16.167	2.015	12.137	20.197
C1	6 years	18.833	2.015	14.803	22.863
	10 years	20.833	2.015	16.803	24.863
	14 years	20.000	2.015	15.970	24.030
C2	6 years	19.833	2.015	15.803	23.863
	10 years	21.333	2.015	17.303	25.363
	14 years	21.833	2.015	17.803	25.863
DE	6 years	21.167	2.015	17.137	25.197
	10 years	23.000	2.015	18.970	27.030
	14 years	22.333	2.015	18.303	26.363

Figure 14.8 *Couch potato*: Means, SEs and 95% confidence intervals for *SES*, *age* and *SES × age*

below for how to obtain these). Note how the significant main effect of *SES* in the ANOVA summary table is reflected in the relative lack of overlap in the confidence intervals, as compared to those for *age* which did not produce a significant main effect. Notice also that the interaction means reflect a non-significant interaction term.

Unplanned (post hoc) tests

As noted above, the *F* ratio for the *main effect* of *SES* does reach the level required to be statistically significant (the *p* value is just below .05), while neither the *main effect* for *age*, nor the *interaction* between *SES* and *age*, is statistically significant. Applying *Tukey's HSD test* to the significant main effect of *SES* gives the results shown in Figure 14.9 (note, there is no need to perform *post hoc* tests on either *age* or *SES* × *age*, as these effects are not significant). As can be seen, there is only one pairwise comparison that is statistically significant (AB v DE), suggesting that the effect of *SES* is driven by this difference.

Multiple Comparisons

Hours of TV watched per week
Tukey HSD

(I) SES	(J) SES	Mean Difference (I − J)	Std. Error	Sig.	95% Confidence Interval	
					Lower Bound	Upper Bound
AB	C1	−2.50	1.645	.432	−6.85	1.85
	C2	−3.61	1.645	.136	−7.96	.74
	DE	−4.78*	1.645	.026	−9.12	−.43
C1	AB	2.50	1.645	.432	−1.85	6.85
	C2	−1.11	1.645	.906	−5.46	3.24
	DE	−2.28	1.645	.514	−6.62	2.07
C2	AB	3.61	1.645	.136	−.74	7.96
	C1	1.11	1.645	.906	−3.24	5.46
	DE	−1.17	1.645	.893	−5.51	3.18
DE	AB	4.78*	1.645	.026	.43	9.12
	C1	2.28	1.645	.514	−2.07	6.62
	C2	1.17	1.645	.893	−3.18	5.51

Based on observed means.
The error term is Mean Square(Error) = 24.356.
*The mean difference is significant at the .05 level.

Figure 14.9 *Couch potato*: Tukey's HSD tests for *SES*

Effect sizes

Using the appropriate sums of squares from the summary table in Figure 14.7, we can calculate the proportion of the total variance accounted for by each of the systematic effects, as follows:

$$\text{For } SES: \eta^2 = \frac{SS_{SES}}{SS_{total}} = \frac{224.56}{1735.11} = \mathbf{.129}$$

For *age*: $\eta^2 = \dfrac{SS_{age}}{SS_{total}} = \dfrac{24.11}{1735.11} = \mathbf{.014}$

For *SES* × *age*: $\eta^2 = \dfrac{SS_{SES×age}}{SS_{total}} = \dfrac{25.11}{1735.11} = \mathbf{.014}$

The η^2 values show that *SES* explains almost 13% of the total variance, and *age* and *SES* × *age* approximately 1.4% each. The η^2 values represent a medium-to-large effect size for *SES* and small effect sizes for *age* and the interaction (see also the corresponding value of *r* values below).

In terms of *r* as a measure of effect size, taking the square root of the three η^2 values, we obtain .36, .12 and .12 for *SES*, *age* and *SES* × *age*, respectively. Note that the former equates to a moderate-to-strong effect, and the latter two to weak effects, based on Cohen's guidelines for effect sizes based on *r* (see p. 215).

Reporting the results of two-factor between groups ANOVA

Alert

There are no hard and fast rules for presenting two-factor ANOVA results, although there are strong conventions. We adopt a similar format to Brace et al. (2009) with two differences. First, we do not give η_p^2 as the measure of effect size. Instead, we suggest η^2. Second, since the interpretation of main effects is subject to the presence or absence of an interaction effect, we suggest that you begin by reporting the interaction, followed by the main effects. If the interaction is significant, it is almost not worth reporting the main effects, since one or both will have been modified by the interaction. However, as a learning exercise, we suggest you do so.

Technophilia/Technophobia

There was no significant interaction between *faculty* and *gender* ($F(2,167) = 1.008$, $p = .37$, $\eta^2 = .01$). The main effect of *faculty* was not significant ($F(2,167) = 0.107$, $p = .90$, $\eta^2 = .001$). The main effect of gender was not significant ($F(1,167) = 0.203$, $p = .65$, $\eta^2 = .001$).

Couch Potato

There was no significant interaction between *SES* and *age* ($F(6,60) = 0.172$, $p = .98$, $\eta^2 = .01$). There was a significant main effect of *SES* ($F(3,60) = 3.073$, $p = .03$, $\eta^2 = .13$). There was no significant main effect of *age* ($F(2,60) = 0.495$, $p = .61$, $\eta^2 = .01$).

Making sense of SPSS

Two-factor between groups designs

Note: For further information on 2-way between groups ANOVA, we recommend you consult Brace et al. (2009), pp. 218–221.

Also for economy of space, we present only strictly relevant screen shots and diagrams not presented earlier in the book. We suggest you refer to relevant SPSS examples in Chapter 12 and elsewhere for more general shots of data structure and top level dialogue windows.

1. **Data files**

For the *Technophilia/technophobia* example, we did not present all of the data in Chapter 13, so it was not possible to code these data. Here, we use a data file already created which is available on the website. For the *Couch potato* example, you require the data file coded as indicated in Chapter 13 (p. 285).

2. Calculating two-way between (independent) groups ANOVA

Technophilia/technophobia

The routine for this analysis is located in **Analyze** > **General Linear Model** > **Univariate ...**. Although we have two independent variables, we select **Univariate ...**. This refers to the *dependent* variable, not the independent variables and, therefore, reflects the fact that each participant produces a single score in fully between groups designs.

Having reached the **Univariate** dialogue window, assign the variables as indicated below.

Also select **Post Hoc...**, move *faculty* and *gender* into the box on the right as shown and choose **Tukey**. Click **Continue**.

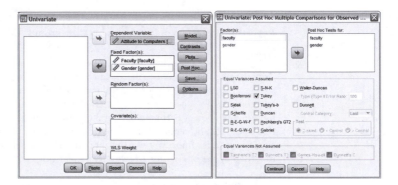

Now, click on **Plots...**. Here, each graph that you wish to obtain must be specified by allocating the relevant variables to the **Horizontal Axis:** and **Separate Lines:** boxes and then adding the selection(s) to the **Plots:** box by clicking on **Add** button. In the example below, the two univariate graphs have already been added by assigning the variable in question to the **Horizontal Axis:** box and clicking **Add**. So too for the *faculty* × *gender* graph, by adding *faculty* to the **Horizontal Axis:** box and *gender* to the **Separate Lines:** box and clicking **Add**. The *gender* × *faculty* graph has yet to be added to the **Plots:** box. When all desired graphs have been chosen, click **Continue**.

Click on **Options...** and select **Homogeneity tests** and, for good measure, **Descriptive statistics**. Also move the three effects into the **Display Means for:** box. Click **Continue**.

Click **OK**.

A mass of output will appear in the **SPSS Statistics Viewer** window, much unnecessary and some repeated. You should simply extract the information you require rather than being dictated to by SPSS.

The ANOVA summary table in Figure 14.2 will appear, as will the three tables of means, SEs and confidence intervals in Figure 14.4 (although these will not be together). The Tukey HSD table for *faculty* (Figure 14.5) can also be found – remember, SPSS will not have carried out Tukey HSD for *gender*, since it is redundant.

One table that will not have been presented above is the result of the homogeneity test (Levene's test). This appears below and shows that there are no significant differences in the variability in the scores of the six groups of participant (*remember, no significance is good news for homogeneity tests!*). This result is reassuring and adds validity to the ANOVA result.

Levene's Test of Equality of Error Variances[a]
Dependent Variable:Attitude to Computers

F	df1	df2	Sig.
.874	5	167	.500

Tests the null hypothesis that the error variance of the dependent variable is equal across groups.
[a]Design: Intercept + faculty + gender + faculty * gender

Finally, the four graphs selected have been thumbnailed below to illustrate the various graphical representations available directly from the ANOVA calculation. These are in the 'raw' state in which they appear, but can be edited to appear more viewer-friendly.

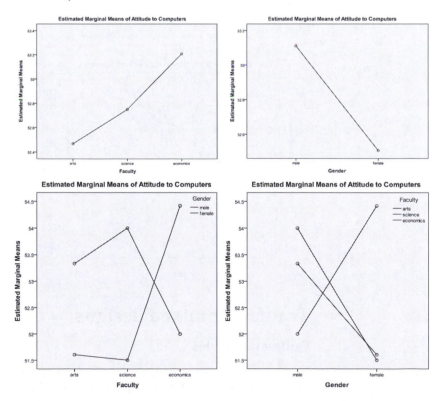

Couch potato

Here, the procedure for carrying out the ANOVA is identical to the *Technophilia/ technophobia* example. Again, among the output will be the tables shown in Figures 14.7 to 14.9. The Levene's test of homogeneity will appear as below. Again, the absence of significance is a welcome result which confirms homogeneity of variance across our groups.

Levene's Test of Equality of Error Variances[a]
Dependent variable:Hours of TV watched per week

F	df1	df2	Sig.
.773	11	60	.665

Tests the null hypothesis that the error variance of the
dependent variable is equal across groups.
[a]Design: Intercept + SES + age + SES * age

As before, the four available graphs are thumbnailed below. These can be useful visual references when considering the summary statistics in the tables above.

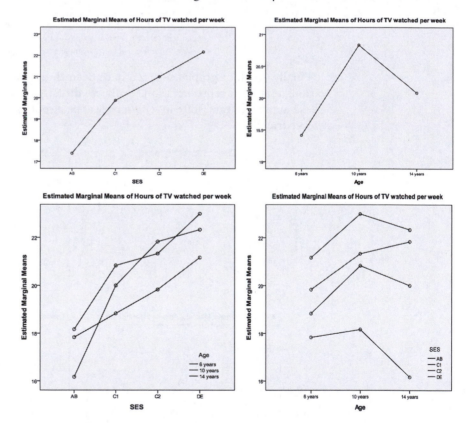

Two-factor mixed designs

Fading memories

Figure 14.10 again shows the graph for the example involving memory deterioration over time for an experimental group given training in a mnemonic strategy and a

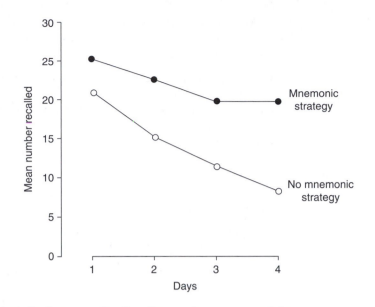

Figure 14.10 *Fading memories*: Recall scores by *strategy* and *day*

Source of Variation	Sum of Squares	df	Mean Square	F	p
Strategy	880.071	1	880.071	29.642	.0001
Error	356.286	12	29.690		
Day	668.357	3	222.786	118.443	.0000
S× D interaction	98.929	3	32.976	17.532	.0000
Error	67.714	36	1.881		
Total	2071.359	55	37.661		

Strategy Means	
No training	13.93
Training	21.86

Day Means	
1 day	23.07
2 days	18.86
3 days	15.57
4 days	14.07

Figure 14.11 ANOVA summary table for *fading memories* data

control group given no such training. By contrast with the first two examples, which involved two between groups factors, this is an example of a **mixed design**, with one between groups factor (*strategy*) and one within-subjects factor (*day*). The ANOVA summary table is as shown in Figure 14.11.

Note that there are two error terms in this table, one for working out the *F* ratio for the main effect of the between groups factor (*strategy*), and the other for working out the *F* ratio for those effects which involve any repeated measures variable (here, the main effect of the within-subjects factor, *day*, as well as that for the *strategy* × *day* interaction). An explanation of why this is so will not be offered! Suffice it to say that the different error terms are a consequence of the fact that one factor is between groups and the other within-subjects. In practice, it makes no difference whatsoever to the way you should go about interpreting the *F* ratios in the summary table.

All three *F* values are high, and the associated *p* values are very small; that is, all three are statistically significant. These results confirm the strong indications from the graph that

- being taught the mnemonic strategy improves retention, *irrespective of day* (main effect of *strategy*);
- memory deteriorates progressively across days, *irrespective of strategy* (main effect of *day*); and
- the rate of deterioration of memory is faster for the no mnemonic group (*strategy* x *day* interaction).

> **Before reading on...**
>
> Think about the *strategy* × *day* interaction. Is there another way of expressing the nature of this interaction? Jot down your thoughts.
>
> **... now read on**

An alternative way of describing the interaction between *strategy* and *day* would be to say that the magnitude of the *strategy* effect differs across *day* – specifically, the impact of the mnemonic is greater as the time elapsed increases. Remember, again, that this is simply another way of expressing the same idea and, while it may seem to be labouring the point in this case, there may be occasions when it is necessary to look at patterns of interaction from more than one perspective in order to understand them fully.

> **Lecturer:** *Remember in the last chapter we were wondering whether this interaction was sufficiently strong to be statistically significant?*
> **Student:** *Yep – we agreed that it was certainly apparent from the graph, but that is not the same as formal significance.*
> **Lecturer:** *No indeed. But here it is confirmed that the lack of parallelness is highly statistically significant.*
> **Student:** *I noticed that, in the previous two examples, the interaction was also analysed in terms of effect sizes. I didn't quite expect that.*
> **Lecturer:** *It's entirely appropriate to think in terms of the strength of the effect of the interaction. Remember, we analyse the interaction just like a main effect. We can even describe the interaction in terms of the confidence intervals of the interaction means.*
> **Student:** *Yes, I saw that too in the earlier examples.*

Confidence intervals

Figure 14.12 presents SPSS calculations of 95% confidence intervals for the means of each main effect and for the eight interaction means (again, see *Making sense of SPSS* below for how to obtain these). As seen, the population mean for the no mnemonic treatment is estimated to lie between 11.69 and 16.17, with 95% confidence, and, for the mnemonic condition, between 19.61 and 24.10. Note how the significant main effect of *strategy* in the ANOVA summary table is reflected in the relative lack of overlap between the two confidence intervals.

Estimates				
Measure:MEASURE_1				
			95% Confidence Interval	
Strategy	Mean	Std. Error	Lower Bound	Upper Bound
no mnemonic	13.929	1.030	11.685	16.172
mnemonic	21.857	1.030	19.614	24.101

Estimates				
Measure:MEASURE_1				
			95% Confidence Interval	
day	Mean	Std. Error	Lower Bound	Upper Bound
1	23.071	.759	21.417	24.726
2	18.857	.882	16.936	20.778
3	15.571	.795	13.838	17.304
4	14.071	.733	12.474	15.669

Strategy * day					
Measure:MEASURE_1					
				95% Confidence Interval	
Strategy	day	Mean	Std. Error	Lower Bound	Upper Bound
no mnemonic	1	21.000	1.074	18.660	23.340
	2	15.143	1.247	12.426	17.859
	3	11.286	1.125	8.835	13.737
	4	8.286	1.037	6.027	10.545
mnemonic	1	25.143	1.074	22.803	27.482
	2	22.571	1.247	19.855	25.288
	3	19.857	1.125	17.406	22.308
	4	19.857	1.037	17.598	22.116

Figure 14.12 *Fading memories*: Means, SEs and 95% confidence intervals for *strategy, day* and *strategy × day*

Before reading on...

Look at the confidence intervals for the remaining two systematic effects (*day* and *strategy × day*). Reflect on the population means, the interval widths and the extent to which these statistics reflect the ANOVA summary.

... now read on

Alert

For reasons first discussed in Chapter 10 (p. 208), it is important to be aware that the confidence intervals for the effects involving within-subjects variables, that is *day* and *strategy × day*, are only meaningful for considering the variability of data separately at each level of the source of variance in question. The overlap of the confidence intervals between levels, or lack thereof, does not provide information about the likelihood that the means differ significantly. This is in contrast to the between-groups variable (*strategy*) for which such overlap is meaningful.

Unplanned (post hoc) and planned tests

In principle, the between groups effect (*strategy*) can be analysed using Tukey's HSD test. However, since there are only two levels in this factor, this is redundant and, for this reason, SPSS does not carry out such an analysis.

Regarding the within-subjects factor of *day*, as we have seen previously, we can 'unpick' the means of a within-subjects factor by choosing Bonferroni or Sidak adjusted multiple comparisons in SPSS (see pp. 276–277). Results of Bonferroni tests for *day* are shown in Figure 14.13. These tests may be thought of as 'conservative' paired *t*-tests, that is, with certain adjustments made to take account of the fact that several tests are being carried out, which would otherwise increase the likelihood of a Type 1 error.

The Bonferroni comparisons show highly significant differences between all of the four days, in every permutation. This is not entirely evident from Figure 14.10 which clearly shows *no* difference between days 3 and 4 for the mnemonic condition. Bear in mind, of course, that the main effect of *day* is averaged across both *strategy* conditions, producing a significant difference between days 3 and 4 overall (though note the slightly elevated *p* value, reflecting the mnemonic means for days 3 and 4.

Of course, arguably more importantly, the main effect of *day* can be investigated through a linear trend test (see Figure 14.14, ANOVA summary table). The method for obtaining this test, and for extracting the relevant information from the myriad output, is shown in *Making sense of SPSS* below.

Pairwise Comparisons

Measure:MEASURE_1

(I) day	(J) day	Mean Difference (I – J)	Std. Error	Sig.[a]	95% Confidence Interval for Difference[a]	
					Lower Bound	Upper Bound
1	2	4.214*	.467	.000	2.743	5.685
	3	7.500*	.668	.000	5.396	9.604
	4	9.000*	.612	.000	7.072	10.928
2	1	−4.214*	.467	.000	−5.685	−2.743
	3	3.286*	.452	.000	1.861	4.710
	4	4.786*	.465	.000	3.321	6.251
3	1	−7.500*	.668	.000	−9.604	−5.396
	2	−3.286*	.452	.000	−4.710	−1.861
	4	1.500*	.393	.015	.260	2.740
4	1	−9.000*	.612	.000	−10.928	−7.072
	2	−4.786*	.465	.000	−6.251	−3.321
	3	−1.500*	.393	.015	−2.740	−.260

Based on estimated marginal means
*The mean difference is significant at the .05 level.
[a] Adjustment for multiple comparisons: Bonferroni.

Figure 14.13 *Fading memories*: Bonferroni-adjusted pairwise comparisons for *day*

Source of Variation	Sum of Squares	df	Mean Square	F	p
Strategy	880.071	1	880.071	29.642	.0001
Error	356.286	12	29.690		
Day	668.357	3	222.786	118.443	.0000
Linear trend	*642.057*	*1*	*642.057*	*206.639*	*.0000*
Error linear	*37.286*	*12*	*3.107*		
S × D interaction	98.929	3	32.976	17.532	.0000
Error	67.714	36	1.881		
Total	2071.359	55	37.661		

Figure 14.14 ANOVA summary table for *Fading memories* data, including linear trend test for *day*

> **Student:** *I'm a bit confused about how this linear trend fits into the ANOVA summary table.*
> **Lecturer:** *You'll notice that it has been italicized and indented.*
> **Student:** *Yeh, that's part of the confusion. And also, the total sums of squares don't add up correctly now.*
> **Lecturer:** *Ah, that why it's been italicized. This is not an extra term as such. Rather, it is a part of the main effect of Day. So it indicates how much of the main effect is driven specifically by a linear trend.*

Effect sizes

Using the appropriate sums of squares from the summary table in Figure 14.14, we can calculate the proportion of the total variance accounted for by each of the systematic effects, as follows:

$$\text{For } \textit{strategy}: \eta^2 = \frac{SS_{strategy}}{SS_{total}} = \frac{880.07}{2071.36} = \textbf{.425}$$

$$\text{For } \textit{day}: \eta^2 = \frac{SS_{day}}{SS_{total}} = \frac{668.36}{2071.36} = \textbf{.323}$$

$$\text{For } \textit{strategy} \times \textit{day}: \eta^2 = \frac{SS_{strategy \times day}}{SS_{total}} = \frac{98.93}{2071.36} = \textbf{.048}$$

$$\text{For linear trend of } \textit{day}: \eta^2 = \frac{SS_{linear}}{SS_{total}} = \frac{642.06}{2071.36} = \textbf{.310}$$

The η^2 values show that the main effect of *strategy* accounts for 42.5% of the total variance, a large proportion by any standards. *Day* also explains an impressive proportion of total variance (32.3%), while *strategy* × *day* accounts for 4.8%.

In terms of *r* as a measure of effect size, taking the square root of the three η^2 values, we obtain .65 for *strategy* (strong effect), .57 for *day* (also a strong effect), and .22 for the interaction between the two (a weak-to-moderate effect). Note that, although statistically highly significant, the effect size for the *strategy* × *day* interaction suggests that it is a relatively unimportant result. As discussed elsewhere, the fact that this relatively weak effect was found to be statistically highly significant is most likely due to the relatively high power associated with the design of the study and the type of analysis. Although there were only 14 participants in total, each produced four scores (one for each day), giving 56 data points in all. This, combined with the fact that the analysis involved more powerful repeated measures, resulted in a relatively powerful analysis.

Incidentally, with 31% of total variance explained by the linear trend of *day*, this represents 96% of the variance explained by the main effect. Hence, it is clear that this main effect is driven almost entirely by the linear trend.

Before reading on...

Think about the *strategy* × *day* interaction. Is there another way of expressing the nature of this interaction? Jot down your thoughts.

... now read on

An alternative way of describing the interaction between strategy and time would be to say that the magnitude of the strategy effect differs depending on time elapsed – specifically, the effect of strategy is greater as the time elapsed increases. Remember, again, that this is simply another way of expressing the same idea and, while it may seem to be labouring the point in this case, there may be occasions when it is necessary to look at patterns of interaction from more than one perspective in order to understand them fully.

Settling more differences: Simple effects

A further useful set of follow-up tests goes by the name of **Simple Effects**. What this approach does is to look at the effects of each factor, not overall, but *separately* for each level of the other factor. Think of simple effects as a series of *mini ANOVAs*.

In our example, we can look at the effects of *strategy* separately after 1 day, after 2 days, after 3 days, and after 4 days. Conversely, we can look at the effects of *day* for the no mnemonic group and the mnemonic group separately. These two versions of simple effects reflect the above exercise of describing our interaction from two perspectives. The result is a bunch of *F* ratios, which are summarized in Figure 14.15.

Thus, *strategy* has a significant effect whether the time elapsed is 1 day, 2 days, 3 days or 4 days. However, note the increasing *F* ratios, reflecting the trend visible in the graph (Figure 14.10), that the separation between the groups increases over time (this is what constitutes the interaction, in fact). Similarly, looking at the interaction the other way round, *day* is significant for both the no mnemonic group and the mnemonic group separately.

Simple Effects	F	df	p
Strategy at day 1	7.442	1,12	.018
Strategy at day 2	17.751	1,12	.001
Strategy at day 3	29.032	1,12	.000
Strategy at day 4	62.288	1,12	.000
Day at no mnemonic	92.832	3,18	.000
Day at mnemonic	30.191	3,36	.000

Figure 14.15 *Fading memories*: Simple effects

Note that, when factors have only two levels (like *strategy*), simple effects allow unambiguous interpretation. For factors with more than two levels (such as *day*), however, they may need to be used in conjunction with paired comparisons, such as paired *t*-tests or Bonferroni tests, since the various levels of the factor(s) may need to be unpicked further in order to reveal the source of an interaction.

SPSS does not offer simple effects straightforwardly. A somewhat tortuous method for obtaining these statistics is shown in the *Making sense of SPSS* example below).

Before reading on...

Spend some time thinking about this last point. Make sure you understand when it might be necessary to use multiple comparisons in conjunction with simple effects.

... now read on

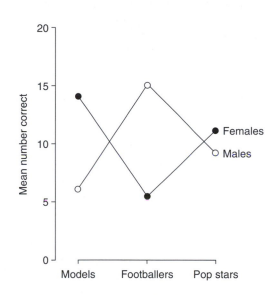

Figure 14.16 *Fame and recognition*: **Identification scores by gender and type of photograph**

Fame and recognition

Figure 14.16 again presents a graph for the data on the recognition of photographs by male and female students (between groups factor) for three categories of photo (within-subjects factor). Looking at the ANOVA summary table (Figure 14.17), we see no main effects, but a huge *F* ratio for the interaction. This is in line with what the graph, and the patterns of means, suggest strongly.

Confidence intervals

Figure 14.18 presents SPSS calculations of 95% confidence intervals for the means of the two main effects and for the six interaction means (again, see *Making Sense of SPSS* below for how to obtain these). Note that the confidence intervals for population means of males and females overlap almost completely. This is with the non-significant main effect of *gender*. Note again, however, that the confidence intervals for *category* and *gender × category* are only meaningful for considering the variability of data at each level of *category* and the interaction. The overlap of the

Source of Variation	Sum of Squares	df	Mean Square	F	p
Gender	0.184	1	0.184	0.010	.9228
Error	284.130	15	18.942		
Category	0.801	2	0.402	0.100	.8541
G × C interaction	680.723	2	340.361	134.731	.0000
Error	75.787	30	2.526		
Total	1041.625	50	20.833		

Gender Means

Male	10.42
Female	10.30

Category Means

Models	10.18
Footballers	10.47
Pop stars	10.42

Figure 14.17 ANOVA summary table for *Fame and recognition* example

1. gender

Measure:MEASURE_1

			95% Confidence Interval	
gender	Mean	Std. Error	Lower Bound	Upper Bound
male	10.417	.888	8.523	12.310
female	10.296	.838	8.511	12.082

2. category

Measure:MEASURE_1

			95% Confidence Interval	
category	Mean	Std. Error	Lower Bound	Upper Bound
1	10.181	.688	8.713	11.648
2	10.465	.640	9.101	11.829
3	10.424	.730	8.868	11.980

3. gender * category

Measure:MEASURE_1

				95% Confidence Interval	
gender	category	Mean	Std. Error	Lower Bound	Upper Bound
male	1	6.250	1.002	4.115	8.385
	2	15.375	.931	13.390	17.360
	3	9.625	1.062	7.361	11.889
female	1	14.111	.944	12.098	16.124
	2	5.556	.878	3.684	7.427
	3	11.222	1.002	9.087	13.357

Figure 14.18 *Fame and recognition*: Means, SEs and 95% confidence intervals for *gender*, *category* and *gender × category*

confidence intervals, or lack thereof, does not provide information about the likelihood that the means differ significantly.

Simple effects

The impressions are further confirmed by carrying out tests for simple effects, with the results as shown in Figure 14.19. Note the statistically significant differences between males and females for both models and footballers (note too that the differences are in opposite directions) but a non-significant difference for pop stars. Note also that the effect of *category* – which was non-significant for the main effect – is statistically significant for both males and females when looked at separately.

Simple Effect	F	df	p
Gender at models	32.610	1,15	.000
Gender at footballers	58.845	1,15	.000
Gender at pop stars	1.197	1,15	.291
Category at male	57.563	2,14	.000
Category at female	79.362	2,16	.000

Figure 14.19 *Fame and recognition*: Simple effects

Other *post hoc* tests: multiple comparisons

Since the simple effects of *gender* reveal male/female differences at two of the three levels of *category*, further *post hoc* tests would be redundant. However, the significant simple effects of *category* do warrant further unpicking, since we do not know the precise nature of these effects revealed by the 'mini ANOVAs'. Again, as category is a within-subjects factor, we report Bonferroni-adjusted tests.

Somewhat tediously, it is not straightforward in SPSS to compare the six interaction means with each other, which is what we need to be able to do if we wish to compare the means for category separately for males and females. First, we must split the data into two separate data subsets (male and female), then carry out the Bonferroni tests as normal. Figure 14.20 presents the results of these paired comparisons.

As seen, all six paired comparisons are significant, indicating that the significant **simple main effects** of *category* for both males and females are contributed to by all three levels of *category*.

Effect sizes

From the sums of squares in the summary table in Figure 14.17, we can calculate the proportion of the total variance accounted for by each of the systematic effects, as follows:

$$\text{For } gender\text{: } \eta^2 = \frac{\text{SS}_{gender}}{\text{SS}_{total}} = \frac{0.184}{1041.625} = \textbf{.0001}$$

$$\text{For } category\text{: } \eta^2 = \frac{\text{SS}_{category}}{\text{SS}_{total}} = \frac{0.801}{1041.625} = \textbf{.001}$$

Pairwise Comparisons (Males only)

Measure:MEASURE_1

(I) category	(J) category	Mean Difference (I – J)	Std. Error	Sig.[a]	95% Confidence Interval for Difference[a]	
					Lower Bound	Upper Bound
1	2	−9.125*	.766	.000	−11.521	−6.729
	3	−3.375*	.885	.020	−6.143	−.607
2	1	9.125*	.766	.000	6.729	11.521
	3	5.750*	.921	.001	2.870	8.630
3	1	3.375*	.885	.020	.607	6.143
	2	−5.750*	.921	.001	−8.630	−2.870

Based on estimated marginal means
*The mean difference is significant at the .05 level.
[a] Adjustment for multiple comparisons: Bonferroni.

Pairwise Comparisons (Females only)

Measure:MEASURE_1

(I) category	(J) category	Mean Difference (I – J)	Std. Error	Sig.[a]	95% Confidence Interval for Difference[a]	
					Lower Bound	Upper Bound
1	2	8.556*	.729	.000	6.358	10.753
	3	2.889*	.857	.029	.304	5.474
2	1	−8.556*	.729	.000	−10.753	−6.358
	3	−5.667*	.408	.000	−6.898	−4.435
3	1	−2.889*	.857	.029	−5.474	−.304
	2	5.667*	.408	.000	4.435	6.898

Based on estimated marginal means
*The mean difference is significant at the .05 level.
[a] Adjustment for multiple comparisons: Bonferroni.

Figure 14.20 *Fame and recognition*: Bonferroni-adjusted pairwise comparisons for *category*, separate analyses for males and females

$$\text{For } gender \times category: \eta^2 = \frac{SS_{gender \times category}}{SS_{total}} = \frac{680.723}{1041.625} = .654$$

The eta squared values show that the main effect of *gender* accounts for a minuscule 0.01% of the total variance and *category* an almost equally tiny 0.1%. By contrast, the interaction between the two factors explains a massive 65.4% of the total variance in the data. In terms of *r* as a measure of effect size, taking the square root of η^2 for the interaction, we obtain a value of 0.81, suggesting that, not only is this result statistically significant, it represents a very large effect size according to Cohen's guidelines.

Student: I can see I shall have to be careful in interpreting ANOVA summary tables. When I first looked at this one, I thought there were no effects of either gender or category, and that was more or less end of story.

Lecturer: It's certainly true that, in a formal sense, the main effects of gender and category are not even approaching significance, but the highly significant interaction hides a multitude! In fact, it is completely obscuring strong effects of both gender and category.

Student: So any time I see a significant interaction, an alarm bell should ring?

Lecturer: Absolutely. If you have a significant interaction you must *look at the data in more detail.*

Student: Precisely how should I go about it?

Lecturer: As our example illustrates very well, the obvious first step is to draw a graph. Spend some time looking at it in order to get a sense of the nature of the interaction – maybe even plot the two versions of the graph. Then choose appropriate follow-up tests formally to confirm or disconfirm your conclusions about the true nature of your results.

Student: So, if I want to know if some means differ significantly from others, I would choose multiple comparisons or *simple effects?*

Lecturer: Or sometimes both, and if you were interested in, say, a linear trend, you would test for that.

Student: Life would be much simpler if interactions were not significant.

Lecturer: Indeed, but much less interesting as well!

Reporting the results of two-factor mixed ANOVA

Fading memories

There was a significant interaction between *strategy* and *day* ($F_{(3,36)}$ = 17.532, $p < .0001$, η^2 = .05).

The main effect of *strategy* was significant ($F_{(1,12)}$ = 29.642, $p = .0001$, η^2 = .43).

The main effect of *day* was significant ($F_{(3,36)}$ = 118.443, $p < .0001$, η^2 = .32). This factor produced a significant linear trend ($F_{(1,12)}$ = 206.639, $p < .0001$, η^2 = .12). The number of words remembered decreased linearly from day 1 through day 4.

Fame and Recognition

There was a significant interaction between *gender* and *category* ($F_{(2,30)}$ = 134.731, $p < .0001$, η^2 = .65).

There was no significant main effect of *gender* ($F_{(1,15)}$ = 0.010, $p = .92$, η^2 = .0001).

There was no significant main effect of *category* ($F_{(2,30)}$ = 0.100, $p = .85$, η^2 = .001).

Making sense of SPSS

Two factor mixed designs

Note: For further information on 2-way mixed ANOVA, we recommend you consult Brace et al. (2009), pp. 238–240.

Again, for economy of space, we present only strictly relevant screen shots and diagrams not presented earlier in the book. We suggest you refer to relevant SPSS examples in Chapter 12 and elsewhere for more general shots of data structure and top level dialogue windows.

1. Data files

For both examples, you require the data file coded as indicated in Chapter 13 (p. 294 for both *Fading memories* and *Fame and recognition*).

2. Calculating two-way mixed ANOVA

Fading memories

The routine for this analysis is located in **Analyze > General Linear Model > Repeated Measures…**. This refers to the fact that each participant produces more than one score – it is not necessary that all factors are repeated measures – it can be one or more.

The first dialogue window to appear asks you to specify your repeated measures factor(s). There is no need to define any between groups factors since these will already have been specified at the data coding stage using coding variables. Here, we have one repeated measures factor with four levels. Enter the details as shown below using the **Add** button and click **Define**.

In the resulting **Repeated Measures** dialogue window, move the four levels of the repeated measures factor *day* and the between groups factor *strategy* into the appropriate boxes as shown.

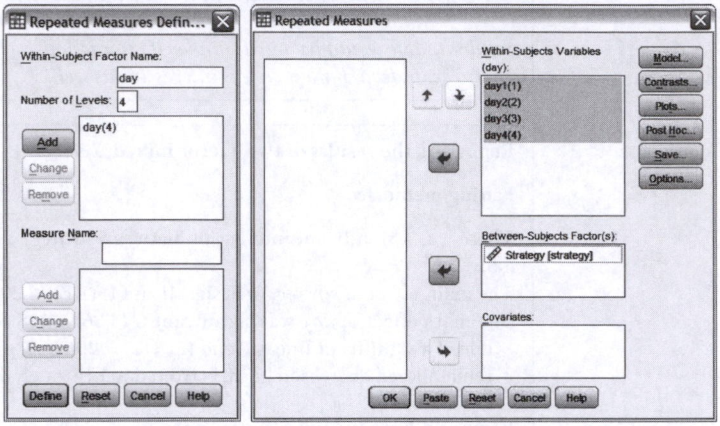

There is no need to select **Contrasts...**, since these will be calculated for both factors (including a redundant calculation for strategy which only has two levels).

Choose **Plots...** and, as described in the *Technophilia/technophobia* example above (p. 310), specify the four graphs: *strategy*, *day*, *strategy × day* and *day × strategy*. When all graphs have been specified, click **Continue**.

There is no need to choose **Post Hoc...** for the between groups factor *strategy*, since it has only two levels and, therefore, SPSS will not calculate Tukey HSD or any other paired comparison.

Next, choose **Options...** and select those options in the window below, including Bonferroni tests for *day* and *strategy × day*.

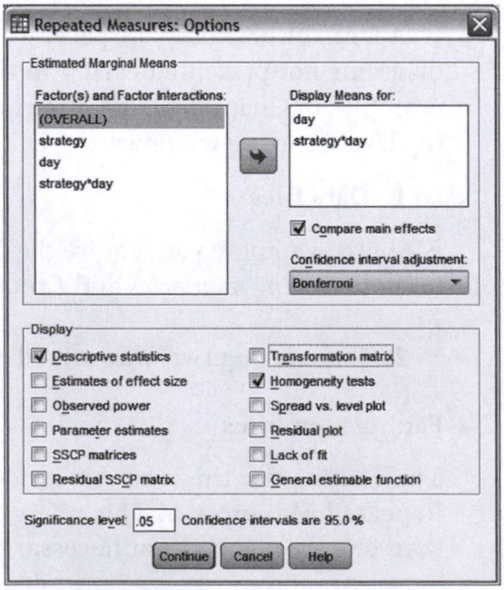

Click **OK** to run the ANOVA.

Again, a mass of output will appear in the **SPSS Statistics Viewer** window. You should simply extract the information you require rather than being dictated to by SPSS.

Jumping ahead a little, the tables of means, SEs and confidence intervals which appeared in Figure 14.12 are provided (although these will not be together). The Bonferroni table for *day* (Figure 14.13) can also be found – remember, SPSS will not have carried out Tukey HSD for *strategy*, since it is redundant. The additional term for the linear trend of day in the ANOVA summary table in Figure 14.14 can also be extracted from the output.

The simple effects in Figure 14.15 are not available. These have to be calculated by splitting up the data and carrying out separate one-way ANOVAs. We do not provide the details here, as this is likely to promote confusion. Such manipulations will come quite naturally as you grow in confidence with SPSS.

Frustratingly, the complete ANOVA summary table in Figure 14.11 is not presented (don't ask us why not, we don't know!). Instead, you must compile it from the two tables below.

Tests of Within-Subjects Effects
Measure:MEASURE_1

Source		Type III Sum of Squares	df	Mean Square	F	Sig.
day	Sphericity Assumed	668.357	3	222.786	118.443	.000
	Greenhouse-Geisser	668.357	2.140	312.359	118.443	.000
	Huynh-Feldt	668.357	2.835	235.735	118.443	.000
	Lower-bound	668.357	1.000	668.357	118.443	.000
day * strategy	Sphericity Assumed	98.929	3	32.976	17.532	.000
	Greenhouse-Geisser	98.929	2.140	46.235	17.532	.000
	Huynh-Feldt	98.929	2.835	34.893	17.532	.000
	Lower-bound	98.929	1.000	98.929	17.532	.001
Error(day)	Sphericity Assumed	67.714	36	1.881		
	Greenhouse-Geisser	67.714	25.677	2.637		
	Huynh-Feldt	67.714	34.022	1.990		
	Lower-bound	67.714	12.000	5.643		

Tests of Between-Subjects Effects
Measure:MEASURE_1
Transformed Variable:Average

Source	Type III Sum of Squares	df	Mean Square	F	Sig.
Intercept	17928.643	1	17928.643	603.852	.000
strategy	880.071	1	880.071	29.642	.000
Error	356.286	12	29.690		

Before reading on...

Look at the tables below and match up the relevant values with those in Figure 14.11. Notice how much redundant information is presented above.

... now read on

The choice of 'Sphericity Assumed' or one of the other three versions of the ANOVA component calculations will depend on the table below headed **Mauchly's Test of Sphericity** which addresses the homogeneity of the within-subjects samples (days). Here, Mauchly's *W* is not significant, which is good news, so homogeneity can be assumed.

Incidentally, the Levene's table, also shown below, adds further reassurance regarding the homogeneity of the between groups factor, *strategy*, on each of the four days. Note, though, that a minor violation of the assumption is evident on day 4, although ANOVA is robust enough to cope with this.

Mauchly's Test of Sphericity[b]
Measure:MEASURE_1

Within-Subjects Effect	Mauchly's W	Approx. Chi-Square	df	Sig.	Greenhouse-Geisser	Huynh-Feldt	Lower-Bound
					Epsilon[a]		
day	.563	6.164	5	.292	.713	.945	.333

Tests the null hypothesis that the error covariance matrix of the orthonormalized transformed dependent variables is proportional to an identity matrix.
[a] May be used to adjust the degrees of freedom for the averaged tests of significance. Corrected tests are displayed in the Tests of Within-Subjects Effects table.
[b] Design: Intercept + strategy
Within-Subjects Design: day

Levene's Test of Equality of Error Variances[a]

	F	df1	df2	Sig.
day1	.445	1	12	.517
day2	.002	1	12	.969
day3	1.907	1	12	.192
day4	5.442	1	12	.038

Tests the null hypothesis that the error variance of the dependent variable is equal across groups.
[a] Design: Intercept + strategy
Within-Subjects Design: day

Finally, the four graphs available have been thumbnailed below. Again, these are in the 'raw' state in which they appear, but can be edited to appear more viewer-friendly.

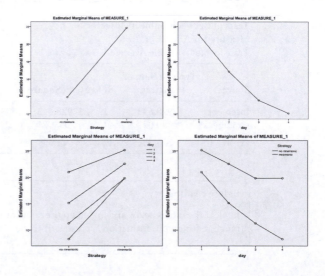

Fame and recognition

Here, the procedure for carrying out the ANOVA is identical to the *Fading memories* example. Again, the ANOVA summary table in Figure 14.17 has to be compiled and simple effects (Figure 14.19) are not available. The Mauchly's and Levene's tests of homogeneity appear below. Again, the absence of significance is a welcome result which confirms homogeneity of variance across our samples.

Mauchly's Test of Sphericity[b]
Measure:MEASURE_1

Within-Subjects Effect	Mauchly's W	Approx. Chi-Square	df	Sig.	Epsilona		
					Greenhouse-Geisser	Huynh-Feldt	Lower-Bound
category	.916	1.235	2	.539	.922	1.000	.500

Tests the null hypothesis that the error covariance matrix of the orthonormalized transformed dependent variables is proportional to an identity matrix.
[a] May be used to adjust the degrees of freedom for the averaged tests of significance. Corrected tests are displayed in the Tests of within-subjects effects table.
[b] Design: Intercept + gender
Within-subjects design: category

Levene's Test of Equality of Error Variances[a]

	F	df1	df2	Sig.
models	.252	1	15	.623
footballers	2.605	1	15	.127
pop stars	.464	1	15	.506

Tests the null hypothesis that the error variance of the dependent variable is equal across groups.
[a] Design: Intercept + gender
Within-subjects design: category

As before, the four available graphs are thumbnailed below.

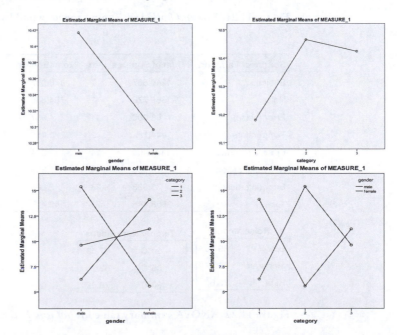

Two-factor within-subjects designs

Hot and bothered

Figure 14.21 presents the graph for the example about the effects of *noise* level (a within-subjects factor, remember) and *temperature* (also a within-subjects factor) on typing performance. The summary table this time (Figure 14.22) has three error terms, because the ANOVA design is **two-factor within** (again, it is beyond our aims of this book to explain why).

In this example, consistent with the patterns evident in the graph, both main effects are statistically significant, but the interaction between the factors does not produce a statistically significant result. This allows for a much more straightforward interpretation of the main effects, since the absence of interaction means that the effect of *noise* is the same for all three levels of *temperature*. Also the effect of *temperature* is the same for all levels of *noise*.

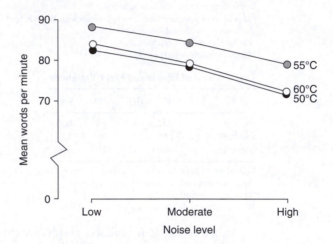

Figure 14.21 *Hot and bothered*: Typing speed (wpm) by *noise* and *temperature*

Source of Variation	Sum of Squares	df	Mean Square	F	p
Subjects	1246.667	7	178.095		
Noise	1569.778	2	784.889	161.595	.0000
Error (noise)	68.000	14	4.857		
Temperature	444.111	2	222.056	30.780	.0000
Error (temperature)	101.000	14	7.214		
N × T interaction	3.556	4	.889	0.330	.8552
Error (interaction)	75.333	28	2.690		
Total	3508.445	71	49.415		

Noise Means		Temperature Means	
Low	85.00	50°C	77.58
Moderate	80.67	55°C	83.25
High	73.67	60°C	78.50

Figure 14.22 ANOVA summary table for *hot and bothered* example

Confidence intervals

For this example, Figure 14.23 presents SPSS calculations of 95% confidence intervals for the means of the two main effects and for the nine interaction means (again, see *Making sense of SPSS* below for how to obtain these). Thus, the 95% interval estimates of the population means for *noise* are 81.2 to 88.8 for low noise, 76.8 to 84.5 for moderate noise and 69.9 to 77.5 for high noise. Note again that, because this is a within-subjects factor, the overlap in these intervals is not useful in indicating the significance of the differences between means. They do, however, give an indication as to the overall spread of scores for each of the nine conditions.

1. noise

Measure:MEASURE_1

noise	Mean	Std. Error	95% Confidence Interval	
			Lower Bound	Upper Bound
1	85.000	1.609	81.196	88.804
2	80.667	1.623	76.828	84.505
3	73.667	1.613	69.851	77.482

2. temperature

Measure:MEASURE_1

temperature	Mean	Std. Error	95% Confidence Interval	
			Lower Bound	Upper Bound
1	77.583	1.572	73.866	81.301
2	83.250	1.367	80.018	86.482
3	78.500	1.919	73.962	83.038

3. noise * temperature

Measure:MEASURE_1

noise	temperature	Mean	Std. Error	95% Confidence Interval	
				Lower Bound	Upper Bound
1	1	82.500	1.793	78.261	86.739
	2	88.375	1.375	85.124	91.626
	3	84.125	1.777	79.923	88.327
2	1	78.500	1.452	75.068	81.932
	2	84.250	1.250	81.294	87.206
	3	79.250	2.366	73.655	84.845
	1	71.750	1.645	67.861	75.639
3	2	77.125	1.630	73.270	80.980
	3	72.125	1.931	67.558	76.692

Figure 14.23 *Hot and bothered:* Means, SEs and 95% confidence intervals for *noise*, *temperature* and *noise × temperature*

Post hoc tests

Again, since both factors are within-subjects, *post hoc* tests are not directly available from SPSS. Instead, the results of Bonferroni tests are as shown in Figure 14.24.

Here, pairs of means within each main effect are compared in turn that is, averaging across the levels of the other factor. It is important to note here that, even if we had wished to, we cannot obtain *post hoc* tests for the nine **interaction means**. Admittedly, this would produce 36 different comparisons, excluding all of the repetition typical of such tables.

As it happens, we can avoid having to produce such an unwieldy analysis because the interaction was not significant in this case. Had there been a significant interaction, we would have needed to drill down into the interaction means and this would have to be done through a succession of paired *t*-tests.

> **Before reading on...**
>
> Examine the two Bonferroni tables carefully. What difference do you notice between them, and how would you explain it?
>
> The *Student/Lecturer* dialogue below should help clarify the issue. How much of this had you anticipated when thinking about the above question?
>
> **... now read on**

Pairwise Comparisons

Measure:MEASURE_1

(I) noise	(J) noise	Mean Difference (I − J)	Std. Error	Sig.[a]	95% Confidence Interval for Difference[a] Lower Bound	Upper Bound
1	2	4.333*	.403	.000	3.072	5.595
	3	11.333*	.779	.000	8.896	13.770
2	1	−4.333*	.403	.000	−5.595	−3.072
	3	7.000*	.667	.000	4.915	9.085
3	1	−11.333*	.779	.000	−13.770	−8.896
	2	−7.000*	.667	.000	−9.085	−4.915

Based on estimated marginal means
*The mean difference is significant at the .05 level.
a Adjustment for multiple comparisons: Bonferroni.

Pairwise Comparisons

Measure:MEASURE_1

(I) temperature	(J) temperature	Mean Difference (I − J)	Std. Error	Sig.[a]	95% Confidence Interval for Difference[a] Lower Bound	Upper Bound
1	2	−5.667*	.693	.000	−7.834	−3.499
	3	−.917	.503	.333	−2.490	.656
2	1	5.667*	.693	.000	3.499	7.834
	3	4.750*	1.035	.008	1.514	7.986
3	1	.917	.503	.333	−.656	2.490
	2	−4.750*	1.035	.008	−7.986	−1.514

Based on estimated marginal means
*The mean difference is significant at the .05 level.
a Adjustment for multiple comparisons: Bonferroni.

Figure 14.24 *Hot and bothered*: Bonferroni tests for the main effects of *noise* and *temperature*

Planned comparisons

Trends

Lecturer: Look back at the means in Figure 14.22. Tell me what you see.

Student: Well the three means for the main effect of noise are roughly 85, 81 and 73 going from low to high noise and, for temperature, they are 78, 83 and 79 going from 50 to 60 degrees centigrade.

Lecturer: Any comment?

Student: Blimey, I didn't notice this because it is not at all apparent from the graph. The noise means decrease gradually – possibly linearly? – from low to high noise, but the temperature means change in a very different way – first increasing from 50 to 55, then falling back to virtually where they began at 60.

Lecturer: Be careful – it is not appropriate to think in terms of a linear effect for noise, since we have no way of knowing whether the intervals between low, medium and high noise are equal. Temperature is fine in this respect, but the shape is far from linear! This is more apparent if we re-plot the graph roughly with the variables switched on the axes...

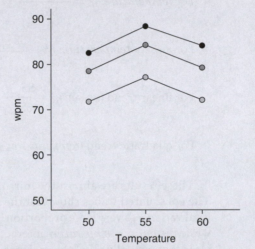

Student: No doubt about it – the temperature means are curved – a sort of upside down V or U.

Lecturer: That's exactly what they are – an inverted V or U. There is actually a technical term for this – **quadratic** and we can actually test how well data fit a quadratic shape, just as we can with a linear fit.

Student: How do we do that then?

Lecturer: Well, you know when we ask SPSS for a linear trend test – actually we are not asking precisely for that. What SPSS does is to fit all sorts of shapes to the data – linear, quadratic, and other types of curve. The name for this big family of shapes is **polynomial**.

Student: Ah – I noticed that term when we used SPSS to do a linear trend test previously. I did wonder at the time.

Lecturer: Let me show you some of what you get from SPSS when you ask for this polynomial test for temperature.

Tests of Within-Subjects Contrasts
Measure:MEASURE_1

Source	temperature	Type III Sum of Squares	df	Mean Square	F	Sig.
temperature	Linear	10.083	1	10.083	3.322	.111
	Quadratic	434.028	1	434.028	38.096	.000

> **Student:** So, for temperature, *it suggests a poor linear fit, but a significant quadratic fit? That's consistent with what we guessed from the graph.*
>
> **Lecturer:** *Correct, and we can insert the relevant term into the ANOVA summary table to reflect this.*

Effect sizes

Using the sums of squares in the summary table in Figure 14.25 (or 14.22), we can calculate the proportion of the total variance accounted for by each of the systematic effects. Thus:

$$\text{For } noise: \eta^2 = \frac{\text{SS}_{noise}}{\text{SS}_{total}} = \frac{1569.78}{3508.45} = .447$$

$$\text{For } temperature: \eta^2 = \frac{\text{SS}_{temperature}}{\text{SS}_{total}} = \frac{444.11}{3508.45} = .127$$

$$\text{For } noise \times temperature: \eta^2 = \frac{\text{SS}_{noise \times temperature}}{\text{SS}_{total}} = \frac{3.56}{3508.45} = .001$$

$$\text{For linear trend } (noise): \eta^2 = \frac{\text{SS}_{linear}}{\text{SS}_{total}} = \frac{1541.333}{3508.45} = .439$$

$$\text{For quadratic trend } (temperature): \eta^2 = \frac{\text{SS}_{quadratic}}{\text{SS}_{total}} = \frac{434.028}{3508.45} = .124$$

These results are almost the mirror image of the *Fame and recognition* example. The eta squared values show that the main effect of *noise* accounts for 44.7% of the total variance, a very large proportion by any standards. *Temperature* explains 12.7%, while the *noise × temperature* interaction accounts for a tiny 0.1%. Additionally, it is clear that virtually all of the variance explained by *temperature* is accounted for by the quadratic trend.

Source of Variation	Sum of Squares	df	Mean Square	F	p
Subjects	1246.667	7	178.095		
Noise	1569.778	2	784.889	161.595	.0000
Error (noise)	68.000	14	4.857		
Temperature	444.111	2	222.056	30.780	.0000
Error (temperature)	101.000	14	7.214		
Quadratic trend (temp)	*434.028*	*1*	*434.028*	*38.096*	*.0005*
Error quadratic	*79.750*	*7*	*11.393*		
N × T interaction	3.556	4	.889	.330	.8552
Error (interaction)	75.333	28	2.690		
Total	3508.445	71	49.415		

Figure 14.25 ANOVA summary table for *Hot and bothered* example, quadratic trend test for *temperature*

In terms of *r* as a measure of effect size, taking the square root of the three η^2 values, we obtain 0.67 for *noise* (very strong effect), 0.36 for *day* (also a moderate-to-strong effect), and.03 for the interaction between the two (effectively, no effect).

Pictures in the mind

In the final example (Figure 14.26), the graph shows a consistently longer, though not apparently massively so, decision time for reversed figures, and a clear relationship between the angle of rotation and the decision time. (Again, it's a *two-factor within-subjects design*).

The ANOVA table is shown in Figure 14.27. It confirms that both the main effects are statistically significant, but not the interaction. Again, you will see that, because it is a two-factor within-subjects design, each systematic source of variation has its own separate error term. This is different from the two-factor mixed design, which in turn is different from the two-factor between groups design. Remember that, irrespective of the number of error terms, the principles governing the interpretation of *F* ratios associated with the systematic sources of variation are identical in all cases.

You may note that there are some enormous sums of squares and mean squares values. These are purely a function of the nature of the dependent variable which, because it is a measure of response time in milliseconds, is typically in the high hundreds or more than one thousand (see data table in Chapter 13).

As in the previous example, the absence of an interaction permits a straightforward interpretation of the main effects. Since there is a significant main effect of *type* (and no interaction), we can conclude that the effect of *type* is pretty much the same for all levels of *angle*. Similarly, we can conclude that the effect of *angle* is the same for both levels of *type*.

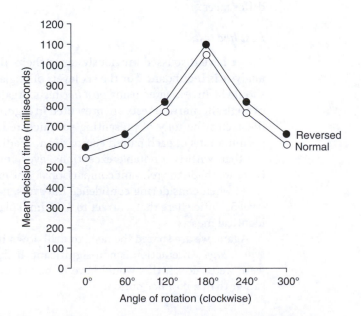

Figure 14.26 *Pictures in the mind*: **Response time (m.sec.) by** *angle* **and** *type*

Source of Variation	Sum of Squares	df	Mean Square	F	p
Subjects	32064.778	5	6412.956		
Type	44104.500	1	44104.500	4708.665	.0000
Error (type)	46.833	5	9.367		
Angle	2012295.444	5	402459.089	4495.968	.0000
Error (angle)	2237.889	25	89.516		
T × A interaction	29.833	5	5.967	0.922	.4833
Error (interaction)	161.833	25	6.473		
Total	2551727.277	71	35939.821		

Type Means	
Normal	727.36
Reversed	776.86

Angle Means	
0°	576.08
60°	634.58
120°	793.50
180°	1078.25
240°	792.83
300°	637.42

Figure 14.27 ANOVA summary table for *pictures in the mind* example

Confidence intervals

Figure 14.28 presents SPSS calculations of 95% confidence intervals for the means of the two main effects and for the 12 interaction means (again, see *Making sense of SPSS* below for how to obtain these). The 95% interval estimates of the population means for *type* are 703.2 to 751.5 for normal figures, and 752.5 to 801.2 for reversed figures. Again, these give an indication of the spread of scores in each treatment, but do not indicate the likely significance or otherwise of the mean differences.

Post hoc tests

As we have discussed previously, since there are only two levels of *type*, follow-up analysis is redundant. For the six levels of angle, however, the nature of differences should be investigated using *post hoc* tests. Again, due to the within-subjects nature of angle, Bonferroni tests are presented in Figure 14.29. First and foremost, the table illustrates the folly of presenting so much redundant information involving both permutations of each paired comparison. Wading through the results, however, we see that, with two notable exceptions, every mean differs from every other mean (here we shade the relevant comparisons). The exceptions are those we already identified when considering confidence intervals, namely, level 2 v level 6, and level 3 v level 5. Notice here that, correct to 3 decimal places, $p = 1.000$, indicating effectively identical means.

Again, we are spared the need to drill down into the interaction means, since the *type* × *angle* interaction is non-significant. It should be noted again, however, that, were we to do so, this would have to be achieved through a succession of *t*-tests, rather than a *post hoc* option.

1. type

Measure:MEASURE_1

Type	Mean	Std. Error	95% Confidence Interval	
			Lower Bound	Upper Bound
1	727.361	9.402	703.193	751.529
2	776.861	9.487	752.474	801.249

2. angle

Measure:MEASURE_1

Angle	Mean	Std. Error	95% Confidence Interval	
			Lower Bound	Upper Bound
1	576.083	10.145	550.004	602.162
2	634.583	9.641	609.802	659.365
3	793.500	10.056	767.651	819.349
4	1078.250	10.765	1050.576	1105.924
5	792.833	8.217	771.712	813.955
6	637.417	9.556	612.851	661.982

3. type * angle

Measure:MEASURE_1

type	angle	Mean	Std. Error	95% Confidence Interval	
				Lower Bound	Upper Bound
1	1	551.167	9.799	525.977	576.357
	2	609.833	9.779	584.696	634.971
	3	768.333	10.314	741.820	794.846
	4	1052.500	10.689	1025.024	1079.976
	5	769.000	8.390	747.432	790.568
	6	613.333	9.098	589.946	636.721
2	1	601.000	10.555	573.868	628.132
	2	659.333	9.563	634.752	683.915
	3	818.667	9.838	793.378	843.955
	4	1104.000	10.927	1075.911	1132.089
	5	816.667	8.082	795.892	837.441
	6	661.500	10.029	635.719	687.281

Figure 14.28 *Pictures in the mind*: Means, SEs and 95% confidence intervals for *type*, *angle* and *type* × *angle*

Planned comparisons

While a trend test across all six levels of *angle* would not produce evidence of a linear trend, separate trend tests for 0–180 and 180–300 would be likely to reveal highly significant linear trends (you can try this for yourself). Furthermore, as we saw in the previous example, since SPSS tests not only for a linear trend but for other shapes of trend, there may be something interesting in a trend analysis.

Figure 14.30 re-displays the ANOVA summary table with the outcome of a polynomial trend test for *angle* included. Note the very large F ratio associated with this

Pairwise Comparisons

Measure:MEASURE_1

(I) angle	(J) angle	Mean Difference (I − J)	Std. Error	Sig.ᵃ	95% Confidence Interval for Differenceᵃ	
					Lower Bound	Upper Bound
1	2	−58.500*	3.413	.000	−76.411	−40.589
	3	−217.417*	4.905	.000	−243.154	−191.679
	4	−502.167*	5.988	.000	−533.590	−470.743
	5	−216.750*	5.869	.000	−247.547	−185.953
	6	−61.333*	3.296	.000	−78.627	−44.040
2	1	58.500*	3.413	.000	40.589	76.411
	3	−158.917*	2.488	.000	−171.972	−145.861
	4	−443.667*	3.293	.000	−460.947	−426.386
	5	−158.250*	3.430	.000	−176.247	−140.253
	6	−2.833	1.931	1.000	−12.965	7.298
3	1	217.417*	4.905	.000	191.679	243.154
	2	158.917*	2.488	.000	145.861	171.972
	4	−284.750*	1.811	.000	−294.252	−275.248
	5	.667	2.906	1.000	−14.582	15.915
	6	156.083*	3.184	.000	139.374	172.793
4	1	502.167*	5.988	.000	470.743	533.590
	2	443.667*	3.293	.000	426.386	460.947
	3	284.750*	1.811	.000	275.248	294.252
	5	285.417*	3.546	.000	266.810	304.024
	6	440.833*	4.430	.000	417.586	464.081
5	1	216.750*	5.869	.000	185.953	247.547
	2	158.250*	3.430	.000	140.253	176.247
	3	−.667	2.906	1.000	−15.915	14.582
	4	−285.417*	3.546	.000	−304.024	−266.810
	6	155.417*	4.508	.000	131.760	179.073
6	1	61.333*	3.296	.000	44.040	78.627
	2	2.833	1.931	1.000	−7.298	12.965
	3	−156.083*	3.184	.000	−172.793	−139.374
	4	−440.833*	4.430	.000	−464.081	−417.586
	5	−155.417*	4.508	.000	−179.073	−131.760

Based on estimated marginal means

* The mean difference is significant at the .05 level.

a Adjustment for multiple comparisons: Bonferroni.

Figure 14.29 *Pictures in the mind*: Bonferroni tests for the main effect of *angle*

trend and the corresponding *p* value. (Incidentally, SPSS produced an even better fit for a very complex trend that is far beyond the scope of this text.)

Effect sizes

For this example, we can estimate the proportion of the total variance (eta squared) accounted for by each of the systematic effects, as follows:

Source of Variation	Sum of Squares	df	Mean Square	F	p
Subjects	32064.778	5	6412.956		
Type	44104.500	1	44104.500	4708.665	.0000
Error (type)	46.833	5	9.367		
Angle	2012295.444	5	402459.089	4495.968	.0000
Error (angle)	2237.889	25	89.516		
Quadratic trend (angle)	1157847.787	1	1157847.787	4892.836	.0000
Error quadratic	1183.207	5	236.641		
T × A interaction	29.833	5	5.967	0.922	.4833
Error (interaction)	161.833	25	6.473		
Total	2551727.277	71	35939.821		

Figure 14.30 ANOVA summary table for *Pictures in the mind* example, with quadratic trend test for *angle*

For *type*: $\eta^2 = \dfrac{SS_{type}}{SS_{total}} = \dfrac{44104.50}{2551727.28} = .017$

For *angle*: $\eta^2 = \dfrac{SS_{angle}}{SS_{total}} = \dfrac{2012295.44}{2551727.28} = .789$

For *type* × *angle*: $\eta^2 = \dfrac{SS_{type \times angle}}{SS_{total}} = \dfrac{29.83}{2551727.28} = .00001$

For quadratic trend of *angle*: $\eta^2 = \dfrac{SS_{quadratic}}{SS_{total}} = \dfrac{1157847.79}{2551727.28} = .454$

The η^2 values show that, in spite of its significance ($p < .0001$) the main effect of *type* accounts for only 1.7% of the total variance. This is likely to be due to the relatively high statistical power associated with the repeated measures analysis. *Angle*, on the other hand explains an enormous 78.9%, while *type* × *angle* accounts for a positively microscopic 0.001%. Rarely have two lines been more parallel on a graph! Furthermore, the quadratic trend accounts for 45.5% of the variance, some 58% of the variance explained by the main effect of *angle*.

In terms of *r* as a measure of effect size, taking the square root of the η^2 values, we obtain 0.13 for *type* (weak effect), 0.89 for *angle* (huge effect), and 0.003 for the interaction between the two (tiny effect). Most striking here is that, although statistically highly significant, the effect size for *type* points to a weak effect of this variable.

Reporting the results of two-factor within-subjects ANOVA

Hot and bothered

There was no significant interaction between *noise* and *temperature* ($F_{(4,28)} = 0.330$, $p = .86$, $\eta^2 = .001$).

The main effect of *noise* was significant ($F_{(2,14)} = 161.595$, $p < .0001$, $\eta^2 = .45$). Typing speed (wpm) decreased linearly from low noise through to high.

The main effect of *temperature* was significant ($F(2,14) = 30.780$, $p < .0001$, $\eta^2 = .13$). This factor produced a significant quadratic trend ($F(1,7) = 38.906$, $p = .0005$, $\eta^2 = .12$). Typing speed (wpm) was fastest at 55° and slower for both 50° and 60°.

Pictures in the mind

There was no significant interaction between *type* and *angle* ($F(5,25) = 0.922$, $p = .48$, $\eta^2 = .00001$).

There was a significant main effect of *type* ($F(1,5) = 4708.665$, $p < .0001$, $\eta^2 = .02$).

There was a significant main effect of *angle* ($F(5,25) = 4495.968$, $p < .0001$, $\eta^2 = .79$). This factor produced a significant quadratic trend ($F(1,5) = 4892.836$, $p < .0001$, $\eta^2 = .45$). Response time increased gradually from 0° to 180° and decreased again in a similar pattern to 300°.

Making sense of SPSS

Two-factor within-subjects designs

Note: For further information on 2-way within-subjects ANOVA, we recommend you consult Brace et al. (2009), pp. 228–237.

1. Data files

For both examples, you require the data file coded as indicated in Chapter 13 (p. 298 for *Hot and bothered* and p. 299 for *Pictures in the mind*).

2. Calculating two-way within-subjects ANOVA

Hot and bothered

The routine for this analysis is located in **Analyze > General Linear Model > Repeated Measures…**. This refers to the fact that each participant produces more than one score – it is not necessary that all factors are repeated measures, although, in this case, both factors are.

The first dialogue window to appear asks you to specify the repeated measures factors. Here, we have two repeated measures factors, each with three levels. Enter the details as shown below using the **Add** button and click **Define**.

In the resulting **Repeated Measures** dialogue window, move the levels of the repeated measures factors into the **Repeated Measures Factors:** box as shown.

Alert

Note, that the order of the two factors and their levels in the left-hand window (before transferring them across) reflects the order in which you entered the scores when creating the data file. This may be different from the order in which you have defined the factors and levels in the ANOVA, although with some care, both should be the same. Whether you can transfer the levels directly, *en bloc*, to the **Repeated Measures Factors:** box will depend on the consistency of the order of columns in your data file and the order required by the ANOVA based on your variable definitions. *It is essential to keep your wits about you at this stage.*

There is no need to select **Contrasts...**, since these will be calculated automatically for both factors.

Choose **Plots...** and, as described in previous examples, specify the four graphs: *noise*, *temperature*, *noise × temperature* and *temperature × noise*. When all graphs have been specified, click **Continue**.

The **Post Hoc...** routine does not work for within-subjects designs.

Instead, choose **Options...** and select those options in the window below, including Bonferroni tests for *noise, temperature* and *noise × temperature*. Also select **Homogeneity tests** and **Descriptive statistics**, but not **Estimates of effect size**.

Click **OK** to run the ANOVA.

Again, a mass of output will appear in the **SPSS Statistics Viewer** window. You should simply extract the information you require rather than being dictated to by SPSS.

Again, the complete ANOVA summary table which appeared in Figure 14.22 is not presented and you must compile it from the two tables below. First, however, notice that the Mauchly's test, although not significant for *noise* and *noise × temperature*, *is* significant for *temperature*. Strictly, therefore, when compiling the ANOVA summary table, we should not use the 'Sphericity Assumed' values for *temperature* and its error term, but instead, for example, the Greenhouse-Geisser adjusted values.

Below, we have shaded the appropriate rows with which to compile the summary table. You can see that, in practice, it does not appear to make a blind bit of difference – simply, that the degrees of freedom have been modified, but the *F* ratio remains the same and, although not identical, the corresponding *p* value is still highly significant. You could be forgiven for concluding 'much ado about very little'.

Mauchly's Test of Sphericity[b]
Measure:MEASURE_1

Within-Subjects Effect	Mauchly's W	Approx. Chi-square	df	Sig.	Epsilon[a] Greenhouse-Geisser	Huynh-Feldt	Lower-Bound
noise	.588	3.181	2	.204	.708	.836	.500
temperature	.343	6.417	2	.040	.604	.661	.500
noise * temperature	.312	6.303	9	.723	.639	1.000	.250

Tests the null hypothesis that the error covariance matrix of the orthonormalized transformed dependent variables is proportional to an identity matrix.

[a] May be used to adjust the degrees of freedom for the averaged tests of significance. Corrected tests are displayed in the tests of within-subjects effects table.

[b] Design: Intercept
Within-subjects design: noise + temperature + noise * temperature

Tests of Within-Subjects Effects
Measure:MEASURE_1

Source		Type III Sum of Squares	df	Mean Square	F	Sig.
noise	Sphericity Assumed	1569.778	2	784.889	161.595	.000
	Greenhouse-Geisser	1569.778	1.417	1107.877	161.595	.000
	Huynh-Feldt	1569.778	1.672	938.813	161.595	.000
	Lower-bound	1569.778	1.000	1569.778	161.595	.000
Error(noise)	Sphericity Assumed	68.000	14	4.857		
	Greenhouse-Geisser	68.000	9.918	6.856		
	Huynh-Feldt	68.000	11.705	5.810		
	Lower-bound	68.000	7.000	9.714		
temperature	Sphericity Assumed	444.111	2	222.056	30.780	.000
	Greenhouse-Geisser	444.111	1.207	367.907	30.780	.000
	Huynh-Feldt	444.111	1.322	335.989	30.780	.000
	Lower-bound	444.111	1.000	444.111	30.780	.001
Error(temperature)	Sphericity Assumed	101.000	14	7.214		
	Greenhouse-Geisser	101.000	8.450	11.953		
	Huynh-Feldt	101.000	9.253	10.916		
	Lower-bound	101.000	7.000	14.429		
noise * temperature	Sphericity Assumed	3.556	4	.889	.330	.855
	Greenhouse-Geisser	3.556	2.555	1.392	.330	.773
	Huynh-Feldt	3.556	4.000	.889	.330	.855
	Lower-bound	3.556	1.000	3.556	.330	.583
Error(noise*temperature)	Sphericity Assumed	75.333	28	2.690		
	Greenhouse-Geisser	75.333	17.885	4.212		
	Huynh-Feldt	75.333	28.000	2.690		
	Lower-bound	75.333	7.000	10.762		

Tests of Between-Subjects Effects
Measure:MEASURE_1
Transformed Variable:Average

Source	Type III Sum of Squares	df	Mean Square	F	Sig.
Intercept	458243.556	1	458243.556	2573.025	.000
Error	1246.667	7	178.095		

Before reading on...

Look at the tables below and match up the relevant values with those in Figure 14.22.

... now read on

Regarding the remaining ANOVA output, the tables of means, SEs and confidence intervals in Figure 14.23 are provided (although these will not be together). The Bonferroni tables for *noise* and *temperature* (Figure 14.24) can also be found – remember, *post hoc* tests are not directly available for the interaction means. The planned comparisons (contrasts), including those shown in the *Student/Lecturer* dialogue above (p. 331) are also presented and these in turn can be included in the ANOVA summary table as shown in Figure 14.25.

Finally, the four graphs available have been thumbnailed below.

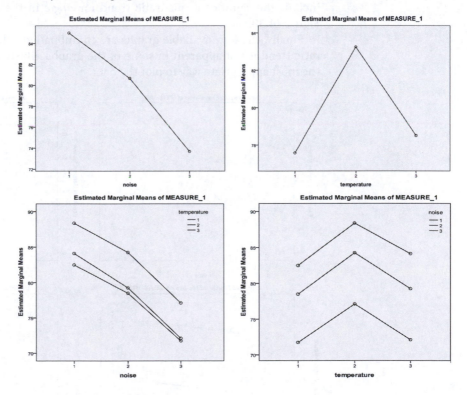

Pictures in the mind

Here, the procedure for carrying out the ANOVA is identical to the *Hot and bothered* example. Again, the ANOVA summary table in Figure 14.27 has to be compiled. The Mauchly's tests of homogeneity appear below (do not worry about the odd looking result for *type*). Again, the absence of significance is a welcome result which confirms homogeneity of variance across our samples.

Mauchly's Test of Sphericity[a]
Measure:MEASURE_1

Within-Subjects Effect	Mauchly's W	Approx. Chi-Square	df	Sig.	Epsilon[b]		
					Greenhouse-Geisser	Huynh-Feldt	Lower-Bound
type	1.000	.000	0	.	1.000	1.000	1.000
angle	.005	16.331	14	.433	.403	.675	.200
type * angle	.082	7.757	14	.942	.600	1.000	.200

Tests the null hypothesis that the error covariance matrix of the orthonormalized transformed dependent variables is proportional to an identity matrix.

[a] Design: Intercept

[b] May be used to adjust the degrees of freedom for the averaged tests of significance. Corrected tests are displayed in the tests of within-subjects effects table.

Within-subjects design: type + angle + type * angle

The output also includes the tables shown in Figures 14.28 and 14.29. A table of contrasts (linear, quadratic and other trends) is also available and allows us to include the significant quadratic trend for *angle* in the summary table shown in Figure 14.30.

Finally, the four available graphs are thumbnailed below. Notice how the quadratic trend is not apparent in some of the graphs, illustrating the need to consider the most appropriate way to plot the data.

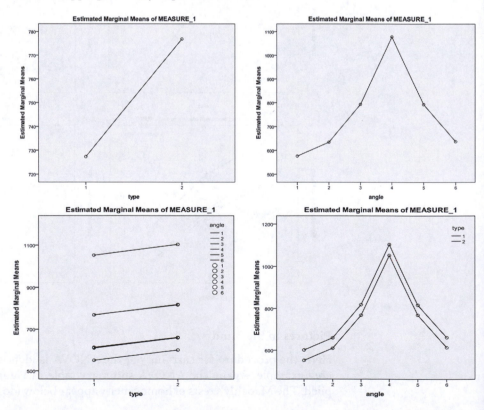

Chapter review

This chapter has gone through the same examples as in the previous chapter, but this time looking at the ANOVA results for statistical significance or otherwise, and introducing various follow-up methods that help to tease out the details of the salient patterns in the data. Careful study of these examples will pay dividends – noting the relationships between the raw data and various derived means, graphical representations, and the results from the ANOVA tables and follow-up tests. Everything contributes to the art of interpreting the evidence.

Relating: Multiple variables

In this chapter

... the topic of regression analysis is extended beyond the simple case introduced in Chapter 8. Paralleling the extension of ANOVA from one to more than one independent variable, Multiple Regression Analysis (MRA) allows the relationship between several independent variables and a dependent variable to be investigated. Following an introduction to the concept of a *regression model*, a variety of examples are presented, illustrating the flexibility of the technique. Contrasts between ANOVA and MRA are discussed briefly.

Introducing multiple regression analysis

In Chapter 8, we introduced the idea of fitting a regression line to a scatterplot showing the relationship between two variables. When these two variables are correlated, and related in a more-or-less linear fashion (as a scatterplot will show), the fitted line summarizes the relationship between them – the closer the correlation to ±1, the more exact the relationship, the closer to 0, the less linear. Now we show how this form of analysis can be extended to examine the relationship among more than two variables – analogously to the extension within ANOVA to more than one factor.

Predicting test performance

The initial example for this purpose concerns a study of what characteristics of students may affect their performance on a practical statistics test in which they are asked to use a statistical package to carry out analysis of data provided and to interpret the results. The specific aspects to be considered are *IQ*, our now familiar measure of *Attitude to Computers*, and the number of hours spent practising with the software (*Practice*). Figure 15.1 presents the data.

To begin with, we can consider the variables *IQ*, *Attitude to Computers*, and *Practice* separately in relation to performance on the test (*Mark*), in terms of the product-moment correlation coefficients, shown at the bottom of Figure 15.1. For $N = 18$, the

	Predictor Variables		Criterion Variable
IQ	**Attitude to Computers**	**Practice**	**Mark**
121	49	10	61
106	43	14	58
140	41	34	67
111	60	22	41
121	41	9	44
124	56	6	52
104	52	13	46
131	56	17	75
130	61	27	72
138	47	8	25
137	53	12	66
128	45	18	54
127	64	31	85
117	57	21	60
129	56	23	62
113	44	14	30
143	46	11	20
138	54	24	54

.582

.490

.054

Correlations with criterion variable

Figure 15.1 *IQ, Attitude to Computers, Practice* and test performance (*Mark*)

critical value for r is .468, so the correlations of *Attitude to Computers* with *Mark*, and *Practice* with *Mark* are both statistically significant at the .05 level. The correlation between *IQ* and *Mark* is low, and not statistically significant.

The next step is to examine how *IQ*, *Attitude to Computers* and *Practice* relate to *Mark*, *collectively* rather than separately. Traditionally, in such a case, *IQ*, *Attitude to Computers*, and *Practice* are called **predictor variables**, and *Mark* is called the **criterion variable**. **Simple Regression Analysis**, described in Chapter 8, deals with the relationship between one predictor variable and a criterion variable. As an extension, **Multiple Regression Analysis (MRA)** is concerned with the relationship between a several predictor variables amalgamated in a way we shall describe below, and a criterion variable.

To work through this extension, we'll start with the combination of *Attitude to Computers* and *Practice*. The standard method used is to create a combination of the general form:

$$Y' = a + b_1 X_1 + b_2 X_2$$

where a, b_1 and b_2 are specific numbers, and X_1 and X_2 are two predictor variables. Before we explain how the numbers a, b_1 and b_2 are determined, consider how this equation resembles the simpler case of the straight-line equation from Chapter 8:

$$Y' = a + bX$$

where a is the intercept and b the slope. Note that when this notation was introduced, it wasn't necessary to number either the slope, b, or the predictor variable, X, since there was only one of each. You should be able to see that the more complex formula is just a generalization of the simpler one. For the more complex formula

$$Y' = a + b_1 X_1 + b_2 X_2$$

the meaning of the intercept, a, generalizes in the sense that it is the value of Y' when X_1 and X_2 are both zero. The slopes, b_1 and b_2, are the increases in Y' for every unit increase in X_1 and X_2, respectively.

The mathematics, as you might expect, is more complicated than it is for the case of simple regression. However, the same basic principle applies. Think of Y' as a new variable constructed by amalgamating X_1 and X_2 according to the general formula, with the numbers a, b_1 and b_2 open to us to choose, according to whatever criterion we apply. A standard criterion that is adopted is to choose those precise values of a, b_1 and b_2 that will make the predicted Y' value as good an approximation to the actual Y value as possible – in the sense that $\sum (Y' - Y)^2$ is as small as possible. This method is called the method of **least squares**, since it minimizes the sum of the squared differences between the actual individual values of the criterion variable and the values predicted by the formula. The least squares criterion is analogous to the criterion used in the simple case with a single predictor (see pp. 165–166).

The method for calculating the values of a, b_1 and b_2 is quite straightforward. In practice, we do not expect you to be doing multiple regression without computer software, so we simply state that the equation that results for our example is

$$Y' = -3.334 + 0.778 X_1 + 0.995 X_2$$

where X_1 is *Attitude to Computers*, and X_2 is *Practice*.

Figure 15.2 lays out in some detail how this works. X_1 and X_2 are shown as columns, each column consisting of the 18 values for the respective predictor variable. On the right is the criterion variable Y, similarly represented as a column containing the values for that variable, *Mark*. The data are aligned, participant by participant; that is, the data in any given row are for the same person. Y' is formed by amalgamating X_1 and X_2 according to the formula. Specifically, this works by applying the formula to each participant's data in turn, that is, row by row. For example, the first

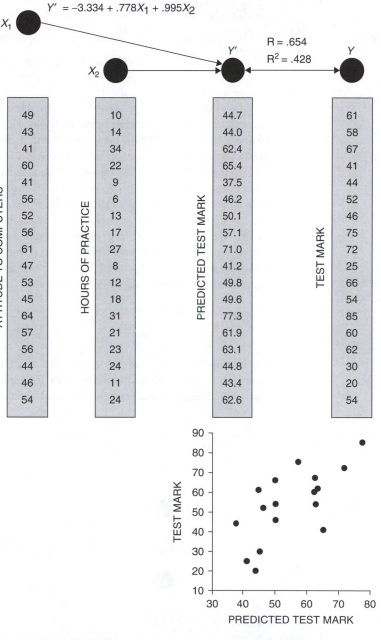

Figure 15.2 Predicting *Mark* **from** *Attitude to Computers* **and** *Practice*: **Regression model and multiple correlation** (R) **between 'predicted** *Mark*' **and** *Mark*

value of X_1 is 49, and the corresponding value of X_2 is 10. Putting those values into the formula:

$$Y' = -3.334 + (0.778 \times 49) + (0.995 \times 10)$$

gives a corresponding value of 44.7 (to 1 decimal place) for Y' for the first participant listed. The rest of the data for the column Y' are calculated in the same way.

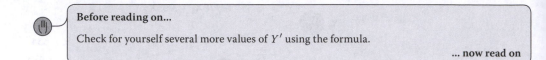

Before reading on...

Check for yourself several more values of Y' using the formula.

... now read on

To see how closely Y' relates to Y, we can use a scatterplot, as shown in Figure 15.2, and calculate the correlation between them. Here we see that there is a moderately strong positive correlation between Y' and Y. Because Y' is formed from multiple predictors (in this case, two), this correlation is called a **multiple correlation**, and R is used as notation for it. Here $R = .654$, and its square $R^2 = .428$ – the use of R^2 in this context, and not simply R, is discussed shortly. (Note that R^2 is numerically less than R, which will always be the case for R lying between 0 and 1 – make sure that you understand why this is necessarily the case).

We shall use the term **regression model** to refer to a regression equation with one or more predictors, and the associated multiple correlation between Y' and Y, and represent it as in Figure 15.3. We can test for the statistical significance of such a model using a statistic defined in general as follows:

$$F = \frac{R^2/m}{(1 - R^2)/(N - m - 1)}$$

where m is the number of predictors, and N is the number of cases. In our example, replacing the general components of the formula R^2, m, N with their particular values 0.428, 2 and 18, respectively, this works out as follows:

$$F = \frac{0.428/2}{(1 - 0.428)/(18 - 2 - 1)} = \mathbf{5.612}$$

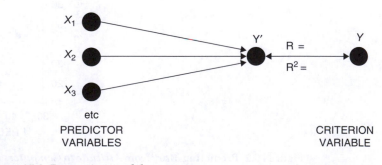

Figure 15.3 Regression model

Although it would not have been apparent to you, this F statistic is, in fact, the statistic as used in ANOVA in Chapters 12 and 14. As with ANOVA, the F statistic here has two associated degrees of freedom, which are given by the general formula $(m, N - m - 1)$, becoming $(2,15)$ for our example. The obtained value of $F = 5.612$, with these df, is statistically significant.

What does statistical significance mean here? As usual, it refers to the probability of getting a result (here a value of F) as extreme as the one we obtained from the data, if the null hypothesis is true. Here the null hypothesis, roughly speaking, is that the predictors, collectively, are not related to the criterion. Assuming H_0 to be true, the probability of the F ratio (taking into account the degrees of freedom) exceeding 3.68 is .05 (3.68 being the critical value for 2,15 df). If that critical value is exceeded (which happens in this case) then the result is statistically significant at the .05 level.

In practice, as is the usual story, the software you use is likely to give an exact probability (p). In this case, $p = .015$, which means that, if the null hypothesis is true, the probability of a value of F as extreme as 5.612 is .015 (and since this is less than .05, the result is statistically significant at the .05 level). Another way of saying this is that there is a probability of .015, or 1.5%, that we could have obtained this result by chance (that is, when H_0 is true).

Now let's consider what happens if IQ is also included as a predictor. For three predictors, as you might expect, the general form of the regression equation is:

$$Y' = a + b_1 X_1 + b_2 X_2 + b_3 X_3$$

with a, b_1, b_2, b_3 determined so as to minimize $\sum (Y' - Y)$ in a way that parallels the previous cases with one or two predictors.

For this example, with *Attitude to Computers*, *Practice* and *IQ* as predictors of *Mark*, the relationship between the variables is shown by the model in Figure 15.4.

Before reading on...

Work out the F ratio, and associated df, for this model.

... now read on

You should get $F = 3.497$, with (3,14) degrees of freedom. This is statistically significant at the .05 level (the exact p value being .0442).

So the three predictors, *Attitude to Computers*, *Practice* and *IQ* collectively predict *Mark* to a statistically significant degree. Recall, however, that the correlation between IQ and *Mark*, as shown in Figure 15.1, is close to zero ($r = .054$), suggesting

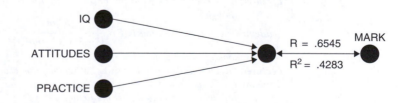

Figure 15.4 Regression model for predicting *Mark* from *Attitude to Computers*, *Practice* and *IQ*

that *IQ* is not an important determinant of *Mark*. The low value of this correlation suggests that *IQ* is not 'pulling its weight' in terms of the 3-predictor model, and that it is essentially *Attitude to Computers* and *Practice* that are providing the *predictive power*. We can analyse this apparent pattern by comparing the 3-predictor model with the previous 2-predictor model.

Figure 15.5 shows us that the addition of *IQ* as a third predictor increases R^2 by only a very small amount. We can test for the statistical significance of this increase by using the formula:

$$F = \frac{(R_2^2 - R_1^2)/k}{(1 - R_2^2)/(N - (m + k) - 1)}$$

where *m* is the number of predictors in the first model and *k* is the number of *extra* predictors in the more inclusive model. Again, as with ANOVA, *F* has two *df* given by the general formula $(k, N - (m + k) - 1)$.

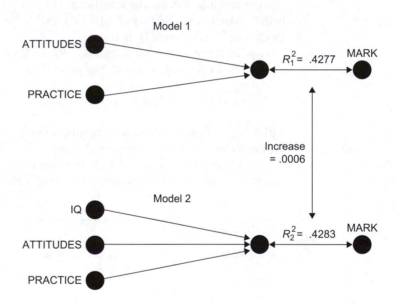

Figure 15.5 **Predicting *Mark*: Assessing the predictive power of IQ by comparing 2- and 3-predictor models**

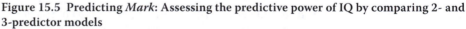

For those who wish to dig a little deeper

Lecturer: Look back at the equation on page 348 and compare it to the equation above. Any thoughts?

Student: The earlier equation is $F = \dfrac{R^2/m}{(1 - R^2)/(N - m - 1)}$ which is obviously less complicated looking than the one above. But beyond that...

Lecturer: OK let's think about it this way. What does the second equation tell us?

Student: It tells us about the change in the regression model following the addition of a further predictor or several further predictors.

Lecturer: Good, now what does the earlier, simpler looking, equation tell us?

Student: Well it just tells us about the significance of a regression model calculated from scratch.

Lecturer: What do you mean 'from scratch'?

Student: Well, you don't start with an existing model and add to it, you simply carry out a regression model without adding to anything.

Lecturer: Great! Let me put that another way for you. 'From scratch' means that you begin with zero predictors and then you see how the model fit changes following the addition of one or more predictors.

Student: You mean, see how the model has changed from no model at all?

Lecturer: You've got it! So in this light let's look again at the more complicated looking equation for model change.

Student: Right, so $F = \dfrac{(R_2^2 - R_1^2)/k}{(1 - R_2^2)/(N - (m+k) - 1)}$

Lecturer: Here you have R_1^2 and R_2^2 indicating the multiple R^2 before and after the addition of further predictors. If you begin with no predictors, what would you expect the to be?

Student: Zero, because initially there are no predictors explaining zero percent of the variance?

Lecturer: Correct, so what does the equation become as a result?

Student: Right, so $F = \dfrac{(R_2^2 - 0)/k}{(1 - R_2^2)/(N - (m+k) - 1)}$

Lecturer: Right, in fact, we can call it R^2, since there is no need to distinguish two R^2s anymore. Now, m represents the number of predictors in the initial model which we know to be zero. So, what does the equation now become?

Student: $F = \dfrac{(R^2 - 0)/k}{(1 - R^2)/(N - (0+k) - 1)}$

Lecturer: Now get rid of all the unnecessary zeros, brackets and the like.

Student: OK, so $F = \dfrac{R^2/k}{(1 - R^2)/(N - k - 1)}$

Lecturer: Remind you of anything?

Student: Ah – the simpler equation on page 348. Cool!

Lecturer: Cool indeed! So the formula on page 348 is actually a specific case of the more general equation, representing the change in model fit from an initial model with no predictors.

Before reading on...

Work out the *F* ratio, and associated degrees of freedom, for the comparison of the two models, by substituting the particular values in the general formula.

... now read on

You should have obtained:

$$F = \frac{(.4283 - .4277)/1}{(1 - .4283)/(18 - (2+1) - 1)} = \frac{.0006/1}{.5717/14} = \frac{.0006}{.0408} = \mathbf{0.015}$$

with (1,14) *df*, which is nowhere close to being statistically significant. The appropriate interpretation is that *IQ* does not add significantly to the predictive power already produced by *Attitude to Computers* and *Practice*.

Conceptual understanding and computational practice

As emphasized throughout this book, our assumption is that you have access to computer software to carry out statistical computations and we show how to use SPSS to do so. Here we are attempting to provide a conceptual understanding of the key ideas of MRA through representing the results of analyses in terms of regression models and comparisons between such models. As you will see in the *Making sense of SPSS* illustration below, the output from SPSS will not resemble our form of representation. However, the specific information that you need on multiple correlations, *F* values for testing the significance of models and differences between models, associated *p* values, and so on, will be provided.

An important point of detail here is that any calculations involve approximations. For example, if a correlation, or a squared correlation, is given even to 4 significant figures, for example, .3062, that is an approximation. If approximate figures are used in calculating an *F* ratio using one of the standard formulas (as done throughout this chapter) the result will be slightly inaccurate (technically known as rounding error). Thus, if you re-analyse the data for some examples with a computer package – which works to a much more exact approximation – the values of *F* that it produces will differ slightly from those given here (as well as being more accurate).

Making sense of SPSS

Coding data and carrying out multiple regression analysis

Note: We recommend you also consult Brace et al. (2009), pp. 211–215, 248–251 and 256–258 who provide further information.

Predicting test performance

1. Creating the data file

The same principles apply in coding data for MRA. We remind you of the golden rule that *each individual participant (case) occupies a single row of their own in the data file*. In this example, we have 18 participants, each of whom provides scores on four measures: *IQ*, *Attitude to Computers*, *Amount of Practice* (*Practice*), and *Statistics Test Performance* (*Mark*). Therefore, the data file will have 18 rows and, since each participant produces four scores, we will have four columns. We do not need any additional coding columns, since we have no between groups variables. *So, the final data table will have 18 rows and four columns.*

Create the data file as you were shown in Chapter 3, pp. 35–38). Your **Data View** should resemble that shown below. Remember to save the data giving the file an appropriate name.

	IQ	att_comp	practice	mark
1	121	49	10	61
2	106	43	14	58
3	140	41	34	67
4	111	60	22	41
5	121	41	9	44
6	124	56	6	52
7	104	52	13	46
8	131	56	17	75
9	130	61	27	72
10	138	47	8	25
11	137	53	12	66
12	128	45	18	54
13	127	64	31	85
14	117	57	21	60
15	129	56	23	62
16	113	44	14	30
17	143	46	11	20
18	138	54	24	54

Recall that the purpose of this example is to use the measures *IQ*, *Attitude to Computers* and *Practice* to predict *Mark*. Not surprisingly, the first three are known as **predictor** variables and, perhaps less obviously, the fourth a **criterion** variable. We began by simply correlating each predictor separately with the criterion, in order to assess how each variable in isolation was related to *Mark* (see Figure 15.1). Let's do this.

Select **Analyse > Correlate > Bivariate...** to reveal the following dialogue window:

Move the four variables into the box as shown and click **OK**. The correlation matrix below will appear. The correlations of interest are shaded, namely those between the criterion and the three predictors, as seen in Figure 15.1.

Correlations

		IQ	Attitude to computers	Hours of practice	Performance on test
IQ	Pearson Correlation	1	−.028	.190	.054
	Sig. (2-tailed)		.912	.450	.831
	N	18	18	18	18
Attitude to computers	Pearson Correlation	−.028	1	.365	.490*
	Sig. (2-tailed)	.912		.137	.039
	N	18	18	18	18
Hours of practice	Pearson Correlation	.190	.365	1	.582*
	Sig. (2-tailed)	.450	.137		.011
	N	18	18	18	18
Performance on test	Pearson Correlation	.054	.490*	.582*	1
	Sig. (2-tailed)	.831	.039	.011	
	N	18	18	18	18

*Correlation is significant at the 0.05 level (2-tailed).

When we considered this example above, we began with a regression involving only the two predictors that correlated significantly with *Mark*, namely *Attitude to Computers* and *Practice*. Let's calculate this regression using SPSS.

Select **Analyse > Regression > Linear...** and, in the resulting dialogue window, as shown, move the criterion variable, *Mark*, into the box labelled (somewhat unhelpfully) **Dependent:** and *Attitude to Computers* and *Practice* into the one labelled (equally unhelpfully) **Independent(s):**. Click **OK**.

The regression analysis will appear in the **SPSS Statistics Viewer** as below. For this first example, we include all of the tables that appear in the output and indicate those that are most important for reporting the results of the regression. Key statistics are shaded.

The second table headed **Correlations** displays a subset of those presented above. Notice that, for no particularly good reason, these are in a different format, with the correlation coefficients in one block and the p values and Ns in separate blocks below. The redundant correlations of each variable with itself are also shown. Obviously, correlations involving IQ are not presented, since this predictor was not selected for the regression analysis.

The table below, headed **Variables Entered/Removed**, lists the variables (and by this SPSS means the predictor variables) entered into the regression analysis, confirming that the two predictors have been entered.

The table labelled **Model Summary** gives the multiple correlation, R, and the multiple R^2. This latter value is the one shown in Figure 15.5 above for the 2-predictor model (Model 1), albeit to three, rather than four, decimal places.

The table headed **ANOVA** shows the outcome of applying the formula for F as demonstrated on page 248. Notice again that there is a minor discrepancy due to rounding error. The associated p value of .015, indicates that the 2-predictor regression model is significant.

The final table, labelled **Coefficients**, presents the values of a, b_1 and b_2 in the equation $Y' = a + b_1X_1 + b_2X_2$ discussed on page 346, giving the best-fit linear model representing the 2-predictor regression as $Y' = -3.334 + 0.778X_1 + 0.995X_2$.

Descriptive Statistics

	Mean	Std. Deviation	N
Performance on test	54.00	17.344	18
Attitude to computers	51.39	7.138	18
Hours of practice	17.44	8.111	18

Correlations

		Performance on test	Attitude to computers	Hours of practice
Pearson Correlation	Performance on test	1.000	.490	.582
	Attitude to computers	.490	1.000	.365
	Hours of practice	.582	.365	1.000
Sig. (1-tailed)	Performance on test	.	.020	.006
	Attitude to computers	.020	.	.068
	Hours of practice	.006	.068	.
N	Performance on test	18	18	18
	Attitude to computers	18	18	18
	Hours of practice	18	18	18

Variables Entered/Removed[a]

Model	Variables Entered	Variables Removed	Method
1	Hours of practice, Attitude to computers[b]	.	Enter

[a] Dependent variable: Performance on test
[b] All requested variables entered.

Model Summary

Model	R	R Square	Adjusted R Square	Std. Error of the Estimate
1	.654[a]	.428	.351	13.969

[a] Predictors: (Constant), Hours of practice, Attitude to computers

ANOVA[b]

Model		Sum of Squares	df	Mean Square	F	Sig.
1	Regression	2187.045	2	1093.523	5.604	.015[b]
	Residual	2926.955	15	195.130		
	Total	5114.000	17			

[a] Dependent Variable: Performance on test
[b] Predictors: (Constant), Hours of practice, Attitude to computers

Coefficients[a]

Model		Unstandardized Coefficients B	Std. Error	Standardized Coefficients Beta	t	Sig.	95.0% Confidence Interval for B Lower Bound	Upper Bound
1	(Constant)	−3.334	24.671		−.135	.894	−55.920	49.251
	Attitude to computers	.778	.510	.320	1.526	.148	−.308	1.864
	Hours of practice	.995	.449	.465	2.218	.042	.039	1.951

[a] Dependent Variable: Performance on test

We could of course repeat this analysis in SPSS, this time including all three predictors. Then, we could compare the results with the 2-predictor analysis to see whether the three predictors produce an improved model compared to only two, as we showed in Figure 15.5. This would be indicated by any difference between the R^2

values (and the *F* values). There is, however, a neater method in SPSS for doing this, within a single analysis, which we describe next.

Before reading on…

For practice, why not use SPSS to calculate the 3-predictor regression.

… now read on

Predicting test performance: Comparing two regression models

First, as before, we instruct SPSS to enter only the two predictors. Select **Analyse > Regression > Linear…** and, in the resulting dialogue window, again, move the criterion variable, *Mark*, into the **Dependent:** box and *Attitude to Computers* and *Practice* into the **Independent(s):** box, as shown.

Now, here's the clever bit. Click on the Next button located between the two variable boxes. Nothing much appears to happen, but the more eagle eyed of you will have noticed that the **Independent(s):** box appears to have been emptied as shown below. This is not so, because the difficult-to-spot label just under the **Dependent:** box has changed from **Block 1 of 1** to **Block 2 of 2**. So, the 2-predictor regression has been tucked away for the time being.

This now allows us to instruct SPSS to add another predictor and to carry out a 3-predictor regression after the 2-predictor one (see below). Notice that you do not have to specify the three predictors – SPSS will simply add the third predictor to the two already entered.

Before proceeding, we need to choose a useful statistic which will tell us about the effect of adding the third predictor. Click on the **Statistics...** button to reveal the dialogue window below and select **R squared change** (**Model fit** and **Estimates** are already selected by default).

Click **Continue**, followed by **OK**.

The following output will appear in the SPSS Statistics Viewer window (we have been more selective than in the illustration above). The first table confirms that two regressions have been carried that. In the first regression (Model 1), the predictors *Practice* and *Attitude to Computers* have been entered. In the second regression (Model 2) a *further* predictor has been entered, *IQ*, giving a 3-predictor model.

Variables Entered/Removed[a]

Model	Variables Entered	Variables Removed	Method
1	Hours of practice, Attitude to computers[b]	.	Enter
2	IQ[b]	.	Enter

[a]Dependent variable: Performance on test .
[b] All requested variables entered.

The second table labelled **Model Summary** shows the R and R^2 values associated with both the 2- and 3-predictor models. Interpretation is a little hampered by the fact that SPSS presents the values correct to three decimal places, suggesting no difference between the two models when, in fact, there is a very small difference.

This table is in two halves. The left half shows the overall statistics for the two regression models. The second row of the table (Model 2) shows R and R^2 following the introduction of *IQ*. It is clear that, to three decimal places, the three predictor model does not result in a higher R^2. Actually, to four decimal places, the values are .4277 and .4283 for Models 1 and 2 respectively.

More revealing is the right half of the table labelled *Change Statistics* which shows **R Square Change** and **F Change** resulting from the introduction of the third predictor. For Model 1, these are merely the values obtained for the 2-predictor regression (if you like, showing the change from no predictors to two). These confirm that the model is statistically significant ($p = .015$) and that, together, the two predictors explain 42.8% of the variation in test performance ($R^2 = .428$).

For Model 2, that is, following the introduction of *IQ*, R^2 is seen to have increased by a mere .001 (actually, .0006 to four decimal places as shown in Figure 15.5), and the *F* value associated with this change is 0.016. Recall that this was the value that we calculated by hand using the formula on page 351 (the actual value there was .015). The associated *p* value is .900, confirming the meagre nature of the increase, which has a 90% probability of occurring by chance.

As before, therefore, we can conclude that the 3-predictor model does not improve the predictive power already produced by *Practice* and *Attitude to Computers* together.

Model Summary

Model	R	R Square	Adjusted R Square	Std. Error of the Estimate	R Square Change	F Change	df1	df2	Sig. F Change
					Change Statistics				
1	.654[a]	.428	.351	13.969	.428	5.604	2	15	.015
2	.654[b]	.428	.306	14.451	.001	.016	1	14	.900

[a] Predictors: (Constant), Hours of practice, Attitude to computers
[b] Predictors: (Constant), Hours of practice, Attitude to computers, IQ

An analogy: Loose change

At this point, we introduce an analogy that we hope may give you some intuitive feeling for how a regression equation works. Imagine 11 people turning out their pockets to see how much cash they have, in terms of £1 coins, fifty-pence (50p) pieces, twenty-pence (20p) pieces, and smaller change. The data are shown in Figure 15.6.

Number of £1 coins	Number of 50p	Number of 20p	Change (in pence)	Total Amount (in pence)
3	3	2	15	505
12	8	3	25	1685
4	1	4	21	551
6	4	2	26	866
8	7	3	7	1217
8	2	1	18	938
5	10	6	14	1134
6	3	4	7	837
7	1	2	27	817
2	5	3	39	549
0	3	3	4	214

Figure 15.6 Breakdown of cash in pocket: How many £1 coins, 50p pieces, 20p pieces and smaller coins (10p or less)?

Before reading on...

Think about the logic of this situation. What would you expect to happen if the separate correlations between the first four variables and the total amount of money (the last variable) are calculated?

... now read on

You should be able to reason that the number of £1 coins is a major determinant of the total amount of money, so the correlation between number of pounds and total amount should be high. The number of 50p pieces is less important in determining the total, but still has some bearing on it, so the correlation of that with total amount should be less. After that, the correlations should become small. The actual correlations are as shown in Figure 15.7.

	Correlation with Total Amount
Number of £1 coins	.9207
Number of 50p	.6479
Number of 20p	.1342
Change	.0799

Figure 15.7 Correlations between numbers of each coin and total cash in pocket

Now consider a sequence of regression models in which total amount of money is treated as the criterion variable and the other variables are added in sequentially as predictors (see Figure 15.8). The number of pounds already correlates highly with total amount of money. Adding in number of 50p pieces as a second predictor increases the value of R^2 to .9974, and adding the number of 20p pieces as a third predictor increases R^2 further to .9994 (getting very close to 1). For practice in using the formula, you might like to see if these increases are statistically significant.

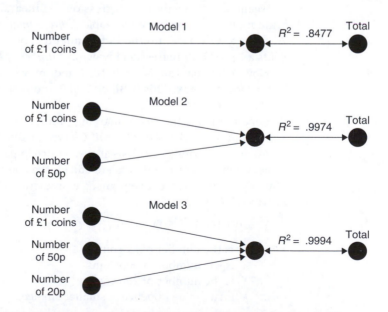

Figure 15.8 Predicting total cash from coinage: Three regression models

> **Before reading on...**
>
> What would happen if the amount of small change was added as a fourth predictor?
>
> **... now read on**

The total amount of money (in pence) is given *exactly* by the formula:

Total = (100 × number of £1 coins) + (50 × number of 50p pieces) + (20 × number of 20p pieces) + (1 × amount of small change),

so in this case, Y' and Y would be identical, there would be a perfect multiple correlation and R^2 would be 1.

If you think carefully about the different components in this analogy and how they are related logically, it should help to give you a feel for what is going on in MRA.

Making sense of SPSS

Loose change: Comparing four regression models

1. Coding the data

Here, we have 11 participants, each producing 5 scores, namely the number of £1, 50p and 20p coins, the value of smaller change in pence, and the total value of loose change in pence. You should know by now that there will be eleven rows in the data matrix and five score columns. Since there are no between groups variables, there will be no further columns needed to code group membership.

2. Calculating the regressions

The method is the same as for the example above, except that, this time, the regression is built up in four blocks, rather than just two. We do not repeat the method in detail here, so, if necessary, re-read the example above.

Again, select **Analyse > Regression > Linear...** and, in the resulting dialogue window, move the criterion variable, *Total Amount*, into the **Dependent:** box and *Number of £1 Coins* into the **Independent(s):** box. This is **Block 1 of 1** and represents a 1-predictor regression involving *Number of £1 Coins* as the only predictor.

Now, click on the Next button and move *Number of 50p Coins* into the Independent(s): box. This is **Block 2 of 2** and represents the 2-predictor regression model.

Repeat this for the two remaining predictors, adding *Number of 20p Coins* in **Block 3 of 3** and *Amount of Small Change* in **Block 4 of 4**. The results are shown below and confirm the analysis above. Notice in particular that, in the **Coefficients** table, when all four predictors are added, the coefficients a, b_1, b_2, b_3 and b_4 are 0, 100, 50, 20 and 1 respectively, giving a prediction of the total value of loose change (Y') as:

$$Y' = 0 + 100X_1 + 50X_2 + 20X_3 + X_4$$

where X_1 is the number of £1 coins
X_2 is the number of 50p coins
X_3 is the number of 20p coins
X_4 is the value in pence of smaller change

which is basically how you calculate exactly the value of your loose change.

Variables Entered/Removed[a]

Model	Variables Entered	Variables Removed	Method
1	pound coins[b]	.	Enter
2	50 pence coins[b]	.	Enter
3	20 pence coins[b]	.	Enter
4	smaller coins[b]	.	Enter

[a] Dependent variable: total cash in pocket.
[b] All requested variables entered.

Model summary

Model	R	R Square	Adjusted R Square	Std. Error of the Estimate	Change Statistics				
					R Square Change	F Change	df1	df2	Sig. F Change
1	.921[a]	.848	.831	165.828	.848	50.102	1	9	.000
2	.999[b]	.997	.997	23.077	.150	456.716	1	8	.000
3	1.000[c]	.999	.999	12.127	.002	21.968	1	7	.002
4	1.000[d]	1.000	1.000	.000	.001	.	1	6	.

[a] Predictors: (Constant), pound coins
[b] Predictors: (Constant), pound coins, 50 pence coins
[c] Predictors: (Constant), pound coins, 50 pence coins, 20 pence coins
[d] Predictors: (Constant), pound coins, 50 pence coins, 20 pence coins, smaller coins

Coefficients[a]

Model		Unstandardized Coefficients		Standardized Coefficients	t	Sig.
		B	Std. Error	Beta		
1	(Constant)	222.397	101.378		2.194	.056
	pound coins	112.568	15.903	.921	7.078	.000
2	(Constant)	67.680	15.857		4.268	.003
	pound coins	97.511	2.323	.798	41.983	.000
	50 pence coins	55.752	2.609	.406	21.371	.000
3	(Constant)	23.133	12.640		1.830	.110
	pound coins	100.117	1.341	.819	74.645	.000
	50 pence coins	50.333	1.793	.367	28.066	.000
	20 pence coins	17.750	3.787	.059	4.687	.002
4	(Constant)	0	.000		.000	1.000
	pound coins	100.000	.000	.818	1.165E8	.000
	50 pence coins	50.000	.000	.364	4.346E7	.000
	20 pence coins	20.000	.000	.067	8052981.720	.000
	smaller coins	1.000	.000	.026	4134771.007	.000

[a] Dependent Variable: total cash in pocket

Variations on the multiple regression analysis theme

A wide variety of useful forms of analysis can be carried out using the basic repertoire we have introduced in terms of regression models and significance tests for either (a) a single regression model; or (b) the comparison between two regression models, one of which contains a subset of the predictor variables in the other. In this section, we illustrate this variety with a number of examples.

Category variables as predictors

In order to use a category (or *nominal*) variable (see p. 18) as a predictor variable in MRA, special steps need to be taken.

Here are some fictitious data for sense of humour, measured on a scale from 0 to 100 (you might like to think about how sense of humour could be measured in practice) for twenty individuals belonging to four different nationalities, which, to avoid possible offence, we have labelled, but not identified (see Figure 15.9).

	Nationality			
	A	B	C	D
	82	42	52	62
	61	66	53	59
	57	61	39	72
	63	50	67	75
	64		54	69
Means	65.4	54.8	52.2	67.4

Figure 15.9 Sense of humour by nationality

What you must NOT do is to code nationalities A, B, C, D as 1, 2, 3, 4 and treat this as a single predictor variable.

Before reading on...

Think about why doing this would be silly.

... now read on

Coding nationality within a single predictor variable as 1, 2, 3, 4 would imply that the four nationalities are ordered and, more specifically, that the differences between A and B, B and C, C and D are all equal (an interval scaled predictor). No such ordered relationship exists. The appropriate way to treat nationality, or any other category variable, as a predictor for MRA is to recode the data by introducing so-called **dummy variables**. Figure 15.10 shows how this works for our example.

There are three dummy variables. The first takes the value 1 if that individual's nationality is A, and the value 0 otherwise. The second and third relate in a similar way to nationalities B and C, respectively. You might be expecting a fourth dummy variable for nationality D, but in fact it is not necessary, because any individual coded as 0, 0, 0 for the three dummy variables must of necessity be of nationality D, by elimination. In general, *if a category variable has k categories, it is coded by k − 1 dummy variables.*

Having recoded the data in this way, the regression analysis proceeds as normal, with the dummy variables being treated as a set of predictors. (Even though these variables are dichotomous, coded as 0 as 1 for each individual, the standard formula for working out the regression equation, multiple correlation, F ratio for testing for significance, and so on, can be applied.) The resulting model is shown in Figure 15.11.

The F ratio to test for significance of the model is 3.625 with (3,16) df and this is significant at the .05 level (the exact p value is .0361). The appropriate interpretation

Dummy 1	Dummy 2	Dummy 3	Humour Score
1	0	0	82
1	0	0	61
1	0	0	57
1	0	0	63
1	0	0	64
0	1	0	42
0	1	0	66
0	1	0	61
0	1	0	50
0	0	1	52
0	0	1	53
0	0	1	39
0	0	1	67
0	0	1	54
0	0	1	48
0	0	0	62
0	0	0	59
0	0	0	72
0	0	0	75
0	0	0	69

Figure 15.10 Recoding nationality: The use of dummy variables

is that we can reject the null hypothesis that the populations from the four nationalities do not differ in terms of sense of humour as measured. Note that this is a general statement, and does not pinpoint where differences exist between the nationalities. Eyeballing the means, it looks as if nationalities A and D have better senses of humour that nationalities B and C. In order to check this pattern of differences more precisely, some follow-up procedures would be needed (as is the case when a significant effect is found in ANOVA) but we're not going to cover that.

In any case where the variable is dichotomous, that is, can only take two values (for example, gender); the variable can be coded simply as a single predictor using 0 and 1 for the two categories (note that this is a special case of k categories requiring $k - 1$ dummy variables; when $k = 2$, $k - 1 = 1$).

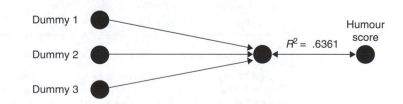

Figure 15.11 Predicting sense of humour from nationality through dummy variables

Making links: MRA and ANOVA

Looking at the original data in Figure 15.9, it should be clear to you that these data could have been analysed as they were, without coding, using one-factor between groups ANOVA. While this is so, it is sometimes necessary to code such data using dummy variables in order that they can be included as part of a larger regression analysis involving other predictors, as in the next example (*Selecting from multiple predictors*). However, the fact that either MRA or ANOVA is appropriate suggests that there must be very clear links between the two forms of analysis.

Lecturer: Informally, have you noticed any clues so far to suggest that regression and ANOVA may be closely related.

Student: As a matter of fact, yes. I was struck right at the start in the Predicting test performance example, where I noticed that the significance of the regression model was tested using F which I naturally associate with ANOVA.

Lecturer: That's right. There is another, more subtle, clue. Have you noticed it I wonder?

Student: Eh, no.

Lecturer: Let me give you a hint – think SPSS.

Student: Eh, still nothing.

Lecturer: OK, what SPSS routine do you select to carry out an ANOVA?

Student: That would be Analyze, then General Linear Model, then either....

Lecturer: Stop there!

Student: General Linear Model? Ah, I see, you don't choose Analyze then ANOVA. General Linear Model sounds very like linear regression.

Lecturer: You've got it! The clue is that there is a large collection of tests that all fall under a rubric that, if not actually *regression*, is very close to it.

Let's illustrate the closeness of the relationship between regression and ANOVA. The relevant parts of the SPSS output for the dummy variable data are given below. These show that the variance in *humour* scores explained by the dummy-coded *nationality*, as indicated by R^2, is 40.5%, and that the regression model is significant, as indicated by the F value of 3.625 (noted above) and associated p value of .036.

Model Summary

Model	R	R Square	Adjusted R Square	Std. Error of the Estimate
1	.636[a]	.405	.293	9.083

[a] Predictors: (Constant), dummy3, dummy2, dummy1

ANOVA[a]

Model		Sum of Squares	df	Mean Square	F	Sig.
1	Regression	897.217	3	299.072	3.625	.036[b]
	Residual	1319.983	16	82.499		
	Total	2217.200	19			

[a] Dependent variable: humour
[b] Predictors: (Constant), dummy3, dummy2, dummy1

Now let's look at the output below from a one-way between groups ANOVA using the original data in Figure 15.9. (Look back at Chapter 12 if you need to be reminded how to perform this calculation using SPSS.) Note that we finish up with the same value of F (and the same degrees of freedom), exemplifying the close link between the two statistical techniques.

Tests of Between-Subjects Effects
Dependent Variable: humour score

Source	Type III Sum of Squares	df	Mean Square	F	Sig.
Corrected model	897.217[a]	3	299.072	3.625	.036
Intercept	70364.180	1	70364.180	852.910	.000
nationality	897.217	3	299.072	3.625	.036
Error	1319.983	16	82.499		
Total	73738.000	20			
Corrected total	2217.200	19			

[a] R Squared =.405 (Adjusted R Squared =.293)

Selecting from multiple predictors

Next we look at a rather more complex example, using real data for 172 psychology students. A small part of the data is shown in Figure 15.12.

The question to be addressed by analysing these data is what variables predict students' *Attitude to Computers*. The variables to be considered are *Faculty* (arts, science or economics), *Gender, IQ, External Locus of Control* (a measure of the degree to which individuals consider that their behaviour is controlled by external events rather than under their own control – commonly abbreviated to *External LoC*), and *Computer Use* (which, in this case, is simply the answer to the question: 'Have you taken a computer course before?'). The first step is to recode *Gender* and *Computer Use* as 0s and 1s, and *Faculty* as 2 dummy variables, *Faculty1* and *Faculty2*, with the result shown in Figure 15.13. When all variables are included as predictors, the model looks like that in Figure 15.14.

Predictor Variables					Criterion Variable
Faculty	*Gender*	*IQ*	*External LoC*	*Computer Use*	*Attitude to Computers*
Science	Female	104	10	Yes	55
Economics	Female	107	10	Yes	58
Arts	Male	97	17	No	41
Economics	Female	97	17	No	43
Arts	Female	87	16	No	52
Science	Female	94	13	Yes	56
Arts	Male	93	16	Yes	61
Arts	Female	104	14	No	45

Figure 15.12 *Faculty, Gender, IQ, External LoC, Computer Use,* and *Attitude to Computers*: **Real data**

Separate correlations between each predictor variable and *Attitude to Computers* are as shown in Figure 15.15. For *Gender, IQ, External LoC* and *Computer Use*, these are simple (bivariate) correlations. The correlation for *Faculty* consists of a multiple correlation produced by combining the two dummy variables.

So it looks as if *External LoC* and *Computer Use* are the important predictors. (Note that the correlation between *External LoC* and *Attitude to Computers* is negative, indicating that, in general, a higher degree of *External LoC* goes with a lower *Attitude to Computers*, and vice versa.) The dominance of the major predictors may

	Predictor Variables					Criterion Variable
Faculty1	*Faculty2*	*Gender*	*IQ*	*External LoC*	*Computer Use*	*Attitude to Computers*
0	1	1	104	10	1	55
0	0	1	107	10	1	58
1	0	0	97	17	0	41
0	0	1	97	17	0	43
1	0	1	87	16	0	52
0	1	1	94	13	1	56
1	0	0	93	16	1	61
1	0	1	104	14	0	45
.	.	.	.	.	.	.
.	.	.	.	.	.	.
.	.	.	.	.	.	.
.	.	.	.	.	.	.

Figure 15.13 Recoding *Gender, Computer Use* and *Faculty*

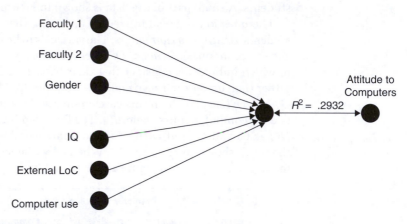

Note: Faculty counts as two predictors because of use of dummy variables.

Figure 15.14 6-predictor regression model: Predicting computer attitude from *Faculty, Gender, IQ, External LoC* and *Computer Use*

	Correlation with *Attitude to Computers*	Squared Correlation
Faculty 1 + Faculty 2	.0961	.0092
Gender	.0706	.0050
IQ	.0533	.0028
External LoC	−.3136	.0983
Computer Use	.4572	.2090

Figure 15.15 Separate correlations between attitude and the five variables

be confirmed by comparing the model that contains just those two predictors with the original model containing the full set of predictors (Figure 15.16).

The two predictors in this model give a value for R^2 of .2793, which is only marginally less than the value of .2932 given by the full set of predictors (see Figure 15.14). Note that the correlation coefficient for *External LoC* in Figure 15.15 is negative, reflecting the inverse relationship between this predictor and the criterion variable.

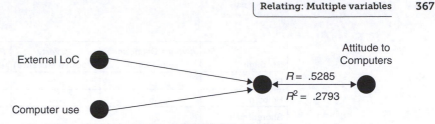

Figure 15.16 Predicting computer attitude using just *External LoC* and *Computer Use*

We may use this example to explain further how it is possible to test for **interaction** within MRA. By way of example, we shall show how to test for an interaction between *External LoC* and *Computer Use*. What would an interaction mean in this case? It can be expressed in various ways, but perhaps the clearest would be to say that there would be an interaction if the relationship between *External LoC* and *Attitude to Computers* differed depending on whether or not the individual had previous experience of computers. This reflects the general meaning of an interaction between two variables, discussed extensively in relation to ANOVA (Chapters 11 to 14), that the effects of one variable differ depending on the value of the other variable.

In practical terms, the procedure for testing for a statistically significant interaction between two predictor variables, X_1 and X_2, goes as follows. A new variable is created by multiplying the value of X_1 by the value of X_2 for each individual. Then a comparison of models is carried out using the usual formula, the first model having X_1 and X_2 as predictors, and the second X_1, X_2 and X_1X_2. In the case of the example, the resulting models are as seen in Figure 15.17. You will see that adding X_1X_2 as an extra predictor increases the squared multiple correlation only slightly, and an F test will confirm that this small increase is far from statistically significant. We conclude therefore that there is no evidence in these data of an interaction between *External LoC* and *Computer Use*.

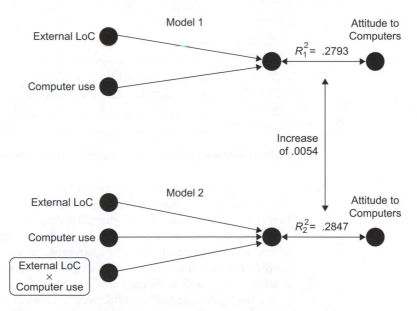

Figure 15.17 Investigating a possible interaction between *External LoC* and *Computer Use*

The complication of correlated predictors: Burt data

To illustrate another key point about MRA, we return to the data from Burt's study (Figure 15.18) already analysed quite extensively in Chapter 8.

Borough	Juvenile Delinquency (per 10,000)	Poverty (Booth's Measure)	Poor Relief (per 1000)	Percentage Overcrowding
Finsbury	42	37	22	34
Holborn	36	49	16	20
Shoreditch	28	42	51	32
Bermondsey	23	44	46	23
St. Pancras	21	30	20	22
Southwark	18	49	32	24
Stepney	17	38	20	29
Battersea	16	38	43	12
Deptford	16	40	40	13
St. Marylebone	15	27	8	18
Westminster	15	35	5	10
Paddington	14	22	15	15
Bethnal Green	14	45	25	28
Islington	14	31	26	19
Hammersmith	13	34	17	14
Lambeth	12	26	21	13
Poplar	12	36	83	21
Kensington	12	25	10	17
Chelsea	12	25	13	14
Greenwich	11	37	16	14
Camberwell	10	29	34	13
Fulham	9	25	14	13
Woolwich	9	25	27	8
Hackney	8	24	18	12
Lewisham	7	18	23	5
City of London	5	32	4	7
Wandsworth	4	27	8	7
Hampstead	2	14	3	7
Stoke Newington	0	19	8	8

Figure 15.18 Burt's data on *Juvenile Delinquency, Poverty, Poor Relief* and *Overcrowding*

Given the generally high correlations between *Poverty, Poor Relief* and *Overcrowding*, separately, and *Juvenile Delinquency* – r = .66, .42 (ignoring the outlier) and .77, respectively (see Figure 8.18, on p. 162) – and, given that it is plausible to consider the measures of poor social conditions as causally contributing to the level of *Juvenile Delinquency*, it would seem sensible to combine those three variables as predictors in an MRA, with *Juvenile Delinquency* as the criterion variable. Doing so produces the model in Figure 15.19.

So, the trio of predictors collectively predict *Juvenile Delinquency* to a considerable degree, with R^2 = .660 (which is statistically significant). But what if we want to tease the predictors apart and evaluate the importance of the contribution of each one independently? The contribution of any one predictor that can be *uniquely* attributed to that predictor can be found by comparing two models – one that contains all the predictors, and another that contains all of them except the one under consideration. Figure 15.20 shows the result for the Burt data.

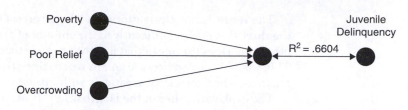

Figure 15.19 Regression model for predicting *Juvenile Delinquency* from *Poverty, Poor Relief* and *Overcrowding*

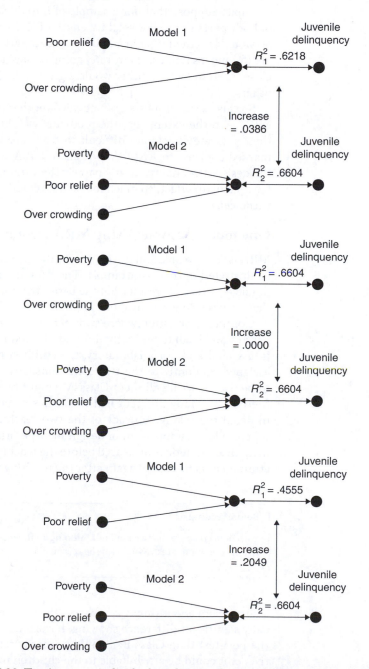

Figure 15.20 Teasing apart individual predictions from multiple regression (Burt data)

The result is not straightforward to interpret. *Overcrowding* is the only one of the three that *adds* significantly to the amount of predictive power produced by the other two. Does this mean that it is the only one that predicts *Juvenile Delinquency*? This would be an odd conclusion to reach, since the other two also have high correlations, when correlated separately with *Juvenile Delinquency*.

The explanation lies in the fact that in this example the predictor variables are all highly correlated, not just with the criterion variable, but with each other, something known as **colinearity** or **multicolinearity** (again, see Figure 8.18, on p. 162). To get a feel for the implications of this, consider the following glaringly obvious example. Suppose that, for a sample of individuals, you were using measurements of body parts to predict height. Length of left arm would be a very good predictor. So would length of right arm. But because length of right arm and length of left arm are (for most samples, at any rate) going to have a very high correlation – extremely close to +1, in fact – neither would significantly add to the predictive power of the other.

So this example shows dramatically another prominent characteristic feature of MRA – to the extent that the predictor variables are correlated with each other, their separate effects are difficult to tease apart. In this respect, MRA stands in marked contrast to ANOVA. For an ANOVA with equal numbers in each cell of the design, the analysis neatly parcels the variance into separate chunks – so much for each main effect, so much for each interaction, and so much unexplained (error variance).

One more example: Using MRA for analysis of covariance

MRA is very flexible and has many specific useful applications, and one in particular is illustrated in this last example. The data are made up to illustrate four different possible patterns of results, but the basic structure of the experimental design is one that occurs frequently in applied research.

Consider a situation where two methods of teaching arithmetic are being compared – we'll call them Method A and Method B. Because this sort of study is done in a school and not a laboratory, the children being taught would usually not be assigned randomly to the two conditions. Instead, two existing classes are likely to be used – we'll call them Class A (taught by Method A) and Class B (taught by Method B). Many different methodologies could be brought to bear to investigate in detail the relative efficacy of the two teaching methods, but for our purposes we consider a simple form of design incorporating a *pre-test* (the children's attainment in arithmetic is measured before the teaching takes place) and a *post-test* (their attainment is measured again after the teaching takes place).

Before reading on...

You could compare the two methods by doing an independent *t*-test to compare the scores of the two classes at post-test. Would this be reasonable? If not, why not?

... now read on

The problem about simply comparing the post-test scores is that if there is a statistically significant difference showing, for example, that Class A performed better on the post-test than Class B, it could be attributable to Method A being more effective, or it could be attributable to the children in Class A being better at arithmetic to begin with (or both). Conversely, failure to find a significant difference when Method A is 'really' better than Method B could be because the children in Class B were better at arithmetic to begin with.

> **Before reading on…**
>
> Think very carefully through the logic and the implications of the two scenarios just described.
> … **now read on**

The point of carrying out a pre-test now becomes apparent. It can be used to adjust statistically for any initial differences between the classes in arithmetic attainment. A simple way to do this would be to work out, for each child, the difference between pre-test and post-test scores, representing the improvement during the teaching. These improvement scores could then be compared for the two classes.

A more sophisticated method of taking the pre-test scores into consideration is called **Analysis of Covariance (ANCOVA**, for short). A **covariate**, in general, is some variable that, for one reason or another, cannot be controlled for in carrying out the experiment (for example, by random assignment of participants to conditions) but which can be measured and so taken into account in the statistical analysis. *Prevention is better than cure, so to speak, but if prevention isn't possible, then cure is advisable.*

To make important points about ANCOVA, four possible data sets are to be contrasted (see Figure 15.21). To work out what's going on in each case, it's helpful to have scatterplots for the four data sets, showing the relationship between pre-test and post-test scores for Class A and Class B (see Figure 15.22). Additionally, on the right-hand side in each case, a representation of post-test scores alone for each class is provided.

| | Data set 1 | | Data set 2 | | Data set 3 | | Data set 4 | |
	Pre-	Post-	Pre-	Post-	Pre-	Post-	Pre-	Post-
Class A	22	19	22	27	14	19	30	27
	23	30	23	38	15	30	31	38
	33	35	33	43	25	35	41	43
	29	25	29	33	21	25	37	33
	19	24	19	32	11	24	27	32
	12	15	12	23	4	15	20	23
	13	22	13	30	5	22	21	30
	20	31	28	39	20	31	36	39
Class B	16	18	16	18	16	18	16	18
	18	27	18	27	18	27	18	27
	34	32	34	32	34	32	34	32
	30	37	30	37	30	37	30	37
	26	21	26	21	26	21	26	21
	19	23	19	23	19	23	19	23
	10	17	10	17	10	17	10	17
	25	28	25	28	25	28	25	28

Figure 15.21 Illustrating the use of pre-test as a covariate: Four contrasting data sets

Before reading on...

Look carefully at each of the plots and consider what the data in each case suggest about the relative efficacy of the two teaching methods.

... now read on

We now analyse each of the data sets in turn.

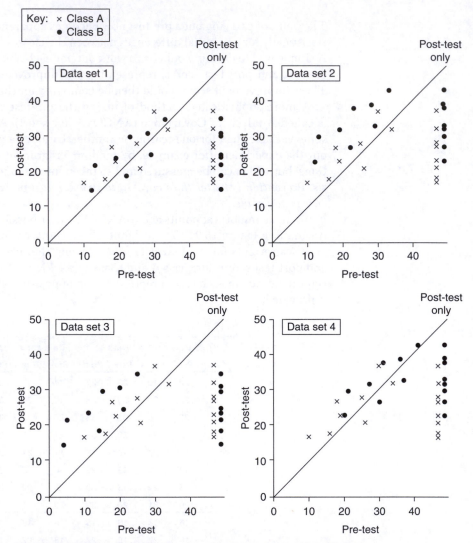

Note: Each graph also shows differences in post-test scores between A and B classes.

Figure 15.22 Scatterplots of post-test against pre-test for the four data sets

Making links

Note that this is an example of the use of scatterplots primarily to represent *differences* between participants' pre- and post-scores, and between classes, rather than *correlations* between sets of scores (although these are also apparent from the graphs).

Data set 1

For this data set, the scatterplot shows that there is a clear correlation between pre-test scores and post-test scores, which is not surprising, if you think about it – students who are relatively good/poor to begin with are likely to remain relatively good/poor after instruction. More interestingly, by taking into account the diagonal line through points showing equal pre-test and post-test scores, it is clear that in most cases (all but four, to be precise) the post-test score is higher. Thus, these data indicate that the effects of the teaching in both classes have generally been positive. There is considerable overlap between the two sets of points within the scatterplot, suggesting that there is no difference between the two teaching methods in terms of efficacy. If the post-test scores are considered in isolation (as represented to the right of the scatterplot) there is also no indication of any difference between the two classes.

Carrying out statistical tests to check these indications from the graphs, the following results are obtained:

- Comparing the post-test scores in isolation: $t = -.0737$, with an associated p value of .9423, so the result is not statistically significant; and
- taking into account the pre-test as a covariate: this is done by comparing two regression models, as in Figure 15.23.

Here, we can see that the (simple) r^2 of .5692 for the first Model 1 has increased to a (multiple) R^2 of .5699 following the addition of *Class* in Model 2. We can test for the statistical significance of this increase by using the formula we used earlier in the chapter (p. 350):

$$F = \frac{(R_2^2 - R_1^2)/k}{(1 - R_2^2)/(N - (m + k) - 1)}$$

where m is the number of predictors in the first model and k is the number of *extra* predictors in the second model. Thus

$$F = \frac{(.5699 - .5692)/1}{(1 - .5699)/(16 - (1 + 1) - 1)} = \frac{.0007/1}{.4301/13} = \frac{.0007}{.0331} = 0.021$$

Degrees of freedom are given by the general formula $(k, N - (m + k) - 1)$ which gives (1,13) *df*. Here, the F value is so small (far less than 1), so we can conclude

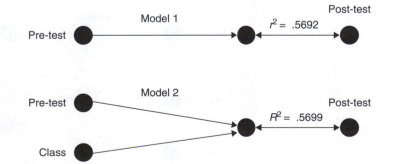

Figure 15.23 Examining the effect of pre-test as a covariate in data set 1: Comparison of two regression models

straight off that the increase in r^2 is not significant. Thus, adding the variable *Class* does not increase significantly the predictive power of the original model with only pre-test (the covariate) as a predictor. *The difference in post-test scores of Classes A and B, with pre-test as a covariate, is not statistically significant.*

For these data, then, the picture is clear and consistent. There is no evidence in the data that the teaching methods differ in efficacy.

Data set 2

The scatterplot again shows that there is a clear correlation between pre-test scores and post-test scores. Except for two cases, the post-test score is higher than the pre-test score in each case. By contrast, there is now a strong visual suggestion of a difference between the two classes, with the points for Class B generally further away from the diagonal line than those for Class A. A similar pattern of higher scores for Class B is evident in the post-test scores considered in isolation.

Carrying out statistical tests to check these indications from the graphs, the following results are obtained:

- Comparing the post-test scores in isolation: $t = 2.284$ with an associated p value of .0385, so the result is statistically significant at the .05 level; and
- taking into account the pre-test as covariate by comparing two regression models, as in Figure 15.24.

Here, we can see that r^2 of .4764 for the first Model 1 has increased to R^2 of .7416 following the addition of *Class* in Model 2. Using the formula to test for the significance of this increase we obtain

$$F = \frac{(.7416 - .4764)/1}{(1 - .7416)/(16 - (1 + 1) - 1)} = \frac{.2652/1}{.2584/13} = \frac{.2652}{.0199} = 13.327$$

With (1,13) *df*, this F value is statistically significant (in fact, SPSS gives an associated p value of .003). So, this time, adding the variable *Class* increases significantly the predictive power of the original model with only pre-test (the covariate) as a predictor. In other words, *the difference in post-test scores, with pre-test as a covariate, is statistically significant.*

Again, the results from both tests point to the same conclusion: Students in Class B did better on the post-test, and their performance was statistically significantly better even when pre-test marks were taken into account.

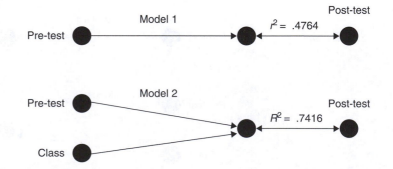

Figure 15.24 Examining the effect of pre-test as a covariate in data set 2: Comparison of two regression models

Data set 3

The scatterplot yet again shows that there is a clear correlation between pre-test scores and post-test scores for each class. With two exceptions, the post-test score is higher. As for the previous data set, there is a strong visual suggestion of a difference between the two classes, with the points for Class B generally further away from the diagonal line than those for Class A. However, the same pattern of higher scores for Class B is *not* evident in the post-test scores considered in isolation.

Carrying out statistical tests to check these indications from the graphs, the following results are obtained:

- Comparing the post-test scores in isolation: $t = -.0737$ with an associated p value of .9423, so the result is not statistically significant; and
- taking into account the pre-test as covariate by comparing two regression models, as in Figure 15.25.

Here, we can see that r^2 of .5105 for the first Model 1 has increased to R^2 of .6455 following the addition of *Class* in Model 2. Using the formula to test for the significance of this increase we obtain

$$F = \frac{(.6455 - .5105)/1}{(1 - .6455)/(16 - (1+1) - 1)} = \frac{.1350/1}{.3545/13} = \frac{.1350}{.0273} = 4.945$$

With (1,13) *df*, this *F* value is statistically significant (SPSS gives an associated p value of .044). Thus, as for Data set 2, adding the variable *Class* increases significantly the predictive power of the original model with only pre-test (the covariate) as a predictor. In other words, *the difference in post-test scores, with pre-test as a covariate, is statistically significant.*

Before reading on...

Given that the *t*-test yields a result that is not statistically significant, and the ANCOVA a result that is statistically significant, which should be followed? Why?

... now read on

The ANCOVA is the appropriate analysis in this case. The lack of a significant result for the *t*-test may be explained by examining the data in the scatterplot. It is true that the post-test scores for the two classes are similar overall, but the pre-test scores for Class B are, on average, considerably lower (further to the left

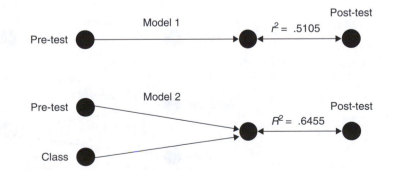

Figure 15.25 Examining the effect of pre-test as a covariate in data set 3: Comparison of two regression models

on the graph). Thus, the children in Class B have, in fact, shown greater improvement, which is what the distance from the diagonal line represents. This example is intended to show one way in which relying on the post-test scores alone would be misleading, and how Analysis of Covariance, taking pre-test scores into account as well, avoids this problem.

Data set 4

As usual, the scatterplot shows a clear correlation between pre-test scores and post-test scores. Apart from four cases, the post-test score is higher. There is no hint in the scatterplot that one of the two classes is generally further away from the diagonal than the other. However, the same pattern is *not* evident in the post-test scores considered in isolation, where there appears to be a clear difference.

Carrying out statistical tests to check these indications from the graphs, the following results are obtained:

- Comparing the post-test scores in isolation: $t = 2.284$ with an associated p value of .0385, so the result is statistically significant; and
- taking into account the pre-test as covariate by comparing two regression models, as in Figure 15.26.

This time, we can see that r^2 of .7278 for the first Model 1 has increased to R^2 of .7416 following the addition of *Class* in Model 2. Using the formula to test for the significance of this increase we obtain

$$F = \frac{(.7416 - .7278)/1}{(1 - .7416)/(16 - (1+1) - 1)} = \frac{.0138/1}{.2584/13} = \frac{.0138}{.0199} = \mathbf{0.693}$$

As for data set 1, this F value is not even close to statistical significance, so, adding the variable *Class* does not increase significantly the predictive power of the original model with only pre-test (the covariate) as a predictor. In other words, *the difference in post-test scores, with pre-test as a covariate, is not statistically significant.*

> **Before reading on...**
>
> Given that the t-test yields a result that is statistically significant, and the ANCOVA a result that is not statistically significant, which should be followed? Why?
>
> **... now read on**

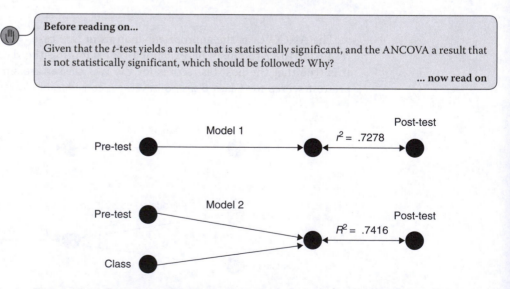

Figure 15.26 Examining the effect of pre-test as a covariate in data set 4: Comparison of two regression models

ANCOVA is again the appropriate analysis. The significant result for the *t*-test may be explained by examining the data in the scatterplot. It is true that the post-test scores for the two classes differ overall, but the pre-test scores for Class B are, on average, generally higher (further to the right on the graph). Thus, the children in Class B have, in fact, shown no greater improvement than those in Class A – they started higher, and they finished higher. This example is intended to show another way in which relying on the post-test scores would be misleading, and how the ANCOVA, taking pre-test scores into account as well, avoids this problem.

The relative strengths and weaknesses of MRA and ANOVA

The first example presented in this chapter gives us a convenient starting point to make some comments about the contrasting characteristics of MRA and ANOVA. In that example, we showed how to analyse the relationship between *Attitude to Computers*, *Practice* and *IQ* as predictor variables, and *Mark* as the criterion variable, using MRA. These data could be analysed using ANOVA but before this could be done they would need to be converted into a form that fits the ANOVA mould. Consider *IQ*, for example. It can be used as a factor in ANOVA, but only if expressed in terms of a relatively small number of levels. For example, we could define high, medium and low *IQ* as follows (the values may appear a little high; however, the mean IQ of our university sample is 125):

High   greater than 135
Medium   between 120 and 135 (inclusive)
Low   below 120

Then *IQ* can be treated as a factor with three levels. Similar treatment for *Attitude to Computers* and *Practice* could be carried out, and the data could then be analysed through ANOVA. However, note that by treating each of the variables in this way, some of the information in the data is being lost: No distinction is made between IQs of 121 and 131, for example. This loss of information inevitably results in a reduction in statistical *power*. A further point is that basic ANOVA treats low, medium, high as simply three different levels, and takes no account of the fact that the levels are ordered. However, that is not a particular problem – to take account of this ordering, follow-up trend tests would be appropriate (see p. 279).

ANOVA and MRA may be contrasted in many ways:

• While they are related mathematically, the basic way of talking about ANOVA analyses is in terms of comparing means (relative to variation), while the basic way of talking about MRA analyses is in terms of correlations. These contrasts reflect the way in which ANOVA may be considered as a generalization of *t*-tests and MRA a generalization of correlation and regression with a single predictor variable.

• ANOVA is best suited for manipulated variables, that is, variables under the control of the experimenter and taking a small number of values. Variables such as *IQ* have to be banded artificially into a small number of intervals (for example, high, medium, low) if they are to be included as factors in an ANOVA design. MRA, on the other hand, is naturally suited to variables such as *IQ* that come with the participants, so to speak.

- Related to the previous point, ANOVA is more suited to controlled laboratory research, whereas MRA is suited to research outside the laboratory, where there is less chance of experimental control.
- There are consequent differences in terminology. Thus, the independent variables for ANOVA are called factors, while for MRA the independent variables are called predictor variables, and the dependent variable is called the criterion variable. As alluded to above, these differences in terminology largely reflect the fact that ANOVA is typically used in an experimental context and MRA in a non-experimental, or correlational, context. If ANOVA were applied to a non-experimental design, it would strictly be inappropriate to talk about independent and dependent variables. Similarly, if MRA were used in an experimental context, which is entirely possible, it would make perfect sense to refer to independent variables or factors.
- An ANOVA design imposes restraints, particularly in the ideal case where the numbers of participants in all cells of a factorial design are equal. The reward for this discipline is that the interpretation of the results is straightforward. ANOVA divides the variation in the data into neat, discrete, packets – a certain amount for each main effect, so much for each interaction, and so much for background variation. By contrast, MRA is much more flexible, but the price paid for this flexibility is that interpretation often is not straightforward, particularly when predictors are themselves highly correlated.

Chapter review

In this chapter, you have been introduced to the techniques of multiple regression analysis, with a range of examples showing its flexibility. The basic building block underlying the logical structure of these examples is the regression model for the relationship between a set of predictor variables and a criterion variable, and comparisons between such models. A survey of the many contrasts between ANOVA and MRA concluded the chapter.

16

Overview

In this chapter

... we review some key ideas in the book and show how these fit within the cyclical process of experimentation and theory-building in psychology. We discuss the centrality of significance testing in traditional approaches to statistical inference in psychological research, the controversies relating to this approach, and various ways to supplement it, indicating the directions in which your statistical knowledge will need to be extended if you want to take your statistical education further. We finish with some reflections on the nature and aims of the book as a whole.

On seeing the wood for the trees: What are the big ideas?

Variability

If we had to nominate one idea as the most important in understanding statistical analysis of data from psychological research, it would be variability. In a nutshell, as discussed in Chapter 1, variability is characteristic of the subject matter of psychology, namely people and, occasionally, other animals. Statistical methods are the techniques devised to cope with this most human of characteristics in attempting to understand people through empirical enquiry, and to establish data-based theoretical generalizations about them.

Variables

To be able to handle variability, both conceptually and mathematically, the building block is the concept of a variable, by which is meant, broadly speaking, any aspect within the experimental situation that varies and can be measured on a single scale.

Subject variables are characteristics of the people being studied (for example, gender, age, IQ, level of anxiety). Whereas a variable such as age or gender may be considered reasonably straightforward to define, examples of variables such as IQ and anxiety are complex and themselves embedded in theory – for example, it is highly controversial whether it is appropriate or not to measure intelligence on a single scale. As discussed in Chapter 2, a major effort of psychologists is in postulating and defining viable and useful variables and then devising, often with considerable ingenuity, ways of measuring them.

Treatment variables are aspects of the experimental conditions under the control of the experimenter, depending on the nature of the experiment such as the nature of reinforcement, whether the participant is given coffee or not, and so on.

Both subject and treatment variables give rise to numbers, which may be as simple as 0 and 1 representing a dichotomous variable, such as gender or having/not having coffee. These numbers, organized variable by variable, are the raw materials for statistical analysis.

Process of experimentation

As has already been seen in Chapters 1 and 9, the process of experimentation broadly follows the stages shown in Figure 16.1.

- A round in the ongoing cyclical process of experimentation and theory-building begins with the posing of a question in the form of a conjectured relationship among two or more variables (the experimental hypothesis).
- In order to be able to investigate this conjectured relationship statistically, it must be possible to measure each variable.
- An experimental design is needed so that the data that the experiment generates appropriately bear on the theoretical question of interest.
- The data collected are analysed, interpreted, and communicated. The interpretation feeds back into theory development.

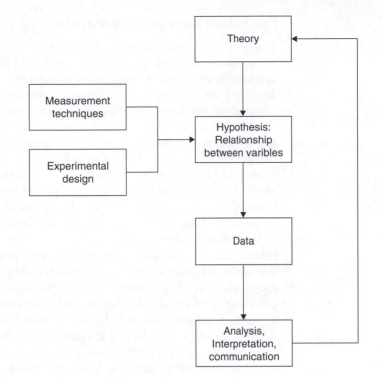

Figure 16.1 The process of experimentation

Inference from sample to population

Given that the aim of building theory is to make statements about people in general, and given that it is obviously impossible to study everyone, psychological researchers have no option but to collect data for only a sample of the people of interest (say 12-year-old children, or left-handed people).

As a natural consequence of variability, a sample may not be representative of the population from which it is drawn – if a different sample is taken, the results may be very different. An intuitive acceptance of sampling variation is one of the key insights in truly understanding the principles of statistical analysis. A second, related, key insight is that, to put in the most general terms, probabilistic phenomena stabilize as the number of cases becomes very large.

By way of example, think of tossing a (fair) coin ten times. The probability that the number of heads will lie between four and six is .66 (to two decimal places). Now think in terms of proportions. In these terms, the probability that the number of heads will lie between 40% and 60% is .66. Now suppose the coin is tossed 100 times. The probability that the percentage of heads lies between 40% and 60% is now greater than .95. Increase the number of coin tosses to 1000 and the probability of the percentage of heads lying between 40% and 60% is extremely close to 1. In fact, there is a probability of about .95 that the percentage of heads in this case (for 1000 coin tosses) lies between 47% and 53%.

This pervasive characteristic of probabilistic phenomena (exemplified at many points throughout this book) explains why the number of participants tested in a given experiment is a vital factor in determining the power of the statistical test carried out (see Chapter 9).

Evaluating the value of a statistic

The term *statistical inference* refers to the necessity of making an inference about a population on the basis of data collected for a sample of that population. Such an inference from sample to population is made through a statistic, which is a number derived from the data that expresses a specific and relevant aspect of the data. Throughout the book, in introducing each statistic, we have emphasized the logic of its definition in terms of what aspect of the data it measures. For example, the Mann-Whitney U statistic (see p. 124) reflects the degree to which data from the two groups being compared are mixed up or not when they are combined and listed in order. The independent t-test (see p. 112) is the ratio of the difference between means for scores from two independent groups to a measure of the variation in these scores within these groups that also takes sample size into account; examples were presented in Chapter 7 to explain the rationale for this definition of the statistic.

In general (all things being equal) the strength of the evidence that the data provide in terms of evaluating the experimental hypothesis is related directly to the size of the statistic, as we have emphasized throughout, in particular through the use of schematic diagrams (see, for example, Figure 7.13, p. 113). For an independent groups design for example, the t statistic can potentially take any value, positive or negative. All else being equal, the further away from zero (whether positive or negative), the stronger the evidence of a difference in the population in the characteristic under study. As repeatedly stressed, the question then is: just how far away from zero does the t value have to be before we consider it as constituting strong enough evidence of a difference?

A similar question arises for each statistic we have dealt with, and we have described in this book the most generally used method in psychological statistics for answering this question, based on the concept of the null hypothesis and examining the implications of assuming it to be true. In fact, such is the ubiquity of the approach, many researchers consider it as the sole method for evaluating data. The null hypothesis method yields a way of deciding what range of values of a statistic is deemed to satisfy the very specific criterion that is termed *statistical significance*. While the approach continues to be dominant, there are major controversies surrounding it, to which we now turn.

Limitations of the null hypothesis approach

The approach we have described for determining whether a statistic is, or is not, statistically significant has been standard for a long time in psychological research. However, essentially for as long as it has been used, it has also been criticized on many counts. Furthermore, whereas, in the past, much publication of statistical experiments concentrated on reporting whether the results of tests were statistically significant or not, there is now considerable pressure to provide further information. If you are going to take your statistics education further, you will need to go deeper into such matters; here we sketch briefly the main forms of criticism, and some suggested ways to meet them.

You may be surprised, and perhaps somewhat dismayed, to be told that what you have painstakingly (we hope) been learning is based on controversial foundations. However, even the physical sciences are built on an edifice that is no longer seen as incontrovertibly true, but rather a set of theories of models that we construct in an attempt to explain the physical world – think of the arguments surrounding Darwinian theories of evolution, for example. Because statistical methods draw on the mathematical theory of probability, it might be imagined that they thereby acquire the certainty of mathematics, but the theoretical foundations of probability are themselves uncertain. In every respect, we live in an uncertain world, and absolute certainty is not even to be found in mathematics.

At the root of the criticism of the statistical approach based on evaluating the null hypothesis is being clear about what 'statistical significance' actually tells us. In Chapter 6, we tried to make this point as clearly as possible. In particular, the statement that a result is *statistically significant at the .05 level* is a statement about the probability of getting a value of the statistic in a certain range, on the assumption that the null hypothesis is true. It is, emphatically, *not a statement about the probability of the null hypothesis being true*. The all-too-easy tendency to slide between the correct interpretation and the incorrect one is an example of confusing conditional probabilities, as explained in Chapter 6. Research has shown that the error is pervasive, even among experienced researchers, and is propagated in some textbooks.

Thus, what the statistical significance of a result tells you is rather limited, and in a sense 'indirect'. It may be regarded as a minimal safeguard against reading incorrectly into data evidence for a systematic effect that is not warranted. If you continue with your statistical education, you will need to extend beyond mere determination of whether a result is statistically significant or not, and consider other aspects of the data.

In particular, in this book, we have touched on the importance of the power of an experiment, yet it is well known that in psychological research many experiments are based on sample sizes which imply that their power is undesirably low. This reality has a cumulatively distorting effect on how experimental data feed back into theory-building, since it implies that many experiments fail to yield statistically significant results that would have been produced by larger samples (or more carefully designed experiments). For your future statistical education, you will need to know more about power and how it can be calculated for specific experimental designs.

Another aspect is that the use of the word 'significance' is unfortunate in that it carries the message that a statistically significant result is significant in the general sense of the word, which is not necessarily the case. Because of the ever present effect of sample size, a statistically significant effect can be obtained with a very large sample which represents a very small difference between two means, for example, or a very small correlation. Indeed, a correlation of .01, or even lower, is statistically significant if the sample size is large enough. In addressing this issue, the concept of effect size has become increasingly important and we have covered the calculation and interpretation of various measures of effect size in this book.

Another way in which more valuable information can be presented is in the form of confidence intervals. Again, we cover the calculation and interpretation of confidence intervals in this book. You may well have seen reports of opinion polls or electoral polls in which, let's say for the sake of example, it is reported that 31% of those polled considered that cats are better companions than dogs, and this is followed by the statement 'margin of error ±3%'. You will certainly realize that this does not mean that the actual percentage of the population who think that cats are better companions than dogs lies in the range from 28% to 34%. What it means is that, roughly speaking (and an exact explanation of what we mean here by 'roughly speaking' is beyond the scope of this book), there is a 95% probability that the percentage lies in that range. The advantage of this extra information is that it not only gives us an estimate of the pro-cat percentage in the population, but also an indication of the precision of that estimate. As another example of the importance of sample size, the margin of error in a case like this is directly related to the size of the poll – interview fewer people and the margin of error increases; interview more and it decreases.

In a similar way, confidence intervals can be calculated for statistics. For example, if a correlation coefficient of .42 is reported, it can be augmented by a statement that the 95% confidence interval is, say, .36 to .48 (the actual value will depend on the sample size, of course), which again means (roughly) that there is a 95% probability that the true value lies in that range.

What the foregoing paragraphs represent, then, are sketchy indications of the ways in which the null hypothesis approach to statistical inference is deemed to be controversial, and of ways in which the reporting of statistical significance can be augmented by other information necessary to evaluate the significance, in the general sense, of the data.

Making sense of a multivariate world

The important questions about people are complex. More specifically, to understand complex aspects of behaviour, many variables need to be taken into account. In Part I of this book, we limited attention to simple experimental designs involving at most two variables – these are important enough in their own right, and serve to establish a foundation for moving on to the more complex experimental designs dealt with in Part II.

In Chapters 11 to 14 on ANOVA, we showed how the analysis of data by comparing means relative to variation within groups could be extended, first by having more than two levels of the independent variable, and then by increasing the number of independent variables to two or more. Such designs allow the effects of several independent variables to be taken into account and, moreover, possible interactions between two or more to be considered, something not enabled by a series of simpler experiments, each with one independent variable. The case of interaction in ANOVA exemplifies the point that, in describing and understanding complex behaviour, intricate patterns within data for many variables need to be teased out. In a relatively simple example (see pp. 291–292) we saw that comparing males and females on recognition of specific sets of photographs could only be interpreted meaningfully by taking into account a third variable, namely the nature of the groups of people in the photographs (in this case, models, footballers, or pop stars).

In Chapter 15, regression analysis was extended in similar fashion to encompass data where multiple variables could be treated as predictors. The examples given to illustrate the flexibility of the approach show various ways in which it serves to tease out the relationships between several variables. For example, on p. 365, when dealing with which factors influence attitude to computers among psychology students, five potentially important predictors were considered, namely Faculty, Gender, IQ, External Locus of Control, and Computer Use. On the basis of the data available for a reasonably large sample of students, it appeared that only External Locus of Control and Computer Use were the important predictors out of the set considered. Again, if you are going to go further with statistics, one direction in which your skill and knowledge will be extended is in learning more multivariate methods designed to cope with our multivariate world.

Figure 16.2 completes the picture of the landscape sketched in this book. Taking account of the contents of Part II, the diagram is an elaboration of Figure 9.10.

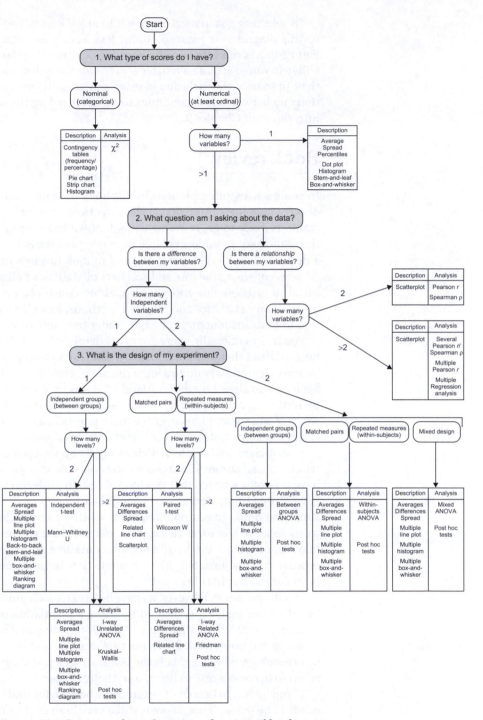

Figure 16.2 Decision chart: Overview of statistical landscape

In selecting a statistical approach to any data set, you may find it useful to refer to this diagram, or Figure 9.10, for less advanced tests. Again for ease of access, Figure 16.2 is reprinted on the *back inside cover*. Regular reference to these figures will help you to acquire a reliable schema for statistics. You may be interested to note that, in spite of the inclusion of more statistical techniques in Figure 16.2, the relationship between tests continues to be governed by the same three basic questions introduced in Chapter 9.

Book review

In some senses, our ambitions in this book have intentionally been limited. In spite of our foregoing comments on the directions in which your future statistical education is likely to go, in terms of content we have conformed largely to, as it were, the orthodoxy in undergraduate psychological statistics. We have tried to balance a desire to break certain moulds, and to look towards future trends, with a realistic sense of what students and teachers of statistics believe they need *now – today*. Mindful of these not entirely compatible concerns, we have attempted to house introductory statistics and research methods, as well as a solid conceptual foundation in post-introductory statistics, under the same roof.

Again, intentionally, there are many details of both elementary and post-elementary statistics that we have omitted – in trying to help you see the wood for the trees, we have cleared away quite a lot of the undergrowth. We don't imagine that you have been cast up alone on a desert island with this book – we expect you to supplement it by additional reading and by benefiting from your statistics instruction. Thus, while we have endeavoured to cover the main points in a coherent way we have, above all, attempted to provide a solid conceptual framework.

Statisticians and mathematicians might be shocked at the lack of formulae and technical derivations throughout the book – on this point we are unrepentant. We have taken for granted that you have access to powerful statistical software, and we have chosen to supplement our material with optional illustrations in SPSS. There is simply no point, in our opinion, in presenting complex formulae to students, when many lack the technical facility to understand the mathematics. In our experience, many introductory texts claim to eschew mathematical complexity in favour of conceptual explanations, but this aim rarely lasts beyond about Chapter 3; we trust we have done better in this respect.

In a deeper sense, however, we have been extremely ambitious. We have attempted, based on our long experience of teaching a population of psychology undergraduates, to present a book that you will find interesting and accessible, and will provide a conceptual framework for, as the title implies, making sense of data and statistics in psychology, whether this is the last statistics you study formally, or whether you go on to become a researcher or a statistical expert.

If you intend to become a researcher, the case for understanding statistics hardly needs to be made. If not, there is still a very high chance that your work will involve dealing with complex issues involving people. Statistical tools for interpreting and communicating data will almost certainly be important in any such career.

Beyond pragmatic considerations of your future career, it is clear that basic statistical literacy is essential in our contemporary world, where there is a proliferation of data, mostly presented by agencies such as governments, pressure groups, the media, or advertisers, that have a vested interest in persuasion. In this environment, a critical disposition allied with a feel for data, and an expectation that it should be possible to make sense of data for yourself, are vital. Given the Internet and other aspects of the information explosion, the ratio

$$\frac{\text{Amount of available information}}{\text{Conceptual tools for making sense of it}}$$

is liable to increase out of control. We hope this book helps.

Index